MORE GROUNDED THEORY
METHODOLOGY:
A Reader

MORE GROUNDED THEORY METHODOLOGY:
A Reader

Edited by

Barney G. Glaser, Ph. D.

Sociology Press
P. O. Box 400
Mill Valley, CA 94942

Sociology Press
P. O. Box 400
Mill Valley, CA 94942
(415) 388-9431

First printing

Library of Congress Catalog Card Number applied for.
ISBN 1-884156-07-X

Printed in the United States of America

TABLE OF CONTENTS

Part III Generating Grounded Formal Theory

MORE GROUNDED THEORY METHODOLOGY:
Introduction

Barney G. Glaser, PhD.

There is no question that *Basics of Grounded Theory Analysis* (Barney G. Glaser, Sociology Press, 1992) has been received virtually all over the world with success for its critique of Strauss and Corbin's book, *Basics of Qualitative Analysis*. It was, as surmised by me, Dr. Glaser, needed and sought after in order to clarify the confusion that so many researchers had with the Strauss - Corbin book; a confusion that left many paralyzed in their research. *Basics of Grounded Theory Analysis* has rescued many dissertations, books and papers, and it has saved careers and promotions which are required by the former writings. People have called me from all over the world to thank me for my corrections and clarifications. Some wondered why I waited so long to make these corrections!

This reader on more grounded theory methodology continues the corrections started in *Basics of Grounded Theory Analysis*. It shows three correctives:

(1) One can use scholarship in advancing grounded theory methodology. Scholarship, it was clearly shown, was bypassed in the Strauss - Corbin book. One can use scholarship in the close sense of taking what was said before on grounded theory and taking it a step further, and in the broad sense, within a context of other work where it can be used for the current purpose of the area.

These authors have varying views of the use of grounded theory and of grounded theory methodology itself. Their use and rendering of the methodology emerges within the context of their area of research. They become their own methodologists to some degree, *but* they stick closely to the essential elements of grounded theory, from start to finish, of their research and of the application of grounded theory. Emergence of categories and properties through constant comparison and coding, theoretical sampling, memo writing, sorting, integration, densification and saturation remain the cornerstones of their research.

It is truly amazing how the core ideas of grounded theory have made *deep impressions* on these authors. These ideas permeate their papers as they engage in their effort to extend grounded theory into their substantive areas of interest. Their ability to follow them as they were traditionally written and meant, and then carefully extend or adjust them to current concerns is remarkable. These are the ideas which Strauss and Corbin, in their book *Basics of Qualitative Analysis*, either forgot or recast like they were never written about in the first place.

These papers are written by sincere researchers with more modest aspirations, but with relevant, important contributions. Their work indicates the benefits of advancing grounded theory methodology with scholarly considerations uppermost in mind. The reader clearly knows where the advance is coming from. Researchers in other substantive areas are doing the same methodological extensions, yet to be published.

(2) In this reader we republish core articles from previous grounded theory books that were neglected by Strauss and Corbin and; except for "Constant Comparative Method of Qualitative Analysis," are seldom referred to in grounded theory research. This revisit is essential to revitalizing traditional grounded theory and increasing the researcher's stockpile of tools of research.

(3) Lastly, we take a look at the generation of formal theory using grounded theory methodology. This effort is not clearly as well formulated as the methodology for generating grounded substantive theory. We hope to bring out some of the problems of formal theory generation, particularly that of the ease of drifting into forcing the data with very abstract logical elaboration.

Forcing becomes imperceptibly easy when data run thin for grounding, the author has a pet interest or bent and/or he has a facile ability to logically elaborate without the corrective of data, or of grounded theory to compare to as he or she extends the generality of emergent focus. Since sociologists are always given to trying to write formal theory one way or another, but usually by logical conjecture, this section on inductive formal theory generation is particularly important and barely a start on formulating this area of grounded theory methodology.

Part I

Methodological Advances and Adaptations

GROUNDED THERAPY[1]

Odis E. Simmons

My introduction to grounded theory occurred in 1967, when Barney G. Glaser and Anselm L. Strauss published *The Discovery of Grounded Theory*, the seminal statement on grounded theory. At the time, I was an undergraduate student in sociology. The book made a deep and lasting impression on me. I determined that I wanted to learn "how to do that." I was given this opportunity in 1970, upon my admission to the Graduate Program in Sociology at the University of California, San Francisco. In addition to other fine faculty members, this program was home to both Barney Glaser and Anselm Strauss. Thus, I was able to learn grounded theory, from the ground up, so to speak, from its originators.

My introduction to therapy[2] occurred during the course of my dissertation research (Bigus, 1974)[3]. The topic of this research was what I came to refer to as "the alcoholic career." I used a qualitative, grounded theory approach, collecting my data through a combination of intensive interviews and participant observation field research. During this research I had the opportunity to observe therapy sessions between alcoholism counselors and their clients, in inpatient settings. At the end of many of these sessions I was able to interview both the client and the therapist, for their impressions and interpretations as to what occurred during the sessions. The disparity of views between the two parties impressed me. In general, the therapists tended to have a much more positive view of what occurred during the sessions than the clients did. The therapists tended to believe that some positive ground was made during the sessions, whereas the clients tended to express varying levels of disappointment and anger about the sessions. This was certainly not always the case, but it was often enough the case, at least in my mind, to point to problems in the therapeutic relationship and approach. Although these issues were not the primary subjects of my research, I couldn't help but take notice of them, out of strong personal curiosity.

In subsequent years, through teaching and consulting work, I had further opportunities to observe and reflect upon the therapeutic relationship and process. Eventually, I became a therapist, myself. Since then, I have had an abundance of opportunities to not only make such observations, but to participate in therapeutic relationships and the therapeutic process.

From the beginning of my experience with therapy, I saw many areas in which it was evident to me that the therapeutic process and the therapeutic relationship could be improved. As I learned more about grounded theory, it also became evident to me that grounded theory might be very useful in this application. Some years later when I became a practicing therapist, I was able to empirically test this supposition. My original hunch has proven to be solidly correct. One of the original promises of grounded theory, "to be usable in practical applications" (Glaser and Strauss, 1967: p.3), has certainly been fulfilled, in this instance.

In fact, this promise has been fulfilled in a way which was evidently not originally perceived. The original thought appears to have been that with grounded theories, "prediction and explanation should be able to give the practitioner some understanding and control of situations" (Glaser and Strauss, 1967: p.3). What I have discovered is that the grounded theory *process* itself (not just grounded theories) is very useful as a model for guiding a grounded *therapeutic* process -- albeit in a modified form to fit the situation. Because of the inherent nature of this relationship, I refer to this approach as *"grounded therapy."* Grounded therapy is a *methodology* by which to achieve therapy.

Because of the requirements and limitations of this format, i.e., a chapter in an anthology, I have limited the breadth and depth of my discussion.[4] My purpose here is not to present a detailed exposition of how to conduct grounded therapy, but merely to present enough of an outline to give the reader an idea as to what sorts of problems it addresses, how it addresses them, and how it proposes to solve them. And, in the course of these tasks, I hope to illustrate a practical application of grounded theory. The intended audience of this book is primarily sociologists interested in grounded theory, not therapists, so to avoid unnecessary digression, I shall assume readers have more than a passing familiarity with grounded theory.

APPROACHES TO THERAPY

Therapy consists of two general, interrelated components -- the "explanatory" (to identify, understand, explain) and the "operative" (to solve, remedy, rectify, heal). In my experience, grounded theory, in modified form as grounded therapy, is useful in the service of both tasks.

A plethora of therapeutic theories, models and paradigms exist for therapists to use. Some are formulated for use in specific substantive areas, and some for more general application. Each consists of some configuration of explanations, concepts, understandings, assumptions, operational prescriptions, proscriptions, and so forth, which if followed promise results. Unfortunately, research on the effectiveness of therapy suggests that often it does not produce the desired results, at least as practiced.[5] It is this problem which I am attempting to address here.[6]

I might add that in this context, I am much more interested in what I have observed therapists actually saying and doing, in practice, rather than what is contained in the literature, as the literature becomes "real" only through its empirical use.

Many therapeutic models are configured as a set of precepts, which some practitioners, usually the novice and less creative ones, use essentially as "formulas." With this approach, the therapist attempts to "stay within the lines," of whatever procedural dictates are espoused by the particular therapeutic model(s) they are using. This general approach to therapy might be referred to as "formula therapy." The essential problem with a formula therapy approach, is that it lacks the flexibility required by an applied enterprise. In therapy, each new situation requires a fresh, yet informed start. However, formula therapy proceeds in an essentially deductive, rather than inductive manner. And, if any enterprise cries out for an inductive, "discovery" approach, it is therapy.

Another, somewhat opposite approach to therapy is what might be referred to as "improvisational therapy." Some therapists attempt to free themselves from formulas by pulling what is useful in a given circumstance from their "menu" of known theories, concepts, approaches, and such, conducting therapy in an extemporaneous manner.[7] With this approach, therapists make up the rules as they go along, so to speak. They pick and choose whichever explanatory or operational construct appeals to them at the moment. This process may be somewhat more inductive and creative than a formula therapy approach, but it may also be uninformed and erratic. In using this procedure, therapists have to rely primarily on their own creative sensibilities. Furthermore, once they have selected a particular therapeutic mode, they may resort to applying it in a formula manner.

What is needed are systematic, yet flexible guidelines with which to avoid the inflexibility of formula therapy and the capriciousness of improvisational therapy. I believe grounded therapy can provide this, by giving "permission" to be creative and by providing a systematic and

6

informed means by which to do it. To demonstrate this, I shall outline what I think are the prominent problems of therapy, as I have seen it practiced, and how these problems may be minimized through the use of a grounded therapy approach.

PRECONCEPTION

One of the primary problems with the way therapy is ordinarily conducted is that it is predicated on a number of a priori assumptions and preconceptions, most of which are unnecessary, and detrimental to the therapeutic process. These preconceptions are detrimental, not only because they have not "earned" their position of primacy, but because many of them are epistemologically and empirically questionable to begin with. This detriment occurs not only to the process of developing explanations for the issues under question, but for the curative process which therapy is presumably all about.

These a priori assumptions and preconceptions consist of concepts, frameworks, models, paradigms, procedures, and so forth, which are presumed to be relevant and useful, without question, nor without having systematically earned their way into relevance. From my observations, the following are the most damaging a priori assumptions routinely made by therapists:

1) One a priori assumption which appears to be almost universally held by therapists is a belief in the notion of "unconscious" (or subconscious") mind. In all the years I have been around the therapy professions, I have seldom heard practitioners (as distinguished from theorists) of therapy seriously question (or for that matter even discuss) this concept. This is made particularly problematic by the way in which I have seen the concept used. It is generally used in such a way as to indicate a belief that there resides somewhere in the human brain a *pro-active* unconscious mind, which is not only capable of, but frequently does "overrule" and even "trick" the conscious mind. The unconscious mind is often given primacy over the conscious mind in explaining, particularly problematic behavior, thoughts, and emotions. However, the existence of a pro-active unconscious mind can only be "known" through inference. In my observations of therapists searching for explanations, this often results in remarkable inferential leaps, in which more obvious variables are ignored in favor of this "hidden" concept. To do this is to treat an empirically unprovable abstraction as more real than that which *is* real (i.e., conscious thought).[8]

The notion of (pro-active) unconscious mind is also often given primacy in the curative (as opposed to explanatory) side of therapy. This results in the use of "indirect" techniques, which are used to presumably "bypass" the conscious mind. This produces a form of "mysteriousness" which may alienate the client from the therapeutic process. The therapist presumably knows what is going on, but the client may not. If the client does "see through" what the therapist is attempting, they may be insulted, annoyed, or in some other way "put off" by the thinly veiled attempt to do something *to* them, rather than *with* them.

I see much less of a problem with the notion of unconscious if it is used as an adjective, to refer to "unconscious mental process" or "below the level of awareness," rather than as a noun, "with connotations of a definite region, a dark and forbidding territory to be apprehensively but courageously explored" (Thornton, p. 254). However, to assume that the unconscious can be conscious and unconscious simultaneously, is oxymoronic.

2) A second a priori assumption, very much related to the concept of unconscious mind, consists of a belief in the primacy of emotions in explaining thought and behavior. It is all too often assumed that the basis of the client's problem is to be found in some aberrant emotional state, usually stemming from problematic early childhood or "family of origin" experiences. Again, there is a tendency to "leap over" more obvious explanations in favor of the less obvious. Psychotherapy may be more glamorous for the therapist, but it is not necessarily what the client needs. As with any other variable, emotional variables must "earn" their way into an explanation.

In the same vein, "systems theorists" sometimes give the same level of primacy to "the system," usually the "family system," as a causal variable. The problem lies not so much in the concept of system, as in the a priori assumption that "the system" is the determining variable. However, if the notion of system is regarded more as an "entity" (common with systems theorists) than as an abstraction which represents a set of dynamic relationships, this presents the problem of reification.

3) Another a priori assumption, also very much related to the concept of unconscious mind, is the notion of "pathology."[9] It is often, in fact in my observation, usually invoked in such a way that some aspect of the client is viewed as pathological. The most common version of this is found in the use of the medical model, wherein clients (referred to as

"patients" are "diagnosed" from the <u>DSM-III-R</u>,[10] as having some sort of a "disorder," which is then "treated." Simply because a person's emotions, thoughts and/or behavior may be problematic for them or others, it does not necessarily follow that some feature of their person is pathological.

In my own practice, I have not once found it necessary, or even useful, to "pathologize" a client, although I have had numerous clients who had previously been pathologized by former therapists. One of the first things I have done with these clients is to "de-pathologize" them.

Even though I frequently have heard therapists condemn labeling and pathologizing, they nonetheless frequently do it. I have heard much mention of "wellness models," but in practice the same therapists often insidiously, and seemingly without awareness, use the notion of pathology. Furthermore, a wellness model presents most of the problems of a pathology model, because it is still a formula full of inherent preconceptions and a priori assumptions. The problem is not just in pathologizing, it is in preconceiving. This is one of the problems that grounded therapy is designed to overcome.

However, regardless of awareness and intent, this concept can be very damaging to the therapeutic process, the therapeutic relationship, and to the client. Probably the most damaging aspect of a pathologizing label is what it can do to the client's own self-concept. The client may come to see themselves as "a co-dependent," "a manic-depressive," a "depressed person," "an enabler," ad nauseam. They may come to see themselves as being "possessed" of an "affliction," over which they may have little or no power (especially without the help of the therapist). This may become the dominant factor in their own self concept, and even the inundating focus of their lives. This can be a very "disempowering" experience.

On the other hand, if the client has reservations about being pathologized, they run the risk of being further pathologized through the therapist invoking such concepts as "resistance," "denial," or even "oppositional disorder." In my experience, however, if an when these phenomena exist, they are most often an artifact of the therapeutic approach, particularly as a response to the experience of being pathologized.

The pathology notion presents a myriad of other problems in the therapeutic process and relationship, which because of space limitations cannot be delved into here. Combined, the above three a priori assumptions (unconscious mind, primacy of emotions, and pathology) present a mountain of difficulties for therapy, as they are usually invoked in concert with one another. In the present venue I am able to only give a brief indication of the types of problems they present.

In addition to the above a priori assumptions, a number of other sources of preconception are endemic to therapy as it is practiced. The most common of these are as follows:

1) Preconception in the therapeutic process usually begins immediately, through the collection of "intake information." Agencies usually require that their therapists complete intake forms on each new client. These forms usually contain "face sheet" types of information, which is preconceived to be of use in the therapeutic process, such as gender, age, income, religious affiliation, race, ethnicity, marital status, parental status, number and ages of children, alcohol an drug use patterns, health status, previous therapy, family of origin material such as birth order, number and gender of siblings, family alcohol and drug use patterns, and so on. Many agencies provide additional forms, which cover more topics in more detail, to be used as a "tool," at the therapist's discretion. Many therapists in private practice also collect such intake information, often using forms identical or similar to those which they have been provided by current or former agency employers (many therapists combine agency with part-time private practice).

In therapy, preconception is simply not viewed as a problem. In effect, it is more often seen as a preference, the assumption apparently being that the more information you have to guide you from the outset, the better.

2) One of the most notable forms of preconception in therapy is what is usually referred to as "the treatment plan." The treatment plan is comprised of preconceived ideas regarding what constitutes "the problem" (or "issue"), as well a what approaches the therapist will take in addressing it. In agencies, the treatment plan is ordinarily part of the intake procedure. The therapist is required to preconceive both the explanatory and operative sides of the therapeutic process, before they have information beyond that collected during the intake process, which itself is preconceived. Although the therapist may alter or ignore this plan as therapy evolves, it may have already done its damage, having served as the foundation for the therapeutic process.

3) Another source of preconception in therapy is an outgrowth of the use of the medical model as it is applied to behavior, thoughts and emotions. Many agencies require their therapists to advance a __DSM-III-R__ diagnosis, either as part of the intake procedure, or for the purpose of third party payment (as a virtually universal requirement of medical insurance companies). Although it is not uncommon for therapists to at least attempt to disregard the diagnosis, just the fact that so early on in the process they are required to frame whatever information about the client they have may present in insidious preconception. They are forced to think about the client and their situation, issues, problems, etc. within the medical model framework, to arrive at a diagnosis that has some semblance of fit.[11] Once this pseudo-analytical process has begun, it may be difficult to completely "erase" the diagnostic framework, particularly for therapists who have little training and experience in analysis (of which there are many). Because they are essential components of the medical model as it is used in therapy, therapists may begin to invoke the a priori assumptions discussed previously (the primacy of emotions, the unconscious mind and the notion of pathology), while consciously rejecting the specific diagnostic label. Although many therapists are inclined to invoke these assumptions regardless, advancing a diagnosis can only reinforce these a priori assumptions, and lend them a sense of legitimacy.

4) Another source of preconception in therapy occurs through the use of psychological tests. Such tests are sometimes given as part of the intake procedure, or early in the therapeutic process. The information derived from psychological tests is presumed to have value in identifying problems and/or providing a "psychological profile" of the client. This once again presents the problems of assuming unearned relevancy.

Most psychological tests classify test takers into "types" (which may or may not impute pathology),[12] provide diagnoses, or assign a score on a scale. With each of these alternatives, all of the problematic implications of a label are brought into play. The client may begin to incorporate the label into their own self-concept, coming to believe that they "are" the label. This presents the risk of the client permanentizing their problem or issue as an endemic part of their self, rather than a phase in their life, or a stage in a process. Moreover, the therapist (and the client) will likely see the test results as verified "fact." The illusion is created that the labeling process is removed from the realm of subjective judgment, and placed into the realm of objective science. Furthermore, the therapist may begin to essentially "treat" the label rather than the person.

5) Like most other cultures, the therapeutic culture experiences its share of fads. This gives rise to another source of preconception in therapy. Diagnostic categories, labels, concepts, models, and so forth (for the sake of brevity I shall refer to them as "explanatory/therapeutic constructs") tend to change over time, sometimes from new knowledge, but more often out of the cultural tendency towards fads. A once popular construct may be replaced by another somewhat analogous or overlapping construct. Some explanatory/therapeutic constructs remain rather stable (e.g., the medical model of alcoholism), but others change frequently. For example, at one time a client may be viewed as an "enabler," at another time they may be viewed as a "co-dependent." This is not to say that these constructs are absolutely interchangeable. They are not. They are, however, similar enough that at one time in the cultural history of the therapy professions there may be a tendency to see clients through "enabler (or whatever) colored glasses," and at another time a tendency to see them through "co-dependency colored glasses." One construct may have no more or less explanatory or therapeutic value than the other, but like with all fads, its users eventually become bored and weary of its imagery, and seize another as it comes along, primarily because of its freshness. This lends a certain capriciousness to the enterprise. And, like all fads, there is a tendency towards overuse when the fad is popular. With explanatory/therapeutic constructs, this exacerbates the tendency towards preconception.

If the conceptual and theoretical side of therapy were better grounded, this would be less likely to occur. Grounded concepts and theories can be moved over time and space. This is one of their strong features. However, because they are grounded, they are much less likely to be employed with such arbitrariness. Ungrounded concepts can too easily become "free floating."

6) Therapists, like all persons, have a tendency to become comfortable with the familiar. This engenders another source of preconception in therapy. When contemplating new information, therapists tend to limit their search for explanatory/therapeutic constructs to those which are available, familiar and comfortable.

A particularly insidious source of preconception occurs in the way in which "the problem" itself is defined. Is a client's essential or core problem "low self-esteem," "depression," "anger," "grief," "substance abuse," or a "dysfunctional relationship?" Frequently, all of these (and more) are present in the lives of one particular client. How is the therapist to resolve which is the "real" problem? Is "anger" a property of "low self esteem," or is "low self esteem" a property of "anger?" Is "substance abuse" a property of "depression," or is "depression" a property of "substance abuse?" Each of these "problems" has overlapping indicators. So, what is an indicator of which? Should the therapist accept the client's definition of "their problem"? What if the client's definition has only tenuous fit with the circumstances? For example, it is not uncommon for clients to "discover" or define "their problem" through reading self-help literature or from talking with friends who have or are currently undergoing therapy.

Therapists are seldom trained at analyzing, generating and synthesizing theoretical constructs. Thus, they have only those with which they are already familiar to choose from. This familiarity usually comes with their training, in graduate school and from courses and workshops subsequent to graduate school. With experience, they may become so comfortable with particular ways of viewing and doing things that it becomes taken for granted. It no longer occurs to them that it may be productive to question their perspectives, assumptions, methods, and so forth. Once therapists routinely use and become familiar with a particular set of explanatory/ therapeutic constructs, it becomes easy for them to begin to force fit them, with no awareness that they are doing so. Their application becomes routine.

In its most extreme expression, this produces a fixation with a particular pet explanation or approach. This is most likely to occur if a therapist comes to identify closely with a particular explanation or approach from their own therapeutic experience, as a client (many therapists have themselves been in or are currently in therapy), or if they become enamored with a particular explanation, approach, or theorist/therapist, from graduate school, workshops, or readings. It is somewhat ironic that such a fixation may be regarded as a "specialty," because to "specialize" in this manner is tantamount to specializing in preconception.

THE THERAPEUTIC CULTURE

Part of the problem with therapy exists in the concepts, models and paradigms themselves, and part exists in the way in which they are employed. Many of the concepts, models and paradigms are simply not well grounded in the meaningful experiences and subjective interpretations and understandings of the client. The perspective of the therapist is often given primacy over the perspective of the client. Indeed, if they are inconsistent, the client's perspective may even be regarded as part and parcel of the problem, through such concepts as "resistance," "denial," "transference," or even "oppositional disorder."

In actuality, the perspectives and interpretations of therapists are grounded in the therapeutic subculture. They make sense to therapists because they are immersed in them during their training and in daily interactions with their colleagues. They take on a semblance of validity and legitimacy primarily through a general social consensus. Most therapy training programs include a requirement that initiates undergo some sort of psychotherapeutic experience themselves. The assumption appears to be that this experience will weed out those who do not possess the personal qualities conducive to being a therapist, and help prepare the remainder for their future role -- sort of an emotional/ psychological "boot camp," as it were.

The training process in toto serves as a socialization experience, in which the initiates become members of the therapeutic "community" or "world."[13] Through this process they become familiar with the knowledge, ways of thinking, feeling, understanding, acting, interacting, and so forth of that culture. What was once generally foreign to them becomes comfortable and taken for granted, in the same manner that the knowledge, ways of thinking, feeling, etc. of any culture become taken for granted by its members. Many therapists lose touch with the fact that clients are not members of this culture, although some clients are somewhat familiar with it, through having read self-help literature, and through conversations with others who have been or are currently in therapy. Such clients are often familiar and comfortable enough with therapeutic jargon and such to in effect become "auxiliary members," so to speak. However, many other clients (in my experience men more so than women) find much of what they are subjected to when they enter the therapeutic milieu to be some combination of uncomfortable, insulting, confusing, intimidating, and sometimes even ridiculous and silly, and generally foreign. They seldom express this to their therapists. Some simply leave. Some feel inadequate and blame themselves for their inability to understand and relate to it. Some learn to tolerate it. Some eventually become more comfortable with it, and are "converted."

However, many clients find that the meanings which they derived from their experience in the therapeutic milieu are of limited value in their real lives. When they are themselves active participants in the therapeutic milieu, its meanings possess an appealing veracity. However, when the leave the aura of this setting and the therapeutic relationship, what they have learned is often less useful than it first appeared. Outside this setting much of what they learned is simply not realistic. Without the weight of the therapist's countenance, these new meanings begin to lose their magic. Unfortunately, many clients see this as their own shortcoming, rather than the therapist's. Others lose faith in the idea of therapy.

This is not to suggest that what they have learned is of no value. It is to suggest that if what clients learned in therapy was more completely grounded in their own experience and meanings, they would benefit a great deal more. I would also point out that many clients are helped a great deal by their therapeutic experience, often more by the relationship itself than by the particular therapeutic mode. And, of course, sometimes there is a gainful fit between a particular therapeutic approach and a particular client.

THE THERAPEUTIC RELATIONSHIP

A third problematic area in therapy occurs within the therapeutic relationship. It has often been stated, probably correctly, that therapy *is* the relationship. To the extent that this is true, it is extremely important that the formation of a therapeutic relationship be accomplished carefully and with consideration to its therapeutic consequences, risks and opportunities. The evolving therapeutic relationship becomes the foundation for the therapeutic process. In fact, the relationship and therapy evolve in an interweaving manner.

In the more than twenty years since I was first introduced to them, I have seized many opportunities to conduct extemporaneous interviews with people who have been on the client side of therapeutic relationships. Never having been a client myself, I have always been most interested in understanding the phenomenological experience of being a client, so my questions have been primarily along these lines.

In terms of the effectiveness of the relationship (the outcome), responses have ranged widely from, "it saved my life," to "it was a complete waste of time and money," to "it made matters worse." In terms of overall satisfaction with the relationship itself, responses have ranged from "it was the best relationship I have ever had," to "it was awful." Although I made no attempts to construct a representative sample (understanding, not generalization, has been my goal), I have received a distressing number of negative responses to my queries about the experience and effectiveness of these relationships.

In the many extemporaneous interviews I conducted, the experience of being on the client side of a therapeutic relationship was often described in less than glowing terms. The following is a list (in no particular order) of the negative words and terms most often mentioned in these interviews (in some instances I have used my own summary terms): feeling disrespected; feeling deceived; being the object of suspicion; feeling mistrusted; feeling blamed; feeling "analyzed" (the feeling of "being under a microscope"); feeling judged, particularly feeling unfairly judged; feeling misunderstood; feeling confused; not knowing what's going on (i.e., feeling mystified); feeling alienated; feeling inferior; receiving no feedback; feeling or being treated passively; not feeling listened to; being treated as an "object"; being treated as if you were "sick" (i.e., feeling pathologized); being treated with indifference; feeling patronized; being neutralized; being invalidated; being disapproved of; having no "boundary rights"; having no rights of grievance; being treated with impatience; being treated as stupid or unaware; not being talked to "directly" (i.e., "beating around the bush"); being asked or "forced" to act in unnatural or affected ways (e.g., talking to an empty chair).

Unfortunately, very few persons I interviewed informed or complained to their therapists regarding these matters. As a result, the therapists were probably left with the impression that "everything is okay." Once again, this was often the case in the instances in which I observed therapy sessions and subsequently interviewed the participants.

The reluctance of clients to complain to their therapists is probably related to the fact that therapeutic relationships are characterized by inherent status differential, to wit, that of "doctor/patient," "helper/helped," "expert/layman," and the like. We all have experienced relationships, even intimate ones, which are characterized by status differential. Most of us are generally comfortable with this, particularly if the relationships are personally rewarding (e.g., parent/child, student/teacher, and coaching relationships). So, the status differential inherent in therapeutic relationships is not necessarily problematic. However, it can become so in at least two ways.

First of all, it may become problematic if the client accepts status asymmetry and gives over autonomy to the therapist. In such instances, the client tends to defer to the therapist's "authority" and "expertise," and accepts what the therapist says, does, or suggests, often blaming themselves if it is ineffective. Some clients initially give a valiant try at maintaining a generally equal relationship, but eventually succumb to the might of the therapist's authority. Others give over their autonomy from the beginning.

Secondly, it may become problematic for some clients if they feel uncomfortable with being on the "lower" side of status asymmetry. In therapy, this often takes the form of the client not wanting to feel as if the therapist has power over them (e.g., the power to ask personal questions, the power to make judgments about them, the power to degrade them, or in the case of relationship therapy, the power to affect the balance of power in the relationship).[14]

In these instances, the client may resist the perceived power asymmetry, which will likely present a myriad of problems in the relationship, such as lack of trust, lack of respect, uncooperativeness, and so forth. This may in turn result in the therapist seeing this resistance as in inherent, problematic feature of the client's personality, language of emotions, and so on, and therefore a property of "the problem" or "the disorder." Such labels as "resistance," "denial," or "transference" may then be invoked. Of course, this will only compound the problem. It is ironic that although the problems may be an artifact of the therapist's approach, the client is essentially held responsible. This may leave the client feeling "blamed."

GROUNDED THERAPY

I have sketched there problematic areas in therapy -- preconception, the therapeutic culture, and the therapeutic relationship. The problems in these three areas cannot be understood in isolation from one another, as they are very much interrelated. The therapeutic culture effectively serves as a global preconception. It provides the explanatory and operative frameworks within which therapists practice their profession. It also provides the everyday understandings, prescriptions and proscriptions -- ways of thinking, acting, interacting, and so forth -- which are inherent to any culture. It is these factors,

combined, which "drive" therapy and the therapeutic relationship.

How then should one construct a satisfactory therapeutic relationship and process? In my view, the best way to accomplish this is to take a grounded approach, by enlisting the following guidelines:

1) *Begin with as few preconceptions about the client and their situation and as few theoretical preconceptions (both explanatory and operative) as possible.*[15]

Glaser and Strauss (1967: p.5) assert that the adequacy of a theory cannot be divorced from the process by which it is generated. I believe the same logic holds true for therapy. Collecting information, defining '' the problem,'' drawing conclusions, and preselecting concepts, theories, and models *before* the therapeutic process, rather than *through* the therapeutic process, may limit, misdirect, or derail therapy. With this approach, it becomes all too easy to slip into the use of ''processing stereotypes,'' (Hawkins and Tiedemen, 1975: p.184) and to view the client, their situation, and problem as an instance of something which is already familiar, and then to take a premature ''leap forward'' in the process, similar to what Lofland (1970/1971) refers to as ''analytic interruptus.''

Furthermore, the *process* of collecting and analyzing ''data'' has great therapeutic potential. It should not, in fact cannot, be separated from the operative side of the therapeutic process. One of the most therapeutic of all experiences is to feel *listened to* and *understood.* If the abstract, conceptualized understandings which evolve out of the therapeutic process are grounded in the client's subjective experience, interpretations, understandings, and meaning system, and are achieved in *partnership* with the client, a large part of therapy will already have been achieved.

Questions asked on intake forms and psychological tests are typically based on preconceived notions about what sorts of explanatory variables are relevant. ''Findings'' are of course always shaped by questions. Therefore, in order for the therapeutic process to remain grounded, not only the answers, but the *questions* must *earn* their way. Their relevancy should be *discovered* through the analytical process. This is not to say that factors which are commonly presumed to be relevant, such as family or origin experiences, cannot be relevant. They certainly can. But, the therapist should not assume their relevancy from the outset, but instead should *remain open to discovery.*

In using a grounded therapy approach, the therapist begins from a framework of presumed ignorance about explanations, solutions, the client, their situation, their problem, and so forth, then proceeds with a primarily *inductive* process, with the full participation of the client. In this manner, the therapeutic process becomes one of *partnership* and *mutual discovery*, in which both therapist and client learn what is relevant and what works.

Another reason to proceed with an attitude of presumed ignorance, is that clients are usually very eager, even impatient, to "tell their story." If the therapist frustrates this urge by immediately administering psychological tests, asking long lists of questions which the client may at this point not see as relevant (even though they may be), and offering "explanations" right from the start, the client may become alienated from the process. This may encourage them to shut down, and become passive recipients of therapy, rather than active, mutual participants. Or, they may feel as if the therapist is not listening and not really concerned with what they think and feel. This may provoke them to seek another therapist, or cease therapy, altogether.

2) *Ground the frame the therapeutic process and relationship within the client's values, subjective understandings, interpretations, and meaning system.*

I once heard a psychiatrist assert, "if your client feels good when they leave a session, you have failed them." I have observed this sentiment to be fairly common in the therapeutic culture, although certainly not universal. In talking and listening to therapists who share this sentiment, it is evident that their assertion is that change and growth are always uncomfortable, even painful, and thus if you are helping the client to feel better you are not tapping into the "real" issues, and therefore are not doing real therapy. The assumption here is that helping clients to consciously think and feel better about themselves and their lives is superficial, because the "real stuff" occurs in the *unconscious*. Another assumption often made here is that clients typically resist attempts to "break through their defenses," even though they may be unaware of it (evidently the unconscious is a "trickster"). Thus, when the therapist attempts to breach these defenses to get at the real pathology, it produces resistance and discomfort in the client.

This approach might aptly be termed "nutcracker therapy." The nutcracker approach focuses on the negative -- i.e., "breaking through" defenses so as to defeat the "pathology" rooted in the unconscious. In my experience, not only is this approach unnecessary, it is very limiting, and often even counter-therapeutic. I believe this approach, more than any other, is apt to generate the kinds of negative responses which I outlined earlier.

The nutcracker approach overlooks what I, and many other therapists who prefer a "cognitive" approach, believe is the most important asset in therapy, the resources of the conscious, subjective self. In my experience, it is most productive in therapy to work on the positive, by reinforcing and enhancing the efficacious resources of the conscious self.

Furthermore, in my view, the nutcracker approach is disrespectful and insulting to clients, as it treats them as "objects" of therapy, whose subjective interpretations, and so forth must be regarded with suspicion (one must beware of "the trickster"), rather than as trustworthy, fully participating, equal partners.

In using a grounded therapy approach, from the outset the therapist seeks "verstehen," or what Rogers (1959 and elsewhere) refers to as "empathetic understanding," by attending closely to the client's *own* subjective view of themselves, their situation, and their problem. In effect, the grounded therapist attempts to "become the other," to the extent this is possible. To have any real, lasting power for the client, the knowledge derived from the therapeutic process must be relevant to the client's everyday life, values and meaning framework.

With a grounded therapy approach, the client's values, knowledge, interpretations, understandings, and meaning system are viewed as central to therapy, and *more* important than the therapist's, as they are what guides both the explanatory and operative components of therapy. This is not to say that the client will necessarily have a fully informed and well articulated view. If they did, they probably wouldn't be seeking the services of a therapist. However, the client will always know the conditions of their life, their values, their experiences, thoughts, feelings, etc. in more immaculate detail than the therapist. The therapist's knowledge, which is more abstract, is initially secondary. As suggested above, to start, therapists should attempt to "suspend" their knowledge, so as to minimize the risk of preconception.

However, the therapist enters the situation with unique and valuable *skills* not possessed by the client. The therapeutic process involves combining the client's knowledge with primarily the therapist's skills, and only secondarily their knowledge, from whence evolves new, hopefully better conceptualized and organized, knowledge (and skills). Knowledge should be abstracted *from* the therapeutic process, not imposed upon it. To be sure, the therapist brings useful knowledge to the process. The therapist enters with abstractions, awareness and understanding of broader patters, processes, conditions, and so forth. But, this pre-existing knowledge should be used merely to sensitize the process, not determine it.

3) *Model the therapeutic relationship after the positive features of functional, healthy, native relationships.*

In my efforts to understand the differences between a productive versus unproductive therapeutic relationship, I have come to the clear conclusion that the contrast lies in where the relationship is grounded. Satisfactory therapeutic relationships resemble satisfactory, "native" (i.e., "real world") relationships. It is important to model therapeutic relationships after relation-ships in the native culture, not the therapeutic culture.

Clearly, therapeutic relationships cannot, nor should they, be exactly of the same nature as native relationships. They are artificially contrived for a specific purpose, so they should include only those components of native relationships which are productive for this purpose. Native relationships, even the best of them, are sometimes characterized by conflict, judgmentalness, impatience, and so forth. Insofar as it is possible, these features of native relationships should not be duplicated.

Therapeutic relationships are, probably more often than not, modeled after "doctor/patient," or "expert/layman," and such, relationships. The therapist is viewed as already possessing the special knowledge which the client needs. The client's knowledge is typically viewed as being secondary, even irrelevant or counter-productive. The therapist is viewed as the "authority," or "expert," the client as the "layman," The therapist is viewed as "the helper," the client as "the helped." Although these things may be essentially true, they do not need to comprise the framework within which the relationship is conducted. Like doctor/patient relationships, such relationships may (or may not) feel relatively comfortable and friendly, but they are limited by their asymmetry. More useful frameworks, such as "partnership," or "co-analyst" are available. Such frameworks encourage the active participation of the client.

In my experience, the most effective therapeutic relationships are those which feel "natural" and generally "equal." Experiencing a relationship which feels natural, healthy, accepting, and nurturing can be therapeutic, in and of itself. Many, if not most, clients have a paucity of healthy relationships in their lives. Like many other therapists, I have had numerous clients mention to me that their relationship with me was the first comfortable, healthy relationship they had experienced, wherein they felt understood, accepted, listened to, respected, and such, and that it was very healing. I believe this is largely what is being referred to with the notion that "therapy *is* the relationship."

What then comprises a natural, healthy relationship? Certainly, it consists of the counterpoints to the previously enumerated list of dissatisfactions. The respondents who expressed satisfaction with their therapeutic relationships, identified essentially the same factors as those who expressed dissatisfaction, but inversely. That is, participants prefer being respected over being disrespected, being trusted over being mistrusted, being listened to over not being listened to, being understood over being misunderstood, ad infinitum. In short, they prefer pretty much the same thing in therapeutic relationships as they do in natural relationships.

It makes sense, then, to nurture and encourage the positive versions of these factors when developing a therapeutic relationship. This is best achieved by grounding the relationship in the client's interpretations and meaning system, rather than the therapeutic culture. In other words, to the extent possible, it is achieved by making the relationship feel natural. This is of course done in pretty much the same manner that one achieves it in healthy native relationships, by attending to the other persons needs, feelings, interpretations, rights, comfort and discomfort, by being respectful, by listening, ad infinitum. It is certainly not achieved by acting in ways which feel to the client as if they are being objectified, patronized, viewed with suspicion, disrespected, and so on. If the therapist grounds the relation-ship, as suggested, these feelings will likely be avoided.

4) *Attend carefully to the client's ongoing experience of the therapeutic relationship and process.*

It is generally regarded as a given in therapy that the relationship is extremely important. As mentioned previously, many therapists maintain that therapy is the relationship. This is a sentiment with which I largely agree. If this is the case, creating a sound therapeutic relationship should take initial priority, as it will serve as a foundation for everything which follows. It is important for the therapist to pace the process on the client's terms. If, as discussed above, the therapist begins by thwarting the client's needs as they perceive them, the therapeutic relationship and process may itself be thwarted. If the therapist proceeds too quickly, the client may be "scared off." If the therapist proceeds too slowly, the client may begin to believe that "therapy doesn't work," and come to view it as "a waste of time and money."

This does not mean, however, that the therapist should always let the client assert complete control over the process and content of therapy. If it becomes evident that a client is trying to control the process for "illegitimate" reasons, the therapist should introduce this as a "therapeutic issue." For example, it is not uncommon in relationship therapy for one person to attempt to control the process and content of therapy, so as to keep or increase power in the relationship. However, if there are not apparent reasons to the contrary, and if such control and power issues are not present, I believe it is best for the therapist to give deference to the client's needs and preferences in this regard.

I have heard many therapists assert that the client should never be allowed to "take charge" of the process. In my experience, if the relationship is on solid ground, very few clients attempt to do this. Most are quite satisfied to be involved in a relationship in which power is shared. It is probably more common for clients to voluntarily lend too much of their power and autonomy over to the therapist, than the reverse.

In using a grounded therapy approach it is important to be constantly aware of the client's phenomenological experience of the therapeutic process, not just to ensure that it "feels good," but because to do otherwise is hazardous. Given that grounded therapy can only be achieved through a generally equal partnership between client and therapist, it is critical that the therapist stay in harmony with the client. Furthermore, if the therapist neglects to attend to the client's ongoing experience of therapy, the therapeutic relationship may be irreparably damaged.[16]

5) Although to some extent therapeutic relationships possess inherent status differential, *develop the relationship mutually so that it feels generally "equal,"* keeping in mind that "equal" does not mean "identical."

It is important for therapists to remember they are being enlisted primarily for their skills, not their knowledge. The client's knowledge and the therapist's skills are equally important to the process. Therefore, therapy must be a *mutual* process, which requires a general *equality* in the relationship. Each party must feel equally invited to contribute to the process, and each party must feel equally entitled to rights of grievance.

An effective therapeutic relationship must be an intimate one. Clients must feel free to discuss subjects, experiences, thoughts, emotions, and so forth with their therapist which they may never before have discussed with anyone.

Relationships are more apt to achieve intimacy within a framework of general equality. This includes therapists sharing something of themselves, rather than remaining aloof. One way for therapist to achieve this, is to use anecdotes from their personal lives, as one would use comparative data in generating a grounded theory, for the purposes of constant comparative analysis, and theoretical sampling. This approach gives analytical value to personal disclosure, as well as enhancing intimacy in the relationship. It also minimizes the likelihood that, although they are incorporating material from their personal life into the process, they will begin to work on their own personal issues, rather than the client's issues.

One of the keys to establishing an effective therapeutic relationship is to achieve intimacy, and all of the positive things that go with it, while minimizing the negative and capitalizing on the positive aspects of status differential. It is important that clients feel as if they are full, equal participants in the process. Yet, it is also important that the client attribute a certain amount of "charisma" to the therapist's role, such that they believe in the process. This is a balancing act which can be more thoughtfully and thoroughly managed with a grounded therapy approach, because such an approach keeps the therapist constantly "in tune" with the client.

6) To the extent possible, *ground the operative side of therapy in the client's everyday life, values, interpretations, understandings and meaning systems.*

Many therapeutic solutions are grounded primarily in the theories, concepts, understandings, meanings, and so forth of the therapeutic culture. For example, if a client's problem is judged to be a function of some pathology of the unconscious, stemming from childhood trauma, the attempted solution(s) will be designed to penetrate the client's defenses, so as to access and affect the unconscious. It is often assumed that, because of defenses, it is difficult to directly access the unconscious. Thus, "indirect" techniques are used, to supposedly circumvent these defenses. For example, some techniques involve the use of symbols, or metaphors, which are presumed to bypass the conscious and work directly on the unconscious. Such approaches are rather mystical. For the uninitiated (usually the layman or client), it appears that some sort of unseen, "magical" variable is at work. Somewhat over-simplistically, the client comes in, the therapist performs "magical incantations," so to speak, and the client leaves "cured," not knowing quite what did the trick -- sort of a "hocus pocus therapy." Only the therapist presumably knows what is occurring. The client is left in the dark, so as to prevent their defenses from coming into play. The client's understandings and interpretations are relegated to a secondary status.

A critical assumption being made here appears to be that not only are the resources of the conscious, interpretive mind essentially irrelevant, they are impotent, and even a potential obstruction to therapy. This appears to be pretty much a universal assumption of theories and approaches which are rooted in the notion of the unconscious.

With a grounded therapy approach, as with cognitive and insight therapies in general, the conscious, interpretive mind is given primacy. The conscious mind is directly accessible. The client and therapist can discover, analyze, discuss, interpret, reinterpret, and so forth, directly and dynamically. Through analyzing patterns of emotion, thought, and behavior, factors which have existed "below the level of awareness" (the "unconscious" as an adjective, rather than a noun) may be brought into the realm of awareness, where change can be consciously and willfully attempted. The client assumes a position of power, as the active author of their own life, rather than a victim of mystical, unconscious forces. The client's interpretations, understandings, beliefs, values, lifestyle, everyday life, and so forth become the context within which solutions are processed. The conscious, interpretive mind is open to new ways of viewing things, through the discovery or introduction of new knowledge and concepts, through appeals to rationality, through "reframing," and so forth. In partnership with the therapist, the client can discover, strengthen, and build on the innate resources of their conscious mind.

The conscious mind is capable of *will*. New awareness combined with will can serve as a catalyst for change. And, such change will be "owned" by the client, as they will have played a primary role in producing it. This is not to say that solutions, healing and change always come easily, or that this approach or any other cognitive or insight approach can solve all problems. But, solutions and change are certainly more likely to occur if the client is an active player, rather than a passive recipient.

Whenever it is possible and appropriate, it is useful to incorporate the client's values, beliefs, and meaning systems into the operative side of therapy. Sometimes, through the therapeutic process, it becomes evident that a client's beliefs, etc., might be problematic. For ethical as well as procedural reasons, in such instances, it is best for the therapist to provide opportunities for the client to discover this (presumably) on their own, whereupon it can then be discussed. From what I have observed, therapists tend too often, and inappropriately, to view client's beliefs, meaning systems, and values as themselves part of the problem, as "defense mechanisms," for example. This is particularly the case if they are seen as being substantially out of the ordinary. This eliminates their potential as resources for therapy.

However, in my experience, if a client has a strong, clear set of beliefs, they may be useful as a resource, to formulate a "reframe," for instance. It is not necessary or important that the therapist agree with these beliefs, only that they respect and understand them well enough to incorporate them into the therapeutic process. In general, if solutions are framed within a meaning system which the client already understands and values, they are more likely to be useful, durable, relevant, and to work.

A client's association with the therapeutic milieu is temporary. And, the therapeutic milieu is artificial. As I mentioned previously, what makes sense to the client during their time in the therapeutic milieu may make less sense when they leave its influence. For this reason, it is important for the client's new skills and knowledge to be grounded in the real world, not the therapeutic world.

Therapeutic solutions must also realistically fit the limitations and resources of the client's everyday life. If they don't, they will likely drift into disuse. What may be appropriate or possible for one client may be impossible for another. For example, a therapist's suggestion that a client do mid-day relaxation exercises to relieve stress may be unrealistic because of workplace conditions. The client's workplace may have no private, quiet location in which to do them. Or, a male client's co-workers may tease and laugh at him when he attempts to do them.

The danger in not fitting solutions to the client's everyday life is not only that the value of therapy will be diminished or lost, but that the client may view themselves as being responsible. They may interpret the outcome as merely one more instance of personal failure.

7) To the extent possible, *model therapeutic solutions after natural, indigenous ones.*

Although their personal experience of it may be unique, most problems for which clients seek therapy are common in society. And, they are commonly solved, indigenously, without enlisting the services of a therapist. It is useful to know something about natural healing and problem solving processes, as they occur in the real world, rather than the artificial milieu of therapy. Whenever possible, I believe it is important to model therapeutic problem solving and healing process after natural, indigenous ones. The closer a therapeutic course of action approximates a natural process, the more relevant, effective and enduring it will be. After all, natural, indigenous solutions have already been shown to *work.*

However, our knowledge of natural, indigenous healing and problem solving processes is inadequate. It would be ideal for practicing therapists if large numbers of well-grounded studies of the kinds of problems which they address were available. Although a fair number of reasonably well-grounded studies are available, they tend to focus on the substantive rather than the generic, and they tend to be somewhat limited in scope, density, and integration. Through no fault of the researchers, they also tend to be read and used by therapists as formulas to be applied, rather than as abstractions to enhance theoretical sensitivity.

PROCEDURES

As I maintained above, in using a grounded therapy approach, one should begin with as few preconceptions as possible. The reigning guideline in gathering information is to proceed from the general to the specific. One should always ask questions in the least leading manner possible. Each new subject area should be introduced with a "grand tour" type of question, which does not guide the client's response. For example, my favorite opening question with a new client is, "to what do I owe the honor of this visit?" My next question is always informed by the client's response to this initial question. And, the following question is then informed by the response to this question, and so forth, with questions always being posed in the least leading way, until the topic feels momentarily saturated. A topic which has already been covered can of course be brought up again, if the ongoing analysis suggests it (for the purposes of constant comparative analysis, theoretical sampling, elaboration, exploring new dimensions, etc.). What is important here is that at this point the process be guided, not by preconceptions or capricious, unguided probing, but the *evolving analysis*.

As with grounded theory, analysis begins immediately, and always guides how and where you do next. As I mentioned at the outset, I am assuming the reader has a general familiarity with grounded theory procedures, so I shall not review them in detail.[18]

The coding process itself is conducted in pretty much the same manner as it is in generating a grounded theory, albeit in truncated form:

1) Start with *open coding*, by coding for anything and everything that seems potentially relevant, without preconceiving problems, solutions, etc.

2) Begin *constant comparative analysis:* (a) Compare each coded incident to similar coded incidents. For example, if you are working with a couple experiencing frequent conflict, you would want to compare each episode of conflict with each other episode. From this you may discover particular properties of the conflict, such as relative power, resentment, fear, anger, or particular substantive issues, such as money, sex, parenting, and so forth. (b) Compare new concepts with new incidents. To continue the above example, upon comparing episodes of conflict, you may discover an underlying common theme, such as misunderstanding. (c) Compare concept to concept. In your coding you may have developed the concept of gender misunderstanding. In comparing the two codes, misunderstanding and gender misunderstanding, it will be apparent that gender misunderstanding is merely one type of misunderstanding. This will cue you to look for other specific types of misunderstanding. In doing this, you may discover patterns of interpretation from previous relationships (often referred to as "old baggage") to be another source of misunderstanding. In any event, constant comparative analysis will increase the breadth of your understanding, while simultaneously allowing you to narrow your focus down to core issues and problems.

At first compare incidents from within the particular case with which you are working, then, if useful, incorporate incidents from other similar cases. An additional technique which I have found particularly useful in therapy is to search your own experience for incidents which are as similar as possible to the client's, for purposes of comparison. This is particularly useful in a therapeutic context because the client's experience of their issues and/or problems is often very deep and intense. Because of the more personal nature of therapy, it is important for the therapist to achieve close "verstehen," or empathetic understanding with each client, at a deeper level than is normally required by research.

3) Once a reasonably clear picture of the relevant issues or problems emerges, then begin *selective coding,* around these matters. If your open coding points to misunderstanding as a consistent theme, as illustrated above, begin coding for different properties and types of misunderstanding.

4) When it feels appropriate, begin exploring how the in vivo and substantive codes relate to each other, through the use of *theoretical codes.*[19]

5) Look for the emergence of a *core variable* or variables.[20] In the above example, through selective coding and constant comparison, you may arrive at "misunderstanding" as a core variable. Although in many instances one core variable will cover matters sufficiently, you must remain open to multiple core variables. The number of relevant core variables will be determined by the particular issues in each particular case. Unlike the theorist, the therapist cannot arbitrarily decide to eliminate a particular core variable and focus exclusively on another. This decision must be made according to the therapeutic needs of the particular client. In some instances this may produce a need to focus on multiple core variables. However, with further analysis, one often finds a relationship between these various core variables, which produces a transcending core variable, which can then become the focus of therapy. This is not a particularly unusual occurrence in therapy. Once clients' immediate issues or problems begin to subside, they often choose to tackle "deeper" personal issues. For example, a client who originally seeks help in processing a divorce may begin to perceive patterns in how they conduct relationships in general, whereupon they will want to shift from the more pragmatic concerns of the divorce to deeper issues of self, relationships, and so forth. Upon delving into these issues, the client may then go full circle, seeing how they contributed to the divorce.

Like the theorist, the therapist must remain open to discovery, throughout the process. Because the aim is different than in generating a theory for publication, and the conditions under which the therapist works are different than those under which the researcher works, modifications to the process must be made, as each situation dictates. As a rule, whenever and to the extent possible, it is best to follow the procedures of grounded theory as closely as one can. This will maximize grounding. However, the extent to which this is possible will vary from one therapeutic situation to another. For example, opportunities for constant comparison and theoretical sampling would vary from individual, to couple, to family or group therapy. The more individuals involved in a particular case, the more one can find such opportunities with that particular case. When conducting individual therapy, such opportunities within the case are limited, as you have only one "respondent." In this instance, one must use other sources, such as the situations of other clients, including the clients of other therapists, through consultation, conversation and routine "case staffings," or as I discussed previously, even one's own personal life. In any event, the therapist must remain creative and flexible.

One clear difference between generating a theory and conducting therapy is that, because of the practicalities of doing therapy, most coding will have to be conducted *in process*, often openly, with the participation of the client.[21] Furthermore, much of the coding must occur solely in the therapist's mind. It is possible to jot down codes in the case notes, or on a separate piece of paper, as they occur in one's mind. But, because of the fluid immediacy of the therapeutic process and the number of matters which the therapist must juggle simultaneously, coding simply cannot be achieved in as thorough a manner as with research, nor for that matter can case notes be as thorough as field notes. Furthermore, given typical client loads, it is simply not practical to spend separate time at the end of each day conducting lengthy analyses.

This mode of "coding from the hip," so to speak, requires a dexterity which can only be achieved through experience. Although in doing ordinary grounded theory research, data collection and analysis are said to occur simultaneously, they do not ordinarily occur *at the same exact time*, as most coding for therapy does.

Furthermore, although it is important to attend to the respondent's ongoing phenomenological experience of an interview, it is not critical, because one is merely gathering information, not intervening in a person's life. In addition, the therapeutic relationship is an ongoing one, whereas the interviewer/respondent relationship seldom is (except in the case of long-term participant observation research). Plus, it is not particularly common for researchers to do group interviews, as therapists commonly do. To complicate matters even further, the therapist also has the ongoing responsibility of arriving at remedies for the client's problem(s) and finding ways in which to introduce them, either covertly or overtly into the process. And, for reasons discussed above, all of this must be accomplished with the active participation of the client, and it must be accomplished with subtlety so as to feel natural. In fact, much of what the therapist does is not visible to the client. The more the client feels the insights, knowledge, ideas for solutions, and so forth are "owned" by them, the more apt they are to be relevant, to fit, and to work. With so many matters to attend to, the grounded therapist must be ever vigilant, balancing numerous levels of thought and action, simultaneously.

Although in some ways the therapist's task is more complex than the theorist's, insofar as elaboration and integration of concepts are concerned, it is also more limited. Because it is not the task of a therapist to generate and theory for write-up and publication, the therapist need only generate a "working theory," for a particular case. A good working understanding and explanation is all that is needed.

Another clear difference between generating a theory and conducting therapy is that therapy has an operative component. In therapy, the point of analysis is not to arrive at a generalizable theory (although with a little extra work that could be accomplished), but to arrive at solutions to the identified issues or problems, in a particular case. Although, while adding another dimension with which to be concerned, it also provides an opportunity that potential solutions can be rolled back into the process. Likely solutions can be tried, examined, refined, modified and retried, in process. Although solutions sometimes have a delayed reaction effect, their potential usually begins to evidence itself during the therapeutic process.

With any particular case, solutions can be either devised, or inherent to the process, or as is usually the case, both. Devised solutions could include anything from strategic "reframing," to "behavior modification," to teaching "communication skills," ad infinitum, depending upon what the situation suggests.

Inherent solutions are an outgrowth of simply participating in the process. For example, as I discussed previously, merely feeling listened to and understood can be very therapeutic. And, careful listening and empathetic understanding are necessary components of the grounded therapy approach. Additionally, the grounded therapy process is inherently "educational." Clients gain both conceptualized, organized knowledge and skills, with which to identify and solve problems. Furthermore, whatever is achieved is "owned" by the client, as it is achieved in full partnership. All of this can be very "empowering" for the client. In fact, most often, it is best to covertly "lead" the client, such that they experience the power of ownership in the process.

CONCLUSIONS

As I mentioned at the outset, the grounded therapy approach was devised in response to what I observed practicing therapists doing, not what is found in the literature. Therapy as it is routinely practiced is replete with a priori assumptions and preconceptions, coming from explanatory/operative constructs, the therapeutic culture and the therapeutic relationship. Less imaginative and novice therapists tend to practice what I characterize as "formula" therapy, by adhering to particular therapeutic modes in a doctrinaire fashion. Imaginative, experienced therapists tend to practice what I characterize as "improvisational therapy," which may be somewhat more creative, but which may also be somewhat erratic. As I hope to have shown here, both approaches have some serious problems and limitations. Over the years, I have integrated the techniques of grounded theory with the best of what I observed other therapists doing, as well as what has worked in my own practice. The result is what I am referring to as "grounded therapy." Although grounded therapy shares a great deal with other modes of therapy, in that it incorporates whatever is useful and fits, it is uniquely formulated to provide therapists with a methodology, a specific set of operational guidelines, by which to conduct both the explanatory and operative sides of therapy with creativity and without orthodoxy. And, in my experience, it is an example of the power of grounded theory.

ENDNOTES

1. I wish to thank my colleagues and clients for providing the arena and experiences from which much of what is contained here was drawn. I also wish to thank my friends and colleagues Kelly Hadley and Gary Sandwick for many informative and enjoyable hours spent discussing therapy. I especially wish to thank Jo Simmons for many informative and

enjoyable years spent discussing about every imaginable facet of therapy, and for contributing to many of the ideas contained herein.

2. When I use the term "therapy," I am referring to psychiatry, clinical psychology, counseling (in its many forms), and the like. My observations, conversations, discussions and interviews have mostly been with practicing counselors, although a fair number have been with psychiatrists and clinical psychologists.

3. To avoid confusion, I might point out that since I completed my Ph.D. I have resumed the use of my birth surname, Simmons.

4. However, a book-length piece on this topic is currently in progress.

5. See Gross (1978), Masson (1988), as well as the many works of Thomas Szasz, amongst others, for discussions and reviews of the research literature concerning the failures of therapy.

6. Some critics, most notably Masson (1988) argue that therapy is useless or impossible in any form. Although I consider myself a critic of therapy as it is practiced, I believe simply eradicating therapy would be tantamount to "throwing out the baby with the bath water." As a practicing therapist, I have seen many instances in which therapy has been undeniably and profoundly helpful to clients. I am not yet ready to give up the idea that one person can help another, even if such help involves a fee.

7. Many therapists, in fact about half of psychologists who practice therapy, call themselves "eclectic" (Masson, 1988).

8. The notion of "unconscious" or "subconscious" mind, although not originated by Freud, was initially central to Freudian psychoanalysis. However, later in his career, it came to play a lesser role, much of what was attributed to it being replaced by the "id." The distinction between the conscious and unconscious was replaced with the three part organization of the "id," "ego," and "superego." The unconscious was "demoted" to the status of merely "a quality of mental phenomena" (Hall, 1954).

9. See Thornton (1986) for a discussion of this connection.

10. The **DSM-III-R** is the Diagnostic and Statistical Manual of Mental Disorders, of the American Psychiatric Association (revised edition).

11. Such diagnoses are sometimes influenced by considerations other than fit, such as minimizing the potential stigma for the client.

12. Therapists would do well to follow Glaser's (1978, p.69) advice for theorists to "...type behavior, not people... This allows the actors in grounded theory to walk in and out of many behavior patterns without being typed as one of them. Our actors can rome unlabeled and unclassified. They can succeed here and fail there and not be failures or successes, deviate here and conform there and not be deviants or conformists, and so forth. This does not offend people, since the emphasis is on behavioral patterns, not personal patterns."

13. See Strauss (1977 and 1984) for discussions of the notion of "social worlds."

14. In my experience, this is more often the case with men than with women, because of cultural expectations regarding the male role.

15. This does not mean each case needs to be re-invented. Knowledge and concepts derived from well-grounded studies and experience at doing therapy can be used to sensitize, but not determine where a given analysis will go. The line between "preconception" and "sensitivity" is somewhat imprecise, but becomes intuitive with experience. The idea is to remain open and flexible, to avoid "pet" and "fad" concepts and explanations, and to refrain from becoming doctrinaire in one's approach.

16. Of the many "horror stories" I have heard from persons who have been on the receiving end of nutcracker therapy, one stands out. This person (a woman in her early sixties) reported that her therapist fell asleep during a session, while she was talking. When she realized he had fallen asleep, she remained in stunned silence for some time. When he finally woke up, he told her he had fallen asleep intentionally, because she was "boring." He explained that if he merely told her she was boring, the experience would not have sufficient impact to break through her defenses, so as to reach her unconscious. She terminated therapy. This experience was so distressing the insulting to her that she didn't seek another therapist, assuming incorrectly, that this approach was universal.

One noteworthy thing about this and many other therapeutic "horror stories" which have been related to me is that in each instance the therapist denied the insult, frequently offering a "therapeutic" justification for thoughtless, disrespectful behavior. To be sure, this problem is not confined to nutcracker therapy. The practitioners of more "humanistic," "client centered" therapies exercise their own forms of insulting insensitivity, usually by mistaking a patronizing, gratuitously sincere attitude and demeanor and a "sing songy" tone of voice for "concern," "caring," "sincerity," and the like.

17. To give a clearer idea of what I mean by "grand tour questions," consider the following (note that each of these examples is more specific a topical than the one I posed in the text):

A. "Please tell me about a typical day in your life."

B. "Tell me about your family, growing up."

C. "What was life like when you were a child?"

D. "What do you think the future holds for you?"

E. "Tell me about your relationship."

F. Etc.

18. Therapists who want to learn and use a grounded therapy approach would do well to learn how to do "pure" grounded theory first. This will allow them to approximate grounded theory procedures to the extent that their particular therapeutic situation allows. For a detailed illumination of the techniques of doing grounded theory research upon which the procedures of grounded therapy are based, see Glaser (1978).

19. For a discussion of theoretical coding "families," see Glaser (1978, pp. 72-82).

20. In therapy, the core variable can be a core problem or issue, or it can be the central variable which "drives" a problem or issue. In either instance it is the (or one of the) variable(s) which is central to the individual's life. Some core variables will be exhibited as strong patterns, which are not necessarily conscious to the client(s). Chronic misunderstanding between parties to a relationship is an example of such a core variable. Other core variables, such as chronic resentment, chronic anger, or chronic feelings of worthlessness, may be closer to a client's consciousness. To discover this second type of variable, while coding, it is useful to address the question "what is the client working on?" (such that they are engaging in a particular pattern of emotion, thought and/or action).

21. For this reason, it is particularly important that concepts have imagery, as well as analytical ability, so they will be understandable, appealing and memorable to clients. As Glaser (1978, p.70) points out, in

vivo codes usually have vivid imagery. Concepts with vivid imagery will have more power in the therapeutic process.

REFERENCES

Bigus, Odis E.

1974, *Becoming "Alcoholic": A Study of Social Transformation*, San Francisco, University of California Ph.D. dissertation.

Glaser, Barney G.

1978, *Theoretical Sensitivity*, Mill Valley, California: The Sociology Press.

Glaser, Barney G. and Strauss, Anselm L.

1967, *The Discovery of Grounded Theory*, Chicago: Aldine Publishing Company.

Gross, Martin L.

1978, *The Psychological Society*, New York: Random House.

Hall, Calvin S.

1954, *A Primer of Freudian Psychology*, New York: The New American Library.

Hawkins, Richard and Tiedeman, Gary

1975, The Creation of Deviance, Columbus, Ohio: Charles E. Merrill Publishing Company.

Lofland, John

1970, "Interactionist Imagery and Analytic Interruptus," in Tamotso Shibutani (ed.) *Human Nature and Collective Behavior: Essays in Honor of Herbert Blumer*, Englewood Cliffs, New Jersey: Prentice Hall, Inc., pp. 35-45.

Lofland, John

1971, *Analyzing Social Settings*, Belmont, California: Wadsworth Publishing Co., Inc.

Masson, J. Moussaieff

1988, *Against Therapy: Emotional Tyranny and the Myth of Psycho-*

logical Healing, New York: Atheneum.

Rogers, Carl R.

1959, ''A theory of Therapy, Personality, and Interpersonal Relationships, as Developed in the Client-Centered Framework,'' in S. Koch (ed.) *Psychology: A Study of a Science, Vol. III; Formulations of the Person and the Social Context*, New York: McGraw-Hill, pp. 184-258.

Strauss, Anselm L.

1978, ''A Social World Perspective,'' in Norman K. Denzin (ed.) *Studies in Symbolic Interaction,* Greenwich, Connecticut: Jai Press, pp. 119-128.

Strauss, Anselm L.

1984, ''Social Worlds and Their Segmentation Processes,'' *Studies in Symbolic Interaction,* pp. 123-139.

Thornton, E. M.

1986, *The Freudian Fallacy*, London: Paladin Grafton Books.

Reprinted from *The Handbook of Social Science Methods: Qualitative Methods*, Irvington Publishers, Inc., 1979

THE STUDY OF BASIC SOCIAL PROCESSES*

Odis E. Bigus, Ph.D.

Stuart C. Hadden, Ph.D

Barney G. Glaser, Ph.D.

INTRODUCTION

One of the fundamental tenets of sociology is that social life is not random; that it exists as sets of behavioral uniformities, which occur and recur over time. One of the primary tasks of sociology should be to systematically study these patterned regularities and their major variations as *social processes*. Although process has been addressed throughout the history of sociology,[1] it has too seldom been studied in a methodical manner in and of itself. This is not so much because of a lack of concern about social process as it is an absence of specific and systematic means of approaching its study.

Recognizing this dilemma, we would like to introduce a specific and systematic approach to the study of social process. We propose that one way social process might be studied is by way of a theoretical construct which we shall refer to as *"basic social process."*[2] The basic social process *conception* (hereafter referred to simply as "BSP") is a generic theoretical construct of the same genre as Weber's (1964) "ideal type" and Schutz's (1971) "homunculus." However, unlike these conceptions, the idea of BSP was developed within and is systematically tied to a specific methodological program for generating theory.

Formulation of the BSP conception arose as a by-product of the ongoing development of what Glaser and Strauss (1967) refer to as "grounded theory" methodology. It is important to underscore the fact that the conception is not a preconception of the methodology, but rather is a product of its empirical application. Consistent with the reasoning to be advanced throughout this paper, the BSP notion was conceived *in the process of doing* grounded theory research.

Briefly stated, BSP's are conceptually developed to account for the organization of social behavior as it occurs over time. That is, BSP sociology is concerned with *dynamics*. Also, BSP's capture both micro and macro phenomena, through a conjoint consideration of both social psychological and social structural variation. These two analytic dimensions are integrated in BSP theories so as to reflect their empirical relationship in the social world. Although either structural or social psychological variation may have primacy in a particular research undertaking (empirically determined), in rendering a structural process theory social psychological variation will be accounted for, and vice versa.

Furthermore, although BSP theories are generated within substantive arenas, they are easily separable from them. The primary concern of BSP sociology is with the *generic*, and only secondarily with the substantive. Since the analytic focus is a *generic process*, formalization of theory can also be readily accomplished. As will be developed more fully later, BSP formal theory is generated from substantive formulations in a manner similar to the development of the original substantive process theory.

Although we are using the term "basic social process" to delineate a particular approach to the development of qualitative theory, we are by no means claiming novelty in this approach. Much work has been produced in qualitative sociology which, to varying extents, is compatible with the BSP notion. Notable examples are Davis' (1961) conception of the "deviance disavowal" process, Lofland's (1966) model of the "conversion" process, and Matza's (1964) conception of the process by which juveniles "drift" into delinquency, and the numerous studies on what might be termed the "becoming" process, such as Becker's (1953) "Becoming a Marihuana User," Olesen and Whittaker's (1968) "The Silent Dialogue," and Weinberg's (1966) "Becoming a Nudist."[3]

Neither are we claiming novelty in our concern for grounded studies which focus on generic variables and on process (cf. Blumer, 1956). These are concerns which have been enduring in sociology. However, the paucity of field studies which clearly and specifically illuminate generic processes testifies to the fact that not all that need be said about these concerns has been said. Generic processes are evident in many qualitative field studies, but in too many instances they remain conceptually underdeveloped.[4] Furthermore, most of the generic conceptualizations in sociology (e.g., functionalism, symbolic interactionism) are not well grounded in field studies. When used in field studies, such conceptualizations are usually used in an appended and/or force-fitted manner. It is our hope that the BSP conception may help focus field studies towards the theoretical development of grounded generic processes, in the tradition of the above-mentioned studies.

In this paper, we shall explore the utility of the BSP approach for generating sociological theory. We shall do this by first comparing process sociology (specifically BSP sociology) with what we shall for convenience refer to as "unit sociology," with respect to durability, generalizability, relationalability, and coverage. Second, we shall discuss, in general terms, the methodology of BSP development. We shall close with a discussion of what effects a well developed process sociology might have on perspectives and conceptions in sociology.

UNIT VERSUS PROCESS SOCIOLOGY

It is sometimes unavoidable that in making conceptual distinctions between real phenomena one must oversimplify or overdraw them for purposes of heuristic comparison. The reader is advised to view the distinction made in this paper between unit and process sociology in this light. Unit and process are tendencies in sociology, with some sociology sharing characteristics of both. Most sociology, however, tends toward the unit side of this distinction.

We use the term "unit sociology" to refer to work in which the basic analytic focus is on a specific sociological unit, such as a population unit (e.g., "Americans," "drug users," "scientists"), cultural units (e.g., "skid row," "mental hospitals," "Universities"), or combinations thereof (e.g., "deviants" as a conceptual category of prostitutes, drug users, check forgers, etc., or "occupations and professions" as the general category for nurses, milkmen, lawyers, etc.). As currently practiced, unit sociology is generally concerned with developing static descriptions and/or conceptualizations of such units and their properties. The imagery suggested by such an approach is one of discrete entities which can be studied and understood in spatial and temporal isolation. In assuming this orientation, dynamic, cross-contextual properties of behavior remain, almost unavoidably, undiscovered.[5]

For example, a researcher with a unit orientation would likely view the recruitment and orientation of nudists, nurses and marihuana users as qualitatively distinct phenomena, requiring separate research efforts and likely resulting in separate and distinct explanatory schemes, emphasizing properties of each unit *per se*. Such an approach is limiting, in that it promotes a tendency to overlook the generic properties of each unit, while developing the substantive properties.

In contrast, BSP sociology takes generic process as its basic analytic *my process is "working together"* *Calvin says you can't work with someone who has to have total control.*

focus and consequent endeavors are directed towards formulating theories about social processes. The referent is the process itself, and not the particular unit or units in which it was isolated. Thus, a process sociologist would view the recruitment and initiation of nudists, nurses, and marijuana users as instances (''strategic settings'') of a generic process like ''becoming.'' Within this orientation, the researcher would search for phenomena in each of these settings which are related to the process of becoming, such as opportunity, acquisition of knowledge, skills and beliefs, justification rhetoric, and so forth. That is, the focus would be on *becoming*, not on nudists, nurses, or marihuana users (or nudism, nursing, or marihuana use) *per se*. BSP theories are, of course, developed through research conducted within such units, and will certainly lend understanding to these units. For example, a study concerning how people become nurses would add to the understanding of nursing schools and the nursing profession, even though the focus might be on becoming.

In themselves, the foci of either unit or process sociology are not intrinsically meritorious. The test of their worth lies in how well they lend themselves to the development of sociological knowledge and theory. In this regard, we will argue that BSP sociology produces significant advantages with respect to the durability of formulations and propensity for theoretical development. By durability, we mean the capacity of a conceptual formulation to remain viable through the passage of time. Theoretical development refers (1) to the ability of formulations to be generalized and formalized, (2) to the extent to which formulations can be related to other formulations in similar contexts, and (3) to the ease with which conceptualization occurs.

Within this foreshortened universe of concern we will deal only peripherally with the formal issues of interest to the philosophers of science, e.g., axiomatizing a body of knowledge, formal cumulative procedures, etc. (cf. Freeze, 1972, Mullins, 1974). Rather, our concern is a prior one, dealing with the effects of analytic focus in research on the ability to generate durable conceptualizations with the capacity to be cumulated. In short, we wish to illustrate that ''unit sociology'' and ''process sociology'' as analytic foci, have particular consequences along the dimensions outlined above.

DURABILITY

It is perhaps axiomatic to say the world changes. In recognition of this, sociologists have parceled out a portion of their domain to deal with such matters -- to wit, "social change." However, it seems somewhat incongruous that, recognizing social change as a crucial sociological concern, we often fail to consider it when pursuing research from a unit orientation. By focusing our efforts on substantive properties of units, we condemn our formulations to eventual obsolescence.

Since units will undoubtedly undergo significant change over time, the most that can be said for most unit formulations is that they illuminate a temporally circumscribed, and thus particularized set of conditions. Explanations of behavior under such conditions rest upon a configuration of variables which may or may not be so aligned in the future. On a descriptive level, a statement about a unit remains intact only so long as the unit itself remains relatively static. As the unit changes, the description becomes increasingly obsolete.

Unit *theories* likewise may become obsolete over time. For example, a review of the sociological literature on opiate addiction (merely one facet of the unit "drug use") shows an enormous change in the characteristics of the substantive unit. From Terry and Pellens' (1970) compendium of drug studies prior to 1928, through the most recent National Commission Report (1973), it is apparent that many variables attributed to opiate addiction (e.g., ethnicity, age, sex, drug of choice, etc.) have undergone radical transformation. It should not be surprising then, that the only theoretical proposition to survive the quicksilver of the changing drug scene is Lindesmith's (1938 and 1968) analysis of the role played by withdrawal distress -- perhaps the only durable static property of opiate use.[6] Such is the fate of unit dependent theories; as the unit undergoes transformation, theory must be developed anew.

Many other examples of unit descriptions and theories are available, but would only belabor the point. Durability is seriously undermined when descriptive and theoretical formulations are dependent upon such capricious properties as are found to constitute a particular unit at a particular time.

In contrast to unit descriptions and theories, BSP theories (BSP sociology does not concern itself with description apart from theory) are quite durable. BSP's as generic processes are part of the basic fabric of social organization. They do not radically change or expire as time passes. Thus, the theories that reflect them merely become extended, deepened, and most importantly *modified* as the data which suggest them changes. The manner in which BSP's exist in particular units may change over time, as conditions may change, but the fundamental core process and its essential properties will remain essentially intact.

This durability is enhanced by the fact that it is not merely the explication of generic properties that is the focus of BSP sociology. One is concerned as well, with the conditions under which such properties may vary across units and through time. That is, BSP's are developed such that change is an oriented-to feature of the analysis. Examples of both a formal and substantive process theory will serve to illustrate this durability.[7]

From Glaser and Strauss' (1971) formal theory of "status passages," it appears that status passages as generic processes, have always existed and always will exist in all cultures at all times. Furthermore, the essential formal properties of status passages are also durable. Status passages will always be repeatable or non-repeatable, voluntary or involuntary, undergone alone, collectively or in aggregate, and so on. Status passages at any time, in any location (i.e., in any unit) may be analyzed in respect to such properties.

In regard to more substantive BSP theory, durability is reduced, but it is nonetheless much greater than with static unit based conceptions. The unit within which a substantive theory was developed may undergo change, but the theory merely need be slightly modified to account for such change.

Bigus' (1972) substantive process theory regarding how milkmen "cultivate" relationships with customers and prospective customers will serve to illustrate. One of the essential stages of relationship cultivation is the development of trust. Milkmen at the time and location where this study was conducted utilized several "trust-inducing" tactics. If conditions were to change such that a particular trust-inducing tactic were to lose its usefulness, the theory could easily be modified to account for the changed *conditions* and whatever resulted (the development of a new tactic, the increased use of already existing tactics, or whatever). Even if conditions in the retail milk business were to change so radically as to eliminate the need for cultivating relationships (or, for that matter, even if the home delivery milk business were to die altogether), a great deal of the original conceptualization of relationship cultivation would remain useful. Even with a substantive BSP theory, the focus is on generic phenomena (e.g., trust development as it relates to relationship cultivation). If relationship cultivation were to be eliminated from the context of the home delivery milk business, it would nonetheless exist elsewhere, under conditions similar to those which originally gave rise to its presence in the milk business (such as low demand and high supply of a service or product, power asymmetry in relationships, and so forth). And, the understanding gained from its study in the context of the milk business would remain essentially intact. We would know at lease some of the essential properties of relationship cultivation, some of the conditions under which it occurs, and so forth. In other words, we would have gained permanent knowledge about the dynamics of one, probably universal, form of social relationship, not merely fleeting knowledge of milkmen and their customers.

GENERALIZABILITY

The foregoing example illustrated the potential generalizability and propensity for formalization of substantive BSP theory. The cultivating process and its essential properties occur in other substantive units (particularly those related to servicing such as automobile repair, undertaking, hairdressing, etc.). The existence of BSP's is not bound by or dependent upon their status in any particular unit. Although a BSP theory might have been originally derived from a particular unit, the conditions, properties, consequences, and so forth of the process transcend the unit. Thus, the conceptualization developed in the original study of the cultivating process as it occurred in the context of the home delivery milk business remains intact when the BSP is applied to other units in which relationship cultivation occurs.

Unit theory is not so unbound. It is limited in its generalizability because a theoretical statement about a unit is bound by the particular configuration of conditions in the unit at a specific time.[8] As such, it cannot be lifted reasonably intact to another unit with a different configuration of conditions, much less a different class of unit, without obscuring the relationship of the theory to the obdurate world. The theory remains ''trapped'' in the unit within which it was developed, and will always be read as a descriptive statement about that particular unit at a specific time.

Historically, the development of unit theory has been along lines of generalizing to larger units of the *same type*, rather than through densification and integration of the concepts themselves.[9] Such generalization is typically attempted in two ways: (1) through enlargement of the same class of population units (e.g., from marihuana users to users of other types of drugs), and (2) through conceptual escalation from a substantive unit to a formal conceptual unit (e.g., drug users as an example of deviance). This type of theoretical development is seldom adequate, because variation in the form of fresh data from different units undermines a developing unit theory. Such variation frequently functions to contradict the theory as it currently exists, rather than to contribute to its modification and elaboration.

Imagine, for instance, a theorist who develops a theory of LSD use, which is to be used as a foundation for developing a theory of drug use in general (a larger unit). Comparative data from other units (barbiturate users, amphetamine users, etc.) is collected for inclusion in the analysis. However, in short order the analyst discovers instances in the data which are counter to the original theory. In the original work (hypothetically) it may have been found that LSD use occurs almost exclusively in subcultures which encourage LSD use. Therefore it was concluded the LSD use is directly related to membership in such subcultures. However, the data from the comparative unit of amphetamine users (hypothetically) indicates that amphetamine users have a very strong tendency to shy away from drug subcultures. The analyst thus concludes (correctly within the framework of unit analysis) that the theory does not pertain to amphetamine users. A theory of amphetamine use must be developed apart from LSD use. The case for escalation of the original theory to a general, or more formal, theory of drug use has been weakened.[10]

The outcome of the above hypothetical example resulted from the researcher attempting to generalize a theory which was originally developed through focusing on substantive properties of a particular unit (LSD use), rather than on phenomena related to generic processes occurring therein. By using a substantive property of the unit (subculture affiliation) as the explanatory variable, the researcher has undermined the generalizability of the developing theory, and has failed to discover similarities in comparative units. If the focus had been on processes occurring within the units, such as getting into drug use (cf. Becker, 1953) getting out of drug use, or whatever, one would more likely have discovered similarities as well as variations between the units which could have been conceptualized and related to a generic process core variable. Within this alternative framework, drug subculture affiliation would be conceived merely as one variation of getting into drug use. Further, similarities between this particular mode of introduction and other variations may also be discovered through closer comparison (which is encouraged, rather than undermined, by the generic process approach). For example, by focusing on avenues into drug use, rather than absence or presence of subculture affiliation, it may be discovered that the persuasion of friends is a key variable in acquiring knowledge about the availability and desirability of a particular drug and its use. One class of users, young persons, for example, may frequently be introduced into drug subcultures and hence into drug use, by friends. Similarly, another quite different class of users, middle class housewives, for example, may also commonly be introduced to drug use through friends. In this instance, the friend may urge the candidate for use to see her family doctor (or a specific doctor who prescribes liberally) for a barbiturate prescription, to "calm her nerves down." She may argue, "I did it, and it worked for me." Either of the above instances of introduction to drug use through friends could result in the routine use of a drug. Additionally, by using a generic process approach, a researcher would more easily avoid being conceptually misled by such common sense categories as "illegal" and "legal" drug use.

We would not argue that it would be impossible for a unit oriented researcher to discover such variations and similarities as suggested above. We would argue, however, that it would be unlikely, because of the tendency in unit research to focus on substantive properties of units. Furthermore, even if one were to discover such variations from a unit perspective, not having a dynamic core variable which cuts across the units would retard the theoretical linkages being seen. One would likely end up with a largely descriptive comparison of the units, with possibly an *appended* theoretical scheme.

The focus on generic process allows BSP's to transcend the boundaries of units (and common sense categories), and facilitates the elevation of the core theoretical properties to a more formal level, as was demonstrated in our previous example of "cultivated relationships." Further, the generalizability of BSP's data and findings, from specific units are cumulative, thus allowing for the development of an integrated, dense theory. For example, the process of "status passage" occurs in contexts of religion, education, marriage, aging, health and illness, alcoholism, etc. Much of what is found in a study of the status passage process as it occurs in religious settings may be carried over to educational settings, in a cumulative fashion. The findings of further studies of status passages in yet other settings may also be integrated into the developing status passage theory. As findings from each study are integrated into the theory, the formal properties of the status passage process will emerge. In this manner, each study will have contributed to the development of the formal process theory.

Integration and densification of a BSP theory is further enhanced because, not being unit dependent, variation in terms of fresh data from new units does not undermine a developing theory. To the contrary, it contributes to its generation, because it gives greater theoretical coverage, and allows for modification and extension of the theory. An example from a BSP oriented study can illustrate this point.

In research conducted in a small community (Hadden, 1973), it was found that local officials relied on a particular evidentiary form in order to provide a "basis" for their assessments of the "extent" of the drug menace in the community. Conceptualized as "evidentiary notions" this form entailed taking a supposed qualitative feature of the phenomenon (e.g., marijuana causes conduct problems), assessing it quantitatively (e.g., no incidents noted), and the asserting a qualitative appraisal of the phenomenon qua problem (e.g., minimal). From the data available in that particular research site, this evidentiary form could be taken to be an invariant pattern in the creation of such problems.

A year after this first study, information on the "rise" of a rape problem in a Southwestern city was reviewed and a second evidentiary form was noted -- the patterning of idiosyncratic events. Here, an unusually brutal rape/murder was widely publicized and immediately seized upon as an indicator of a more pervasive problem. The originally-noted evidentiary form isolated in the drug study was only selectively employed in the initial stages of the career of the rape problem.

In comparing the career of the two separate substantive problems, it can be noted first that the evidentiary form present in the rape career *does not* negate the prior form found in the drug study. Rather it extends the concept of evidentiary notions to include another pattern. Second, in looking at this new variation we can isolate the conditions under which one form will predominate. Such a comparison in the present example indicated that the dictating features of an evidentiary base were conditioned by the degree of visibility of the phenomenon (i.e., how much information was readily available) and the amount of control over this information available to interested parties. In the drug case, officials were dealing with a virtually invisible phenomenon (for the general public) where they held primary control over the availability of information. However, in the rape situation, the original "event" was highly visible (through intense media coverage), with officials having little direct control over public access to information. Correspondingly, the evidentiary bases for the problems took different forms.

From the foregoing example, it is evident that in constructing a process theory, new data collected from comparative units, whether different or similar, merely function to elaborate and extend the theory, rather than to undermine it. Thus, the avenue to generalization and formalization remains open.

RELATING CONCEPTS

With unit sociology, there is typically no theoretical nexus with which to relate separate units to one another in an analytically significant way. Units are ordinarily seen as separate entities with definite boundaries, which can be understood in isolation and which relate in no theoretically important manner to other units. In this sense, theorists create unit theories which operate within a vacuum and imply unwarranted logical assumptions about the scope of the subject matters when generalizations to other units are attempted. For example, most studies of deviant behavior carry with them the implicit assumptions that "deviant" behavior is somehow fundamentally different from "normal" behavior, and the "causes" of deviant behavior are also fundamentally different from the "causes" of non-deviant behavior rather than being two consequences of the same BSP.[11] These assumptions did not result from empirical investigation. They derived, instead, from the fact that sociologists have somewhat arbitrarily divided social behavior into two units, "deviant" and "normal."

The most superficial investigation shows, however, that deviant behavior does not occur in a vacuum inhabited only by "deviant" persons who engage only in deviant behavior. What sociologists refer to as "deviant behavior" ordinarily develops and is acted out in the same settings as "normal" behavior (cf. Lofland, 1969: 62-69). Furthermore, it often develops in interaction with "normal" persons as consequences of the same BSP, e.g., "achieving prestige," or "achieving upward mobility" (cf. Bell, 1953). Despite rather obvious relationships, many theories of deviant behavior disregard phenomena which are not deemed to be direct properties of "deviants" or "deviant behavior." As such, theoretical integration between "normal" and "deviant" behavior as two dimensions of a BSP remains unachieved, despite the potential empirical relationship.

We realize one can argue that instances of deviant behavior share at least one commonality which would facilitate theoretical integration -- presumed rule violation of some sort.[12] However, even if we ignore that this is probably more of a legalistic or moralistic description of a unit, the "rules in use" nature of the phenomenon (Garfinkel, 1967) are typically taken in most research as an unexplicated, defining feature of the subject being studied. Consequently, the relationship(s) the behavior may have with more fundamental patterns of behavior is again obscure.

A partial exception to this general trend, the labeling perspective, takes as an object of study the interaction between rules, rule-making, rule-enforcement, and rule-breakers -- in short, a process. Yet, it is one of the consequences of the way we delineate the sociological world, and a testimony to the channeling of research dictated by unit analysis, that even when process models or theories are advanced (such as labeling) they are still taken as descriptive of a particular population or conceptual unit.

We would argue that labeling is a BSP (however ill-defined or specified at the present time) with strong carry-through outside the substantive field of deviance. However, since labeling was conceived from deviance studies, it is primarily taken as tied to that conceptual unit. In our analysis, labeling (or some variant thereof) could indeed become a major theoretical contribution if this process were to be studied in the manner advocated in the final portions of this paper.[13] One of the problems with "labeling theory" at present is that it is the result of studies where the primary concern has been the explanation of the conceptual unit, deviance. Hence, the reference for the theory has been a unit to be explained in process terms and not *the process itself*.

The paucity of well-integrated propositions stems in our view, from the failure to systematically focus on process -- analyzing conditions, properties, consequences, etc. -- regardless of the common-sense categories and predetermined conceptualizations about the nature of the social world. By cutting across and transcending the boundaries of separate units, BSP's provide a way of relating different units to each other. For example, cultivating a clientele in our one example above is a way of relating the activities of milkmen to those of doctors.

Besides BSP theories relating diverse units to each other, analytically distinct BSP's relate to one another through the empirical world of units. Often one BSP is a property or condition which affects another BSP within a particular unit. For instance, the longitudinal study of the career of a "drug problem" in a small community, referred to earlier, yielded the conceptualization of an "alarming process." This process was characterized as the movement of a phenomenon from a position of little or no concern for the community through its "discovery as a matter of 'concern'," the mobilization of resources to meet the situation, and finally, the "demise" of the phenomenon qua community problem (Hadden, 1973). One of the major properties of this broad processual model was the notion of "pronouncing prevalence." This term refers to the social dimensions associated with certain behavior being made problematic, i.e., who can, under what conditions, successfully promote a phenomenon as worthy of attention -- to wit, a problem. While the notion of "pronouncing prevalence" was isolated and developed within the context of the larger concern with the alarming process it may also be developed in its own right as a BSP.

Pronouncing prevalence of phenomena is pervasive within social life as individuals, organizations, and their leaders furnish evidence to themselves and others of the "good life," decide on appropriate courses of action, and in general, elevate phenomena from mundane to noteworthy status. If one were to develop this BSP theory of "pronouncing" it would certainly pertain to all problem areas (including social problems), although sampling in other areas would yield a wider applicability of the process as one would be specifically looking for the conditions under which pronouncing takes on different dimensions.

For example, in the original research where pronouncing was used to inform the alarming process, a notion of vulnerability was seen as necessary for successful pronouncements. Such pronouncements were couched in a rhetoric which connoted an inevitable spread of a problem on both a territorial and personal basis, unless social action was taken. In other words, "everyone" was depicted as potentially affected. However, in developing the process of pronouncing in different contexts (i.e., non-alarms) we would probably find this "vulnerability" requirement to be but one of a number of strategies under which pronouncing took place.

The discovery of empirical relationships between BSP's within units, whether similar or diverse can lead to a new development in theory. As seen above, it was through the discovery of pronouncing practices as a major property of the alarming process, that it became evident that pronouncing was itself a basic social process, worthy of individual development.

THEORETICAL COVERAGE

One remaining aspect of theoretical development in which BSP sociology possesses major advantage over unit sociology concerns the problem of "immaculate coverage." Immaculate coverage refers to the emphasis in unit sociology on developing fully the properties of the unit under study to satisfy criteria of either logical or descriptive completeness. This emphasis is not of any necessity related to theoretical coverage. With regard to theoretical development, such a requirements impedes rather than fosters conceptualization.

Consider again the area of drug using behavior. With the emphasis on the unit drug use, a well-developed theory would logically have to include the isolation of variables on the physician-addict, the garden-variety street user, the occasional marihuana smoker, the barbiturate abusing housewife, etc. The enormity of such a task is staggering. However, the difficulty for well-developed theory does not lie in the work requirements. Rather, it would appear that many properties of the unit are simply not theoretically related to one another. On a common sense level, only one property seems to bind the above-mentioned housewife to the marihuana smoker to the physician as a unit. They all ingest substances called "drugs." Despite this, a theory would somehow have to relate fundamentally diverse properties to account for all facets of the area under study. Perhaps for this reason, most unit analysis produces a few concepts, maybe a stunted theory, and a tremendous amount of substantive description.

When conducting research and analysis, a process theorist need only attend to those phenomena occurring in the unit(s) in which the research is located, which appear to be theoretically pertinent to the process being studied. Although the research is conducted within particular units, *one is not studying the units per se; incumbent process(es) is the focus.* Therefore, that which does not relate to the BSP does not relate to the study. This allows the theorist to achieve sufficient theoretical coverage of the subject matter without researching the unit in immaculate *descriptive* detail. It also frees one from having to account for the great amount of behavioral variation (much of it theoretically unrelated) found in the unit.

METHODOLOGY OF BSP DEVELOPMENT

Having outlined what we purport to be the advantages of BSP sociology in regards to theoretical development, we will now turn to the methodology of BSP development. As mentioned earlier, the BSP notion was developed in the process of *doing* "grounded theory" research, and is thus both methodologically and theoretically linked to that particular methodology. While this is not an appropriate forum for entertaining a programmatic account of "how to generate grounded theory," a slight digression into the methodology is warranted in order to demonstrate its departure from more traditional modes of research within the unit orientation, and more importantly, its congruence with the logic of basic social processes.

Briefly stated, the intent of grounded theory methodology is the inductive generation of theory "from data -- systematically obtained and analyzed in social research" (Glaser and Strauss, 1967:1). In such formulations, the hypotheses, conceptual categories, and their properties are derived, tested and refined through a detailed and continuous inspection of comparative collected data. A "discovery" model of research is employed in generating BSP's in contrast to the more usual verification and descriptive model used in unit oriented research. The general rationale for this type of research in an elemental science is succinctly captured by Glaser and Strauss in their advocacy of an inductive methodology. For them:

> "Verifying a logico-deductive theory generally leaves us with at best a reformulated hypothesis or two and an unconfirmed set of speculations; and at worst, a theory that does not fit or work... A grounded theory [read BSP theory] can be used as a fuller test of a logico-deductive theory pertaining to the same area by comparison of both theories, than an accurate description used to verify a few opropositions would provide. Whether or not there is a previous speculative theory discovery gives us a theory that 'fits or works' in a substantive or formal area (though further testing, clarification, or reformulation is still necessary) since the theory has been derived from research data, not deduced from logical assumptions about it." (Glaser and Strauss, 1967: 29-30).

Consistent with this notion of an inductive methodology, a researcher employing grounded theory will not preconceive the important properties and processes of the study area. However, one does not enter the research arena as a blank slate. Rather, the BSP conception provides the research with an initial focus *without* having to preconceive the eventual theory. The researcher has something specific to look for (a process), yet sufficient latitude to allow the theory to emerge inductively. More concretely, since there is an attempt to discover some sort of BSP, the researcher will begin the search for the process (i.e., core variable) which accounts for the most variation in the data, and to which other variables appear to be related. In accomplishing this end, data collection, coding, and analysis occur jointly,[14] such that freshly collected data informs the emerging theory, and in turn, the emerging theory guides further data collection. Glaser and Strauss (1967:45) refer to this process as "theoretical sampling."

> "Theoretical sampling is the process of data collection for generating theory whereby the analyst jointly collects, codes and analyzes his data and decides what data to collect next and where to find them, in order to develop his theory as it emerges. This process of data collection is *controlled* by the emerging theory, whether substantive or formal.""

Congruent with the BSP conception, theoretical sampling involves sampling for variation to achieve *theoretical coverage*, and not descriptive or population (i.e., unit) coverage. For example, Bigus (1972), in his study of milkmen, discovered that most of the milkmen's time and energies of the job were consumed with "cultivating relationships" (the BSP) with customers and prospective customers. This was the major "problem" confronting the milkmen on a day-to-day basis and almost everything which transpired was related or affected by cultivating relationships. Consequently, Bigus' analysis was directed towards discovery of the generic properties of this process and *not* towards characteristics of milkmen, the occupation milkman, or the like. At this point, the concern with the social phenomenon we call milkman was limited to the theoretical insights it could shed on the cultivating process. In this sense, milkmen and their occupation had become a "strategic" research arena in which to study the emerging theory on cultivating.

As implied in the above example, theoretical sampling is not concerned with fully describing any particular unit or units in the conventional sense. Its primary function is to provide the analyst with the opportunity to discover properties of the core variable being studied (which in the case of the process analyst will be a BSP), so as to densify or fill out the emergent theory. When generating a grounded theory, the sample size is determined only by the necessity of theoretical coverage. When sampling no longer produces new ideas (i.e., when "theoretical saturation" is reached), the need for further sampling ceases. Under this scheme, it is not uncommon for major categories to begin manifesting themselves during analysis of the first several interviews or observations. The task at that point is to sample the research arena so as to provide the constituent properties of those categories and in so doing accomplish at the same time intra-research verification on the emerging theory. It should not be surprising that a seemingly small sample (from a conventional perspective) would enable the process theorist to achieve sufficient theoretical coverage to generate a dense, well-integrated grounded theory, since each stage of the research is being guided by a parsimonious search for variation around emergent process characteristics.

It should be noted that at times more than one BSP may be found to be important in a give situation or set of data. The choice of which to study as the major focus of a particular project is both an empirical and personal decision. On the empirical level, one looks for the variable which accounts for a great deal of variation in the data. In other words, can its properties be sufficiently developed. On a personal level, the choice becomes more arbitrary. Quite simply, one chooses whatever is of personal interest. The choice made, the analyst develops the second process only insofar as it relates to the one commanding primary attention. The other(s) may, of course, be similarly developed at another time.

Once a particular substantive unit or area is sufficiently exploited to discover a BSP and its major properties, a theorist is free to theoretically sample in other diverse kinds of units to begin formalizing the theory. This can be specifically accomplished in a number of ways, the details of which are beyond the scope of this paper.[15] Generally, however, formalization of a BSP theory can be achieved through analyzing data from a number of diverse classes of comparative groups and drawing out variables and properties which are shared by and vary within all comparative units, because of differing underlying conditions. In this manner, the most general, cross-contextual (i.e., formal) properties of the process may be discovered. For example, a theorist constructing a formal theory of "cultivating" may discover that in all comparative instances, one stage of relationship cultivation concerns the establishment of trust.

Trust may then be seen as a formal property of the theory of "cultivating." Similarly, a theorist may develop a formal theory of status passage and discover that in some units with some types of status passages the individual has no control over whether or not he/she enters the status passage, while in other units the individual maintains a high degree of control over the process. Even though events occur differently in each comparative unit, the theorist can ascertain that the extent to which a status passage is voluntary (or involuntary) is a formal property of the process of status passage. Thus, although great variation occurs, a common property is present -- the extent of voluntariness. Concomitantly, the conditions under which a status passage is voluntary or involuntary and the consequences of that variation further illuminates the process of "status passage."

As previously mentioned, our discussion of the manner in which BSP theory is generated must necessarily be truncated. However, the foregoing discussion should demonstrate the general manner in which such theory is capable of being generated. Further, our sketch of the inductive procedures of grounded theory methodology as they relate to the development of BSP's should sensitize one to the quite different appearance sociological renderings of the world might take if BSP analysis were pursued. It is to this topic that we now focus attention.

SOCIOLOGY ALONG PROCESS LINES

To this point, we have suggested that focusing on process as opposed to units will facilitate theoretical development. Implicit in this argument is the notion that generic process, as an explicit focus of any research inquiry, will alter the conceptual world of the discipline by cutting across and transcending traditional sociological boundaries. Again, a comparison with unit analysis should serve to underscore this point.

Much of unit sociology is delineated along lines which are *not* theoretically contiguous, although they are treated as such. For example, if a unit sociologist were to begin a study of "whorehouses" the study would probably be placed in the conceptual category of "deviant behavior" or possibly "social problem" (*a priori*, static conceptions). In doing so, the presumption is that the essence or at least a primary property of the behavior to be studied is that it is deviant or socially problematic. Concomitant results will explain the motivations, attitudes, or other social characteristics of a person who engage in such practices as distinct from non-practitioners (i.e., "normals"). However, in categorizing whorehouse activities as merely another instance of deviant behavior, other, perhaps more central characteristics of the phenomenon are denied serious consideration by the researcher.

If we hold in abeyance the deviance assumption about whorehouses, we note that the area to be studied is an organized activity, established for the expressed purpose of exchanging a "service" for remuneration. Viewed in terms of process, it would be found that the structural properties of the whorehouse are akin to servicing operations in general -- a basic social process.[16] Quite simply, the whorehouse exists to provide a service(s) which happens to be sex. One property of a servicing process in this particular context is that the service being provided is generally considered deviant in the everyday world. The "fact" that it is so conceived may have some consequences for the organization of some of its publicly visible activities, such as making it necessary to maintain a low profile, putting limits on public advertising, necessitating payoffs to the police, etc. However, the deviant conception of whorehouse activities is only one among many conditions and properties in this and other servicing contexts. Compared to other possible characteristics of the general process of "servicing" such as power symmetry, role of expertise, specialized knowledge, rights of grievance, etc., the primacy afforded the role of deviance in a unit analysis seems more reflective of common sense considerations than theoretical fit. Conceptualized from a generic process orientation, the behavior of prostitutes and their customers has more in common theoretically, with the behavior found in garages and beauty parlors than it does with check forgery, alcoholism, and the vast array of other instances ordinarily conceptualized as deviant behavior.

One further observation seems warranted. From our example of whorehouse activities, it might be concluded that we have merely transposed a hypothetical social psychological study into one focusing on organization. We would answer that this is again an *a priori* characterization.[17] One of the strengths of BSP's are their ability to conjointly render both structural and social psychological variables in terms of social process. It may be the case that either structural or social psychological variation has primacy in a given area, but that is a data-related question.

Essentially, what we are arguing is that regardless of the usual sociological interests, whether it be deviance, religion, or collective behavior; and regardless of the usual primary focus as either organizational or social psychological, the referent for BSP theory is always generic process and *not* the particular substantive or conceptual unit involved. This does not mean that the analyst will be unable to explain how the particular research unit functions. Quite the contrary! Theoretical renderings in terms of BSP's contribute substantial insight into the practical realities of the day-to-day world by explaining its variation. However, as mentioned earlier, the analytic focus seeks theoretical coverage and not descriptive completeness (which is seen as impossible). As such, no claim is being made that "servicing" in our prior example, is the only theoretically significant feature of whorehouses. The only claim being advanced is that "servicing" explains much of the variation to be found in the actions, interactions, and perceptions found in the collected data from that research site. The process illuminates organizational features about the house, interactional patterns between prostitute and customer, prostitutes' conceptions of their roles, and a wide variety of less obvious variables. As such, "servicing" is not to be taken as a "theory" about whorehouses (or deviance), but rather as a theoretical statement about processes which occur therein and which occur in other areas of social life, as well.

SUMMARY

In this paper, we have tried to accomplish three tasks. First, we introduced the concept of Basis Social Process (BSP) as a generic theoretical construct and argued for its utility in building theory in sociology. Part of this argument was a critique of what we characterized as unit sociology. From our view, unit sociology is inherently limited in its capacity for theoretical development since referents are not provided to transpose features found in one arena to other arenas, thus forestalling cumulative development of theory. Further, we argued one of the prime reasons for this incapacity to integrate unit theory in a cumulative fashion is because the subject matter involved is more reflective of common-sense considerations than theoretical fit, i.e., behavior in the world does not seem to be divided into discrete units of deviance, religion, etc. In contrast, BSP's are trans-situational and sensitized to temporal considerations, thus allowing theoretical development through comparison of generic process under different conditions.

Secondly, a strength of the BSP conception is its linkage to a specific methodological program -- grounded theory methodology. We have attempted to provide an encapsulated account of this linkage to illustrate the manner in which process can be investigated without relying on logical elaboration, intuitive insight, or other quasi-mystical techniques. In other words, grounded theory methodology provides a means by which BSP's can be a consistent analytic focus rather than a serendipitous finding.

Finally, we attempted to illustrate the consequences BSP sociology would have for the manner in which the discipline theoretically divided the empirical world. In doing so, we argued that BSP's as basic uniformities of social life, cut across the boundaries by which sociology as traditionally been subdivided. If they didn't, the world would be infinitely more intricate and unpredictable. It seems reasonable, then, that one of the major ways in which we render the world sociologically should reflect this fact of uniformity.

ENDNOTES

1. Concern with social dynamics is found in the works of many early sociologists, such as Comte, Marx, and Simmel. For surveys of earlier studies of cyclical processes, see Sorokin (1927 and 1928). For a short survey of American conceptions of process, see Buckley (1967: 17-23).

2. The basic social process notion was originally conceived by Barney Glaser.

3. The "becoming process" is, of course, a socialization process. The term "becoming" is frequently used by those who study the process (the aforementioned studies, for example). We prefer the term as a substitute for the more general term "socialization." The term "socialization" is generally used in the framework of larger social and cultural units (usually socialization into "society"), and particularly in reference to childhood socialization. We think the term "becoming process" is appropriate to distinguish a particular type of socialization process. The studies which have used the term "becoming" share several commonalities which differentiate them significantly from the broader usage of the term "socialization." First, they invariably concern adult socialization. Second, they concern socialization into relatively small social and cultural units (nursing profession, marihuana smokers, nudism, etc.). Third, the participants are ordinarily undergoing socialization into the particular role or setting voluntarily. Fourth, the socialization process is characterized by a constant interpretive process, in which candidates are continually faced with moral dilemmas and choice ("Is becoming a nurse

worth all this work?'', ''Is a marihuana high pleasurable'', ''Is going naked in front of others immoral?''). And, fifth, as Olesen and Whittaker (1968: 13) point out, ''From the standpoint of the candidates' progress and outcome, the movement forward is constantly and continually problematic.''

4. For a discussion of ''Styles of Reporting Qualitative Field Research,'' see Lofland (1974). The BSP orientation would fall under Lofland's classification of ''the generic style.''

5. While it is conceivable that generic unit theory and concepts can be developed, they would usually remain static (and probably reified) formulations, unable to systematically account for change. Cicourel (1970) has made an observation similar to the one here in arguing for the insights afforded from an ethnomethodological perspective. An explicit task of this latter perspective is the discovery of invariant practices -- a direct reflection of our concern for general process. However, as argued elsewhere (Hadden and Lester, 1976), the ethnomethodologists could reasonably profit (especially with regard to theoretical development) from the analytic procedures developed later in this paper.

6. A recent article by McAuliffe and Gordon (1974) suggests a modification of Lindesmith's theory so as to include the desire for euphoria in explanations of opiate addition. Their study, citing a study of a small sample of addicts in Baltimore and reinterpreting previous research findings they found consistent with their own position does not undermine Lindesmith's proposition concerning withdrawl distress, but does address this latter proposition's universality. At this point, given available contradictory evidence, McAuliffe and Gordon's proposition is best viewed as suggestive.

7. We use the terms ''substantive'' and ''formal'' in the sense that Glaser and Strauss (1967: 32-33) used them.

''By substantive theory, we mean that developed for a substantive, or empirical, area of sociological inquiry, such as patient care, race relations, professional education, delinquency, or research organization. By formal theory, we mean that developed for a formal, or conceptual, area of sociological inquiry, such as stigma, deviant behavior, formal organization, socialization, status congruency, authority and power, reward systems, or social mobility. Both types of theory may be considered as ''middle-range.'' That is, they fall between the ''minor working hypotheses'' of everyday life and the "all-inclusive" grand theories."

8. Generalization from a "representative sample" to a population may appear to be an instance in which statements about one unit (i.e., the sample) may be generalized intact to another unit (i.e., the population). However, this is not the case. The sample is not the unit of analysis, the population is. The sample is merely assumed to be representative of the population, in that it supposedly possesses the same properties and conditions. In short, the sample is presumed to be a microcosm of the population unit, not a separate unit in and of itself.

9. The term "densification" refers to the proliferation of concepts -- the development of the sub-properties, conditions, consequences and so forth of a particular concept. The term "integration" refers to the process of drawing the relationship(s) between conceptual categories -- demonstrating how they relate to one another in a systematic fashion.

10. If formal unit theory cannot be generated from substantive theory (which has its roots in actual behavior) in the above manner, or through densification and integration of concepts, the only recourse left open for formalization is logical elaboration. The end result is reified theories. Such logically elaborated theories are more the products of vivid imaginations and personal genius than the products of systematic empirical research. This, we believe, accounts in large part for the lack of integration between substantive and formal unit theory, as well as the tremendous gap between formal unit theory and actual social behavior.

11. This assumption is so strong in some instances that the "cause" of certain types of non-deviant behavior are not even considered as pertinent sociological concern. For example, sociologists frequently interest themselves in the "causes" of homosexuality, which is implicitly assumed to be "natural" and therfore presumably not of sociological concern. A noteworthy exception to the above assumption is found in Simons (1969: 51), who noted:

"Since virtually any behavior is deviant from the moral perspective of some judge, virtually everything causes deviance. That is, since deviant behavior includes virtually all human behavior, its causes are the causes of all human behaviors."

Another noteworthy exception is found in "differential association" theory (Sutherland, 1939: 4-9), which asserts that persons become deviant through essentially the same process as they become conformist.

12. As many have noted, "rule violation" is not unique to deviant behavior, but rather, also characterizes other "conflict" situations; e.g., Democrats vs. Republicans. See Lofland (1969: 13-16) for this basic argument.

13. Work in this direction has been done by symbolic interactionists (cf. Strauss, 1959: 15-30 and Foote, 1951) and ethnomethodologists (cf. Garfinkel, 1967 and the various articles by Douglas, 1970), in their studies of "naming," "identification," the "documentary method," and related terms which refer, essentially, to the process by which meanings and their resultant actions are constructed. This process is probably the most basic of all basic social processes. See Hadden and Lester (1976) for a further discussion of this point.

14. The actual coding and analytic procedures are discussed in detail by Glaser (1966). These procedures are referred to as "the constant comparative method."

15. For a more elaborate account of the process by which substantive theory can be generated into formal theory, see Glaser and Strauss (1967: 79-99) and Hadden and Lester (1976).

16. Much of the following discussion on the dimensions of "whore-houses" draws upon a rudimentary analysis of data collected by Lee Stewart (for Stewart's own rendering of segments of this set of data see Steward, 1972).

17. In line with our previous discussion, one could develop a social psychological process from the whorehouse data which would transcent that unit. But again, this is a data-related decision.

REFERENCES

Becker, Howard S. "Becoming a Marihuana User," *The American Journal of Sociology*, LIX (November, 1953), 235-242.

Becker, Howard S. *Outsiders*. New York: The Free Press, 1963.

Bell, Daniel. "Crime as an American Way of Life," *Antioch Review*, XIII (Summer, 1953), 131-154.

Bigus, Odis E. "The Milkman and His Customer: A Cultivated Relationship," *Urban Life and Culture I* (July, 1972), 131-165.

Blumer, Herbert. "Sociological Analysis and the 'Variable'," *The American Sociological Review,* XXII, 1956.

Buckley, Walter. *Sociology and Modern Systems Theory.* Englewood Cliffs, New Jersey: Prentice-Hall, Inc., 1967.

Cicourel, Arron V. "Basic and Normative Rules in the Negotiation of Status and Role," in H. Dreitzel, *Recent Sociology*, No. 2. New York: The MacMillan Co., 1970.

Davis, Fred. "Deviance Disavowal: The Management of Strained Interaction," *Social Problems*, IX (Fall, 1961), 120-132.

Douglas, Jack D. *Understanding Everyday Life.* Chicago: Aldine Publishing Co., 1970.

Foote, Nelson N. "Identification as the Basis for a Theory of Motivation," *The American Sociological Review*, XVI (February, 1951), 14-21.

Freeze, Lee. "Cumulative Sociological Knowledge," *The American Sociological Review*, 37 (August, 1972), 412-482.

Garfinkel, Harold. *Studies in Ethnomethodology.* Englewood Cliffs, New Jersey: Prentice-Hall, Inc., 1967.

Glaser, Barney G. "The Constant Comparative Method of Qualitative Analysis," *Social Problems*, 12 (1965), 436-445.

Glaser, Barney G. and Strauss, Anselm L. *The Discovery of Grounded Theory: Strategies for Qualitative Research.* Chicago: Aldine Publishing Co., 1967.

Glaser, Barney G. and Strauss, Anselm L. *Status Passage.* Chicago: Aldine Publishing Co., 1971.

Hadden, Stuart C. *The Social Creation of a Social Problem.* Doctoral Dissertation, Washington State University, 1973.

Hadden, Stuart C. and Lester, Marilyn. "Ethnomethodology and Grounded Theory Methodology: An Integration of Topic and Method." American Sociological Association Meetings, New York, 1976.

Lindesmith, Alfred R. "A Sociological Theory of Drug Addiction," *The American Journal of Sociology*, 43 (1938), 593-613.

Lofland, John. *Doomsday Cult*. Englewood Cliffs, New Jersey: Prentice-Hall, Inc., 1966.

Lofland, John. *Deviance and Identity*. Englewood Cliffs, New Jersey: Prentice-Hall, Inc., 1969.

Lofland, John. "Styles of Reporting Qualitative Field Research," *The American Sociologist*, 9 (August, 1974), 101-111.

Matza, David. *Delinquency and Drift*. New York: John Wiley & Sons, Inc., 1964.

McAuliffe, William E. and Gordon, Robert A. "A Test of Lindesmith's Theory of Addiction: The Frequency of Euphoria Among Long-Term Addicts," *The American Journal of Sociology*, 79 (January, 1974), 795-840.

Mullins, Nicholas C. "Theory Construction From Available Materials: A System for Organizing and Presenting Propositions," *The American Journal of Sociology*, 80 (1974), 1-14.

National Commission on Marijuana and Drug Abuse. *Drug Use in America: Problem in Perspective*. Washington, D.C.: U.S. Government Printing Office, 1973.

Olesen, Virginia L. and Whittaker, Elvi W. *The Silent Dialogue*. San Francisco: Jossey-Bass, Inc., 1968.

Schutz, Alfred. *Collected Papers, Volume I*. Edited by Natanson. The Hague, Netherlands: Martunus Nijhoff, 1971.

Simmons, J. L. *Deviants*. Berkeley: The Glendessary Press, 1969.

Sorokin, Pitirim A. "A Survey of the Cyclical Conceptions of Social and Historical Process," *Social Forces* (September, 1927).

Sorokin, Pitirim A. *Contemporary Sociological Theories*. New York: Harper & Row Publishers, Inc., 1928.

Strauss, Anselm L. *Mirrors and Masks: The Search for Identity*. Glencoe, Illinois: The Free Press, 1959. Currently published in San Francisco: The Sociology Press.

Stewart, George Lee. "On first Being a John," *Urban Life and Culture*, I (October, 1972), 255-274.

Sutherland, Edwin H. *Principles of Criminology*. Philadelphia: J.B. Lippincott, 1939.

Terry, Charles E. and Pellens, Mildred. *The Opium Problem*. Montclair, New Jersey: Patterson-Smith Publishing, 1970.

Weber, Max. *The Theory of Social and Economic Organization*. New York: The Free Press, 1964.

Weinberg, Martin S. "Becoming a Nudist," *Psychiatry: Journal for the Study of Interpersonal Processes*, 29 (February, 1966).

Reprinted from *Soc. Sci. Med.*, Vol. 30, No. 11, pp. 1161-1172, 1990

'DISCOVERING' CHRONIC ILLNESS: Using Grounded Theory

Kathy Charmaz, Ph.D.

ABSTRACT

This paper focuses on using the grounded theory method to study social psychological themes which cut across chronic illnesses. The grounded theory method is presented as a method having both phenomenological and positivistic roots, which leads to confusion and misinterpretations of the method. A social constructionist version and application of grounded theory are introduced after brief overviews of the methods and of the debates it has engendered are provided. Next, phases in developing concepts and theoretical frameworks through using the grounded theory approach are discussed. These phases include: (1) developing and refining the research and data collection questions, (2) raising terms to concepts, (3) asking more conceptual questions on a generic level and (4) making further discoveries and clarifying concepts through writing and rewriting. Throughout the discussion, examples and illustrations are derived from two recent papers, 'Disclosing Illness' and 'Struggling for a Self: Identity Levels of the Chronically Ill'. Last, the merits of the method for theoretical development are discussed.

INTRODUCTION

The grounded theory method provides a set of useful research strategies for studying the experience of chronic illness [1-5]. This paper focuses on using the grounded theory method for studying people with a wide range of chronic illnesses to address how *chronicity affects ill people's self-concepts*. Throughout the paper, ways of using grounded theory to develop social constructionist analyses are explored. As used here, the term social constructionist means: (1) Ill people's creation of taken-for-granted inter-actions, emotions, definitions, ideas, and knowledge about illness and abut self and (2) Researchers' sociological constructions which they develop, in turn, by studying chronically ill people's constructions.

Chronically ill people, like most everyone, experience their constructions as reality; their constructions are neither convenient fabrications not idiosyncratic inventions. Rather, ill people's constructions reflect their understandings of their experiences as well as the diverse situations in which they have them

[6].Further, their friends and family often support their constructions even when these constructions challenge or contradict those of medical professionals, and even when ill people cannot make their constructions credible or negotiable. Grounded theory analyses can then provide physicians with alternative understandings of patients' beliefs and actions than those readily available in clinical settings. Subsequently, physicians may use these understandings to improve communications with patients and to act on problems which patients define.

Like Foucault's [7] argument about the conditions giving rise to discursive practices, this constructionist view acknowledges that outcomes result from social interactions, negotiations and power. However, my application of grounded theory derives from a symbolic interactionist perspective tempered by Marxism and phenomenology. Symbolic interactionism assumes that human action depends upon the meanings that people ascribe to their situations [8-11]. These meanings derive from shared interactions, which turn on the pivotal role of language. The symbolic interactionist assumption of the indeterminacy of action rests on the human capacity to objectify self and to ascribe meanings to self like any other object. Such a perspective can lead to an overly rationalized view of the individual which a phenomenological perspective helps to correct. Because phenomenolgy means studying the objects of consciousness, it fosters studying emotions [12-13]. Both symbolic interactionism and phenomenolgy lead the researcher to link closely at the research participants' interpretations of their actions and situations. Marxist theory can then provide tools for linking subjective consciousness and choice to larger social structures. Moreover, Marxist theory brings a critical posture to examining the data.

For the type of social constructionist view taken here, the *assumptions* underlying these theoretical perspectives and the *questions* flowing from them are perhaps, more significant for the resulting grounded theory analyses than are specific concepts inherent within each theoretical perspective. Symbolic interactionists assume that as thinking, acting, creative individuals, human beings respond to the actions of others after interpreting these others' intent and action. A symbolic interactionist perspective leads one to look at self and meaning as processes. Phenomenologists assume that subjective reality may take varied forms. This perspective fosters the researcher's study of the multiple dimensions and realities of a person's lived experience. Marxists assume that individual psychology is both shaped and constrained by social structure. Thus, a Marxist perspective fosters asking critical questions abut how society impinges upon the individual and how individuals reproduce dominant ideas within society.

In keeping with Berger and Luckman [14], such a constructionist view assumes an emergent reality fundamentally shaped by social interaction. Hence, a constructionist approach offers an open-ended and flexible means of studying both fluid interactive processes and more stable social structures [15]. Rather than directly applying concepts such as Meads's "I", "me", and "generalized other", or Schutz' "typification" or "multiple realities", these concepts were used to sensitize me to look for themes and issues within the data [16].

Themes were addressed which cut across diverse chronic illnesses such as multiple sclerosis, diabetes, circulatory disease, renal failure, and cancer. These cross-cutting themes initially included self-esteem, continuity and change of self concept, and relationships between time and identity. After gathering and studying more data, my focus also explicitly included emotions and the self, information-control about self and illness, meanings of chronic illness, and ways of living with it.

Different chronic illnesses give rise to variations and complexity in conceptual development of the cross-cutting themes. For example, some chronic illnesses resulted in periodic, progressive, or permanent visible disabilities; other disabilities remained invisible. The kinds of situations posed by such differences were studied as well as how ill people thought and felt about them, and what effects visible disability made when studying relations between self, emotions, information, and time.

My social constructionist version of using the grounded theory method to study illness makes use of four different phases in developing concepts and theoretical frameworks: (1) creating and refining the research and data collection questions, (2) creating terms of concepts, (3) asking more conceptual questions on a generic level, and (4) making further discoveries and clarifying concepts through writing and rewriting. In this paper, I shall illustrate each phase and will draw my examples and discussion of substantive work mainly from two recent papers, 'Disclosing Illness' [17], an examination of ill people's constructions about what, when, and how to tell others about their illness, and 'Struggling for a Self: Identity Levels of the Chronically Ill' [18], an analysis of how and why ill people construct identity hierarchies with

charmaz' 4 phases of GT research

specific levels. Throughout my analysis below, I stress the *active* stance and approach of the researcher since I see being active as crucial to using the grounded theory method [19].

THE DISCOVERY PERSPECTIVE

The Grounded Theory Method

Before applying the grounded theory method to chronic illness, a brief outline of its defining characteristics will bring it into clearer focus [20-23]. Like other analytic approaches, the grounded theory method itself offers a way of constructing sociological reality; using the method fosters developing analytic and conceptual constructions of the data. In their sociological constructions, grounded theorists aim to create theoretical categories from the data and then analyze relationships between key categories. In short, the researcher constructs theory from the data. By starting with data from the lived experience of the research participants, the researcher can, from the beginning, attend to how they construct their worlds. That lived experience shapes the researcher's approach to data collection and analysis. In comparison, more traditional logical-deductive approaches explicitly derive hypotheses from pre-existing theories, which fundamentally structure both the data collection and analysis toward verification of refutation of these hypotheses (and therefor, the theories from which they were derived).

Grounded theorists affirm, check, and refine their developing ideas, but they do not limit themselves to preconceived hypotheses nor do they follow the prescribed canons of traditional random sampling required for statistical verification.

Grounded theory also differs from other qualitative approaches. Most qualitative approaches stress collecting copious amounts of data before delving into the analysis; researchers using such approaches often complete their major analytic work long after they have left the field. In contrast, grounded theorists use their emerging theoretical categories to shape the *data collection* while in the field as well as to structure the analytic processes of coding, memo-making, integrating and writing the developing theory [20-23]. The 'groundedness' of this approach fundamentally results from these researchers' commitment to analyze what they actually observe in the field or in their data. If they find recurrent themes or issues in the data, then they need to follow up on them, which can, and often, does lead grounded theorists in unanticipated directions. For example, while a

Not conclusive. To spend a long time in the field!

But I didn't in this to some degree.

GT researchers seem to have limited their studies to domestic sites, Nearby locales, where they have time for only

I had some categories from my Bibayn paper but not "tightly-framed pre-conceived hypotheses."

graduate student, I conducted a study of caring for ill and dying elders in working-class families [24]. An unexpected theme emerged about the role coroner's deputies played in notifying families about the death of their relative. Checking out that theme led me to further comparative research with coroner's deputies in different settings about their strategies for announcing death [25].

Grounded theorists begin with general research questions rather than tightly framed pre-conceived hypotheses. If, perchance, those research questions are irrelevant in the field, then they develop new, suitable ones or find another field. For example, my prior experiences as an occupational therapist and as a researcher in rehabilitation led me to expect to find chronically ill people suffering gradual or rapid decline. However, suffering and decline varied enormously despite routine clinical descriptions of specific illnesses as downhill and physicians' dire predictions for certain patients. Hence, the research lived experiences and their constructions of them.

tests ada ohes

Throughout the research and writing processes, grounded theorists follow interests, leads, and hunches that they find or identify in the data. Then they may gather more data, ask more questions, and check their developing categories. Their emergent categories explain and conceptualize (1) the data, (2) common sense understandings of the stat, and, likely, (3) other theoretical interpretations. For example, some people seem to 'deny' illness. But when viewed from an ill person's vantage point of desiring to realize identity goals and struggling to have a valued self, that person's behavior becomes understandable, rather than standing as evidence of 'denial of illness' [18]. To illustrate, an ill woman continues to work while having a serious episode of illness. She does so because she wishes to avoid having illness inundate her life and her identity, not because she disavows its presence.

With grounded theory strategies, theoretical development turns on *theoretical* sampling [20-23]. Here, the researcher collects new data to check, fill out, and extend theoretical categories. In contrast to Strauss [23], I conduct theoretical sampling only after I have defined key concepts. Delaying focused theoretical sampling fosters gaining an in-depth understanding of the realities and issues at hand, Hence, theoretical sampling fits into the research and analytic process much later than initial sampling of sites, people, or documents. By the time theoretical sampling is planned, a researcher would have some hunches

Disagrees with Strauss

or even hypotheses which he or she wishes to check. Thus, theoretical sampling shapes further data collection as the researcher pursues developing conceptual ideas rather than amassing general information. For example, my research led to gathering more materials to specify and clarify the conditions under which ill people form identity goals and to delineate conditions when they revise their goals.

When developing formal theory and forming more generic concepts, grounded theorists take their substantive analysis from one area and conduct theoretical sampling in other substantive areas. Then, they develop and refine their original analysis by using constant comparative methods [22]. For example, my concept of an identity hierarchy [18] reflects ill people's rankings of their identity goals after experiencing loss and uncertainty. To develop the concept identity hierarchy for a formal theory, one could check the concept first with people who face issues of unexpected change, loss, and uncertainty. Thus, a grounded theorist could apply the concept to people who with little warning: (1) lose seemingly secure jobs without having ready access to equivalent positions and (2) must immigrate such as certain central Americans or Southeast Asians. By studying these people, the grounded theorists might discover other contributing conditions which influence the creation of an identity hierarchy. Then data from contrasting sources could be sampled to help develop variation [26]. Moving across substantive areas fosters developing conceptual power, depth, and comprehensiveness.

The strategies of grounded theory can yield rich data, elaborated categories, and dense analyses with applications across substantive fields. These strategies do not yield statistically verified results, which require random sampling of a clearly identified population. However, survey researchers may test reported grounded theories through standard logical-deductive verification procedures.

Grounded theory studies aim for analytic power and conceptual grasp which synthesize, explain, and interpret the data. The rigor of the grounded theory method depends upon developing the range of relevant conceptual categories, saturating (i.e. filling, supporting, and providing repeated evidence for) those categories, and explaining the data. Similar to quantitative studies, or any other research, the quality of grounded theory studies varies according to the methodological thoroughness, the significance of the research questions, and the incisiveness of the analysis. Generally, much qualitative research depends on implicit methods and thus, *but if you have intuition and Talent, why not rely on it. why be structured into a set of explicit procedures?*

relies on the researcher's intuition and talent. In contrast, grounded theory specifies an *explicit* set of analytic guidelines and procedures which can help any qualitative researcher develop more or less fruitful conceptualizations of his or her data.

Debates and Dilemmas

Clearly, grounded theory differs from survey research and from other types of qualitative research such as ethnomethodology. Variations also exist among proponents of the grounded theory method and within the same proponent at different points in time. My social constructionist perspective represents one variation. Glaser and Strauss' [22] early work represents another. They [22] developed grounded theory when formal theory was becoming more arid and distant from the worlds of interacting people, when the primary value of qualitative research lay in sharpening later 'rigorous' quantitative research, and when field research studies generally remained ethnographic or consisted of analytic description. They attempted to demonstrate that the strategies of grounded theory: (1) brought the researcher close to basic processes and issues that people experience; hence, theoretical constructs at once revealed and covered those realities; (2) provided a method for identifying, capturing and rendering *processual* rather than static analyses; (3) fostered developing a rigorous qualitative methodology with its own integrity and intrinsic values distinct form quantitative research; and (4) offered possibilities form moving qualitative research more definitively toward dense, durable, substantive and formal theories [27].

Misunderstandings and criticisms. Like all other methods in social research, the grounded theory method has strengths and weaknesses. A number of the criticisms of grounded theory reflect an incomplete understanding of the logic and strategies of the method.

Such partial understanding can lead to applying inappropriate criteria on which to judge the method [28-30]. For example, Bulmer [28, p. 667] states that Glaser and Strauss's [15] "tabula rasa view of inquiry is open to serious doubt." He accuses them of espousing pure induction since they purpose reading the literature in the relevant fields *after* having developed a set of categories.

Instead, reading and integrating the literature later in the research process is a strategy to prompt *exploring* various ways of analyzing the data. But it means only *delaying* the literature review, not overlooking it,

— * I did my "review of literature" (synergize literature) after my field research.

I did delay reading Corey & Kontler

"the literature review"

Bible is not "the literature"
Bible was part of my "field" work

or failing to use it. Delaying the literature review decreases the likelihood that the researcher will already be locked into preconceived conceptual blinders upon entering the field and in interpreting the data. Once the researcher has developed a fresh set of categories, he or she can compare them with concepts in the literature and can begin to place his or her study appropriately within it. As Glaser [21] stresses, grounded theorists must do their own analytic work; if they 'borrow' concepts form the literature, then they should ensure that these concepts merit a place in their analysis.

Although Glaser and Strauss are not explicit in *The Discovery of Grounded Theory,* they do assume that researchers have had solid training in their fields. Also, they assume that such training provides researchers with perspectives from which to observe and on which to *build* analyses, not merely to apply them. Glaser and Strauss' method fosters both using disciplinary and theoretical perspectives and contributing to their *development* with new ideas, dense analyses, and theory construction. Emerson [29] and Katz [30] reveal another misinterpretation. Emerson [29, p.97] states "while grounded theory glorifies and tries to further generate theory in its own right, it also treats discovery as a stage prior to verification. This rigid divorce between discovery and verification lends support to the critique of fieldwork as insightful but not rigorous."

First, Glaser and Strauss [22] portray the contrast between discovery and verification approaches starkly because they see the need for developing new lines of theoretical development in the discipline. Second, qualitative research generally, and grounded theory specifically, derive from different canons than logico-deductive verification models. Qualitative research typically stresses inductive, open-ended, intuitive approaches to data-gathering and analysis, particularly in the early stages of both. Third, precisely what grounded theory provides *is* a rigorous method for qualitative studies. Hence, grounded theory must be assessed from internal logic of its own method, not by the inappropriate application of external criteria founded in other methods [31].

How researchers actually *use* the method remains a different issue than whether the method itself possesses rigor and logical consistency. Here, Katz and Emerson come close to reifying traditional verification methods as the only scientific method and therefore, as the only legitimate scientific work.

Most criticisms of grounded theory turn on misunderstandings or misuse of the method. However, the major problems with the grounded theory method lie in glossing over its epistemological assumptions and in minimizing its relation to extant sociological theory. The relation between subjectivist and objectivist realities and levels of explanation remains unspecified. And ways in which grounded theorists use their prior theoretical perspectives remain somewhat ambiguous.

Potential weaknesses in using the method. Weaknesses in *using* the method may have become equated with weaknesses inherent in the method. Such weaknesses may also be found in most other types of qualitative research and in quantitative research as well. These weaknesses include: premature commitment to a set of analytic categories [29, 30], unnecessary jargon, and a lack of clarity about key terms such as theory, category, and saturation. Premature commitment to categories means that the researcher has not fully explored the issues, events, and meanings within the research problem or setting and has not gained what Lofland call "intimate familiarity" with it [32].

Like other sociological perspectives, the grounded theory method does lend itself to generating unnecessary, esoteric jargon for labeling categories. Instead, researchers can label their categories with simple, direct, and vivid words. My earlier jargon included "mobilizing the self" [33], and "encapsulated time" [33], which I have since dropped, and in these two more recent pieces, "supernormal social identity" [18] and "cathartic spilling" [17]. Several more vivid terms include "the restored self" [18], "merged identities" [18,33], "making a comeback" [33] and "the salvaged self" [18].

In addition to the weaknesses in using the method, problems also may arise from lack of clarity about key terms in grounded theory. Then, such questions arise as: "When has a researcher achieved saturation of a category?," or "What stands as a theory?" One researcher's conceptual framework may resemble another researcher's theory [35]. Qualitative "theorizing" often remains discursive and imbedded in description, which may reduce it to a loosely integrated conceptual framework. In my view, a theory explicates a phenomena, specifies concepts which categorize the relevant phenomena, explains relationships between concepts and provides a framework for making predictions.

Phenomenological and positivistic emphases in grounded theory. The grounded theory method of analysis is just that, a method. My social constructionist version of grounded theory has a phenomenological cast

What a theory should do

73

[36]. Glaser and Strauss' earlier works [21, 22] have both phenomenological and positivistic emphases and therefore, sometimes may seem confusing and even inconsistent. They claim to be phenomenological, yet a strong positivistic thread runs through their work. On the phenomenological side, Glaser and Strauss have always emphasized going directly to the real world and starting with issues in it. They then went into hospitals and studied expectations of death from detailed first-hand field observations and interviews [37].

On the positivistic side, the early works on the grounded theory method suggest that the method takes on a life of its own, independent of its proponents and independent of the researcher. Glaser and Strauss [22, p.34] state, "Our approach, allowing substantive concepts and hypotheses to emerge first, on their own, enables the analyst to ascertain which, if any, existing formal theory may help him generate his substantive theories." Similarly, Glaser [21, p.5] reiterates, "Grounded theory arrives at relevance, because it allows core problems and processes to emerge." Also, Glaser implies that core processes and problems will similarly reveal themselves, rather than be defined by actors and analysts. Hence, Glaser and Strauss lean toward assuming that the theoretical categories derive from the data and that the researcher remains passive [21, 22]. Here, they come close to positing an external reality, unaltered by the observer's presence. Whether they intended to do so or simply had a theoretical lapse in the midst of methodological claims-making is itself open to construction. Clearly, however, Strauss' [23] recent explication of grounded theory now reveals an actively involved researcher who constructs categories and concepts. Yet, as Denzin [38] observes, Strauss' [23] grounded theory approach remains within the empirical science tradition and displays the tension between being simultaneously subjectivist and scientific.

A SOCIAL CONSTRUCTIONIST GROUNDED THEORY

A social constructionist grounded theory views the process of categorization as dialectical and active, rather than as given in the reality and passively observed by any trained observer. Hence, a social constructionist perspective assumes an active, not neutral, observer whose decisions shape both process and product throughout the research [30]. In short, the research report is also a social construction of the social constructions found and explicated in the data.

The *interaction* between the researcher and the data result in 'discovering', i.e. creating, categories. In short, the 'discovery' process consists of the researcher creating discoveries about the data and constructing the analysis. How the analyst uses the method and *which questions* he or she brings to the data shape the results. Certainly having a store of sociological concepts cues a researcher to look for constructions around status, power, hierarchy, and self-concept [40]. In addition, the researcher's perspective leads to asking certain kinds of questions [41]. In my studies, they include; How do chronically ill people construct definitions of their illness, recovery, self and situation? Who benefits from their definitions? How do their definitions compare with larger cultural themes and social values? What do these people take as real in their situations; of what are they aware; unaware? How do they feel about others, themselves, their plans, hopes and prospects? Under which conditions do ill people have relative autonomy and control? Under which do they not?

From a social constructionist view, the researcher takes those questions a step further. Whether addressing definitions, awareness, feeling, control, or any experience, the social constructionist attempts to find how each develops, changes and gives rise to consequences. For example, what do ill people believe contributes to their having control over their lives? How do they define that control? In which ways do their conceptions of control reflect larger ideologies? How do their constructions of control develop and change over time and over the course of their illness? What consequences emerge from their constructions of control?

Whatever their particular philosophical stance, grounded theorists build in special data-gathering questions, based on their assumptions and substantive interests. For example, given my substantive interests in the social psychology of time and in the sociology of emotions, I often ask questions such as: "What was time like for you during your hospitalization?" "How did you feel about telling your parents about your diagnosis?" "Tell me about what time was like when things were so uncertain."

The researcher's perspective consists of more than philosophical stance, school of thought, and methodological strategies. It also consists of experiences, values, and priorities. Upon reading my data, a colleague interested in the family sees how family interactions affect communications and decisions about illness. One could take that perspective and examine how families construct definitions of illness and decisions about the ill person. Another colleague interested in science sees these ill people's inventiveness. One could then look at how ill people invent liveable worlds.

Similarly, having had considerable experience with chronically ill people may foster developing certain lines of analysis, depending on the nature of that experience. For example, Lubkin's [42] nursing text ''which does not take a social constructionist view) stresses both patient compliance and professional advocacy. A social constructionist could take those topics and analyze how professionals construct and act upon their definitions of and criteria for patient compliance and professional advocacy.

The researcher's values - in the case of chronic illness, toward aging, disability and death - may shape the research process in taken-for-granted ways. Further, an over-riding interest in one concept such as stigma or, for that matter, in one specific chronic illness, fundamentally shapes the later analysis [43].

Perhaps most crucial is the researcher's school of thought, which provides the conceptual roots for the categories to grow. Following a social constructionist perspective fosters creating categories of the research participants' beliefs and actions. In order to create categories, the researcher already must have a firm grounded in sociological concepts without being wedded to them. This stance implies a delicate balance between possessing a grounding in the discipline and pushing it further. In my work, concepts such as identity, stigma, awareness, and meaning inform both the data collection and the analysis.

When wedded to concepts in their disciplines, researchers may neither see beyond them nor use them in new ways. For example, a medical sociologist who uses stigma as a definitive concept [16] to order and integrate data, rather than as a sensitizing concept [16], may only apply it as given in the literature instead of using it to ask new questions and to form new leads. Sensitizing concepts [16] alert researchers to central issues to tap without committing them to reproducing the initial set of concepts.

Using the grounded theory method, on the one hand, necessitates developing, refining, revising, and transcending concepts within the discipline. Often, a social constructionist stance elicits a fresh look at existing concepts. That alone contributes to revising and refining them. On the other hand, using grounded theory means dealing with the rendering the actual research data (i.e. interviews, documents, case histories, accounts etc.). When social constructionists study their data, they continually raise the questions: *"How?"; "Why?"; "Under which conditions?"; "With which consequences?" How do people construct beliefs? How do they manage their lives? Why do they think, feel, and act the way that they do? Under which conditions do they think, feel, and act that way? What are the consequences of their beliefs, feelings, and actions?* The 'grounded' nature of this research strategy is three-fold: (1) researchers attend closely to the data (which amounts to 'discoveries' for them when they study new topics or arenas), (2) their theoretical analysis build directly on their interpretations of processes within *those* data, and (3) they must ultimately compare their analyses with the extant literature and theory.

In short, the flexibility inherent in field work more generally assumes special importance in grounded theory. Grounded theorists start with what they see happening sociologically, and then they interpret it. What happens in the setting or to the research participants shapes the collected materials. For example, studying chronic patients' motivations for being productive did not interest me, despite practitioners' urging me to pursue the topic. Yet over and over again, ill people tried to explain their hopes, plans and intentions - in short, motivations. Hence, the data drew me to address this topic.

Again, the researcher's perspective influences whatever he or she sees within the data. Certainly Mead's [9] theory of emergence, analysis of action, and perspective on the development of self and Strauss' [10] explication of identity shaped my perspective. Since my study focused on issues around self-concept and identity, some questions where asked around those topics and respondents volunteered much other information. Their responses indicated that their motivations vitally concerned them. In addition, their motivations were intertwined with their identity goals. Without an initial theoretical interest in identity, one might miss that connection.

These interpretations of the data dovetailed with my theoretical interests in ways which spurred conceptual development. My questions reflected social constructionist concerns and often rapidly built on my developing concepts. This strategy led to shaping data collection around sociological and analytical interests rather than, in this case, gathering quasi-medical information, or making strictly behavioral recordings. From the beginning of the research, the grounded theory approach fosters the researcher staying on an analytic path, albeit he or she may identify a range of possible analytic paths.

DEVELOPING AND REFINING RESEARCH AND DATA COLLECTION QUESTIONS

The research questions

By asking how, why and under which conditions an existing sociological concept works in this specific field, social constructionists can use existing concepts as sensitizing concepts as Blumer [16] urges. Such sensitizing concepts become translated into general research questions and into more concrete data collection questions. How pointed these questions are depends on the type and level of theoretical development that the researcher has reached. *I'm exploring links between diversity, unity, + mess*

Generally, grounded theorists start with a set of experiences they wish to explore - in this case, chronic illness and how it affects the self. From the beginning of my doctoral research, I wished to explore links between having chronic illness, experiencing time, and shaping the self. Hence, these research questions initiate the inquiry: How do chronically ill people view living with chronic illness? In which ways does having a serious chronic illness affect an individual's shaping of self? How is the shaping of self related to the individual's experience of time? After completing one study [33] on those topics, another study was initiated later with 70 more interviews of ill people and caregivers and a repertoire of published and unpublished accounts about or by people with chronic illness.

Exploring the thematic questions led me to asking a set of interview questions that tapped people's chronologies of illness and how it impinged upon their lives. The chronologies gave some sense of the range of experiences people have had as well as how they cast them. Given my interests, questions about identity and self were built in from the beginning. From those questions and the spontaneous remarks ill people made about themselves, codes and categories were developed describing, synthesizing and explaining the data. *Given my interest, question about diversity*

Developing interview questions *synergy, + unity were built in*

To use the grounded theory method effectively, the researcher needs rich, detailed data. Grounded theorists have been accused of not attending carefully to data collection and of skimping on sampling [32]. However, grounded theorists need detailed, vivid data on which to base their analyses. Unlike some qualitative researchers, grounded theorists may show less concern with ascertaining the 'accuracy' of a specific piece of data than with its theoretical relevance. Two people, such as an ill person and his or her caregiver, may give different account for the ill person's activities. Here, whose rendering of reality comes closer to 'truth' has less importance than the analytic issues raised within each view, as well as the conflicting definitions of each participant. The possibility of someone's account being inaccurate raises interesting theoretical considerations for constructing an identity.

In order to develop durable, useful grounded theory, however, the data must provide a variety of complete accounts of major issues and processes. By obtaining these data, the grounded theorist can then depict their research participants' worlds. Such data results in developing analyses more easily with more convincing arguments.

Unlike most other types of qualitative data, grounded theorists explicitly shape the materials they gather. Learning to shape the materials well from the start provides the basis for later coding and categorizing. Further, interviewing works well in studies of chronic illness since the researcher often wants to obtain detailed individual chronicles. In addition, participant observation may be impossible for certain types of research problems in this area.

Framing, pacing, and managing the interview questions all affect the type and quality of material the researcher obtains [32, 44, 45]. Since my studies relied heavily on interview data, the incisiveness of the analysis turned on developing suitable questions and knowing when to ask them. Given the nature of chronic illness, several interviews may be needed with a respondent just to get through the basic information about the course of his or her illness, much less tap all the areas the researcher needs to cover.

As Lofland and Lofland [32] put it, the interview should be a "directed conversation". How to direct the conversation depends on the respondent's present psychological and physical status, the relationship between researcher and respondent, the researcher's theoretical perspective, and the topic. Being too directive poses hazards when interviewing chronically ill people. The overly-directive researcher can cut off the most interesting leads and rich data. Further, the researcher may load assumptions into the questions without being aware of doing so [44].

Asking "How did you decide to have the surgery?" assumes that the respondent decided. In contrast, "How did you come to have the surgery?" leaves things open. "Who was most helpful to you during the crisis?" assumes that others were involved. "Tell me what happened when you had the crisis" allows the researcher to piece events and people together before asking about helpful participants. Both loaded questions above may prove to be useful, when suitable and when raised in logical sequence, i.e. if the researcher senses that the patient played a part in the decision or already knows that other people were involved in the crisis. If not, both questions may raise sticky issues at a time the respondent may not be able to face them.

Briefly, interview questions can be framed and ordered by developing these kinds of questions and leads: (1) short face-sheet, (2) informational, (3) reflective, (4) feeling, and (5) ending. The short face-sheet questions are intended to be neutral, factual and limited to necessary information. These questions set the tone for the interview, so researchers need to be aware of *their* tone and mode of asking them.

The informational questions bring the respondent further into the interview and establish chronology, types of events, degrees of awareness, cast of participants, and the like. If a researcher has established rapport, he or she can bring in reflective and feeling questions. When trust and ease come more slowly, then sequencing them carefully works better.

Given my theoretical interests, the reflective questions may often serve as transitions to address direct issues about self: "How did - affect you?" "How did you see yourself then?" "How would you compare the person you were - years ago with the person you are now?" Similarly, feeling questions also often directly elicit data about self. "Tell me what you were feeling when you learned the diagnosis." "How did you feel about taking the early retirement?" All of these questions help to elicit the narrative of the respondent's story with only minimal framing by the researcher [46]. Ending questions are designed to complete the interview on a positive note [44]. The more intense the interview, the more questions and comments needed to end the interview with the person feeling positive about self. These questions also elicit insights about self. "What have you learned about yourself over the past - years?" "How have you grown as a person after having these experiences?" Such questions elicit interesting data on symbolic meanings of illness and self as well as accomplishing positive closure.

Coding and categorizing the data

To the extent possible, the codes and categories reflect emerging ideas rather than merely describing topics. For example, I coded some observations of elderly married couples as "merged identities" [18, 33] rather than as family relationships, a more general topic. The codes and categories then help the researcher begin to take the data apart and frame analytic questions about it. In that way, the codes and categories help the researcher to build an *analysis* of the data rather than remain at the level of ethnographic description.

By grounding the categories in the data as specifically yet analytically as possible, the grounded theorist can then sharpen the category, suggest its parameters, begin to outline the *conditions* under which the category develops, and start to look for consequences of it. Conditions mean those prerequisites which influence and shape views, interactions, and events, rather than determine them. By maintaining this type of analytic posture, even the initial ways of handling the data can enhance developing a theoretical analysis out of it.

A few suggestions for coding. Line by line coding during the initial coding prompts the researcher to study the data, to dispel earlier preconceived assumptions about the data, and to begin viewing the data analytically [20-22]. As a grounded theorist begins to render some codes into categories, he or she defines them analytically and delineates their properties. However implicitly,. the researcher's definitions of reality clearly shape what categories he or she constructs. Line by line coding keeps the researcher examining the *collected* data, rather than lapsing entirely into theoretical flights of fancy which have little connection to the data. Yet the researcher can invoke his or her theoretical perspective to raise questions about the data. My theoretical interests, for example, lead to such questions as: (1) Of what larger process is this action a part? (2) How did this action (belief, definition, relationship, pattern or structure) evolve? (3) What do these data state or assume about self and about relationships? By examining the collected data with the theoretical eye, the set of categories developed remains closer to the actual data and simultaneously, moves beyond description. *Am I coding only for topics?*

Coding for processes, actions, assumptions, and consequences rather than for topics leads to greater analytic precision. Coding for processes assists in defining major activities and issues; such coding also helps the researcher to discern connections between structures and events. It helps to look at topics processually. Thus, rather than treating my code, supernormal identity [18] only as a topic, I treated it more processually by looking at the development and abandonment of supernormal identities. Doing so fosters studying the conditions which gave rise to these identities. Similarly, coding for actions fosters the researcher's search for processes. The researcher can then look for phases, contributing conditions and consequences of those actions.

A major strength of the grounded theory method is its open-endedness and flexibility. Since analysis and data collection proceed simultaneously, a researcher can follow up on ideas as he or she creates them. Thus, researchers may use the method to examine an issue thoroughly rather than to rely on previously collected data, which may address the issue incompletely. A grounded theorist may sculpt fully contoured ideas throughout the analysis rather than only suggesting or alluding to them at the end.

The open-endedness of grounded theory allows researchers to pursue leads and ideas as they develop. For example, most of the people who wished to lead conventional lives recounted incidents concerning either disclosing illness to others or avoiding disclosure entirely. Whatever they did, issues around telling people about their illness loomed large to them. Hence, I went back through earlier interviews and sorted material on disclosing and avoiding disclosure. Looking through the interviews with this interest now in mind caused me to find numerous comments and accounts of incidents concerning disclosing or avoiding disclosure. (Data coded in one way earlier can be coded several other ways. Similarly, the same anecdote may point to several different conceptual issues.'' Subsequently, I built questions about disclosing into later interviews. Doing so helped me to frame a more complete picture of it. *I built questions about diversity, unity, spirituality into interviews*
The level of skill of the researcher in collecting data enters here too. As a doctoral student, I knew little about interviewing and initially, felt uncomfortable in doing it. As a result, the quality of the early data differed strikingly with that of the later interviews. In the interim, I had gained both skills and confidence. Since then, I have discovered that many researchers are neither particularly skilled at interviewing nor do they design artful questions. Even practiced interviewers may lapse into 'do you' questions which elicit 'yet' or 'no' answers with limited elaboration.

RAISING TERMS TO CONCEPTS

Raising terms to concepts means that the researcher takes a term or code, defines it succinctly, and analyzes it. The wording of the term is important since the researcher now intends to treat it as a *conceptual category,* rather than merely as a *descriptive topic,* or code. In contradistinction to quantitative studies, here a code means a label applied to certain data; a code remains less abstract than a conceptual category. In turn, a conceptual category is part of the researcher's larger theoretical framework in which he or she specifies conditions, offers explanations, and makes predictions. When treating a term as a conceptual category, the researcher specifies its properties, notes the conditions under which it arises, relates how it changes, describes its consequences, and ultimately, specifies its relationship to the other conceptual categories. Descriptive topics, in contrast, may provide vivid accounts but are not integrated into a set of specified and inter-related concepts from which the researcher develops explanations or predictions. For example, I referred to each rung of the identity hierarchy as an identity level [18] and categorized each level. Then, I specified the conditions under which someone moved up or down the identity hierarchy as an identity level [18] and categorized each level. Then, I specified the conditions under which someone moved up or down the identity hierarchy in order to realize a preferred identity. In that way, a set of related conceptual categories were developed and subsequently, the relations between them could be developed.

Two analytic processes contribute to raising terms to concepts - constant comparison and continued questioning. The comparisons include data with data, category with category and concept with concept [20-23]. In my study, comparing data with data means: (1) comparing different people's situations, beliefs, behavior or accounts of the same type of event or issue, (2) comparing data from the same people at different times and (3) comparing properties found in the data with other properties.

Comparing different people's accounts means taking some topic such as an experience, issue, period of time, relationship, or stage and juxtaposing data from each person against each other one. For example, comparisons were made of ill people's experiences of discovering and defining illness. Then accounts were compiled to compare the circumstances under which they discovered and defined illness, how they felt,

i.e. intra's Kids college tuition

thought and dealt with it, what they faced at that time, who became involved, and so forth. Just looking at such basic issues systematically yields thick description and often, analytic insights. On a more abstract level, comparing identity goals as illness changes became another unit of comparison [18]. Thus, I learned that some people do plummet down the identity hierarchy as they experience their illnesses. Moreover, a few others start at the bottom of the hierarchy and over months or years move up in it.

Raising a term to a conceptual level means making a series of *decisions* about it. Again, the researcher actively shapes the research process. The researcher creates an explication, organization, and presentation *of* the data rather than discovering order *within* the data. The discovery process consists of discovering the ideas the *researcher* has about the data after interacting with it. Raising a term to a conceptual level first means deciding that the term reflects a significant process, relationship, event, or issue. Second, it means explicitly deciding to follow up on it in subsequent data collection. Third, it means making connections between it and other conceptual categories.

Again, such terms are not always ones a researcher expects to study. For example, I did not intend to study disclosing illness nor did I have any particular interest in that topic until issues around difficulties in disclosing or avoiding disclosure appeared in many interviews. Ill people attached such significance to these issues, which, in turn, caused me to look at them more systematically and to raise new questions about them.

To raise the term disclosing to a conceptual level, I looked first at my data and then to the literature in medical sociology. I first asked basic questions such as:

(1) What did disclosing mean to ill people?

(2) When were they concerned about it?

(3) What were the consequences of it?

(4) How did they handle disclosing?

(5) When did ill people view disclosing as irrelevant?

For many of these people, disclosing meant revealing something private, often potentially discrediting, about themselves. The link between disclosing and ill people's emotions was clear. Later, how these issues intertwined with self-images and self-concept became evident. Therefore, I looked at how people managed disclosing. This meant studying how ill people constructed their actions of disclosing. I raised questions about other ways of telling: were there other types of telling and, if so, how did they compare and contrast with disclosing? My awareness of modes of telling was heightened by an earlier study of coroner's deputies announcing death to survivors [2]. I had long realized that physicians and other practitioners announce, inform, impart, or even reveal bad news. But they seldom disclose for disclosures reveal something about self.

Memo-writing

Memo-writing provides the pivotal step of breaking the categories into components and elaborating the codes [20]23]. Through memo-writing, the researcher moves directly into analysis of the data. Bits of data and early codes are systematically examined, explored and elaborated upon. Through memo-writing, the researcher takes his or her emerging ideas apart, checks them, and outlines further data collection. During each stage of memo-writing, the researcher may use his or her theoretical background to deepen the analytic insights of his or her developing grounded theory. My interest in constructions of reality, for example, alerted me to compare people's accounts of disclosing or avoiding disclosure and thereby, to assess the relative amount of reality that they granted to illness.

Basically, memo-writing gives the researcher a tool for engaging in an extended on-going dialog with self [47, 48]. By committing ideas, hunches, questions, and elaborated categories to organized memos, the researcher *defines* what is implicit and what is explicit in the data. In that dialog with self, the researcher looks at the data from a variety of perspectives and analyzes them. Later, the researcher may impose organization upon the memos by ordering them to best capture the data and communicate with the audience. In the meantime, memo-writing gives the researcher an analytic handle on the materials and a means of struggling with discovering and defining hidden or taken-for granted processes and assumptions within the data. For example, my initial respondents' statements led me to sense that the concept of identity encompassed more for them than social location or personal definition. But what was it? As I gathered more data, I realized that they formed identity goals, which took a hierarchical form [18, 33].

The dialog with self through memo-making typically helps to separate the researcher from the researched, thereby reducing problems of immersion in the setting or data, 'going native', assuming the stance of the practitioner and the like. The finished memos form a repository of ideas, which the researcher can then rethink, revise, toss out, organize, and present in varied ways. In a larger sense, memo-writing may never have closure since a researcher may make continued theoretical discoveries as his or her memos become increasingly conceptual. The later memos then may include, incorporate, and transcend extant theory as the researcher develops his or her grounded theory.

WRITING AND REWRITING

The discovery process also extends into writing and rewriting drafts for publication. The researcher gains further insights and creates more ideas about the data while writing. Hence, writing and rewriting actually become crucial phases of the analytic process. Through writing and rewriting, a researcher can identify arguments and problems, make assumptions explicit, and sharpen the concepts [48]. Further, the writing process gives the researcher the opportunity to link his or her work with other theories by integrating them into the discussion and analysis.

At this point in the analytic process, the researcher may have a theoretical grasp of the material. But he or she may not have formed the analysis into an argument or presented it as a problem of interest to colleagues or practitioners for publication. Now, the researcher needs to do a thorough review of the literature in the field. Then he or she can frame the study within that literature and show where and how it fits. The following excerpts show how I located my study on identity and framed the problem [18, p. 287].

People with serious chronic illnesses struggle to have valued lives and selves. Those who love with serious chronic illness experience disrupted plans and altered lives. Their illnesses may cause setbacks, flare-ups, complications, impaired functions and disabilities as well as have social, psychological, and financial consequences. All these experiences and consequences of illness affect whether ill persons lead valued lives and realize their hopes to live on their own terms. Their illnesses pose identity problems that often are left entirely to them and their significant others. How do they handle these identity problems? I answer this question by analyzing the experiences of chronically ill people whose former identities and future plans become questioned, undermined, altered, or negated. By addressing their elusive struggle for a self, my analysis focuses on the consequences of experiencing illness for creating self and identity rather than concentrating primarily on the practical struggles of managing life with chronic illness.

This paragraph sets the stage for studying the problems of struggling for a self and creating valued identities. The category of people who have these problems are specified - those with serious chronic illnesses whose former identities have become questioned. In addition, the focus of the analysis is pinpointed, as contrasted with another major theme in studies of chronic illness - managing to live with it.

In that article, I turn next to the theoretical analysis of identity and introduce the major ideas and arguments. Hence, the reader can discern the framework of the analysis and how the pieces fit together.

Key ideas are as follows [11, pp. 283-285]:

Chronically ill persons' accounts of their experiences reveal two new interconnected issues for studying identity: the role of preferred identities and the development of identity hierarchies. First, individuals choose identities by outlining plans and assessing prospects. The chronically ill people whom I interviewed implicitly developed preferred identities as they attempted to construct lives apart from illness. Their preferred identities symbolize assumptions, hopes, desires and plans for a future now unrealized. In short preferred identities mean identity goals.. the concept of identity encompasses the person's vision of future selves, reflecting his or her hopes, aspirations, objectives and goals. In this sense, preferred identities serve as a source of motivation.

Second, an identity hierarchy becomes visible as ill people, over time, choose different types of preferred identities, reflecting relative difficulty in achieving specific aspirations and objectives. The types of preferred identities constitute particular identity levels in the identity hierarchy. These identity levels include: (1) the supernormal social identity, an identity demanding extraordinary achievement in conventional worlds: (2) the restored self, a reconstruction of previous identities before illness: (3) contingent personal identity, a hypothetically possible, though uncertain, identity, because of further illness: and (4) the salvaged self, retaining a past identity based on a valued activity or attribute while becoming physically dependent. Experiencing progressive illness often

This is about individuals — I'm writing about organizations

means reducing identity goals and aiming for a lower level in the identity hierarchy. In short reducing identity goals means aiming for a less preferred identity.

Through writing and rewriting, the researcher can bring out implicit arguments, provide a context for them, make links to the literature, critically examine the categories and concepts, and present the data cogently [49]. In writing the article cited above, renaming three of my categories enhanced clarity and vividness. Hence, the 'reconstituted self' (it sounded like processed food) became the 'restored self', which captured the idea of returning to a past self and reclaiming former identities. The 'possible personal identity' became the 'contingent personal identity' since the possibility remained contingent upon no further episodes or complications. A 'preferable self-view' became the 'salvaged self' because ill people did more than offer a self-image they preferred; they tried to salvage prior defining traits to claim a valued self now.

Writing and rewriting certainly fosters analytic clarity. These processes also prompt gaining more theoretical comprehensiveness and precision as the researcher grapples with increasingly more abstract theoretical questions and hones his or her responses to them.

SUMMARY AND DISCUSSION

Explicating use of a social constructionist version of grounded theory method to study chronic illness reveals issues concerning the method more generally as well as offering some specific guidelines for sociological research in chronic illness. Rather than reflecting a *tabula rasa*, grounded theorists bring to their studies the general perspectives of their disciplines, their own philosophical, theoretical, substantive, and methodological proclivities, their particular research interests, and their biographies. They do not bring, however, a set of finely-honed preconceived concepts and categories to apply automatically. Should grounded theorists apply such concepts and categories - even their own previous ones - to new data, they must justify them. *OK, I will justify them - I'm dealing in roles*

When using the grounded theory method, researchers actively form questions and seek data. The experiences of people with chronic illness do not entirely unfold before researchers' eyes. Rather, researchers create their analyses. The questions that researchers put to the world, how they collect their data, and which issues and processes they see within it all fundamentally shape their analyses. Further, researchers create a conceptual

(theology)

interpretation of the data, impose an order on it, explicate the relationships between categories, and organize those relationships to communicated their ideas to audiences. Thus, like quantitative researchers [50], grounded theorists make decisions throughout the research process that shape their research products. Also like quantitative researchers, grounded theorists' research reports may take an objectified form and tone that belies the actual research process.

Using the grounded theory method to study chronic illness offers the researcher strategies for focusing and controlling large amounts of data in ways that render it conceptually and, in turn, move the emergent conceptualizations toward more general theoretical statements. Such statements not only deepen sociological understanding of the experience of chronic illness, but also, contribute more generally to the discipline.

The grounded theory method provides the possibility of theory development. The analyses flowing from this approach are ones with conceptual power and durability. But, like other analyses, they can always be refined and modified.

Since grounded theorists believe in studying process, they realize that theories cannot be frozen in time. Certainly changing historical conditions can alter any area of inquiry. Grounded theory analyses can be adapted to changing conditions and can either take historical change into account - or even focus upon it. Grounded theory analyses can also provide future researchers with sources of conceptual, explanatory, and predictive comparison.

From my perspective, grounded theory analyses can be enriched by clarifying the researcher's epistemological premises and by reaching back into extant theory. To date, grounded theorists have not explicated a shared set of epistemological premises. Perhaps there should not be such a set of premises, for researcher from varied backgrounded with diverse research problems can use the strategies of grounded theory. If so, then individual researchers need to examine their own epistemological premises as well as those imbedded in their use of the grounded theory method. Doing so could clarify the relation between the subjective and objective, sharpen the research process, and delineate the theory of reality to which the researcher subscribes. Currently, most grounded theory pieces, including my own, assume a theory of reality. Similarly, some pieces seem to assume the discovery of objectified truth, rather than the discovery of the researcher's more or less useful theoretical categories.

Researching back into extant theory might seem to contradict the entire grounded theory approach. I think not. As noted throughout the above analysis, a strong theoretical perspective can guide questions - from the basic research outline directly into the data gathering and analysis. In that way, a strong theoretical perspective fosters giving the research greater *conceptual* depth and breadth while firmly situating it within the discipline. More direct ties back to their Meadian heritage could, for example, sharpen grounded theorists' theory of action and assumptions about human nature implicit in their studies. Further, a greater attention to contemporary developments in Marxist and critical theory might foster closer connections between microscopic and macroscopic structures in grounded theory analyses. Such emphases would neither contradict nor negate prior work, but would supplement and extend earlier ground-breaking efforts.

Nonetheless, bringing a strong theoretical perspective to grounded theory studies does pose some knotty problems. Prior theoretical socialization in a researcher may produce ideational and ideological baggage which inhibits forming fresh ideas and promotes tunnel-vision. Yet, theoretical sophistication in classical and contemporary sociological theory can also foster asking fundamental questions throughout the research and analytic processes. Such sophistication leads the researcher beyond training for theoretical sensitivity to create sound analytic questions. Rather, such sophistication leads the researcher to address basic questions of value and meaning. To discover the conditions which promote this theoretical sophistication instead of theoretical tunnel-vision may, in itself, require grounded theory research.

Acknowledgements - Thanks are due to Adele Clarke, Uta Gerhardt, Anna Hazan, Marilyn Little and Barbara Rosenblum for reviewing an earlier version of this paper and to Uta Gerhardt and Anselm Strauss for their comments on the preceding draft. I also wish to thank Adele Clarke for rewording the title of the paper.

REFERENCES

1. Strauss A.L. *et al., Chronic Illness and the Quality of Life,* Mosby, St. Louis, MO, 1984.

2. Fagerhaugh S. Getting around with emphysema. In *Chronic Illness and the Quality of Life* (Edited by Strauss A.), pp. 99-107, Mosby, St. Louis, MO, 1975.

3. Reif L. Ulcerative colitis: strategies for managing life. In *Chronic Illness and the Quality of Life* (Edited by Strauss A.), pp. 81-88. Mosby, St. Louis, MO, 1975.

4. Weiner C.L. The burden of rheumatoid arthritis. In *Chronic Illness and the Quality of Life* (Edited by Strauss A.), pp. 71-80. Mosby, St. Louis, MO, 1975.

5. Charmaz K. Loss of self: a fundamental form of suffering in the chronically ill. *Social. Hlth Illn.* 5, 169-195, 1983.

6. Shutz A. *Collected Papers. Volume 1: The Problem of Social Reality.* Martinus Nijhoff, The Hague, 1971; Berger P. and Lueckmann T. *The Social Construction of Reality,* Doubleday, New York, 1966.

7. Foucault M., *The Birth of the Clinic.* Pantheon, New York, 1973.

8. Lindesmith A., Strauss A. and Denzin N. *Social Psychology,* Prentice-Hall, Englewood, Cliffs, NJ, 1988.

9. Mead G.H. *Mind, Self and Society.* University of Chicago, Chicago, IL, 1934.

10. Strauss A.L. *Mirrors and Masks.* Sociology Press, Mill Valley, CA, 1969.

11. Weigert A.J., Teitge J. and Teitge D. *Society and Identity.* Cambridge University Press Cambridge, 1986.

12. Denzin N. *On Understanding Emotion.* Jossey-Bass, San Francisco, CA, 1984.

13. Merleau-Ponty M. *Phenomenology of Perception.* Routledge, Kegan Paul, London, 1962.

14. Berger P. and Luckmann T. See Ref. [6],

15. For a counter-argument positing the dismissal of structural issues by social constructionists, see Gerhardt U. *Ideas about Illness: An Intellectual and Political History of Medical Sociology.* Macmillan, London. In press.

16. Blumer H. *Symbolic Interactionism.* Prentice-Hall, Englewood Cliffs, NJ, 1969.

17. Charmaz K. Disclosing illness. Unpublished manuscript, 1986.

18. Charmaz K. Struggling for a self: identity levels of the chronically ill. In *The Experience and Management of Chronic Illness. Research in the Sociology of Health Care* (Edited by Conrad P. and Roth J.). Vol.6, pp. 283-307. JAI Press, Greenwich, CT 1987.

19. A grounded theorist makes decisions, follows leads, organizes data, defines categories, develops concepts and demonstrates the relations between them. A caveat Researchers in other fields may profitably use the grounded theory method. I stick to sociological concerns as they reflect my interests and expertise.

20. Charmaz K. The grounded theory method: an explication and interpretation. In *Contemporary Field Research* (Edited by Emerson R.M.). pp. 109-127. Little Brown, Boston, MA, 1983.

21. Glaser B.G. *Theoretical Sensitivity.* Sociology Press, Mill Valley, CA 1978.

22. For the first statement of the method, see Glaser B.G. and Strauss A.L. *The Discovery of Grounded Theory.* Aldine, Chicago, IL, 1967.

23. A more explicit formulation of steps and techniques clarifies and greatly extends the *Discovery* book. See Strauss A.L. *Qualitative Analysis for Social Scientists.* Cambridge University Press, New York, 1987. In keeping with the grounded theory method, I did not read the then just-published volume of *Qualitative Analysis* until after I had written two drafts of this paper.

24. Calkins K. Shouldering a burden. *Omega* 3, 23-36, 1972.

25. Charmaz K. The coroners' strategies for announcing death. *Urban Life* 4, 296-316, 1975.

26. For a discussion of theoretical sampling, see Ref. [23, pp. 276-277].

27. Bigus O., Hadden S.C. and Glaser B.G. Basic social processes, In *Qualitative Methods: Volume 11 of Handbook of Social Science Methods* (Edited by Smith R.B. and Manning P.K.), pp. 251-272. Ballinger, Cambridge, MA, 1982.

28. Blumer M. Concepts in the analysis of qualitative data. *Social. Rev.* 27, 651-677, 1979.

29. Emerson R.M. (Ed.) Introduction, Part II: theory and evidence in field research. In *Contemporary Field Research,* pp. 93-108. Little brown,

Boston, MA, 1983.

30. Katz J.A. theory of qualitative methodology. In *Contemporary Field Research* (Edited by Emerson R.M.), pp. 127-148. Little Brown, Boston, MA, 1983.

31. For another discussion of the application of inappropriate criteria, see Star S.L. Triangulating clinical and basic research: British localizationists, 1870-1906. *Hist. Sci.* 24, 29-48, 1986.

33. Charmaz K. *Time and Identity: The Shaping of Selves of the Chronically Ill.* PhD dissertation, University of California, San Francisco, CA, 1973.

34. I am indebted to Susan Leigh Star for the term.

35. See Clarke A. A social worlds adventure: the case of reproductive science. In *Theories of Science in Society* (Edited by Cozzins S. and Gieryn T.). Indiana University Press. Bloomfield, IN. In press. Given my definition of theory, most grounded theory analyses actually provide incisive conceptual frameworks, which aim toward theory, rather than qualifying as theory.

36. My perspective comes close to phenomenology in that I also emphasize lived experience. It departs from phenomenology in that I do not pursue a quest for essences as phenomenologists do. Adopting a social constructionist perspective leads to a certain reflexitivity in examining one's research methods. For a detailed examination of social constructionism in a medical sociology with an emphasis on medical knowledge, see Bury M.R. Social constructionism and the development of medical sociology. *Social. Hlth Illn.* 8, 137-167, 1986.

37. See Glaser B.G. and Strauss A.L. *Awareness of Dying.* Aldine, Chicago, Il, 1967; and *Time for Dying.* Aldine, Chicago, IL, 1968.

38. Denzin N. Review of Strauss A.L. *Qualitative Methods for Social Scientists.* In *Contemp. Social.* 17, 430-432, 1988.

39. For a critique of value-free sociology, see Gouldner A. *The coming Crisis of Western Sociology,* Avon, New York, 1971.

40. Gerhardt U. The Parsonian paradigm and the identity of medical sociology. *Social. Rev.* 27, 229-251, 1979.

41. Such questions hint of ways that grounded theory may be useful in

looking at social psychological issues in a context which addresses macro structural issues. For a further discussion of analyzing stressful life events in a theoretical context which takes macro issues into account, see Gerhardt U. Coping and social action: theoretical reconstruction of the life-event approach. *Social. Hlth Illn.* 1, 195-225-1979.

42. Lubkin I.M. *Chronic Illness: Impact and Interventions.* Jones & Bartlett, Boston, MA, 1986.

43. Locker D. *Disability and Disadvantage: The consequences of Chronic Illness.* Tavistock, London, 1983.

44. Charmaz K. Intensive interviewing. Unpublished manuscript, 1986.

45. Gordon R.L. *Interviewing.* Dorsey Press, Homewood, IL, 1980.

46. Mishler E.G. *Research Interviewing: Context and Narrative.* Harvard University Press, Cambridge, MA, 1986.

47. Memo-writing comes close to what teachers of writing call pre-writing or free-writing, although memos are focused on a category or code. See, for example, Elbow P. *Writing with Power.* Oxford University Press, New York, 1981. The analyst may write anything in the memo without the constraints of evaluation, or of audiences. Memo-writing helps to reduce writer's block and also helps to bring the fluidity, imagery, and rhythm of spoken language into the work.

48. Becker H.S. *Writing for Social Scientists.* University of Chicago Press, Chicago, IL, 1986.

49. For a way of presenting data on interviews and respondent accounts which specifies the amount, if any, of rendering by the researcher, see Gerhardt U. and Brisekorn-Zinke M. The normalization of hemodialysis at home. In *Research in the Sociology of Health Care* (Edited by Roth J.A. and Ruzek S.). Vol. 4, pp. 271-317. JAI Press, Greenwich, CT 1986.

50. Fletcher C. *Beneath the Surface: An Account of Three Styles of Sociological Research.* Routledge & Kegan Paul, London, 1974.

THE GROUNDED THEORY METHOD:

An Explication and Interpretation

Kathy Charmaz, Ph.D.

Publication of Glaser and Strauss' pioneering book The Discovery of Grounded Theory (1967), provided a strong intellectual rationale for using qualitative research to develop theoretical analyses. The authors were protesting against a methodological climate in which qualitative research typically was viewed as only a helpful preliminary to the "real" methodologies of quantitative research (see, for examples, Hyman et al. 1954; Lazarsfeld 1944; and Stouffer 1962). In addition to providing a powerful rhetoric for qualitative analysis per se, in the Discovery book Glaser and Strauss also began articulating research strategies to codify the analytic process throughout the research project. In the decade that followed, other qualitative researchers who held different perspectives, notably Douglas (1976), Johnson (1975), Katz (this volume), Lofland (1971), and Lofland and Lofland (in press), and Schatzman and Strauss (1973) contributed to the growing literature on collecting and rendering qualitative materials.

Both the assumptions and analytic methods of grounded theory have been criticized by some qualitative researchers on a number of counts. Lofland and Lofland (in press), for example, suggest that grounded theorists fail to give proper attention both to data collection techniques and to the quality of the gathered materials. From Katz's (this volume) perspective, discovery and verification are inseparable and the grounded theory contrast between them in some sense perpetuates the notion that qualitative research is preliminary. These criticisms misinterpret the aims and methods of grounded theory. Unfortunately, several features of the grounded theory method have contributed to such misinterpretation. First, the language of the grounded theory method relies on terms commonly used in quantitative research and, I believe, this language lags behind actual development of the method. To illustrate, the terms such as coding, comparison groups, and theoretical sampling reflect the language of quantitative research and often elicit images of logical deductive quantitative procedures.[1] Second, the method arises from and, to date, relies on Chicago school sociology, which, as Rock suggested (1979), depended heavily on an oral tradition implicitly transmitted to students. I view grounded theory similarly as a practice learned largely through apprenticeship. Although Glaser's (1978) work is a critical step forward in explicating the oral tradition in grounded theory, the work contains many tacit assumptions and speaks most directly to students who worked closely with him or Strauss.

In response to these criticisms and misunderstandings of the grounded theory method, I aim to: (1) explicate key analytic procedures and assumptions often left implicit in earlier statements; (2) offer interpretations which suggest varying approaches to the method; and (3) provide substantive applications of the method to illustrate how it can be used during the analytic process. Because I aim to explicate and interpret the method, I draw heavily on approaches developed by Glaser (1978). Throughout the discussion, I will provide examples and illustrations from my own past and current research using this method.

A PRELIMINARY STATEMENT OF THE GROUNDED THEORY METHOD

The grounded theory method stresses discovery and theory development rather than logical deductive reasoning which relies on prior theoretical frameworks. These two aspects of the method lead the grounded theorist to certain distinctive strategies. First, data collection and analysis proceed simultaneously (see Glaser and Strauss 1967). Since grounded theorists intend to construct theory from the data itself, they need to work with solid, rich data that can be used to elicit thorough development of analytic issues (see Lofland and Lofland, in press). Grounded theorists shape their data collection from their analytic interpretations and discoveries, and therefore, sharpen their observations. Additionally, they check and fill out emerging ideas by collecting further data. These strategies serve to strengthen both the quality of the data and the ideas developed from it.

Second, both the processes and products of research are shaped from the data rather than from preconceived logically deduced theoretical frameworks (see, for example, Biernacki, forthcoming; Broadhead, in press; and Wiener 1981). Grounded theorists rely heavily on studying their data and reading in other fields during the initial stages of research (see Glaser 1978). They do not rely directly on the literature to shape their ideas, since they believe that they should develop their own analyses independently. From the grounded theory perspective, researchers who pour their data into someone else's theoretical framework or substantive analysis add little innovation and also may perpetuate ideas that could be further refined, transcended, or discarded.

Third, grounded theorists do not follow the traditional quantitative canons of verification. They do, however, check their developing ideas with further specific observations, make systematic comparisons between observations, and, often, take their research beyond the confines of one topic, setting, or issue. Perhaps because they make systematic efforts to check and refine emerging categories, their efforts may be confused with traditional verification. From the grounded theory perspective, the method does not preclude verification by other types of researchers; it merely indicates a division of labor.

Fourth, not only do grounded theorists study *process,* they assume that making theoretical sense of social life is itself a process. As such, theoretical analyses may be transcended by further work either by the original or a later theorist by bringing more and different questions to the data (see Glaser 1978). In keeping with their foundations in pragmatism, then, grounded theorists aim to develop fresh theoretical interpretations of the data rather than explicitly aim for any final or complete interpretation of it (see Schwatrz and Jacobs 1979).

CODING *descriptive* *theoretical*

Coding, the initial phase of the analytic method, is simply the process of *categorizing* and *sorting* data. Codes then serve as shorthand devices to *label, separate, compile,* and *organize* data. Codes range from simple, concrete, and topical categories to more general, abstract conceptual categories for an emerging theory.[2] In qualitative coding, researchers develop codes out of their field notes, interviews, case histories, or other collected materials (these could include diaries by participants, journals, interactional maps, historical documents, and so forth). Examples of codes I have used in my studies of chronic illness include self-esteem, sources of support, discovering illness, defining limitations, transitory self-pity, identifying moment, and identity questioning. These codes range from lesser to greater complexity as the analytic process proceeds.

Codes may be treated as conceptual categories when they are developed analytically. This means the researcher defines them carefully, delineates their properties, explicates their causes, demonstrates the conditions under which they operate, and spells out their consequences. A descriptive category such as defining illness applies to the substantive area studied. A theoretical category such as transforming identity, in contrast, is part of a theoretical scheme, and may be applied across diverse substantive areas.

Codes serve to summarize, synthesize, and sort many observations made of the data. By providing the pivotal link between the data collection and its conceptual rendering, coding becomes the fundamental means of developing the analysis. Hence, the categorizing and sorting inherent in coding are more than simply assigning subject headings or topics to data. Researchers use codes to pull together and categorize a series of otherwise discrete events, statements, and observations which they identify in the data.[3] Researchers make the codes fit the data, rather than forcing the data into codes. By doing so, they gain a clearer rendering of the materials and greater accuracy. When reading the data, grounded theorists ask: "What do I see going on here?" To illustrate, when reading a number of interviews with widows who had been housewives, I noted that these women repeatedly mentioned the pressures to establish social and economic independence that they confronted due their husbands' deaths. Although they later enjoyed their new pursuits, they initially were fearful and reluctant to begin independent lives. Here, I coined the term "forced independence" to code their experience into a more abstract conceptual category that described and analyzed the widows' experience (Charmaz 1980a).

Grounded theorists code for *processes* that are fundamental in ongoing social life. These processes may be at organizational or social psychological levels, depending on the researcher's training and interests. To find these processes, grounded theorists carefully scrutinize participants' statements and actions for patterns, inconsistencies, contradictions, and intended and unintended consequences. The initial questions they ask are: What are people doing? What is happening? (See Glaser 1978). What the researcher views the participants as doing may not be the same as what participants claim to do. For example, in a treatment unit, participants may claim that their actions are devoted fundamentally to treating patients, yet the researcher may decide an intense jockeying for power underlies their actions, and thus, is the more significant process to pursue.

The *assumptions* that participants hold provide a fertile field for coding. Seeking to discover, identify, and ask questions about these assumptions keeps the researcher thinking critically and defining what is implicit in the data. The researcher then defines how participants act upon their assumptions in the specific setting, which, of course, helps the researcher convert topics into processes. Further, rather than viewing the participants' assumptions as truth itself, the researcher gains some distance on his or her materials. In this way too the researcher avoids overimmersion, which may lead to taking over the views of participants as one's own. For example, a medical sociologist who uncritically accepts the practitioners' discourse of meaning may shape his or her research around terms such as "coping," "stress," and "stress-reduction" without looking at their underlying assumptions.

When looking for processes, the researcher must also ask: What kind of events are at issue here? How are they constructed? What do these events mean? By looking for major processes, researchers delineate how events are related to each other. In a particular study, a researcher may identify several major processes. If so, then grounded theorists code for all of them and may decide later which ones to pursue. Importantly, a grounded theorist sticks with his or her interpretations of the data and follows leads from them, even when they lead to surprising new research problems.

At times, researchers readily identify basic processes, for example, when they are so visible, stark, and direct that even a naive researcher quickly defines them. But other major processes remain much more implicit and covert. Those which are tacitly shared but remain unspoken sometimes are difficult to pull out. This is particularly the case when participants themselves cannot articulate the assumptions and meanings that they, in fact, hold and act upon. In an earlier project on a rehabilitation institution for the physically disabled, I discovered that middle-class staff held markedly different conceptions of time than most of the lower-class patients whom they served. Professional staff held a linear progressive view of time, with realization of goals in the future. Yet they worked with patients who generally held a cyclic view of time, situated in the present. For the patients, time moved from present to present, from crisis to crisis. Repeatedly, staff became frustrated by these patients' failure to use time in the institution to work on the small incremental gains toward a distant goal that staff viewed as both medically and personally appropriate. Instead, patients simply passed time, waited for change, or killed time with unsanctioned pursuits until discharged (Calkins 1970).

Initial Coding

Coding is a two-phase process: an initial searching phase precedes a later phase of *focused* coding (Glaser 1978). In the initial phase, researchers look for what they can define and discover in the data. They then look for leads, ideas, and issues in the data themselves. Glaser (1978) advocates line by line coding to gain a full theoretical accounting of the data. This prompts the researcher to look at the data with a theoretical eye from the start and actively encourages playing with and developing ideas.

Although every researcher brings to his or her research general preconceptions founded in expertise, theory, method, and experience, using the grounded theory method necessitates that the researcher look at the data from as many vantage points as possible. At this point, the rule for the researcher to follow is: *study your emerging data*. At first, the data may appear to be a mass of confusing, unrelated accounts. But by studying and coding (often I code the same materials several times just after collecting them), the researcher begins to create order.[4] If researchers think that the data suggest more questions than they can answer, then they need to collect more data while simultaneously coding them. Sometimes, neither the data actually collected nor the researcher's emerging ideas are related to the original research objectives or topics. In this case, the researcher either continues with the material on hand or finds more appropriate sources of data for the original topic. In my chronic illness interviews, for instance, I had not anticipated covering either self-pity or social support. Yet both these topics were repeated themes so I followed up on them.

Several further questions from my experience may help. First, I attend to the general context, central participants and their roles, timing and structuring of events, and the relative emphasis participants place on various issues in the data.[5] I also look for connections between individuals' special situations and problems and their interpretations of their experience.[6] For example the problems of leading independent lives become magnified for young adults with serious chronic illnesses who seek simultaneously to develop intimate relationships and to prepare themselves for jobs.

Second, I construct codes to note what participants lack, gloss over, or ignore, as well as what they stress. For example, I note the kinds of information patients possessed or lacked about their illnesses when they first were diagnosed. Also, since I am interested in time perspective, I note the lack of awareness of time when respondents tell me that they did not think about time at all as well as other respondents' descriptions of an intensified awareness of time. On a more concrete level, I code for the absence of attention and assistance from intimates when it is observed, implied, or reported, besides coding the detailed accounts of other patients who had available intimates to visit and help.

==Third, I scrutinize the data for in vivo codes.== Research participants sometimes describe their experiences with imagery and power that far transcend their individual situations. One young diabetic described himself as trying to become "super-normal," an experience that many newly and/our younger chronically ill persons shared. Later, I took the term super-normal identity and raised it to a conceptual level to treat analytically (Charmaz 1973). Many of the chronically ill talked about the significance of others "being there." Subsequently, I took the term "being there" as a code and devised subcodes to pull out its underlying meanings and assumptions.

==Fourth, I try to identify succinctly the process that the data indicates.== Here the onus is on the researcher to identify, through coding, what the data *mean*. For example, some respondents who said they had been "depressed" or "felt bad about myself" described these feelings in ways that were strikingly similar to those who explicitly defined their feelings as self-pity (Charmaz (1980a). *Comparing* bits of data with other data for their similarities and differences helps enormously in developing codes. For example, both "negative" feelings such as self-pity and elusive topics such as experiencing time sometimes prove to be difficult subjects for a respondent to address. So, I compare responses to help me identify what is implicit in one set of data but explicit in another. Then, I may decide to return to earlier respondents with more detailed queries.[7]

Examples of Initial Coding

In the following examples, I show the kind of diversity and number of codes developed in initial coding when the researcher pursues as many diverse avenues as he or she can create. The interview statements below are made by persons with different chronic illnesses. My study centers on experiences of time and self of the chronically ill.

Code: Self-perception; Awareness of difference; Identifying self through ill health; Comparing health to others'.

Interview Statement: *A 29-year-old man with renal failure was discussing his high school years, and events that occurred long before he was diagnosed.*

...I knew I was different. I caught colds very easily and my resistance was very low, and so I knew that generally speaking my health wasn't as good as everybody else's, but I tried to do all the things that everybody else was doing.

Code: Normalizing context of illness; Self esteem: feelings of failure, failure of self; Reality contradicts idealized experience.

Interview Statement: *A 29-year-old woman with colitis was recounting her first episode of illness.*

...I was under a great deal of stress as a result of all this bouncing around and trying to get a job and trying not to have to go home to my parents and admit that I had failed. [I] failed at life. I had left college, and left there saying, "Gee, I can do it on my own," so I was trying this exciting existence I read about and there was something wrong; I had all this pain. I didn't know what to do about it.

Code: Self in retrospect; Self-esteem; Outcome of timed struggle; Improving self-esteem as treatment goal.

Interview Statement: *A 54-year-old woman who had cancer and currently had a crippling collagen disease was explaining her view on why she had had a recurrence of cancer.*

...When I look back on my second bout of cancer, I was not feeling good about myself and the whole struggle of the last three years put me into X (cancer institute) to try to get me to feel better about myself.

Focused Coding

Focused coding is the second, selective and conceptual, phase of the coding process. In focused coding, the researcher takes a limited set of codes that were developed in the initial phase and applies them to large amounts of data. The process is selective because researcher has already weeded through the materials to develop a useful set of categories. It is conceptual because the codes employed raise the sorting of data to an *analytic* level rather than one that is used to summarize large amounts of information.

Focused coding forces the researcher to develop categories rather than simply to label topics. Categories may be taken either from the natural language of the participants (an in vivo code) or from the researcher's analytic interest. For example, I took the term self-pity and treated it as a category (Charmaz 1980a). Then I defined it by analyzing the data systematically. I developed another category out of my analytic interests: "identifying moments." This was not part of the natural language of my respondents. Instead, it reflected my categorization of those moments when

I did this. I did that

participants instantly defined clear meanings about their present identities. Since I was generally interested in relationships between time and identity, I looked for material in the data which illuminated connections between the two. I had heard a number of accounts of moments when identity was at issue before I created a category that reflected the described events.

The purpose of focused coding is to build and clarify a category by examining all the data it covers and variations from it. Frequently, this means going back through the data and resifting it in relation to the newly devised category. New categories may subsume earlier materials that were left uncoded or were coded in different ways.

Researchers also use focused coding to break up the category. They develop subcategories which explicate and exhaust the more general category. I broke my category of "identifying moment" into the rather obvious subcategories of positive and negative identifying moments and coded for them (after I witnessed moments when ill persons were identified positively). *Properties* must be identified for the categories developed through focused coding. The properties define the category, delineate its characteristics, and demonstrate the conditions when it develops. For example, a major property of "identifying moment" is the immediate, direct social identification one interactant confers upon another.

After developing their set of focused codes, the researchers may use knowledge of the literature to expand and clarify the codes and to sensitize themselves to ways of exploring the emerging analysis. Pretend, for example, a group of organizational researchers in a hospital find that nurse participants show much concern about "professionalism" but assume that everyone shares their implied meanings of it. The researchers need to discover precisely which meanings these nurses and other professionals hold. After collecting first-hand data, they may use the literature to compare meanings attributed to the term and the criteria invoked to indicate it with their data. The range of meanings of "professionalism" include: maintaining an objective distant attitude, realizing high-quality craftsmanship with criteria set by members of the occupation themselves, and claiming a high status while simultaneously dissociating from those who cannot also claim it. In this instance, researchers need to portray the meanings of the term held in the setting they study. Hence, they use the literature to help outline and compare these meanings rather than to force them into "correct" interpretations. In other instances, the literature can be used as direct data for focused coding. In both cases, the researcher uses the literature as a source of *questions* and *comparisons* rather than as a measure of truth.

Since the grounded theory approach heavily emphasizes process, the categories developed are not treated separately as single topics; rather, grounded theorists weave them together into a *processual analysis* through which they can abstract and explicate experience. Thus, returning to my earlier example, defining self-pity through data analysis was just the first step. After categorizing types of self-pity and its social sources, I then developed the processual categories of becoming immersed in self-pity and reversing self-pity which were vivid when I directed questions toward them, but only implicitly related in the early data before I systematically explored these areas.

Focused coding helps the researcher to outline a framework that preserves the complexities of everyday life. By showing relationships between categories in ways that explain the issues and events studied, focused coding helps to provide the groundwork for developing explanations and predictions.

When researchers begin to question their data analytically, they are beginning to use it, rather than simply relate to an audience. For example, when organizational researchers investigate a topic such as staff turnovers, they would first define exactly what is meant by the term and cite the conditions under which such turnovers occur. Then they would use their data and their knowledge of the situation to help them determine which leads to follow up from there. Under which structural conditions do turnovers increase? Under which do they decrease? How do supervisors view turnovers? How do staff view them? What effects, if any, do they have on staff and client morale? Are there any subtle properties of turnovers that have direct effects on other parts of the organizational structure? Do supervisors change supervisory styles after a run of turnovers? What are the consequences of turnovers? What are the consequences of turnovers for direct client service? Are turnovers the "real" organizational issue or are they reflections of something else? (See Katz's essay, which follows.)

Many, if not most, researchers do develop or adopt "families" of codes that shape their emerging analyses (Glaser 1978). Among them are those that specify process, causation, degree, dimension, type, or a particular type of ordering such as structural, temporal, or generality (see Glaser 1978). By becoming aware of the elements of the code family invoked, one can raise more questions in research and become a better critic of other research works.

A final comment is in order. When the data are rich and full, the researcher may mine the information repeatedly for diverse foci (see Glaser and Strauss 1965, 1968). What may have been implicit to the researcher becomes explicit when he or she reexamines the data with new focused codes. For example, my interests in the chronically ill were primarily directed to issues concerning identity and time. Although I amassed considerable data concerning social support or its absence, I initially did not look at this topic systematically. As I began to study support and recognized its relationship to trust, I also realized that betrayal was a crucial code for understanding the experience of one group of chronically ill persons (Charmaz 1982). Then I categorized types of betrayal and their consequences. In short, the researcher may engage in focused coding of the same data multiple times as he or she identifies new questions to put to it.

Examples of Focused Coding

In the following examples, I provide several focused codes with their corresponding data. The codes show the selective nature of focused coding.

Code: Identifying moment; Critical failure of self

Interview Statement: *A young woman who had had a serious flare-up of colitis recalled:*

...During this time I was under constant care by an intern who later thought I should see a different psychiatrist when I got out of the hospital because he thought I was coming on sexually to him and the odd thing about that was that I found him not sexually attractive at all - that was sort of an interesting twist to that thing. I mean when you are not in a very good place to be told that you have failed with your psychiatrist is like the parting blow. You know it was awful.

Code: Relation of interactional sources of self-pity and self-blame

Interview Statement: *A young woman with intensive experience in undergoing bureaucratic evaluations responded to my questions about how she felt about being scrutinized.*

...All I can do is dissolve in tears - there's nothing I can do. I just get immobilized - you just sort of reach a point, you can't improve, can't remedy the situation, and you're told you aren't in the right category for getting the services you need and can't get for yourself. It makes me madder and madder at myself for being in the situation in the first place.

Code: Negative identifying moment

Interview Statement: *The following observations were made during an interview with a retired college professor and his wife, both of whom had chronic illness.*

... I asked, "Did you keep up with professional work after you retired?" He said: "I used to teach extension courses but with the budget and the governor, there isn't any money for extension courses." She [his wife] cut in [to me], "Andrei used to be an extremely successful speaker; partly his enthusiasm; partly his articulateness, but with the speech problems, he can't do it..." [He, slowly and painfully] "The schools don't have any money ... I can't speak very well.

I felt desperately sorry for him at this point. Whether or not both factors were at play at the point when they stopped calling him for extension teaching, this was a terrible moment for him when she said it. Regardless of the real reason, at this precise moment knowing what she thought of his deteriorating competence was critical to him. Participating in this short sequence was like watching someone who was observing his own identity crumbling away - it was painful both for him and for me, although I got the impression that she was so caught up in her perceptions of accuracy that she actually didn't see how it defaced him... Acknowledging that he can't speak very well was said like an admission of guilt or inferiority that was previously hidden from view.[8]

MEMO WRITING

Memos are written elaborations of ideas about the data and the coded categories. Memos represent the development of codes from which they are derived. An intermediate step between coding and writing the first draft of the analysis, memo writing then connects the barebones analytic framework that coding provides with the polished ideas developed in the finished draft. By making memos systematically while coding, the researcher fills out and builds the categories. Thus, the researcher constructs the form and substance toward a finished piece of work and develops the depth and scope of the materials.

Through memo writing the questions developed in coding are put into analytic context. The memo tells what the code is about; it raises the code to a category to be treated analytically. To differentiate between descriptive and analytic categories, consider the topic "friends." Descriptive treatment might focus on the link between friends, and their shared activities. Analytic treatment, in contrast, might focus on the implicit criteria for qualifying to be a "friend," the rhetorical uses of the term, the conditions for elevating someone from an acquaintance to a friend, the converse conditions for reducing a friend to an acquaintance or former friend, the mutual obligations necessary to sustain friendship, and the consequences of friendship for other relationships and activities. When treating the topic analytically, the researcher likely generates a set of categories which are more abstract than the original topic, and yet explicate underlying assumptions and processes.

Memo writing takes place throughout the research process starting with the first interviews or observations. These early memos shape aspects of subsequent data collection; they point to areas the researcher could explore further. They also encourage the researcher both to play with ideas and to make early assessments about which ideas to develop. Additionally, early memos provide concrete sources for comparison with materials gathered later. By writing memos throughout the research process, researchers avoid being paralyzed by mountains of unanalyzed data and immobilized by the prospect of needing to complete final papers and reports. As a crucial correction to such problems, writing memos throughout the research process sharpens and directs data collection and coding.

Since it fosters a theoretical rendering of the data, memo writing is a useful strategy at various levels of theoretical development. Some grounded theorists construct many short memos on diverse categories. They gradually build up levels of abstraction. Others write fewer memos but work at a more abstract, comprehensive level from the start. Although each reflects a working style, novices frequently discover that writing many memos helps to expand their theoretical grasp of the materials, keeps their analyses flexible, and provides sharper, clearer guidelines for data collection. Also, developing memos through rewriting gives the novice practice in systematically raising the analytic level of the ideas. A developed memo may become a whole section of a paper since it renders and synthesizes part of the data.

Writing is only one part of the grounded theorist's work with memos. Sorting and integrating memos follows memo writing. These two steps may themselves spark new ideas which, in turn, lead to more memos.

1. Definition
2. Conditions
3. Relationship to other categories
4. Properties

Writing Initial Memos

The first step in writing memos is to take codes and treat them as topics or categories. At the beginning of the memo, the author should title it and describe what it is about. If the grounded theorist already has a precise definition of the category, he or she provides it. If the category is concrete and visible, the researcher likely constructs a precise and immediate definition. If the memo is about some more abstract or ambiguous category - such as transforming identities - then the researcher may develop a precise definition later in the analysis. However, at this point, researchers should explore ideas during the memo-writing process. By keeping work flexible, the researcher may create more innovative and denser (many ideas integrated together) pieces of work.

When a category explicates a major pattern, grounded theorists stop and cite the conditions under which it operates and when it varies. What are the structural conditions giving rise to increased turnovers? What are the structural conditions under which a policy about turnovers is articulated or is reorganized? When writing memos, grounded theorists sometimes discover that they define new patterns and ideas that do not initially tie into their coded topic or category. Even when these connections are not apparent, they pursue the idea anyway but put the memo aside and reexamine it after finishing several other memos. (The ideas may make sense in another section of the work.)

Grounded theorists also explain how the code is related to other previously developed categories and codes. Spelling out the connections between categories assists in creating an integrated "whole," helps to reduce rambling, and aids in identifying implicit links, all of which tighten the work considerably.

Whenever writing a memo, researchers describe and discuss the category by delineating its properties as they are reflected in the data the category represents, or at least note the page and date of the properties in the data so quick retrieval is possible later (Glaser 1978).

Grounded theorists make comparisons explicit through memo writing. They often compare several observations in order to demonstrate the existence of the category they are talking about. For example, I composed a stack of accounts of feelings about illness when I was developing my material on self-pity to separate what constituted self-pity from other responses.

As more data accumulate, grounded theorists refine the earlier memos to account for greater variation, to gain a firmer grasp of the general context, and to understand the specific conditions under which the category works. By this time, the grounded theorist may also understand when the category changes and what its consequences are. For example, by examining the accounts of many patients, I was able to outline what contributed to moving away from self-pity, as well as the consequences of remaining immersed in it.

Sorting Memos

Sorting memos simply means putting those that elucidate the same category together in order to clarify its dimensions and to distinguish it from other categories. By going through accumulated memos and sorting them, researchers gain insight into what the core variables, key phrases in a process, or major issues are in the research.

When analyzing a process, the researcher quickly sorts the memos into phases of that process. Sometimes researchers discover that they actually have several issues or processes that can be covered separately. In that case, sorting keeps the researcher from muddling categories that are logically, if not experientally, distant. Conversely, an important dimension of sorting is to increase analytic precision in handling experientally mixed and muddy categories. In my work on chronic illness, for example, I analyzed the sources of loss of self (Charmaz, forthcoming). Living a restricted life results in loss of self. So does being devalued. Yet several people voluntarily restrict their lives to avoid devaluation. The categories are not entirely distinct, hence sorting helps to provide an analytic handle for communicating the categories in writing.

Grounded theorists sort for both the content of the memos and the ordering of them. The ordering of the memos, which forms the core of the paper, often reflects the ordering of experiences the data represent. The ordering may be explicitly grounded in the data as the researcher discusses steps in a process such as recruiting new workers. Or it may be implicitly grounded through the researcher's own sense of logic. For example, the organizational researcher might order memos on supervising by sorting for its properties, when it varies, its implications for morale, and its significance for getting the actual work done.

Integrating Memos

1. Content
2. Ordering

Sorting the memos helps to prepare for their subsequent integration. By integrating the memos the researcher reveals the relationships between categories. Such integration does not always occur spontaneously; often the researcher has to demonstrate the integration explicitly. Although analyses of processes sort and integrate readily into phases, other analyses require the imposition of a logical order. After writing, sorting, and integrating memos, I sometimes share them with interested respondents to see how my analysis fits with their experiences and views (see Huber 1973).

In the following two memos, I treat the category "identifying moment." The first memo is an initial description of the category as I first developed it when working on my dissertation. The second memo refines and extends the earlier materials; it also takes into account substantial further data collection. In the second memo, I include raw data to illustrate the analytic points. That memo appears in almost identical form in the published paper (see Charmaz 1980a).

An Initial Memo on "Identifying Moments"[9]

Identifying moments, in which the individual is treated in ways which designate new definitions of who he really is, may be captured and dramatized in the person's mind. When the disparity is great between prior valuations of self and present treatment such as of being a person worthy of *respect* and the entire procedure is characterized by *disrespect,* from the long wait to being shunted around and having one's identity questioned and categorized, conditions exist for these individuals to feel that they are losing control of their selves and the form of their existence.

Further, identifying moments when the individual is being defined and categorized may instantaneously flash images of the future and heretofore *unforseen identity.* Consider the impact on the unsuspecting individual who hopes to remobilize later to be told the only category into which he fits is that for the "totally disabled."

A Later Memo on "Identifying Moments"

It became clear to me that how a particular chronically ill person was identified by others sometimes became revealed to them in the course of a moment's encounter or interaction. These moments gave the ill individual new reflections of self, often revealing that he (or she) is not the person he felt he was. Hence, within the course of a few moments, someone's self-image may be radically called into question.

Moments that call into question previously held definitions of self may be identified as either negative or positive, although data describing negative moments are much more extensive (identifying moments may also reconfirm assumptions about self, although these are less likely to be recounted since they are not problematic).

Negative identifying moments are those shrouded in embarrassment and devaluation. They often lead to self-pity and self-blame: self-pity because of the implications of the definitions of the other; self-blame because of being in the situation in the first place. One woman described a demeaning encounter with a social service agency when in the course of a moment, she saw herself as being defined as someone not worth helping. She said,

> All I can do is dissolve in tears - there's nothing I can do. I just get immobilized - you sort of reach a point, you can't improve, can't remedy the situation, and you're told you aren't in the right category for getting the services you need and can't get for yourself. It makes me madder and madder at myself for being in the situation in the first place.

Negative identifying moments that occur in intimate relations are likely to be even more devastating. If ill persons can no longer claim preferred identities in other worlds in the present, although they may have possessed extraordinary identities in the past, they may feel that no recourse exists but to accept the identity thrust upon them since it was defined by those who know them most intimately.

(The observation of the elderly professor and his wife which occurs on pages 119-120 directly follows.)

THEORETICAL SAMPLING

Theoretical sampling means sampling aimed toward the development of the emerging theory (Glaser 1978; Glaser and Strauss 1967). As researchers analyze their materials and develop theoretical categories, they frequently discover that they need to sample more data to elaborate a category. Because researchers only develop theoretical categories through the analytic process, they do not know in advance what they will be sampling. Thus, theoretical sampling differs from the kind of selective initial sampling most qualitative researchers engage in as they set criteria for their research problem (see Schatzman and Strauss 1973).

As an inductive technique, theoretical sampling exemplifies the inductive logic of the grounded theory approach. Since grounded theorists systematically build their theoretical frameworks out of their observations, theoretical sampling is part of the progressive stages of analysis. It becomes necessary to use theoretical sampling when the analyst's present data do not exhaust the theoretical category the researcher is developing. At this point, then, more data are needed to fill out, saturate, and exhaust the category. Subsequently, the researcher samples whichever groups or events will provide the relevant material for the category. Comparison groups are chosen only for their theoretical relevance in theoretical sampling (see Glaser and Strauss 1967). Since I focus upon the chronically ill, I return to them when I use theoretical sampling. The theoretical category gains more scope, however, if the researcher chooses other comparative groups.

The need for theoretical sampling means that the conceptual categories that were inductively constructed have become sufficiently developed and abstract that the researcher can construct specific questions about them. Theoretical sampling then becomes a means for checking out hunches and raising specific questions. Furthermore, it provides a way to check the scope as well as the depth of a category.

CONCLUSION

The above explication of the grounded theory approach derives from the original methods that Glaser and Strauss (1967) and Glaser (1978) have delineated. Although I attempt to be faithful to the form and logic of their approach, over the years I have developed my own style of using grounded theory. Each researcher who adopts the approach likely develops his or her own variations of technique.

Basically, however, any researcher who claims to use the grounded theory approach endorses the following fundamental strategies. First, discovering and analyzing social and social psychological processes structures inquiry. Second, data collection and analysis phases of research proceed simultaneously. Third, analytic processes prompt discovery and theory development rather than verification of preexisting theories. Fourth, theoretical sampling refines, elaborates, and exhausts conceptual categories. And last, systematic application of grounded theory analytic methods progressively leads to more abstract analytic levels.

Although I have outlined how to do substantive analysis using a grounded theory approach, analysis need not remain at the substantive level. By taking the analysis to higher levels of abstraction and conceptual integration, grounded theory methods provide the means to develop formal theories (Glaser and Strauss 1971; Strauss 1978). To do so, the grounded theorist takes the comparative methods further. After developing conceptual categories, he or she refines and reworks the emerging theory by comparing concept with concept. Developing formal theories necessitates sampling a variety of different situational contexts and groups in which the concept applies. That way the theorist analyzes the boundaries and applications of the developing theoretical framework. To date, however, the grounded theory approach has been used primarily to develop rich substantive analyses. A theoretical analysis at the substantive level, though more modest in scope and power than formal theory, gives the analyst tools for explaining his or her data as well as tools for making predictions.

I am indebted to members of the Bay Area SWS writing group for their comments on an earlier draft of this paper, with special thanks to Gail Hornstein for her careful review of it. I also appreciate the critiques provided by Adele Clarke, Robert M. Emerson, Marilyn Little and Susan Leigh Star.

REFERENCES

Not references, but Notes – The references are omitted

1. No doubt this reflects Glaser's rigorous quantitative methodological training at Columbia. To date, the language of grounded theory is largely the language Glaser adopted.

2. Qualitative coding is not the same as quantitative coding. The term itself provides a case in point in which the language may obscure meaning and method. Quantitative coding requires preconceived, logically deduced codes into which the data are placed. Qualitative coding, in contrast, means creating categories from interpretation of the data. Rather than relying on preconceived categories and standardized procedures, qualitative coding has its own distinctive structure, logic and purpose (see Glaser and Strauss 1967, Glaser 1978).

3. Glaser and Strauss (1967) imply that the data speak for themselves. They don't. Since researchers pose questions to the data, the codes they develop directly reflect the questions posed. Similarly, Glaser and Strauss often seem to take a partly objectivist view of the researcher's role. While they encourage researchers to build on their prior experience, they

frequently seem to assume that researchers are interchangeable and remain unaffected by the commitments, interests, expertise, and personal histories. My interpretation and use of the method is more distinctively phenomenological (see Blummer 1969).

4. If the confusion is not worked through analytically, piles of thin, undeveloped data result. Hence, it is important to keep studying and coding data even though it may seem easier to simply collect more. Another problem may occur: In dispelling initial confusion, early analysis may induce an erroneous sense of familiarity with the setting or issue. The fieldworker must persist in efforts to ferret out negative cases, account for variations, and explore the consequences of ideas. In this respect, premature publication is a potential hazard of the method.

5. By context I mean the range of historical, political, economic, and organizational issues relevant to these particular data. The researcher needs to address context (1) to place the study in perspective (2) to collect and understand the data, and (3) to minimize reifying ideas.

6. Glaser (1978) also warns the researcher not to assume that face sheet data are important (age, sex, race, religion, occupation, number of years employed, etc.) until they show up in the data in patterned ways. Thus, face sheet data, like other categories, must also be grounded in the data to merit inclusion in the completed analysis.

7. Furthermore, developing an explicit category for the experience allows the researcher to go back to respondents and ask direct questions. I built rapport with many of my respondents, and I found that I could go back to them to explore many sensitive topics directly. The following statement illustrates the kind of direct response I got when I went back to one woman and asked her if she had experienced self-pity. She replied:

> Oh, yes. How tragic! Why me? Yeah, it's not fair. I get a disease I've never heard of; does anybody else have it? I mean I'm nice to small children and animals. I thought I had good Karma and then I grow up with allergies, get colitis, have back injuries and have migraines. Why do all these other people who are not as nice and far more deserve to be sick, why not them? (See Charmaz 1980a: 126)

8. As I watched Andrei's response to his wife's commentary, I saw him blanch and almost reel as if he had been physically struck. Her statements were so direct that he seemed caught by them, as if there was no escape

then as well as in the future. The defeated tone in his voice when he admitted he could not speak suggested to me how deeply this brief episode affected him. Prior to the interview, I had learned from the couple's physician, who took an unusual personal interest in this elderly couple, that Andrei's speech impairment was never discussed openly. The physician felt that Andrei hid the extent of his loss from himself, which was striking in view of his degree of speech impairment compared with his prior eloquence. (From original field notes.)

9. This memo synthesizes the accounts of patients who described their encounters with agency and hospital clinic personnel. These patients had been financially independent while working but now felt they needed assistance temporarily for medical and/or living expenses.

Reprinted from *Image*, Vol XII, No. 1, February, 1980.

GROUNDED THEORY METHODOLOGY:

Its Uses and Processes

Phyllis Noerager Stern, D.N.S.

This paper was prompted by Ludemann's (1979) article which makes a strong case for multiple methodological styles in nursing research. As a proponent of grounded theory, an inductive research technique which Ludemann points out, is often thought of in our profession as "somehow second class, and a little less than scientific" (p.4), I would like to clarify two points which I believe are problematic for nurse researchers not familiar with this technique: (1) appropriate uses of the method, and (2) a clear description of the method itself. In the first and shorter section of this paper, I attempt to make the point of appropriateness, using as supporting data four studies which employed this method. In the second section, I describe the method in what I believe is a fresh style, translating from the original sociological language, a jargon confusing to the uninitiated, into more familiar terms. In this section, I use examples from my study of stepfather families to illustrate the various stages of the research.

APPROPRIATE USES OF GROUNDED THEORY

Classically, research moves from the inductive to the deductive mode. Hypotheses gleaned either from data or the literature, or a combination of the two, are then tested for verification. Since grounded theory has some elements of both inductive and deductive modes, in grounded theory circles it is acknowledged to be the only true method of research -- a frankly religious point of view.

I think the strongest case for the use of grounded theory is in investigations of relatively uncharted waters, or to gain a fresh perspective in a familiar situation. In the first instance, it can easily be understood that where no theory regarding a situation exists, it is impossible to test theory. It is especially helpful -- even necessary -- in attempting to study complex areas of behavioral problems where salient variables have not been identified. In the second instance, it becomes clear that the value of a fresh perspective in a familiar situation is in its applicability to practical problems.

Testing the Water: Uses in New Situations

When I embarked upon a study of stepfather families (Stern, 1976), I
wanted to find out how a stepfather is integrated into the existing family
system made up of mother and child, so that other such families could try
out strategies which seem to influence successful outcomes. The process
had not been examined before: it is assumed in the literature that families
are integrated. Therefore, I had no basis on which to test existing theory,
nor could I utilize identified existing variables, because none were
identified. In other words, it was first necessary to find out what was going
on in these families. It was appropriate to use Grounded Theory to discover
what problems existed in the social scene, and how the persons involved
handled them.

Similarly, Wilson's (1977) study of Soteria House, an experimental
community for schizophrenics, where "there are no locked doors,
medications, or therapies for controlling the behavior of labeled schizophrenics who live at the setting" (p. 130), examined managing the public
presentation of a radically new treatment facility. The problem here
involved screening the inmates from public view so as to keep the facility
from closing down. Wilson found a system of "limited intrusion"
operating. That is, what the public might not understand and accept in
severely disturbed individuals allowed to act out their anxieties, the public
was not allowed to see. Limiting intrusion, Wilson found, is one way of
preserving autonomy. In the two examples above, hypotheses regarding
previously unexamined situations emerged from the data.

Gaining a New Point of View in a Familiar Setting

Dying is as old as living, but in the classic work of Glaser and Strauss,
Awareness of Dying (1965), the mutual deception operating in the situation
is exposed. When a patient is dying in the hospital, they found, no one can
acknowledge the fact: staff, family, or patient. The investigators identified
"open and closed awareness contexts" which existed, but had not been
previously described. Even though patients were aware that they were
dying, they were not allowed to talk about it, because of tabus against
speaking of death. The impact of this study on nursing and medical care of
the dying has been to effect a reversal of the former style of
non-acknowledgement to one of open communication between patient,
family and staff. Everyone involved in the dying process is now
encouraged to talk out the enormity of feelings surrounding the event.

POLITICS OF PAIN MANAGEMENT

(Fagerhaugh and Strauss, 1977) addresses another familiar situation, the hospital personnel's criteria for controlling the patient's pain. In this prize-winning work, it becomes clear that nurses and doctors administer pain-relieving medication according to their own value system rather than on the basis of what the patient is feeling. Since the individual's pain can't be measured, the nurse or doctor decides good from bad pain. (Pain is legitimate on a burn ward, less so on an orthopedics ward.) Relief is dispensed accordingly. The authors give us a new look at our system of patient care: we decide what hurts and what doesn't. The implications for nursing care in the studies cited above are obvious.

Enhancing the Possibility of a Fresh Perspective

According to the ground rules of grounded theory, the investigator looks for processes which are going on in the social scene. Although measuring is not excluded, it usually becomes the by product of the emerging hypotheses. Because the observer looks at interactions before static conditions, the possibility of gaining a fresh but lasting impression is enhanced. Referring back to the studies above once more, it can be seen that all step families everywhere face the problem of integrating a new member; the process is timeless. Likewise, the process of limiting intrusion to protect an unacceptable situation from public scorn is a variable which gives us an insight into all such situations. In the dying study, the investigators were able to discover ways in which the dying process was denied, and determine the consequences of denial. In the pain study, the researchers looked for the processes involved in relieving pain, the conditions under which pain was legitimate, and the consequences of patient having illegitimate pain. A more detailed account of process vs "unit" research can be found in Glaser's new description of grounded theory (1978, pp. 109 - 115). In summary, then, grounded theory provides a method for investigating previously unresearched areas and a nw point of view in familiar situations. Now we may go to the methodology itself.

The Method

Grounded theory, a form of field methodology, aims to generate theoretical constructs which explain the action in the social context under study. That is to say, it consists of a series of hypotheses linked together in such a way so as to explain the phenomenon. Like most research methods, it is a combination of inductive and deductive approaches, and like all

118

methods, the investigator focuses the research according to a conscious selective process. By this I mean that the investigator decides to study A rather than B. At the conclusion of the study, the grounded theorist must, like researchers everywhere, explain what it all means.

There are several ways in which grounded theory differs from other methodologies. (1) The conceptual framework is generated from the data rather than from previous studies, although previous studies always influence the final outcome of the work. (2) The researcher attempts to discover dominant processes in the social scene rather than describing the unit under study. (3) Every piece of data is compared with every other piece rather than comparing totals of indices. For this reason, the method has also been called "qualitative comparative analysis" (Wilson, 1977), and "continuous comparative analysis" (Maxwell and Maxwell, in press). (4) The collection of data may be modified according to the advancing theory; that is, false leads are dropped, or more penetrating questions are asked as seems necessary. (5) Rather than following a series of linear steps, the investigator works within a matrix in which several research processes are in operation at once. In other words, the investigator examines data as they arrive and begins too code, categorize, conceptualize, and to write the first few thoughts concerning the research report almost from the beginning of the study. This last feature of the methodology is what makes the system so difficult to describe. Wilson made a division between data collection and analysis, while Maxwell and Maxwell described five steps in the process: 1) collection of empirical data, 2) concept formation, 3) concept development, 4) concept modification and integration, and 5) production of the research report. In the present paper, the latter system will be used.

1. Collection of Empirical Data

Data may be collected from interview, observation or documents, or from a combination of these sources. In the stepfather family study (Stern, 1978), some data were gleaned from letters and phone calls. However, the bulk of the data were from 85 hours of intensive interviews conducted with 30 San Francisco Bay Area stepfather families. Whole families were interviewed whenever possible, after the method of Mental Research Institute (Broderick, 1971). However, individual family members were interviewed separately in almost half of the families under study. Face-to-face contact was made with 62 persons, and the study includes data on 132 parents and children. The makeup of the families represented a variety of social classes and ethnic groups. This was appropriate since the study focused on process rather than on unit, and the aim here was to discover variables which transcended class or ethnic boundaries; in other words, processes found in all kinds of stepfather families.

Coding. The grounded theorist looks for process. As data are received, the investigator applies a system of open coding. This means examining the data line by line and identifying the processes in the data. Thus when ten-year-old Eric was asked what he liked about his stepfather, he replied, "I like it when he teaches me stuff and shows me how things work," and this piece of data was coded "teaching". When the stepfather in another family said, "You just have to accept kids they way they are," the remark was labeled, "accepting". These codes are called substantive codes, because they codify the *substance* of the data, and often use the very words used by the actors themselves.

Categorizing. Considerable similarity exists between the treatment of data in the continuous comparative method and in the computer method of factor analysis. However, the investigator's brain serves in place of the computer. Data are coded, compared with other data and assigned to clusters or categories according to obvious fit. Categories are simply coded data which seem to cluster together. For example, household rules formed one category in the stepfather study. The content, formation and acceptability of rules were grouped together. Enforcement techniques clustered into another category. Other persistent categories, including teaching which had been developed into a category of teaching strategies, copying, and accepting in various circumstances, also emerged.

2. Concept Formation

In this stage, a tentative conceptual framework is generated using the data as reference. The investigator attempts to discover the main problems in the social scene from the point of view of the interactants, or actors (or subjects participating in the study), and how these interactants deal with the problems. Carefully comparing all data as they are received, the investigator makes a choice regarding the relative salence of the problems presented in the scene under study. My study was directed at discovering how stepfamilies become a cohesive or integrated unit, and what problems or processes were the major stumbling blocks to integration. Although many problems emerged, discussions concerning the discipline of children brought forth an emotional response from informants, whereas other family processes could be discussed in a relatively emotionless manner. Therefore, at this stage, the discipline of children was considered to be the central focus or framework for the study. Two key processes highlight this phase of analysis: coding and categorizing.

3. Concept Development

In this phase, three major steps serve to both expand and densify the emerging theory: reduction, selective sampling of the literature, and selective sampling of data. The first two processes can be thought of as inductive, because they involve searching for clues. The third takes on deductive aspects, already formed, are now verified. These processes are detailed below. *try to reduce, if at all possible*

Reduction. At this point, the investigator has developed an overwhelming number of categories. Category is now compared with category to see how they cluster or connect. Shatzman and Strauss (1973) called these connections "linkages". Is there, asks one investigator, some higher order of category, some umbrella under which all these categories fit? Reduction is a vital step in discovering the major processes, called "core variables" by Glaser and Strauss (1967), which explain the action in the social scene. In other words, the investigator now says, how does everything fit together? Once again, the reader is referred to the clustering of factor analysis. Clustering categories is a more theoretical form of analysis than clustering coded data. As linkages emerge, categories collapse and form more general categories. In the stepfather study, the categories of teaching, accepting and copying were seen to be linked, since these actions all served to bring stepfather and child closer together. This it was possible to reduce the three categories to form the broader category of affiliating. Teaching, accepting and copying were then called "properties" of the category affiliating. Later, other categories were reduced in a similar nature, so that spending time, leveling, and trusting became properties of the broad category affiliating. *what do several categories have in common?*

Selective sample of the literature. Here the existing literature, used as data, is woven into the matrix consisting of data, category, and conceptualization. Literature is carefully scrutinized, and the concepts compared as data. Bohannan's (1978) finding that the mental health of children in stepfather homes is equal to the mental health of children in intact homes fit comfortably with the emerging theory, and became supporting data for the present study. On the other hand, the advice of Kiely (1976) -- that stepparents must settle differences over discipline before marriage -- did not fit with any data from the present study, and was *my pre research literature searches + set up of tutorials in the PhD proposal does not fit grounded theory research*

therefore rejected as invalid. It should be stressed here that although a review of research is in order before a study is begun, a second search is now necessary as processes begin to emerge. Thus the conduct of the stepfather study was preceded by a search for known studies in stepfamilies. When discipline began to emerge as a dominant process, it was necessary to find out what other authors had to say about discipline generally, and what the prevailing work on child-rearing revealed. As the study proceeded further, human development sources were included. As the picture of the stepfather as a new manager joining a going concern, the household, became clear, studies of management and corporate discipline were found to be valuable to the emerging theory.

Selective Sampling. As the main concepts or variables become apparent, they are compared with the data to determine under what conditions they are likely to occur, and if they are indeed central to the emerging theory. Additional data may be collected at this time in a selective manner for the specific purpose of developing the hypotheses, and identifying the properties of the main categories or variables. This process is also called theoretical sampling, because the data is collected to advance the theory. At this state in the analysis of the stepfather data, it was apparent that disputes over the discipline of children represented a major problem in the integration of a stepfather into the mother-child system. I now began to ask, under what conditions do the variables discipline and integration co-exist? Data were collected with the specific purpose of answering this question, and determining the importance of the variables.

It can be seen that selective sampling is a deductive process. The conceptual framework, developed from the data, is now tested by collecting data which proves or disproves the framework hypotheses. Concepts which cannot be supported by the data are dropped. It is unlikely that the conceptual framework would be discarded entirely at this point, but it may be altered, expanded or juggled. In the stepfather study, it was found that discipline and integration co-exist only in the presence of the variable affiliating. Affiliating then became part of the conceptual framework. Affiliating, it will be remembered, emerged as a major category made up of the sub-categories teaching, accepting, copying, and later, spending time, leveling and trusting.

Selective sampling also has an inductive aspect. Data are collected not only to prove or disprove the importance of the variables but also to identify and elaborate the properties of these variables. Thus, data are now collected to develop the sub-category trusting. How long, I wondered, does it take the child to trust a stepfather? What conditions promote trust? Is trust as an interactional goal as difficult for the stepfather to attain as for the stepchild? Answers to these questions provide dimensions to the categories: in the case of the sub-category trust, a time dimension, a conditional dimension, and an interactional dimension emerged.

Through selective sampling, already discovered categories are expanded, dimensionalized, and limited. This process is called saturation of the categories. That is, data are collected regarding a category until the analyst is satisfied that no new information is being received which further explains that particular aspect of the emerging hypothesis. In the case of trust, for instance, I stopped collecting data about this sub-category when I stopped hearing anything new about it.

Following the processes of reduction, selective sampling of the literature, and selective sampling of data, the theory or conceptual framework attains some consistency but suffers from loose construction. It remains for the investigator to integrate the categories, the variables, into a well-fitting and manageable theory.

Emergence of the core variable. Through the process of reduction and comparison, the core variable for this investigation emerged. Integrative discipline seemed to me to explain most of the variation in the social-psychological problem of the research: it explained most of the ways in which integration is achieved in a stepfather family, given the problem of the discipline of children. Once discovered, the data were reexamined to determine the fit of the core variable. Segments of data and the theoretical scheme were shared with nurses and sociologists, and it was the consensus of these colleagues that the core category did indeed explain the problem.

4. Concept Modification and Integration

Two major processes dominate this phase: memo writing and theoretical coding. It is through these processes that the emerging theory is finally integrated and delimited. Here we compare concept with more highly developed concept to discover their relationship, and once again, related concepts are compared with data for validation. Finally the core variable is identified. The reader is reminded here that continuous comparative analysis is a matrix operation rather than a linear endeavor. Therefore, although stage four is a wrapping-up process, it will have proceeded in concert with the other phases.

Theoretical coding. Codes provide a way of thinking about data in theoretical rather than descriptive terms. This simply means applying a variety of analytical schemes to the data to enhance their abstraction. For the visually inclined, data may be diagrammed, fed into four- or six-fold tables, or drawn into models. Lofland (1971) provides the investigator with a variety of analytical techniques. Glaser (1978) offers a chapter of diagrams and codes. Glaser calls this kind of theoretical coding a "conceptual out" (p. 119). Moving from the descriptive to the theoretical, I considered the variable affiliating in the stepfather study from the point of view of its causes, consequences, contexts, contingencies, covariances and conditions. Glaser lists 18 such "families of theoretical codes."

Memoing. Memoing is a method of preserving emerging hypotheses, analytical schemes, hunches, and abstractions. At certain points when the data are being coded, an idea will strike, and if it is not recorded, the researcher will lose the thought. Memos are ideational, but they are sparked by the data, and in this way they are grounded. As the analysis proceeds, the mind of the researcher becomes steeped in data. Ideas for analysis occur at an uneven pace and at unlikely hours. These ideas are captured first on scraps of paper; later on typewritten pages or cards. The data which sparked the memo are noted. Memos linked with other memos, always grounded in the data, enrich the conceptual schemes of the analysis. These notes can be reworked or sometimes tabled for a future study.

One of the most vital steps in the analytical process is the sorting of memos. This process provides yet another opportunity to cluster concepts. Memos are sorted into piles, and the writing of the manuscript becomes a "write-up" of memos which have been organized in such a way that the best integration of the theory is achieved. To neglect this step yields a linear, schematic report. Sorted memos provide the organization for the manuscript.

5. Production of the Research Report

The research report for a grounded theory investigation presents the substantive theory, substantiated by supporting data from the investigation. As such, it differs in several respects from the more familiar report of quantitative studies. Three such difference are the use of the literature as opposed to the method of utilization of the literature in quantitative studies, the absence of numerical data, and the use of field notes.

Literature, it will be remembered, is used to explain the theory the theory

124

classical Review of Lit is inappropriate

is not derived from it. Therefore, the classic review of the literature is inappropriate. Rather, references are woven into the theory much as they are worked into the study in phase three. Likewise, because the method is one of continuous comparison rather than a comparison of totals of indices, and because concepts are dropped unless they appear throughout the data, numerical data are out of place in the report.

In place of numbers, concepts are supported in the report by examples from the field data. This provides a last check point in the analysis. Concepts must earn their way into the theory by virtue of their relevance to the empirical world. The use of data in the report insures this.

CONCLUSIONS

This paper has been an attempt to demystify the grounded theory method of analysis. I have suggested its uses and attempted to order for the reader its various procedures. To draw the comparison again, as with any research methodology, the living process is less orderly than its written description. In other styles of research, computers break down, judges leave town, data sheets are lost, and schools rescind permission to test their students. The grounded theorist, then, may seem as confused and frustrated in the midst of the research as any investigator (some say more so). Nevertheless, what I have tried to make clear here is that like other methods of inquiry, grounded theory has rules of procedures, which if carefully followed, produce an analysis of a social context which has both accuracy and applicability.

REFERENCES

Bohannan, P.J., and Erickson, R. Stepping in. *Psychology Today*, January 1978, 53-59.

Broderick, C.B. Beyond the five conceptual frameworks: a decade of development in family theory. *Journal of Marriage and the Family*, 1971, 33. 139-159.

Fagerhaugh, S and Strauss, A.L. *Politics of Pain Management,* Menlo Park: Addison-Wesley, 1977.

Glaser, B.G. *Theoretical Sensitivity*. Mill Valley, California: the Sociology Press, 1978.

Glaser, B.G. and Strauss, A.L. *Awareness of Dying,* Chicago: Adeline,

1965.

Glaser, B. and Strauss, A. *The Discovery of Grounded Theory*, Chicago: Adeline, 1967.

Kiely, M. Responsibility is kids' stuff. *Stepparents' Forum,* Montreal, Canada. January, February, 1976, pp. 1-3, 7.

Lofland, John. *Analyzing Social Setting.* Belmont, California, Wadsworth Pub. c 1971.

Ludemann, R. The paradoxical nature of nursing research. *Image*, 1979, 11 (1), 2-8.

Maxwell, E.K,. and Maxwell, R.J. Search and research in ethnology: continuous comparative analysis. *Behavior Science Research*, in press.

Schatzman, L. and Strauss. A.L. *Field Research.* Englewood Cliffs, New Jersey: Prentice-Hall, 1973.

Stern, P.N. Stepfather families: integration around child discipline. *Issues in Mental Health Nursing,* 1978, 1 (2), 50-56.

Stern, P.N. Integrative discipline in stepfather families (Doctoral dissertation, University of California San Francisco, 1976), *Dissertation Abstracts International*, 1977 b, 37. (University Microfilms No. 77-5276).

Wilson, H.S. Limiting intrusion -- Social Control of Outsiders in a Healing Community. *Nursing Research*, 1977, 26 (2), 103 - 110.

Reprinted from *Health Education Monographs*, Vol. 6, No. 3, Fall 1978 pp. 280-94.

THE POTENTIAL OF GROUNDED THEORY FOR HEALTH EDUCATION RESEARCH: LINKING THEORY AND PRACTICE

Patricia Dolan Mullen, Dr. P.H.

Richard Reynolds, Dr. P.H.

This paper offers a critique of present research methods used in the literature drawn upon by health education practitioners, students, and teachers. Weaknesses of deductive methods and of theory which is highly general are noted in terms of their implications for the advancement of health education theory and practice, and in terms of their consistency with traditional principles of practice.

The grounded theory method - an inductive approach usually used with participant observation and interview data - is described, and the major arguments for its value are presented. In particular, the empirical generation of middle-range theory can provide a strong link between more general theory and situations faced by practitioners, and definitions of problems are not prematurely closed to reinterpretation from other perspectives. Several recommendations are given for changing the research orientation of health education.

Are there strong links among theory, research, and practice in community health education? Unfortunately, few health educators would agree that this is the case. This paper will show that the research methods and the generality of theories used in health education help explain these gaps; a rationale and a method will be suggested for developing an empirically-based body of theory relevant to practice and conceptually linked to formal theory.

With the maturation of health education, the usefulness of existing theory and the appropriateness of usual research methods for the needs of practitioners have been called into question.[9,18,26,27,32] Health education has relied heavily upon behavioral and other social sciences and upon related professional fields such as social work and adult education for its theories. While this eclecticism has guaranteed a broad base, there has been movement toward the integration, refinement, and adaptation of these imported theories into a conceptual scheme unique to health education.

The favored modes of research in the health education literature have been deductive and hypothesis-testing; only infrequently, have hypothesis-seeking methods been used. The deductive and hypothesis-testing research approaches often have not been useful for the development of health education practice and theory for the following reasons:

* Researchers often have not made a significant commitment to understanding the perspective of the people being studied or to leaving open a redefinition of the "problem." Many studies of compliance with medical regimens illustrate this difficulty. The term connotes an explanation for as well as a description of the ill person's behavior; and this may have short-circuited the research efforts which as they are depicted in the literature show remarkably little attention to the patient's point of view.[29]

* Studies generally have been static. They take a snapshot to describe conditions or situations at one or several points in time instead of moving pictures of processes as they vary under different conditions and interact with other variables. The status of attitudes or behaviors, for example, is infinitely easier to measure than the dynamics of attitude change, health habit formation, or the stages of redesigning a lifestyle.

* Variables such as demographic characteristics have enjoyed considerable popularity among researchers, but these descriptors provide only a starting point for intervention. A deeper understanding is needed to give greater leverage for change.

* Concepts and theory often have not been generated from data. They have been deduced on too general a level without an adequate empirical base, and this means that little is being added to health education theory.

* The focus frequently has been dictated by logico-deductive theoretical concerns rather than empirical questions. In health education terms this is like a program designed by the staff of an agency without the participation of the community or client group to be served.

* Literature of conceptual relevance to a substantive area of health education theory and practice is sometimes missed. If the theoretical starting point of a deductive study turns out not to be relevant or not to have the best fit, no further literature search is routinely conducted. And without empirically generated concepts, it is difficult to estimate the relevance of new theory or concepts.

* Relevant concepts often have been oversimplified when they were

operationalized for quantitative measurement. (See Blumer[3] for an extended discussion of this point.) This can occur, for example, when learning is indicated only by a score on a true-false knowledge test or when prevention is defined solely in Western health care terms for a study of another cultural group.

In an effort to respond to these problems, the advantages of a promising strategy for empirical inquiry, called the "grounded theory" method will be discussed. This method especially lends itself to what Roberts[26] saw as the alternative to the "basic-applied" distinction in research, insofar as it contributes to systematic knowledge and theory and has practical use.

THE GROUNDED THEORY METHOD

The grounded theory method, as it will be described here, was developed and refined by Glaser and Strauss.[12,15] It was derived primarily from two research approaches-one associated with the analysis of qualitative data, the other associated with analysis of quantitative data. The dominant parent is comparative analysis, a recognized general research method which has been used in sociology and anthropology (e.g., by Weber, Durkheim, Mannheim, and social anthropologists). Its major approach is comparison of several groups or social units of any size - e.g., individuals, roles, groups, programs, institutions, or nations. Strauss' work with George Herbert Mead at the University of Chicago initiated a research career using participant observation and comparative analysis as the major modes of gathering and analyzing data.

The second main contribution originated with Lazersfeld and his associates at Columbia University where Glaser was trained to analyze survey data with the goal of generating core variable theories. The concept of core variable refers to a category which accounts for most of the variation in a pattern of behavior and which helps to integrate other categories that have been discovered in the data. *Comparison*

The grounded theory method then, uses comparison as an analytical tool to generate concepts and hypotheses and to interrelate them through core variables which are both parsimonious and broad in scope. The final goal is middle-range substantive theory[15] in a specific content area such as dying,[13,16] pain management,[11] recovery after a heart attack,[21] or formal theory, that is theory generalized over a number of specific areas such as status passage,[17] life-style redesign, or awareness context.[14]

The procedures of this method are systematic and provide for empirical verification of the hypotheses and propositions developed during the research process. Chronologically, these operations are unlike the linear models used to test or verify hypotheses; data gathering, analysis, and conceptual integration go on simultaneously, although their mix at any one time differs over the course of a study.

The beginning stage consists of discovering categories into which data can be coded (see Fig. 1). Indicators (indicents and definitions in the data) are inspected with the question, "Of what concept is this an indicator?" In the early part of the study, the analyst attempts to discover many categories and to compare them with new indicators to uncover their characteristics and relationships. The data are coded into as many categories as possible. These early codes may be discarded if they lack foundation in the data, and more may be added as the data gathering progresses.

FIGURE 1. CODING SAMPLE

Interview with 27-year-old man (severe MI one year earlier) and wife. They have not told their friends about the MI.

Comparing: Incongruity with *age peers'* level of activity; striking difference because of their youth.

Others' views of them have changed. This is non-generalized since they aren't told why. (Gives patient more ability to manage impressions?)

Conditions for cutting out an activity entirely: (1) strong interrelationship of activities (going to Tahoe and being involved in sports) and (2) comparative problems (old and new activity levels).

Most of their friends are active, engaging in sports, weekends and summer vacations at Lake Tahoe, etc. On turning down invitations, e.g., to Tahoe, "They finally stopped asking; they just said *'We'll never get the Johnsons to Tahoe.'*" John said that Tahoe would be an especially uncomfortable place for him, because he has spent many summer vacations there while he was growing up, and "it's hard to think of being there without associating it with boating and water skiing (all of which he cannot do now - maybe later) so I'd rather cut it all out and go to San Simeon instead."

Comparing: She uses the relative standard-early vs. later resumption; he uses an "old normative" standard for comparison-before the MI vs. after.

The former is more favorable, but less meaningful for him in terms of his old and cherished (see earlier) identity.

...Susan pointed out several times during the interview how much improvement John had made in his activity capacity. For instance, when he told me about his frustration at not being able to run anymore, she mentioned that now he didn't get winded bringing the groceries up one flight of stairs, John acknowledged this and didn't seem to deprecate it, but said that running from the apartment to the front door of the building (not very far) would make him out of breath.

....

First indicators are compared with other indicators with the purpose of establishing underlying uniformity and its varying conditions. Then concepts are compared to new indicators to generate more theoretical properties of the concept and new hypotheses and to verify the concept. (See example in Appendix.) A third level of comparison is concept with concept. This is to establish the best-fitting concept(s) for a set of indicators and to establish the interrelationships among the concepts. One analyst has described this as follows:

I sought to discover multiple and varied relationships between and among concepts rather than attempting to prove a linear causal hypothesis between two. Such an approach is designed to yield "molecular" rather than linear theoretical models.[34]

Substantive categories or codes are of two kinds: (1) those which are taken from the language of the people who were observed or interviewed-such as "budgeting oneself," "convincing," and "cutting out"; and (2) implicit codes such as "social loss," "conditional dependence," and various standards of comparison (as seen in Fig. 1) which are constructed by the researcher based on behavioral science concepts.

This mix of comparisons soon begins to make possible the construction of theoretical properties of categories, and the emergence of major categories. Coding thus leads to conceptual reorganization. Core variables provide the organizing focus and are selected on the basis of pervasive and meaningful relatedness to other categories and frequent occurrence in the data. In grounded theory studies, core variables are most often social processes, because qualitative data frequently have a time dimension. The analysis then traces the emerging process to identify its stages, dimensions, and the characteristics and conditions that vary it.

The types of social processes refer to two levels of sociological analysis. (1) Structural processes are social structure in the making, usually growth or deterioration and are exemplified by the concepts of bureaucratization and debureaucratization, routinization and deroutinization, and centralization and decentralization. (2) Social psychological processes are modal patterns of behavior such as becoming, role taking, cultivating clients, leveraging, cutting back and optimizing health. A core variable may also be any other kind of theoretical category, such as the social structural condition, the awareness context (i.e., who knows that the patient is expected to die which explains the social interaction with and around a dying patient.[14]

Further data gathering is purposefully directed through theoretical sampling to obtain more comparison groups. The sampling in later stages of a study, after identification of a basic social process or other core variable, is directly focused on the developing theory.

For example, after one study was underway, focus narrowed from dying patients in general to awareness contexts in which dying was taking place. The researchers found that the closed awareness or mutual pretense contexts were by far the most common in U.S. hospitals at the time of the study (early 1960s). Thus, the fact of the patient's impending death was either unknown to the patient and/or family or they knew and pretended that they did not. The question which was put forward then was "what happens in an open context where everyone knows and behaves as if the others know also" and "where would one find such examples for study?" Such lines of inquiry can be pursued through theoretical sampling but not through statistical sampling; this approach helps assure that the developing theory will be rich with variation.

Glaser has summarized several important points on the differences between theoretical and statistical sampling strategies:[12]

Theoretical Sampling

Purpose: To discover concepts, hypotheses, and their interrelationships, i.e., theory. The magnitude of the relationships may be, but is not necessarily, a part of the hypotheses.

Adequacy: Judged by how wisely and diversely the analyst has chosen groups for "saturating" categories according to the type of theory-formal or substantive-to be developed. Inadequate sampling is characterized by a theory that is thin and not well integrated and by many unexplained exceptions.

Closure: Must be learned. Data collection for a grounded theory study stops when *new* categories and their related aspects stop appearing in the data.

Judgment is based upon techniques of random and stratified sampling used in relation to the social structure of a group or groups sampled.

Statistical Sampling

To obtain accurate evidence on distributions among categories to be used in descriptions or verifications.

Must continue with data collection until the predetermined sample is achieved.

The aim of grounded theory is not complete coverage in a descriptive, logico-deductive, or scholarly sense - its goal is theoretical completeness, that is, the explanation of social phenomenon in relevant terms. Described another way:

Since the field researcher senses the great complexity of social reality and sees the operational relationship between discovery and creativity, he is less inclined quickly to measure or test his findings-not because he fails to appreciate the need for 'nailing things down'...but because he is never quite sure that his latest 'finding' is critical or is the final one. More important to him than 'nailing it down' is 'linking it up' logically, theoretically, and empirically to other findings or discoveries of his own and others. Then, he may measure or test it. [30] (pp. 8-9)

With more data and adequate sampling, major changes in the categories are less frequent. As the categories become saturated, fewer data come to light that are new or that would cause significant alteration of the properties of a category. Later modifications consist of clarifying the logic, removing irrelevant aspects, and simplifying and integrating the outline of the theory.

Lastly, memoranda written during the analysis process (e.g., Appendix) are sorted. The original list of categories is greatly reduced. Data are now ordered and become a systematic statement of the matter under study. Abstractions have been formed to explain the underlying complexities of the data. Inconsistencies are brought to view to be accounted for or explained. The final form of the theory is an integration of the conditions, contingencies, contexts, consequences, and strategies around one or two core variables which are rich in conceptual detail and adequate to develop testable hypotheses.

ADVANTAGES OF THE GROUNDED THEORY METHOD

Applicability by Practitioners

Presentations of grounded theories to practitioners have shown that they do not require an interpreter to translate the research. The practitioner can hear it, relate it to his or her experience, and apply it. Such conceptual schema have four properties which favor successful application: close fit to the practice area, understandability, generality, and focus on situational structure and dynamics over which users have at least partial control.[15]

Fit and understandability. Grounded theories generally meet the criteria of fit and understandability by definition because of the means through which they are developed. Only those theories which are thin - built with insufficient data and inadequate theoretical sampling - will fall short of the criteria. Use in grounded theories of imagery, examples, and concepts drawn from the contexts on which these theories are based makes them immediately recognizable to practitioners and laypersons who are familiar with the area.

"Shifting gears,"[22] a popular guide on making major life changes (and also a grounded theory) has been helpful to many lay readers; "Taking chances"[20] sheds light on the dynamics of behavior involved in unwanted pregnancies and repeated abortions for a wide range of persons involved in family planning and abortion programs.

Generality. A grounded theory meets the criterion of generality, because it is based upon the accumulation of "a vast number of diverse qualitative 'facts' on many different situations in the area,"[15] or sampling of variables rather than being based upon sampling of people aimed at representativeness of a population. Seeking out as much variation as possible and developing hypotheses to explain the variation helps to guarantee that the theory can be exported from the locale in which it was developed. All the practitioner has to do is to identify what conditions are present in the new situation to understand how the grounded theory will apply. Disadvantages of many deductive and of most purely descriptive studies are that they rapidly become outdated and yield relatively few general concepts. From the standpoint of practice it is more fruitful to know the types, range, magnitude, and conditions of occurrence of a phenomenon rather than merely the frequency of occurrence.

Control. By "control" Glaser and Strauss refer to enabling the person applying the theory:

> ...to understand and analyze ongoing situational realities, to produce and predict change in them, and to predict and control consequences both for the object of change and for other parts of the total situation that will be affected. As changes occur, his theory must allow him to be flexible in revising his tactics of application and in revising the theory if necessary.[15(p.245)]

An understanding of the social process of cutting back,[21] for instance, enables a practitioner working with heart patients to understand and predict situational realities. It is possible for more heart patients to reach an appropriate level of physical activity more easily and quickly by assisting them in learning to discriminate among bodily signs and read warning signals and in reinforcing their judgments. Changing the awareness context of surgery patients from closed to open by telling them what is going to happen to them increases the number of patients who have less severe pain.[10]

Grounded theories also have practice validity. In the process of the original research the theory is subject to verification by those who are immersed in that area of social life; however, the theory can be modified through experiences gained in applying it (this may be thought of as an extension of theoretical sampling, as described above). Another example from the Mullen study[21] will illustrate this process. A practitioner reading her study of heart patients would be sensitized to the propensity of persons confronted with a chronic illness to develop a causal explanation for its occurrence. This is hypothesized to influence the ill person's choice of subsequent behaviors designed to prevent crises and further damage or other worsening of the condition, so it would seem important to learn how patients with another illness viewed the cause of their problem. A health educator working with a hypertensive black population learned that there were not only the levels of causal theories found among other heart patients (i.e., causes of the condition in the individual and causes of short-term fluctuations), but also a new level which is constructed by black patients to explain the high prevalence of the condition among black people.[1] This does not make the original hypotheses invalid. It simply leads to the addition of a new condition; (when the disease appears to strike a particular group disproportionately, there will tend to be causal explanations for this). Once these insights are gained, the practitioner needs to explore the consequences of the various levels of causal theories for regimen-related behavior and the proportion of persons subscribing to certain sets of explanations.

Analysis of Processes Versus Analysis of Units

Processes are a crucial aspect of health education, and the grounded theory method is particularly oriented toward understanding them. As such it meets specifications for a strategy which would

> ...trace the lines of defining experience through which ways of living, patterns of relations, and social forms are developed, rather than to relate these formations to a set of preselected item.[3] (pp.138-9)

Present research strategies are of limited help in this regard, because they are focused on units such as persons and their roles, institutions, subcultures, and so forth. These analyses tend to be bound to finite times, places, and people, and as such, are quickly outdated. (Of course, studies of the beliefs, attitudes, and practices related to family planning or other health concerns of programmers provide baselines for evaluations, and they offer suggestions for program development.) In contrast, the grounded theory approach uses social units to study the movement of social life through time. The unit only provides the conditions under which a process varies, so that grounded theories have greater generality because of their transcendence of the specific identities of particular units, and because processes are more basic objects of research.

Two grounded theories which resulted from analyses confined to the stages of development and types of actors within single institutions illustrate the generalizability of such products: One was set in an anti-psychiatric treatment center for schizophrenic teenagers, focusing upon the subtle process of maintaining control under conditions of freedom.[34]

The other study developed a process model of institution-building from historical documents and participant observation which covered the 12-year history of technical assistance to an overseas family planning research and communication center.[25] Four stages of development were indicated by the data: initiating, transitioning, consolidating, and enabling. The core variable was role-sharing, by which was meant that at any time several persons-advisors and counterparts alike-were performing acts which in their sum represented the performance of an institutional role, such as manager, social scientist, or leader. Other process variables which were managed include orientation toward (another cultural world) balancing priorities; pacing change and development; modeling desired behaviors; coaching others on how to act in new roles; sponsoring or vouching for capabilities of one's counterpart (particularly in public roles); and letting go, which is learning when and how not to act.

Social Psychological Level of Analysis

Choice of level of analysis for the study of a substantive problem area has great influence on the range of solutions which might be developed as a result of the study. One view of research recognized three levels: (1) rates (descriptive, verificational, and distributive); (2) modal patterns of behavior; and (3) personal patterns. While it may be clear that grounded theory is not concerned with rates, it should be stressed that the goal of this approach is to explain modal patterns of behavior, not personal patterns. This distinction is maintained in the definition of the problem by a researcher using the grounded theory approach (see below). With this approach explanations of behavior patterns are viewed as problems with which the individual is coping and not as inherent within him.

The assumption that the individual carries the cause of his problem within himself is common in the literature of deviancy, illness behavior, and mental health. Such work accounts for present behaviors in terms of personality, cultural training, social class, and the like. Lofland has referred to studies which emphasize special, pre-existing proclivities as "dispositionalist," and he notes that this label still applies to work focusing upon "temporally and geographically remote or diffused variables."[19(p.67)]

Grounded theory emphasizes the level of analysis in which situational patterns and their personal and social meanings account for behavioral patterns. These are patterns of people, abstracted from personal identities. Thus, an answer to the question, "Why do juveniles steal stereo sets?" is "Because they are easy to pawn." (Why a particular boy steals a stereo is not explained.) In typing behavior an actor is a free agent who can walk in and out of the process. The person is not typed one-dimensionally. He is not a deviant-rather, he is someone who engages in deviating. The grounded theory approach contrasts with the tendency of agencies of social control (juvenile courts, schools, health departments, and medical care workers, for example) to rush this person into the role of deviant.

Such an explanation is illustrated by Whyte's[33] account of why waitresses cry. He does not discuss the women's personality traits. Instead, he focuses upon the organization of their work which often subjects them to upsetting cross-pressures. The orders from superiors, orders from impatient and demanding customers, and even requests from co-workers sometimes builds up to a point at which a waitress will break down and cry.

Problem Definition: The Victim's Perspective

In using the grounded theory approach the problem is allowed to emerge from the data and is thus defined by the actors in the situation. This is consistent with the traditional philosophy of health education. However, some established research strategies force pre-structured questions and interview schedules upon people without asking them how they define their situations and problems. Health education researchers sometimes find themselves representing established interests in trying to change the wrong people.

Ryan has described a research and program planning formula which is all too familiar, and his perspective surely challenges researchers and practitioners:

First, identify a social problem. Second, study those affected by the problem and discover in what ways they are different from the rest of us as a consequence of deprivation and injustice. Third, define the differences as the cause of the social problem itself. Finally, of course, assign a government bureaucrat to invent a humanitarian action program to correct the differences.[28] (p.8)

The grounded theory approach makes it much less likely that the researcher will blame the victim or recommend solutions which aim to change only the patient, the hard-to-reach, or others who pose problems to health professionals.

Several studies[4-6,8,23-24,31] using this method bear out an important point about grounded theory as illustrated with the chronically ill. Focusing on the core social psychological problems of those who are chronically ill has greater explanatory power-accounts for more of what goes on behaviorally-

than approaches which view the medical problem as central. Actions of the ill person which seem anomalous, inexplicable, or irrational when described in relation to medical objectives, appear quite understandable, appropriate, and predictable when analyzed in terms of the consequences of the illness. Non-compliance could be reconceptualized and re-explained in terms of the patient's selective utilization of the regimen and other strategies perceived to optimize health in order to maximize areas of functioning which have high priority.

Thus, an approach which concerns itself with the meanings, definitions, and interpretations which are made by the subjects of the study has greater potential for depicting their world and priorities more accurately than methods which begin by preconceiving that world and its meaning. And it is this which helps practitioners to see an ill person's or community's situation holistically.

Theory-Building: Selection and Integration of Social Science Theory

Health education could benefit from higher quality decisions about the relevance of existing formal theories, and the grounded approach offers an organizing feature which can bring together a wide range of literature and put the analyst in a better position to judge the usefulness of available theories. The use of a substantive grounded theory as a bridge between data and formal theory largely prevents the distortion, forcing, and neglect of data by a formal theory.

As Mullen conducted a study of heart patients,[21] for instance, the important condition of having an invisible physical handicap led to exploration of the deviance literature for work on situations in which people wish to disguise an aspect of themselves that is socially stigmatized, that is, to "pass." The work of others such as Davis,[7] helped to conceptualize aspects of the data; it then yielded ideas for further literature searches - e.g., on the social and psychological effects of successfully passing and on the attendant problems of selective revealment. Further data collection was then undertaken to ascertain the relevance of the new ideas for heart patients. Another example of the ability of a grounded theory to organize a large number of separate studies is the framework developed by Bigus in his study of alcoholics;[2] this study of the social transformation of alcoholics from persons constrained by normal boundaries of behavior to those engaging in greater and greater deviance has helped to bring together a portion of the diverse literature of alcoholism.

The grounded theory method could be helpful in another important aspect of building theory for health education-in the realm of practice theory. Among the many possible subjects are the processes of:

* organizing persons and units within institutional settings;

* coordinating the efforts of a variety of programs promulgated by different agencies;

* establishing health education programs in relatively new settings such as health maintenance organizations under organizational contexts ranging from compliance with federal regulations to strong support by one or more constituencies; and

* facilitating interdisciplinary cooperation among medical care workers.

Further development of theories of practice would be a significant contribution to program development and evaluation, training new health educators, and setting new priorities for research.

CONCLUDING REMARKS: ANOTHER RESEARCH STRATEGY FOR HEALTH EDUCATION

In summarizing this introduction to the grounded theory approach and its potential for health education, its strengths as a research strategy and its unusual compatibility with the principles of health education practice should be stressed. Substantive grounded theories would flesh out the linkages among theory, research, and practice in community health education to a greater degree. Their empirical roots makes them understandable to those who are involved in that substantive area, and they immediately introduce the reader who is unfamiliar with the area to important variables. Existing social science research and theory can be brought to bear on the problem more fruitfully when they are related to the data by the conceptual bridge of a grounded theory.

While one research strategy should not be emphasized to the exclusion of others, greater interest in the grounded theory method is warranted.

One needed change is wider recognition within the field of health education of inductive, qualitative research as a legitimate mode of inquiry. Too often the labels "soft," "lacking rigor," and "not really scientific" are applied. This appears to be because of exposure to poor examples and/or because of the perpetuation of the bias favoring deductive, experimental designs as the highest form of research which psychology adopted in its drive to move from a philosophical to a scientific discipline. This limited view of scientific inquiry is one which ironically, the physical sciences do not share at all. In biochemistry, for example, inductive development of models is a major part of research activity.

Health education training institutions ought to include the grounded theory approach in research methodology survey courses, (e.g., 15). As a basis for more advanced training and also as valuable skills for health education practice, systematic participant observation and inductive thinking should be taught (e.g., 30). Faculty members should encourage interested students to take more extensive course work in the method at institutions where this is available (e.g., University of California at San Francisco, Berkeley, Davis, and San Diego; Teachers College; University of Washington; and University of Oklahoma). The second of the grounded theory methodology books is now in press,[12] and that together with careful study of completed studies such as those cited in this paper are helpful for self-teaching. Students and practitioners could also benefit from reading more grounded theory studies. In conclusion, then, health education would be enriched greatly if this research method were given more attention.

ACKNOWLEDGEMENTS

The authors wish to acknowledge the contributions of Drs. Barney G. Glaser, Lawrence W. Green, Anselm L. Strauss, and Harold Gustafson, and the members of Dr. Glaser's research seminar 1972-1974. The authors' training in the grounded theory method was undertaken during their doctoral work at the School of Public Health, University of California, Berkeley, and sponsored by U.S. Public Health Service Traineeships.

REFERENCES

1. Arnold GM: A Question of Control: A Study of Black People's Perceptions of and Adaptions to Hypertension. Master's thesis, Department of Health Education, University of Washington, 1978.

2. Bigus OE: Becoming "Alcoholic": A Study of Social Transformation. Doctoral dissertation, University of California, San Francisco, 1974.

3. Blumer H: *Symbolic Interactionism: Perspective and Method.* Englewood Cliffs, New Jersey, Prentice-Hall, 1969.

4. Charmaz KC: Shouldering the Burden. *Omega* 3:23, 1972.

5. Charmaz KC: Time and Identity: The Shaping of Selves of the Chronically Ill. Doctoral dissertation, University of California, San Francisco, 1973.

6. Davis F: *Passage Through Crisis: Polio Victims and Their Families.* Indianapolis, Bobbs-Merrill, 1963.

7. Davis F: Deviance Disavowal: The Management of Strained Interaction by the Visibly Handicapped. In Becker HS (ed): *The Other Side: Perspectives on Deviance.* New York, The Free Press of Glencoe, 1964, P. 119.

8. Davis MZ: *Living with Multiple Sclerosis: A Social Psychological Analysis.* Springfield, Illinois, Charles C Thomas, 1973.

9. Derryberry M: Research procedures applicable to health education. *J Sch Health* 33:215, 1963.

10. Egbert LD, Battit GE, Welch CE, et al: Reduction of postoperative pain by encouragement and instruction of patients. *N Engl J Med* 270:825-827, 1964.

11. Fagerhaugh SY, Strauss AL: *Politics of Pain Management: Staff-Patient Interaction.* Menlo Park, California, Addison-Wesley, 1977.

12. Glaser BG: *Theoretical Sensitivity: Advances in the Methodology of Grounded Theory.* Mill Valley, California, Sociology Press, in press.

13. Glaser BG, Strauss AL: *Awareness of Dying*, Chicago, Illinois, Aldine-Atherton, 1965.

14. Glaser BG, Strauss AL: Awareness contexts and social interaction. Am Sociol Rev 29:669-679, 1967.

15. Glaser BG, Strauss AL: *The Discovery of Grounded Theory: Strategies for Qualitative Research,* Chicago, Illinois, Aldine-Atherton, 1967.

16. Glaser BG, Strauss AL: *Time for Dying*, Chicago, Illinois, Aldine-Atherton, 1968.

17. Glaser BG, Strauss AL: *Status Passage*, Chicago, Illinois, Aldine-Atherton, 1971.

18. Hochbaum GM: Research to improve health education. *Int J Health Educ* 3:141, 1965.

19. Lofland J: *Analyzing Social Settings: A Guide to Qualitative Observation and Analysis.* Belmont, California, Wadsworth, 1971.

20. Luker K: *Taking Chances.* Berkeley, California, University of California Press, 1975.

21. Mullen PD: Cutting back after a heart attack: An overview. *Health Educ Monogr* 6:295-311, 1978.

22. O'Neill N, O'Neill G: *Shifting Gears: Finding Security in a Changing World.* New York, M Evans, 1974.

23. Quint JC: Becoming Diabetic: A Study of Emerging Identity. Doctoral dissertation, University of California, San Francisco, 1969.

24. Reif L: Managing a life with chronic disease. *Am J Nurs* 73:261, 1973.

25. Reynolds R: Institution-Building and the Development Process. Doctoral dissertation, University of California, Berkeley, 1973.

26. Roberts BJ (ed): Health Education in Medical Care: Needs and Opportunities. Berkeley, School of Public Health, University of California, 1962.

27. Roberts BJ: Research in Health Education: Background Paper, Geneva, World Health Organization, 1968.

28. Ryan W: *Blaming the Victim.* New York: Vintage, 1972.

29. Sackett DL, Haynes RB: *Compliance with Therapeutic Regimens.* Baltimore, Johns Hopkins University Press, 1976.

30. Schatzman L, Strauss AL: *Field Research: Strategies for a Natural Sociology,* Englewood Cliffs, New Jersey, Prentice-Hall, 1973, pp. 8-9.

31. Strauss AL, Glaser BG: *Chronic Illness and the Quality of Life.* St. Louis, Missouri, Mosby, 1975.

32. Steuart GW: Scientist and the professional: The relations between research and action. *Health Educ Monogr* 1(29):1-10, 1969.

33. White WF: *Human Relations in the Restaurant Industry.* New York, McGraw-Hill, 1948.

34. Wilson HS: Infra-Controlling: Social Order Under Conditions of Freedom in an Anti-Psychiatric Community, Doctoral dissertation, University of California, Berkeley, 1974.

APPENDIX

MEMORANDUM: PROPERTIES OF CAUSAL THEORIES

(1) Faulting aspect

- *faulting*

self, e.g., *not following doctor's orders* after a previous MI or heart condition or even for another illness; *excessive conditions* for which the patient takes responsibility (over-weight, for example): *wrongdoing* (extramarital affair, etc.)

others, e.g., *chronic problems* in marital or other significant relationships (may be represented in a single incident); more *general social problems* (racial discrimination, social class oppression); and *control agents*-doctor (doctor's inability or unwillingness to have recognized risk factors or otherwise "done something"), employer, institutional administration. (A former mental patient blamed the medications which caused him to gain weight and the deliberate creation of a stressful environment in which patients had to suppress anger.)

- defaulting, e.g., MI as *natural consequence of aging* ("the old engine has run down"); *genetic probability; unusual, difficult circumstances* such as grief and loss or nervousness and stress; *innate characteristics* ("I do everything with all of me," "I hold all my emotions inside.")

Also, *positive or ameliorating causes* - "It was your strong heart/jogging, etc., that saved you from death."

(2) Temporal aspect - Emphasis is often on the brief, immediate causes for immediate consequences.

- *brief*: usually having close temporal proximity or concommitancy to MI.

- *long-term*: chronic conditions which are beyond the patient's control and lifestyle causes.

They are sometimes combined:

I am hard driving and that whole year I was under tremendous stress at the office, working even more than my usual 50-60 hour week, but the thing that brought on the heart attack was an argument with my boss.

(3) Degree aspect - (vs. either the patient's normal or what is normal for age or work peers).

- too much: excessive activities (reinforced by doctors who are always saying to take everything in moderation), e.g., terrible job pressures, too much milk, working two jobs, eating a tunafish sandwich awfully fast; exceeding the limits established by a previous MI.

- too little: exercise, relaxation, internal control, etc.

(4) Multivariate aspect

There is emphasis upon what the patient sees as realistically amenable to change, what the doctor stresses as the cause, the short-term rather than life-style type causes, what is emphasized in the media. Involved here especially are coming to terms with some factors which may be immutable.

(5) Scientized rather than scientific

These theories have the "ring of truth" in that they interrelate and mis-relate physiological states and symptoms.

My lymphatic system got clogged up and that produced a fluid pressure leading to high blood pressure. And, everyone knows that high blood pressure causes heart attacks.

Or, they may be absolutely correct.

Reprinted from *Awareness of Dying*, Barney G. Glaser and Anselm L. Strauss, Aldine Publishing Company, New York, 1965

THE PRACTICAL USE OF AWARENESS THEORY

Barney G. Glaser, Ph.D.

In this chapter we shall discuss how our substantive sociological theory has been developed in order to facilitate applying it in daily situations of terminal care by sociologists, by doctors and nurses, and by family members and dying patients. The application of substantive sociological theory to practice requires developing a theory with (at least) four highly interrelated properties. (As we have demonstrated in this book and will discuss explicitly in the next chapter, a theory with these properties is also very likely to contribute to formal -- *i.e.*, general -- sociological theory.) The first requisite property is that the theory must closely fit the substantive area in which it will be used. Second, it must be readily *understandable* by laymen concerned with this area. Third, its must be sufficiently *general* to be applicable to a multitude of diverse, daily situations within the substantive area, not just to a specific type of situation. Fourth, it must allow the user partial *control* over the structure and process of the substantive area as it changes through time. We shall discuss each of these closely related properties and briefly illustrate them from our book to show how our theory incorporates them, and therefore why and how our theory can be applied in terminal care situations.[1]

FITNESS

That the theory must fit the substantive area to which it will be applied is the underlying basis of the theory's four requisite properties. It may seem obvious to require that substantive theory must correspond closely to the data, but actually in the current ways of developing sociological theory there are many pitfalls that may preclude good fitness.[2] Sociologists often develop a substantive theory -- theory for substantive areas such as patient care, delinquency, graduate education -- that embodies, without his realization, the sociologist's ideals, the values of his occupation and social class, as well as popular views and myths, along with his deliberate efforts at making logical deductions from some formal theory to which he became committed as a graduate student (for example, a theory of organizations, stratification, communication, authority, learning, or deviant behavior). These witting and unwitting strategies typically result in theories too divorced from the everyday realities of the substantive area, so that one does not quite know how to apply them, or in what part of the social structure to begin applying them, or where they fit the data of the substantive area, or what the propositions mean in relation to the diverse problems of the area. The use of logical deduction rests on the assumption that the formal theory supplies all the necessary concepts and hypotheses; the consequences are a typical forcing and distorting of data to fit the categories of the deduced substantive theory, and the neglecting of relevant data which seem not to fit or cannot be forced into the pre-existing sociological categories.[3] In light of the paucity of sociological theories that explicitly deal with change,[4] logical deduction usually is carried out upon static theories which tends to ensure neglect, distortion, and forcing when the deduced theory is applied to an ever-changing everyday reality.

Clearly, a substantive theory that is faithful to the everyday realities of the substantive area is one that is carefully *induced* from diverse data gathered over a considerable period of time. This research, usually based primarily on qualitative data gathered through observations, interviews and documents and perhaps later supplemented by surveys, is directed in two ways -- toward discovering new concepts and hypotheses, and then continually testing these emerging hypotheses under as many diverse conditions as possible. Only in this way will the theory be closely related to the daily realities (what is actually "going on") of the substantive area, and so be highly applicable to dealing with them. After the substantive theory is sufficiently formulated, formal theories can be scrutinized for such models, concepts and hypotheses as might lead to further formulation of the substantive theory.[5] We have described in the appendix on method how we have proceeded in developing our theory to fit the realities of terminal care in hospitals. Readers who are familiar with this area will readily be able to judge our degree of success in that enterprise.

UNDERSTANDING

A substantive theory that corresponds closely to the realities of an area will be understood and "make sense" to the people working in the substantive area. This understanding is very important since it is these people who will wish either to apply the theory themselves or employ a sociologist to apply it.[6] Their understanding the theory tends to engender readiness to use it, for it sharpens their sensitivity to the problems that they face and gives them an image of how they can potentially make matters better, either through their own efforts or those of a sociologist.[7] If they wish to apply the theory themselves, they must perceive how it can be readily mastered and used.

In developing a substantive theory that fits the data, then, we have carefully developed concepts and hypotheses to facilitate the understanding of the theory by medical and nursing personnel. This, in turn, has ensured that our theory corresponds closely to the realities of terminal care. Our concepts have two essential features: they are both analytic and sensitizing. By *analytic* we mean that they are sufficiently generalized to designate the properties of concrete entities -- not the entities themselves -- and by *sensitizing* we mean that they yield a meaningful picture with apt illustrations that enable medical and nursing personnel to grasp the reference in terms of their own experiences. For example, our categories of "death expectations," "nothing more to do," "lingering," and "social loss" designate general properties of dying patients which unquestionably are vividly sensitizing or meaningful to hospital personnel.[8]

To develop concepts of this nature, which tap the best of two possible worlds -- abstraction and reality -- takes considerable study of one's data.[9] Seldom can they be deduced from formal theory. Furthermore, these concepts provide a necessary bridge between the theoretical thinking of sociologists and the practical thinking of people concerned with the substantive area, so that both parties may understand and apply the theory. The sociologist finds that he has "a feeling for" the everyday realities of the situation, while the person in the situation finds he can master and manage the theory. In particular, these concepts allow this person to pose and test his "favored hypotheses" in his initial applications of the theory.[10]

Whether the hypotheses prove somewhat right or wrong, the answers still are related to the substantive theory; use of the theory helps both in the interpretation of hypotheses and in the development of new applications of the theory. For example, as physicians (and social scientists) test out whether or not disclosure of terminality is advisable under specified conditions, the answers will be interpretable in terms of awareness contexts (Chapters 3 and 6) and the general response process (Chapter 8). This, in turn, will direct these people to further useful questions as well as lead to suggestions for changing many situations of terminal care.

In utilizing these types of concepts in our book, we have anticipated that readers would almost literally be able to see and hear the people involved in terminal situations -- but see and hear in relation to our theoretical framework. It is only a short step from this kind of understanding to applying our theory to the problems that both staff and patients encounter in the dying situation. For instance, a general understanding of what is entailed in the mutual pretense context, including consequences which may be judged negative to nursing and medical care, may lead the staff to abandon its otherwise unwitting imposition of mutual pretense upon a patient. Similarly, the understanding yielded by a close reading of our chapters on family reactions in closed and open contexts should greatly aid a staff member's future management of -- not to say compassion for -- those family reactions. A good grasp of our theory, also, will help hospital personnel to understand the characteristic problems faced on particular kinds of hospital services, including their own, as well as the typical kinds of solutions that personnel will try.

GENERALITY

In deciding upon the analytic level of our concepts, we have been guided by the criteria that they should not be so abstract as to lose their sensitizing aspect, but yet must be abstract enough to make our theory a general guide to the multi-conditional, ever-changing daily situations of terminal care. Through the level of generality of our concepts we have tried to make the theory flexible enough to make a wide variety of changing situations understandable, and also flexible enough to be readily reformulated, virtually on the spot, when necessary, that is, when the theory does not work. The person who applies our theory will, we believe, be able to bend, adjust, or quickly reformulate awareness theory as he applies it in trying to keep up with and manage the situational realities that he wishes to improve. For example, nurses will be able better to cope with family and patients during sudden transitions from closed to pretense or open awareness if they try to apply elements of our theory (see Chapters 3, 8, 9), continually adjusting the theory in application.

We are concerned also with the theory's generality of scope. Because of the changing conditions of everyday terminal situations it is not necessary to use rigorous research to find precise, quantitatively validated, factual, knowledge upon which to base the theory. "Facts" change quickly, and precise quantitative approaches (even large-scale surveys) typically yield *too few* general concepts and relations between concepts to be of broad practical use in coping with the complex interplay of forces characteristic of the substantive area. A person who employs quantitatively derived theory "knows his few variables better than anyone, but these variables are only part of the picture."[11] Theory of this nature will also tend to give the user the idea that since the facts are "correct" so is the theory; this hinders the continual adjustment and reformulation of theory necessitated by the realities of practice. Because he is severely limited when facing the varied conditions and situations typical of the total picture, the person who applies a quantitatively derived theory frequently finds himself either guideless or applying the inapplicable -- with (potentially) unfortunate human and organizational consequences. This kind of theory typically does not allow for enough variation in situations to take into account the institution and control of change in them. Also, it usually does not offer sufficient means for predicting the diverse consequences of any action, done with purpose, on those aspects of the substantive area which one does not wish to change but which will surely be affected by the action. Whoever applies this kind of theory is often just "another voice to be listened to before the decision is reached or announced" by those who do comprehend the total picture.[12]

Accordingly, to achieve a theory general enough to be applicable to the total picture, we have found it more important to accumulate a vast number of *diverse* qualitative "facts" on dying situations (some of which may be slightly inaccurate). This diversity has facilitated the development of a theory that includes a sufficient number of general concepts relevant to most dying situations, with plausible relations among these categories that can account for much everyday behavior in dying situations. Though most of our report is based on field observations and interviews, we have used occasional data from any source (newspaper and magazine articles, biographies and novels, surveys and experiments), since the criterion for the credibility and potential use of this data is how they are integrated into the emergent substantive theory.[13]

The relations among categories are continually subject to qualification, and to change in direction and magnitude due to new conditions. The by-product of such changes is a correction of inaccuracies in observation and reintegration of the correction into the theory as it is applied. The application is thus, in one sense, the theory's further test and validation. Indeed, field workers use application as a prime strategy for testing emerging hypotheses, though they are not acting as practitioners in a substantive area. In the next section, by illustrating how our theory guides one through the multifaceted problem of disclosure of terminality, we indicate how one confronts the total picture with a theory that is general enough in scope to be applicable to it.

This method of discovering and developing a substantive theory based on a multitude of diverse facts tends to resolve two problems confronting the social scientist consultant, who, according to Zetterberg, is "dependent on what is found in the tradition of a science" and, when this fails, is apt to "proceed on guess work" so as not to "lose respect and future assignments."[14] Our method resolves these problems in large measure because it is not limited by the dictum that Zetterberg's consultant must follow: "Only those details were assembled by the consultant and his co-workers that could be fitted into the categories of sociology, i.e., phrased in sociological terminology.[15] As stated earlier in the section on fitness, we do not believe that the categories of sociology can at the outset be directly applied to a substantive area without great neglect, forcing, and distortion of everyday realities. A substantive theory for the area must first be *induced,* with its own general concepts; and these concepts can later become a bridge to more formal sociological categories if the latter can be found. As Wilbert Moore has noted, however, we still lack the necessary formal categories to cope with change adequately.

CONTROL

The substantive theory must enable the person who uses it to have enough control in everyday situations to make its application worth trying. The control we have in mind has various aspects. The person who applies the theory must be enabled to understand and analyze ongoing situational realities, to produce and predict change in them, and to predict and control consequences both for the object of change and for other parts of the total situation that will be affected. And as changes occur, he must be enabled to be flexible in revising his tactics of application and in revising the theory itself if necessary. To give this kind of control, the theory must provide a sufficient number of general concepts and their plausible interrelations; and these concepts must provide him with understanding, with situational controls, and with access to the situation in order to exert the controls. The crux of controllability is the production and control of change through "controllable" variables and "access" variables.

Controllable variables. Our concepts, their level of generality, their fit to the situation, and their understandability give whoever wishes to apply them, to bring about change, a *controllable theoretical foothold* in the realities of terminal situations. Thus, not only must the conceptual variables be controllable, but their controllability must be enhanced by their integration into a substantive theory which guides their use under most conditions that the user is likely to encounter. The use of our concepts may be contrasted with the unguided, *ad hoc* use of an isolated concept, or with the use of abstract formal categories that are too tenuously related to the actual situation.[16]

For example, the prime controllable variable of our study is the "awareness context." Doctors and nurses have much control over the creation, maintenance, and change of awareness contexts; thus they have much control over the resultant characteristic forms of interaction, and the consequences for all people involved in the dying situation. Also, the interactional modes we have specified are highly controllable variables; doctors and nurses deliberately engage in many interactional tactics and strategies.

If a doctor contemplates disclosure of terminality to a patient, by using our theory he may anticipate a very wide range of plausibly expected changes and consequence for himself, patient, family members and nurses. By using the theory developed in Chapter 8, he may judge how far and in what direction the patient's responses may go and how to control these responses. By using the theory in Chapter 3, he may judge what consequences for himself, nurses and patients will occur when the context is kept closed; and by referring to Chapter 6, he may weigh these against the consequences that occur when the context is opened. Also, he may judge how advisable it is to allow the characteristic modes of interaction that result from each type of awareness context to continue or be changed. From these chapters he also may develop a wider variety of interactional tactics than ordinarily would be in his personal repertoire. If maintaining a closed context will result in too great a management of assessment (an interactional mode) by the nurse -- which might decrease the patient's trust in the whole staff when he discovers his terminality -- it may be better to change the context to allow the nurse to respond differently.

The doctor may also review Chapters 9 and 10 for judging to what degree opening the context by disclosure will lead to problems in controlling family members, and how the disclosure may affect their preparations for death. Resting this decision upon our theory allows him much flexibility and scope of action -- precisely because we have provided many general concepts and their probable interrelations closely linked to the reality of disclosure, in order to guide the doctor in considering the many additional situations that will be affected by disclosure. Simply to disclose in the hope that the patient will be able to prepare himself for death is just as unguided and *ad hoc* as to not to disclose because he may commit suicide. To disclose because the patient must learn, according to formal theory, '' to take the role of a terminal patient,'' is too abstract a notion for coping with the realities of the impact of disclosure for all people concerned.

This example brings out several other properties of controllable variables and, thus, of our substantive theory. First, the theory must provide controllable variables with much *explanatory power*: they must "make a big difference" in what is going on in the situation to be changed. We have discovered one such variable -- awareness contexts. As we have reiterated many times, much of what happens in the dying situation is strongly determined by the type of awareness context within which the events are occurring.

Second, doctors and nurses, family and patients are already purposefully controlling many variables delineated in our substantive theory. While the doctor exerts most control over the awareness context, all these people have tactics that they use to change or maintain a particular awareness context. The patient, for example, is often responsible for initiating the pretense context. However, all these people are, in our observation, controlling variables for very limited, *ad hoc* purposes. Our theory, therefore, can give staff, family and patients a broader guide to what they tend to do already and perhaps help them to be more effective.

Controllable variables sometimes entail controlling only one's own behavior and sometimes primarily others' behavior -- the more difficult of the two. But, as we have tried to show, control usually involves the efforts of two parties; that is *control of the interaction* between two people by one or both. In the dying situation it is not uncommon to see patient, family, doctor, and nurse trying to control each other for their own purposes. Those who avail themselves of our theory may have a better chance in the tug-of-war over who shall best control the dying situation.

In the hospital, material props and physical spaces are of strategic importance as variables which help to control awareness contexts and people's behavior.[17] We have noted how doctors and nurses use spatial arrangements of rooms, doors, glass walls, rooms and screens to achieve control over awareness contexts. By making such controllable variables part of our theory we have given a broader guide to the staff's purposeful use of them. Thus, to let a family through a door or behind a screen may be more advisable than yielding to the momentary urge of shutting out the family to prevent a scene. Letting in family members may aid their preparations for death, which in turn may result in a more composed family over the long run of the dying situation.

Access variables. The theory must also include access variables: social structural variables which allow, guide and give persons access either to the controllable variables or to the people who are in control of them. To use a controllable variable, one must have a means of access to it. For example, professional rules give principal control over awareness contexts to the doctor; therefore the nurse ordinarily has a great deal of control in dying situations because of her considerable access to the doctor, through or from whom she may try to exert control over the awareness context. Professional rules forbid her to change the context on her own initiative; they require her to maintain the current one. Thus the organizational structure of the hospital, the medical profession, and the ward provide degrees of access to control of awareness contexts by both doctor and nurses -- and our theory delineates this matter. Family members have more access to a private physician than to a hospital physician; thus they may have more control over the former. Sometimes they can demand that their private physician keep a closed awareness context because of the control they exert over him through the lay referral system (upon which he may depend for much of his practice).[18] The patient has little access in the closed context to a doctor in order to control changes of context. However, like the nurse, he has much access to everyday cues concerning his condition -- they exist all around him and he learns to read them better and better. Thus, his access to strategic cues gives him an opportunity to control his situation -- and we have discussed at length how he can manage cues to gain controls. Access variables also indicate how best to enter a situation in order to manage a controllable variable while not otherwise unduly disrupting the situation. Thus, we have delineated the various alternatives that a nurse may use to gain control over the "nothing more to do" situation in order to let a patient die.

CONCLUSION

Throughout our monograph we have indicated many strategic places, points and problems in dying that we feel would profit from the application of our theory. By leaving these short discourses on application *in context* we trust they have had more meaning than if gathered into a single chapter.

We have made this effort to establish a "practical" theory also because we feel, as many sociologists do and as Elbridge Sibley has written: "The popular notion that any educated man is capable of being his own sociologist will not be exorcised by proclamation; it can only be gradually dispelled by the visible accomplishments of professionally competent sociologists."[19] By attempting to develop a theory that can also be applied, we hope to contribute to the accomplishments of sociology. Social theory, in turn, is thereby enriched and linked closely, as John Dewey remarked thirty years ago, with the pursuit and studied control of practical matters.[20]

Two properties of our type of an implied theory must be clearly understood. First, the theory can only be developed by trained sociologists, but can be applied by either laymen or sociologists. Second, it is a type of theory which can be applied in a substantive area which entails interaction variables. Whether it would be a useful type of theory for areas where interaction is of no powerful consequence (that is, where large scale parameters are at issue, such as consumer purchase rates, birth control, the voting of a county, desegregation of a school system, and audiences for TV) remains unanswered.

REFERENCES

1 Applied theory can be powerful for exactly the reasons set forth by John Dewey, some years ago: "What is sometimes termed 'applied' science ... is directly concerned with ... instrumentalities at work in effecting modifications of existence in behalf of conclusions that are reflectively preferred ... 'Application' is a hard word for many to accept. It suggests some extraneous tool ready-made and complete which is then put to uses that are external to its nature. But ... application of 'science' means application in, not application to. Application in something signifies a more extensive interaction of natural events with one another, an elimination of distance and obstacles; provision of opportunities for interactions that reveal potentialities previously hidden and that bring into existence new histories with new initiations and endings. Engineering, medicine, social

arts realize relationships that were unrealized in actual existence. Surely in their new context the latter are understood or known as they are not in isolation." *Experience and Nature* (Chicago: Open Court Publishing Company, 1925), pp. 161-162.

2 For many years, Herbert Blumer has remarked in his classes that sociologists perennially import theories from other disciplines that do not fit the data of sociology and inappropriately apply sociological theories developed from the study of data different than that under consideration. Cf. "The Problem of the Concept in Social Psychology," *American Journal of Sociology* (March, 1940), pp. 707-719. For an analysis of how current sociological methods by their very nature often result in data and theory that does not fit the realities of the situation see Aaron V. Cicourel, *Method and Measurement in Sociology* (New York: Free Press of Glencoe, 1964).

3 Our position may be contrasted with that of Hans L. Zetterberg who, after some exploratory research to determine problems, bypasses development of substantive theory and goes directly to formal theories for help. He says, "We must know the day-by-day issues facing the practitioner and then search the storehouse of academic knowledge to see whether it might aid him." *Social Theory and Social Practice* (New York: Bedminster Press, 1962), p. 41.

4 This is noted by Wilbert Moore in "Predicting Discontinuities in Social Change," *American Sociological Review* (June, 1964), p. 332, and in *Social Change* (Englewood Cliffs, N.J.: Prentice-Hall, 1963), preface and Chapter I.

5 Thus, in contrast to Zetterberg who renders his data directly with a formal theory, we first develop a substantive theory from the data which then becomes a bridge to the use of what formal theories may be helpful. By bridging the relation of data to formal theory with a carefully thought out substantive theory the forcing, distorting and neglecting of data by rendering it with a formal, usually "thought-up," theory is prevented in large measure. See Zetterberg, *op cit.,* Chapter 4, particularly pp. 166-178.

6 In contrast, both Zetterberg and Gouldner imply by their direct use of formal theory that the practical use of sociological theory is the monopoly of the sociologist as consultant, since, of course, these formal theories are difficult enough to understand by sociologists. Zetterberg, *op*

cit. and Alvin W. Gouldner, "Theoretical Requirements of the Applied Social Sciences," *American Sociological Review,* Vol. 22 (February, 1959). Applying substantive theory, which is easier to understand, means also that more sociologists can be applied social theorists than those few who have clearly mastered difficult formal theories to be "competent practitioners of them." Zetterberg, op cit., p. 18.

Another substantive theory dealing with juvenile delinquency, in David Matza, *Delinquency and Drift* (New York: Wiley, 1964), provides a good example of our point. This is a theory that deals with "what is going on" in the situations of delinquency. It is not another rendition of the standard, formally derived, substantive theories on delinquency which deal intensively with classic ideas on relations between culture and subculture, conformity, opportunity structures, and social stratification problems, such as provided in the formal theories of Merton and Parsons and as put out by Albert Cohen and Richard Cloward and Lloyd Ohlin. As a result two probation officers of Alameda County, California, have told us that at last they have read a sociological theory that deals with "what is going on" and "makes sense" and that will help them in their work. Thus, they can apply Matza's theory in their work!

7 See Rensis Likert and Ronald Lippitt, "The Utilization of Social Science" in Leon Festinger and Daniel Katz (eds.) *Research Methods in the Behavioral Sciences* (New York: Dryden Press, 1953), p. 583.

8 On sensitizing concepts see Herbert Blumer, "What is Wrong with Social Theory," *American Sociological Review,* 19 (February, 1954), pp. 3-10, quote on p. 9.

9 Zetterberg has made this effort in choosing concepts with much success, *op cit.,* p. 49 and passim.

10 Gouldner (*op. cit.,* pp. 94-95) considers in detail the importance of testing the favored hypotheses of men who are in the situation. However, we suggest that the person can test his own hypotheses too, whereas Gouldner wishes to have a sociologist do the testing.

11 Zetterberg, *op. cit.,* p. 187.

12 *Ibid.*

13 This theme on integration into a theory as a source of confirming a fact or a proposition is extensively developed in Hans L. Zetterberg, *On*

Theory and Verification in Sociology (New Jersey: Bedminster Press, 1963).

14 Zetterberg, *Social Theory, op. cit.*, pp. 188-189.

15 *Ibid.*, p.139. This dictum is based on the idea: "The crucial act here is to deduce a solution to a problem from a set of theoretical principles." Theoretical principles refer to laws of formal theories.

16 At a lower level of generality, in much consulting done by sociologists to industrial firms, hospitals, social agencies, and the like, what is usually offered by the sociologists is "understanding," based upon an amalgam of facts intuitively rendered by references to formal theory and some loosely integrated substantive theory developed through contact with a given substantive area over the years. (Sometimes this is abetted, as in consumer research, by relatively primitive but useful analyses of data gathered for specific purposes of consultation.) Providing that the amalgam makes "sense" to the client and that he can see how to use it, then the consultation is worthwhile. Conversely, no matter how useful the sociologist may think his offering is, if the client cannot "see" it then he will not find the consultation very useful. See also Zetterberg, *op cit.*, Chapter 2.

17 Elements of "material culture" should not be neglected in development of substantive theory. Gouldner suggests they are the "forgotten man of social research": *op. cit.*, p. 97.

18 On the lay referral system see Eliot Freidson, *Patients' Views of Medical Practice* (New York: Russell Sage Foundation, 1961), Part Two.

19 *The Eduction of Sociologists in the United States* (New York: Russell Sage Foundation, 1963), p. 19.

20 See "Social Science and Social Control" in Joseph Ratner (ed.), *Intelligence in the Modern World, John Dewey's Philosophy* (New York: Modern Library, 1939), pp. 949-954.

GROUNDED THEORY METHODOLOGY AS A RESOURCE FOR DOING ETHNOMETHODO-LOGY

Stuart C. Haddan and Marilyn Lester

INTRODUCTION

This paper will explore the potential of grounded theory methodology for generating systematic ethnomethodological theory. Unlike previous attempts at linking ethnomethodology to other sociologies (cf. Denzin, 1970; Handel, 1974; Molotch and Lester, 1973, 1974; Sallach, 1973) which were done only at the programmatic level, the link we seek to effect is an empirically formulated one, arising from actually using grounded theory to study an ethnomethodological topic, i.e., the practices which people employ to "talk" their identities. There is a second distinction between our work and that of others who have sought to articulate ethnomethodological concerns with other sociologies. The antecedent attempts at linkages were between what most of us would take to be competing sociological perspectives, with differing assumptive bases and differing problematics, which result in divergent conceptions of social order, of interaction, etc., such that both ethnomethodology and the other sociology being addressed lose their recognizable characters. Our work leaves the ethnomethodological concern with members' fact-creating and sense-making practices (at several levels of analysis(in tack, and rather seeks to provide a methodology by which these concerns can be explored more systematically and in greater detail.

From our standpoint, ethnomethodologists have paid less than warranted attention to analytic procedures and methods of generating ethnomethodological theory, at least in their *published* works. If discussed at all, such usually consists of a very general statement. We suspect that at least in part this condition has arisen because an explication of those methods is seen to constitute just another "account" with all the properties of accounts so far elucidated in those same studies. In other terms, there is a hesitation to discuss analytic procedures due to ethnomethodological critiques of same. To that position we respond that, "yes, as members we are largely condemned to the same kind of interpretive work that we seek to analyze."

However, ignoring a discussion of methods does not eradicate the similarity between ours and members interpretive work, but it does tend to mystify the "doing" of ethnomethodology for others. Within this spirit, we see a focus on methodology and formulating a systematic one at that, may help to advance the enterprise. In proposing and explicating a coherent, systematic methodology, ethnomethodological topics will be available for study without having to either intuit the analytic procedures, resort to logical elaboration of preconceived categories, or be situated in the California Sun. Hoosiers as well as students of the California groups will be able to conduct ethnomethodological inquiry.

This need to explicate analytic procedures, whether they be from grounded theory or other analytic modes is clearly demonstrated in a question which appeared on a Ph.D. preliminary examination in a major university. Ethnomethodology was seen as an important topic which students should know something about, but there were no ethnomethodologists to conduct training or to write an answerable question. The question went like this:

Because of his training in ethnomethodology, a researcher plans to employ the documentary method of interpretation for interpreting his observations. In the context of this problem (e.g., examining the societal impact of a norm-oriented social movement), just what is the documentary method? *In what ways is it superior or inferior to conventional modes of analysis using literal observation?*

We would hope that explicating whatever methods ethnomethodologists use may eradicate such inanity. In this regard, we do not advance grounded theory as *the only* useful methodology for exploring ethnomethodological-informed topics. We do not intend to take issue with phenomenological modes of discovery, nor with procedures developed by Garfinkel, Cicourel or the conversational analysts. However, we do see grounded theory as a useful and codifiable program of research for extending our knowledge of members interpretive practices. Further, effective theoretical integration of work where other analytic procedures are employed may be established with a grounded approach.

There is a further reason to consider such a program. At present, our studies often result in "rediscoveries" of the "discovered" (e.g., "here's the documentary method again, the accomplishment of social facts, etc., in a different substantive arena,") followed by several citations of previous studies. Rediscovery is in contradistinction to *discovering* other practices of members (perhaps less generic ones), to *elaborating* those (as well as previously discovered ones), to finding *conditions* under which a practice might take varying forms, to discovering the "work" that the practice might take varying forms, to discovering the "work" that the practice accomplishes (otherwise know as "consequences"), and perhaps most importantly, to *integrating* what often appears to others to be a set of isolated concepts or propositions. An analytic mode of the sort proposed by grounded theory will facilitate these latter endeavors.

In order to illustrate our position via grounded theory, the remainder of this paper will follow a somewhat circuitous route. First, we will briefly characterize the aims of grounded theory methodology as a theory-generating enterprise. Second, using our own study on "talking identities" as "data", we will show how the set of analytic procedures can generate ethnomethodological theory. Finally, we will return to a formal discussion of what we take to be the contribution of grounded theory methodology to ethnomethodology.

Time does not permit a full exposition of our analysis of identity production since our concern here is with the general link between grounded theory and ethnomethodology per se. Thus, we will only refer to that empirical work as it helps to illustrate the point we are trying to elucidate. For this reason, we have made the more complete analysis of identifying available before this session (1975).

A PRIMER IN GROUNDED THEORY

The Goals

The aim of grounded theory is the systematic generation of social theory accomplished through a sequence of analytic procedures. By "systematic generation of social theory" we mean several things. First, as a package, grounded theory constitutes a research program which takes one from the initial collection of data through analysis and write-up, although it provides for some variation at each step in the program. Second, at each stage of the research, theoretical concepts are developed in response to the data, but are never left as a set of isolated conceptual ideas. Indeed, no concept is left unlinked; *integration* of concepts is a primary concern in conducting grounded research. Ideally, what results is a multi-level conceptualization of a *basic social process,* (or core process), including the conditions under which the process occurs (or under which its form might vary), the properties of the process, and its consequences for other interactional work. Third, and partly as a consequence of the above, cumulative development of theory is facilitated under the same program.

We have made reference to the notion of "basic social process." The idea connotes generic phenomena, analogous to Garfinkel and Sacks' conceptualization of "formal structures" (1970) and to ethnomethodological concerns more generally. Thus the interest of grounded theory is not in exhaustive description of a specific unit of analysis, but in the trans-unit character of the process.

The trans-unit property of analysis is derived from what Glaser and Strauss (1967) call the *constant comparative method* which entails several analytic procedures. Theory is seen as and every-developing entity, where data and conceptualization are constantly being compared so as not to fall prey to logically elaborating categories in a deductive manner with concomitant loss of linkages to available data. Instead of exhaustively collecting data in one substantive area, data is theoretically sampled. That is the analyst jointly collects, codes and analyzes data which informs what data to collect next, with the goal of refining and elaborating an emerging conceptual scheme. It is likely that several sets of data from different "areas" in the conventional sense will be sampled to varying degrees, depending on the stage of the research and the analytic level desired. This variation incumbent in theoretical sampling will be explicated in more detail when we discuss the procedures entailed in the research program.

As characterized thus far, it should be apparent that grounded theory departs from other analytic modes. For example, many empirical studies attach an explanation and interpretation of findings at the end which are logically deduced rather than being generated by the data. Another similar technique is referred to as "exampling" where the researcher finds illustrations of theory that was formulated in an apriori way. Other studies serve only a verification rather than a theory-generating function, or basically describe rather than conceptualize phenomena. On the other hand it is often suggested that analytic induction is synonymous with grounded theory. While it is true that analytic induction is concerned with generating many categories and hypotheses about a specific population or conceptual unit through comparative procedures, grounded theory differs substantially in at least two major respects. First, grounded theory analysis in *any particular study* has a process as its focus which moves beyond the fairly truncated concern of analytic induction with causality into the multi-variate realm of explicit exposition of conditions, consequences, dimensions, strategies, and the like. Hence there is a significant increase in breadth of purpose. Second, since analytic induction attempts to ascertain universality of propositions there is a required consideration of all available data (the search for the negative case) in a particular substantive concern. Grounded theory on the other hand, makes no claim to either exhaustive logical or descriptive coverage of any one substantive unit. Rather, the task through this latter research mode is to theoretically saturate with available data. Additional development elaboration, or refinement of the resultant theoretical scheme can be accomplished as more data (i.e., different conditions) are brought to bear by others in formalizing the theory. Since the theoretical scheme is "grounded" and not dependent on a singular substantive concern or type of data one would be hard pressed to "falsify" the model although it can certainly be modified.

DOING GROUNDED THEORY

In this second part of our adumbrated primer on grounded theory, we discursively outline the procedures for conducting a grounded analysis, using our own research on "talking identities" to illustrate the research process.[1]

A. *The Starting Point: Data Collection and Sociological Problem (maybe)* In the fall, Hadden, some graduate students and Lester formed a seminar in grounded theory. While there were two preliminary classes on grounded theory per se, Hadden wanted the class to "learn by doing," the usual technique for teaching the method. At the end of the first class, he asked if anyone had some data that the seminar could analyze. One student, interested in ethnomusicology, said she had been reading some interviews with jazz musicians that she found "interesting". In the beginning of the second class, transcripts of interview with several musicians were disseminated to wit. The first data collection phase was complete for us. (Clearly one possible variation at this stage is collection of primary rather than secondary data.)

This might appear to be a peculiar way to begin a study. We had not formulated a sociological problem, no hypotheses to test, no paradigmatic frameworks, no "check" (as yet) on validity and reliability of the data. Although one might begin with a general phenomenon of interest in grounded theory, the relevant core process is still not preconceived. Core processes and their properties are developed in response to the data. It is thus the opposite of logical deduction. Although Hadden wanted the data to be initially interesting in some way to some member, that was as far as preconceptions went. As to the data itself, one of the tenants of grounded theory is that there is no "bad data", although some will be easier to work with, yield different levels of analysis, etc. First, the notion of "bad data" is usually defined with respect to the problem at hand, hypotheses, etc., and since those are absent, the data will yield information on *some* process. Second, the constant comparative method takes no one data set as definitive with respect to process analysis, only as plausibly suggestive.

B. *Substantive Coding*. The next phase in the research process is called substantive coding. In a "non-training" grounded theory production, this phase is usually initiated after 4-8 interviews; or, where data already exists en tot, a "sample" of about 20-30 pages of data is drawn. This coding entails reading the materials very judiciously and noting "what is happening" or what is being said in each line. (Ideally, for this purpose, "data" appears on one side of the page leaving room for coding on the other.) In doing this, one attempts to use the same code when the same process or phenomenon recurs: and conversely, does not employ the same code when seemingly diverse things are happening. Codes, at this point, stay very close to the data--i.e., are fairly literal reductions of the substantive matter although rudimentary conceptualizations are also noted as they are suggested to the analyst.

It might seem at this point, that grounded theory's nose gets rubbed in the ethnomethodological analysis of coding and its critique of coding-as-literal-description (cf. Cicourel, 1964; Garfinkel, 1967; Leiter, 1969). We want to take up some of the most salient issues in this regard. In some sense, ethnomethodology and especially grounded theory are slightly recast.

Glaser and Strauss (1967), followed by their students, saw the possibility in coding "what was really happening on each line" --i.e., "happenings" were factual states of affairs, although independently, particular happenings are but one index of a derived concept. After lengthy discussions between the authors of this paper, (which are not resolved "once and for all"), a different conclusion has been reached, rooted in some ethnomethodological insights into the status of coding as well as the authors' experience with using grounded theory. Description, and thus coding, do not stand as mirrors to the world, to the data here. While substantive coding is seen by other grounded theorists to merely "reduce the data," from our standpoint, what the data "really is" and what is "most important" in each segment of data is context-sensitive in the most global sense. "What is really happening", is dependent on typification of "what is really important" in the occasional coding of taken-for-granted ideas held by the analyst which informs as to what stands as important, and on previous coding. To some significant degree, what is "really important" to code is an ongoing assembling activity on the part of the analyst. So, for example, what might have been seen as previously unnoteworthy (i.e., not necessary to code), might in light of later analysis, be retrospectively viewed as "important after all," or the reverse.

Given these features, coders, especially those not schooled in the problematics of ethnomethodology, and who thus analyze the data from a normative standpoint, invariably "fill in" assumed but unstated meanings. They take for granted that they can access and share the intentional schemes of subjects in the latter's interpretive work; i.e., there is the assumption of common understanding and suspension of knowledge of the indexical character of any account such that the content of subjects' accounts become the codable features.

As we began substantive coding in the fall with Lester promoting an ethnomethodological analysis of same, there was understanding of the features of coding just noted, but disagreement and later recasting of our enterprise as well. For example, insofar as possible substantive coding is totally grounded in the data--we attempt to prevent logical elaboration of codes from the data; so even if different coders see different things as "important" to code, each is rooted in the data. In the present case, the first statement by a musician in the data, as nearly all the data, was substantively coded by each member of the seminar in seemingly the same way: e.g., "About his recent musical changes, Coryell said..." was coded as "change in music." But it is also true that this seeming inter-coder reliability was *only* on the face of it. That is, when we moved to the next phase, theoretical coding, what "change in music" "really meant" was transformed by different analysts who were interested in the data in different ways. Thus, substantive codes do not have a self-evident status but are particulars to be assembled into "good gestalts." The connections between the particulars are to be grounded in the data, but here is more than one possible ensemble of codes. For the two of us, for example, those substantive codes became processual accomplishments, e.g., "changes in music" became "identifying change," while other people took the "change" as a factual product because their interests were essentially substantive and normative.

Here is where we effect a transformation of sorts in grounded theory. For Glaser and Strauss, "what is happening in each line" is an observable, literally describable and self-evident phenomenon. So "change in music" would ordinarily be seen as a "fact in the world" apart from its production by people in verbal interaction. As soon as it became clear that we could employ grounded theory for ethnomethodological concerns, the interests in substantive coding switched to people's interpretive practices for producing what others analyze as self-evident facts. In this transformation our concerns directly dovetail with those of other ethnomethodologists. The interest was in the formal structure of peoples interpretive work, rather than the content per se, which in effect, eradicates some of the problems with "filling in" work, assuming common intentionality, etc.

There is another way to look at the problem of coding. Except for the systematic nature of substantive coding in grounded theory, we ask how our procedures at this stage differ from the way in which ethnomethodologists go about discovering that a stretch of talk exhibits "this" or "that" property of talk, of accounts, etc. That is, for example, to use a protocol as reflexively tied to the phenomena being talked about entails, in its formal structure, the self-same practices--i.e., coding. When ethnomethodologists document their theoretical point with an illustration coding of the illustration as an instance of the theoretical phenomena is taking place. In every sense, coding *is* employing the documentary method of interpretation; and since that is everyone's mode of sense-making, all ethnomethodological inquiries employ the practice too, whether analyzed as such or not.

Since we are all condemned to the documentary method, of which coding is just an instance, there is every reason to introduce *systematic* explicit coding into ethnomethodological research, unless one wanted to postulate that systematic coding has a fundamentally different structure than intuitive unexplained coding!!! As it occurs in grounded theory, explicit and systematic coding leads to discovery of previously unanalyzed processes, their interrelationships, conditions under which they appear and consequences for social interaction. In short, this second step sets the stage for well-integrated and densified social theory.

C. *Initial Theoretical Development.* Once the first data are substantively coded, interest shifts to a more theoretical level. This does not mean that the grounded character of the analysis is laid by the wayside, or that we "intuit" theory. Rather, we start to ask some theoretical questions about the data and substantive codes, beginning with "what is *the* or *a* core process contained in the data" to which the most substantive codes appear related?

Actually, in the present project, a core process was discerned before the substantive coding on the first data was competed (a fairly common occurrence). Independent of each other, Hadden saw a configuration in the substantive codes which he termed "locating": i.e., the musicians were seeking to produce verbal documents of who they are and, also produced various assemblings of those documents into gestalt-like phenomena. Simultaneously, Lester had conceived a seemingly more generic practice--*identifying*--that on initial inspection seemed to incorporate Hadden's "locating" as one of its major components. Lester saw segments of data that dealt not only with documenting who the musicians "are" (locating"), but who they *were, how* they got to be located as musicians with various characteristics, and who they aspired to be. At this point, it is important to note that instead of taking identifying as our emergent process and seeking its dimensions, we could have focused on just the locating practice. Indeed most of the substantive codes in *this* data dealt with pronouncements of who the subjects are, with much less emphasis on who they were and aspired to be-- what later became our retrospecting strategies, respectively--with some modification.

Just as we transformed the substantive codes into products of ongoing documentary work by the musicians, so some students in the seminar found an entirely different process, and substantive codes came to mean different things for them. This is to suggest that the same data will yield information on more than one core process, at more than one analytic level, and the choice of which to pursue is a personal one. Rather than be disturbed by this rather personalistic criteria, we feel it is merely an explication of what goes on everywhere. To our way of thinking, to insist or even intimate that only one researchable problem is evident in a set of data is one of the ultimate vulgarities thrust on the social world by sociologists of several ilks.

Theoretically, we had a core process and a whole host of substantive codes which we thought were related to identifying, to people's practices for "talking identities". But as yet, we did not have the codes linked at a theoretical level. There were ideas, such as locating in the present and retrospecting identities. We asked further questions about Identifying--what makes up the process? What are its properties? Under what conditions does it occur? What are its consequences? But it was premature to discern variation or the relationship among the several features of Identifying. Thus, the next phase of the process was begun while still analyzing and trying to integrate substantive codes from the initial data on musicians' Identifying practices.

D. *Theoretical Sampling.* In grounded theory, the interest is not in a specific population unit. One would not be interested in musicians' identifying per se, nor in exhaustively describing musicians. Rather a population or conceptual unit is analyzed only in so far as it elucidates features of the emergent core process of interest. But of course, the process will in turn reflect back on and provide analysis of the unit. So it was that we wanted to sample other kinds of data in order to refine, elaborate, and perhaps to reformulate the configuration of properties, strategies conditions and consequences relevant for the generic process of talking identities. We collected and substantively coded ethnographic data on institutionalized alcoholics. This data was selected because we wanted more unstructured data in contrast to the magazine interview and a seemingly contrasting population as well.

Each of us substantively coded this data and were to come up with, and bring to the seminar, an initial schematic of features of the Identifying process. This data was rich in people's practices for articulating who they *were,* or so it seemed, as opposed to creating and assembling features of who they *are,* as in the case of the musicians. As well, the alcoholics talked future identities. The Identifying process was now tentatively dimensionalized into three sub-strategies: Locating, Retrospecting and Prospecting. Further, each for these strategies were analyzed for *its* constituent features. For example, people locate themselves in social networks of others. Actually they continually constitute themselves as members of different networks. And they further assemble features of those networks (i.e., establish networks as such) which elaborates their initial locating-in-a-network. Their production of -in-order-to motives renders their initial locating as sensible, rational and competent--an important way to Identify. In retrospecting, as we saw it at the time, people isolate "influencers", "inciting events", etc., in their autobiographies.

We also began to discern some conditions under which one or another Identifying strategy is prominent. So, for example, Identifying can occur as an explicit oriented-to topic in conversation, or it can occur as a by-product or tangential feature to other interactional work. And Identifying will take rather different forms under these conditions. As well we noted a general property of Identifying at this time--identities are a continual ongoing assembling process, where on one occasion for one purpose at hand, with one sequential organization to talk, one identity will be assembled; another in a different setting; and perhaps conjoint rendering on still other occasions. In a similar vein, social networks, significant others, etc., are also continually assembled and reassembled dependent on the nature of the Identifying occasion at hand (cf. Hadden and Lester, 1975), for a more complete analysis).

An integrated conceptualization was emerging, but the constant comparative method dictated yet further sampling; as the strategies for Identifying and their features were still considered very tentative. Some features of Identifying didn't fit and we suspected that we did not have all the relevant variation on the process and its constituent features. Hence, five more data sets were sampled. There was an ethnography of a speech colloquium, transcripts of interviews with mothers about children, with a waitress, and the like. This time only data possibly pertinent to Identifying was substantively coded.

These five data sets reinformed the conceptualization and added properties, conditions, consequences, etc.--i.e., densified the core process. So for example, we had initially conceived the three primary strategies for Identifying--Locating, Retrospecting and Prospecting--as defined along a temporal dimension. Locating was present Identifying, retrospecting was Identifying the past, where it was assumed that when retrospecting as past occurred, it would have been preceded by present locating. But in the new data, some of the subjects were Identifying a past, "e.g., I was a waitress...", but it had the same structure to it as locating *except* for the temporal dimension. And what we had called retrospecting before had "all along" an implicit *connotation* that it was tied to present locating by the actor. That is, the musicians and alcoholics "talked the past" as filling in work for the previous locating activity. The identifying work of the waitress was of a different sort than the retrospecting of the alcoholics: she didn't tie having-been-a-waitress to any account of present identity. As a result of this variation the locating code lost the temporal dimension as its defining characteristic. Locating can assemble both present and past identities and it is the *connection* that the identifier makes between temporal periods that differentiates locating and retrospecting. Thus, for example when an alcoholic assembles features of that located status and then proceeds to pronounce biographical explanations for that location, both locating and retrospecting occur. But when locating is done in present and/or past, with no oriented-to tie between them, both are instances of locating.

In this reformulating stage, another important feature emerged. The retrospecting of the musicians differed significantly from that of the alcoholics. In essence, the musicians retrospected only by describing "how" the past helped them get to where they were; and in general they located much more than they retrospected. But the alcoholics were explicitly providing the "why"-- explaining their locating as their major identifying mode. The result was that retrospecting was dimensionalized into two forms--explicating which connotes describing work, and warranting, which provides explicit "because motives." Aside from just describing that variation, a condition was found to set the stage for engaging in one form of retrospecting or the other--assumption on the part of the identifier about what she and the hearer take as the valued or de-valued character of the location. When ego assumes that alter sees the locating as relatively valued, only explicating will occur. When there is the assumption of a devalued status warranting work takes place.

One last data set, received several months later, filled out this variation. There had been concern about the nature of the data--relative to everyday conversation, all our data was structured. This concern derived from Sacks, et al. (1974) and West and Zimmerman (1974, 1975) explicit focus on "naturally occurring talk" where they suggest that it has a different structure than "programmed interaction". We were fortunate to gain access to some transcripts or more "routine talk". For us, it was the final check on our conceptualization. Virtually all the same practices, properties, conditions appeared in this last data set. Of great interest was the fact that the data confirmed our differentiation of explicating and warranting under the retrospecting code. We had been worried that perhaps the respective interviewers of the musicians and alcoholics had *elicited* the differential pattern--that the difference was due to the nature of the data and not an actual trans-unit condition. But we found the same pattern in naturally occurring talk. For example, two women met for the first time and were engaging in Identifying work. One woman said she lived in a sorority house, which is generally devalued on the university campus. The second speaker directly affirmed that assumption and both located (i.e., assembled) negative features of the sorority/fraternity networks. This was followed by the resident of a sorority house retrospecting in the warranting mode--i.e., "there was no other kind of housing available" when she needed a place to live. Other conversations in this data set focused around Identifying, manifested explicating as the major retrospecting mode, where the located status was relatively valued. Not only were our conditions for undertaking the two forms of retrospecting verified, but there also emerged the idea that the valued or devalued character of the located identity can be *accomplished* in the course of talk, rather than being brought to the setting and assumed as an operating feature, as in the case of the alcoholics' assumptions about the ethnographer's evaluation of them.

Several months prior to obtaining this conversational data, the last step in the research process was begun: memo writing.

D. *Memo writing, "et cetera"*. As the core process and its attendant features are being integrated and densified, the memowriting stage ensues, coterminous with continuing other phases of the research (e.g., theoretical sampling, continual refinement of scheme, etc.). In general, memos are written about the core process, its constituent features and their linkages. So, for example, we write memos on Identifying, what it means, noted its strategies, conditions, and consequences. That one long memo proliferated further memos in two directions: first we moved up generically to talk about the relationship between Identifying, ethnomethodology and grounded theory; second, and most importantly, for the empirical analysis, memos were written on each strategy, sub-strategy, condition, property, etc., until we had effectively exhausted what we deemed to be relevant for analyzing Identifying. I having to explicate codes, their meaning, and linkages, one can discern weak points in the analysis which can send the researcher back to the data for refinement, then to new memos once again. In order to avoid logically elaborating theoretical codes at this stage, we continually extracted illustrations of the code being discussed which may also lead to further refinement, when, for example, the process of writing a memo and articulating it with the data leads one to see a new property of a theoretical code, which generates a new memo and so on. Ideally, memos, theoretical scheme and data continually reinform each other until the best fitting configuration is obtained.[2]

Memos are then sorted. All memos dealing with the same code or set of codes are placed together. Sorting enables one to insure that she/he is not using two different codes for the same process; and conversely that the same code is not in fact referring to different processes. As well, sorting memos within and between theoretical codes elucidates points at which linkages between codes are absent. Sorting can thus send one back to the data, to substantive and theoretical codes for re-analysis, refinement or reformulation. In the end, memos on the core process are linked to those on conditions, properties strategies and consequences, which results in a relatively integrated conceptual scheme.

With elaborate memos, writing for publication can consist primarily of cutting and pasting xerox of memos or parts therein, with an introduction and conclusion *appended*. One will notice that we have so far made no reference to the "literature in the field." If one were to start with that work, the grounded character of the research would recede and logical deduction would assume prominence. It is after one's own analysis is complete that the literature review occurs, and then typically, as in our case, it was literally appended to the beginning of our analysis such that the analysis of Identifying looked like the typical ASR paper even though the latter is usually a deductive enterprise, where the literature actually suggested the study. Were journals more sensitive to this type of work, it would be perfectly reasonable to tie the research into the literature at the end of the paper, for that is what actually happens in grounded theory, where the literature is treated as supplementary data, and in inductive research generally. But as Hadden would say, "SO IT GOES!!"

ETHNOMETHODOLOGY AND GROUNDED THEORY: THE POTENTIAL LINK

We have so far characterized the aims of grounded theory and traced the steps in its research programs they were used to generate a conceptualization of identity production. This research is, in fact, the first time that grounded theory has been used to conduct ethnomethodological inquiry. At this point, we want to discuss, in a more explicit fashion, what we take to be the potential of grounded theory for ethnomethodology.

Fundamental to grounded theory is the interest in basic social process--i.e., generic process. While this has usually meant either social structural or social psychological process in the ordinary sense in which those terms are employed, it is also amenable to ethnomethodological problems or what we might refer to as basic interpretive practices. As such grounded theory methodology dovetails directly with ethnomethodology's paradigmatic interest in generic or formal structure of practical actions. Actually, we believe grounded theory not only can be employed on a par with other research methodologies, but can *enhance* the analysis of ethnomethodology's problematics by rectifying what we see as two problems in the present state of the art. Insofar as many published and unpublished works are concerned, there has been a dual and polar tendency in the past several years to: (1) proliferate programmatic statements, and (2) discard the early interest in discovery and analysis of members' generic interpretive work and rather has rediscovered those practices in different research settings or among different population units.

Programmatic statements have been employed to assemble and reassemble the boundary lines of ethnomethodological inquiry, to suggest theoretical handles or the theoretic attitude to be assumed in undertaking research, and to assemble the "real ethnomethodologists". Were these statements used merely as suggestive of problems of study, of modes of inquiry, there would be no problem. But instead, they have been reified (usually not by the author) for the purposes of criticism (cf. Attawell, 1974); Carpenter, 1975) of our problematic, and/or they are elaborated through logical deduction into hypotheses to be tested. We end up in a modus operandi that has been heavily critiqued by ethnomethodologists themselves, i.e., logical deduction. Were more of us to adopt a grounded approach, programmatic statements, if they occurred at all, would attain a different status. They would be grounded in research, and hence, not really constitute programmatic statements at all, but perhaps function to link at a conceptual level, studies of different ethnomethodological analysis.

On the other hand, a good portion of the ethnomethodological research has moved to an interest in specific population units (e.g. school teachers, newsworkers) or conceptual units (e.g., deviance) rather than exploiting these units for purpose of generating previously seen but unnoticed interpretive practices (e.g., theoretically sampling), or densifying, elaborating and integrating previously discovered ones. So, for example, once Garfinkel elucidated the documentary method of interpretation, characterized some of its properties and consequences for the social world, more than one of us went on to show that it operates in the newsroom (Lester, 1974), among elementary school teachers (Leiter, 1970), and among cops (cf. Sanders, 1975). Each study essentially concluded that "this group's major fact-creating and sense-making practice was the documentary method of interpretation," which had most of the same features as when it was first articulated, except in one case it was used to create evidence of crimes, in another to generate new stories, etc. In so far as this becomes a major mode of inquiry, there will be continual movement from discovery to a "rediscovery" approach and to unit analysis.

In part, we suspect that it was the very success of the early work which lead to this focus on units per se as opposed to continuing to develop conceptions of formal structures. As properties of the documentary method and of accounts more generally were discovered, they were taken as exhaustive and became constituted as a paradigm for others to verify and rediscover in setting after setting, even though one of the major properties of these practices is that they are generic, e.g., transcends units. Ethnomethodological ideas became apriori assumptions about the data and were basically enumerated into testable hypotheses, though not usually related as such. This is not to say that there is anything intrinsically faulty about unit analysis. To be sure this approach is the standard fare in sociology,to wit, sociology of deviance, of organizations, etc. However, proliferating rediscoveries and unit analyses is not facilitative insofar as generic process is the desired goal.

Employing a grounded approach, one may, and an ethnomethodologist will, attend to the constitutive character of the data, to the "doing" as opposed to the product as such. However, preconceptions of what the data will yield ceases there. Because they are not serving primarily a verification function, substantive followed by theoretical coding and theoretical sampling of data can yield information on and lead to conceptualization of yet undiscovered or unstudied facets of interpretive work, or at least to elaboration, densification and integration of already-noted practices. Perhaps,as with the identifying process, these will be less generic than the global "reflexivity of accounts," and "the documentary method," etc., but nonetheless they constitute formal structures. In our study, these latter essential properties of accounts were of course also major properties of Identifying. Were we to have focused on the documentary method as the basic social process so our results might well have come to the same conclusion as other rediscoveries except for the variation in the conceptual unit of analysis. In employing grounded theory, we went on to capture the more specific process by which all identities are talked. We also suspect that we could have analyzed the documentary method via grounded theory and perhaps elaborated and integrated its features beyond work already done.

Aside from being adaptable for generating conceptualization of variety of generic practices, we argue that employing a grounded analysis will result in a level of theoretical integration not so far achieved--i.e., will cement as well as analyze features of the paradigm, and will allow for cumulative development of ethnomethodological theory. This is perhaps particularly important at this point in time while ethnomethodologists are pursuing research in seemingly disparate directions, where there are differing problematic and thus differing features seemingly taken as resource. So, for example, to take the production of accounts-as-fact-creating-work as a problematic usually entails employing the social organization of talk as a resource, as pointed out by Carpenter (1975). Similarly, to take even higher level process, e.g., Identifying, status passage, or the social construction of social problems are typically seen to fall outside the domain of ethnomethodology altogether. Even though there is a fundamental concern with members' fact-creating and sense-making in these latter problems they are seen to take talk, accounts and their attendant properties as resource.

These variations can result in rather fruitless debates about the "real" ethnomethodology or about who constitute the "real" ethnomethodology or about who constitute the "real" ethnomethodologists. That is, conflict rather than complementarity, and integration of different level processes has generally characterized the "accounts" of our individual efforts. If carried to its logical conclusion, we will inevitably get lost in the regress problem. In so far as we take the distinction between topic and resource as the ultimate criterion for ethnomethodology, then when *any* social accomplishment of members is not rendered analytically in *any one study*, the study will be faulted. Taken to such extremes, ethnomethodology will come to constitute only the study of talk, until someone levels the critique that the conversational analysts are employing a fundamental accomplishment as their resource. Indeed, Mehan and Wood (1975) suggest just that, although they also suggest that the conversational analysts employ common sense knowledge as their resource.

Our conceptualization of the meaning and consequences of the differences amongst us takes a different turn. Such is rooted in taking our whole identifying scheme as data for analysis. That is, we asked questions about *that* process, analogous to those we asked about the original data. We wanted to understand the relationship of Identifying to ethnomethodology, to its "good fit" with other ethnomethodological studies, etc. "What properties did Identifying share with analysis of other practical actions?"

With further data, Identifying self might well come to be seen as a variant of *Rendering* anything--other people, social organization and so on. That is, cursory inspection of our's and other's data and analyses suggest that locating, retrospecting and prospecting, so far seen as strategies for self production, are similarly members' practices for rendering other things as factual, patterned, sensible and the like, although the substrategies of those would vary. Thus, this process could be made even more generic. In so doing, Rendering would be analyzed for its properties, conditions, consequences and the like, i.e., would come to be an analyzed basic social process. Identifying people, would likely share all the features of the more general process of Rendering, but would have features in addition which are specific to "people production".

This is an instance of both vertical and horizontal integration. We could move up generically, through the method of constant comparison to analyze the whole Rendering process, and similarly move horizontally to take into account the variation encountered in Identifying people, Identifying self, Identifying objects removed in space and time, etc. In analyzing the most generic process, the characteristics of "rendering talk" would be analyzed, the forms that the documentary method takes in this work, and the reflexive character of "rendering accounts" with what is being rendered, etc. (We cannot at this time really suggest the properties of that process since our data was analyzed at a more substantive level.) However, in studies of the more substantive process--e.g., Identifying "self", "others", etc., the analysis would not rediscover the properties of the formal rendering process (unless new properties of this generic process were discovered in the course of this work), but would look at the form that these practices take--their properties, conditions and consequences. It is not the case that "talk" is being used as a mere resource, but that it has been analyzed in previous work, and here is the opportunity to build on that work and to dimensionalize the properties of the substantive Identifying practices. This work in turn would reflect back on and enrich the initial analysis of Rendering. One could as well work in the opposite direction and build from substantive to formal theory. In either case, Identifying self and others, etc., would be linked together, as well as to the overall Rendering process--the beginning of integration and cumulative development of theory.

There are other possibilities, using the analysis of the more generic Rendering process. If we had analyzed that process, we could have moved in a different direction vertically. For example, Hadden's dissertation, *The Social Creation of Social Problems* (1973) can be seen to analyze, through grounded theory, the process of identifying social problems. That process included practices such as "alarming", that is seeking to produce the sense in which there is an urgent problem, which, in turn, consists of practices such as "pronouncing prevalence" of a problem, "providing indicators" of a problem and, more generally, doing production work to create the sense in which the problem has a stable, objective, transpersonal character. The analysis of the social creation of social problems can be seen to derive from what was previously unexplicated, and is now an explicit analysis of Identifying. This is to say that with an eye toward theoretical integration and cumulative development of theory, phenomena typically unanalyzed by ethnomethodologists will be made available for study and will be linked to other studies of ethnomethodological problems.

Much of the foregoing is at a relatively macroscopic level compared to many ethnomethodological works, but the potential for integration and cumulative development of theory does not start and stop at this level. Indeed, if it did so, our resource would be the more general phenomena of interpretive work. The general nature of interpretive work and its properties, etc.--e.g., the documentary method, the embedded character of accounts, the assembled nature of any phenomena--have and will undoubtedly continue to form problematic for research. But in so far as they are indeed the formal, i.e., transsituational structure of practical actions, they are also attendant properties of Identifying, of creating social problems, etc. By nothing that foundation, less generic problems need not rediscover and reanalyze the formal structure of the more generic practices. That is, "Identifying" partakes of all the discovered features of accounts and practical actions in general and so our analysis focused about the more precise mechanisms by which identities are preferred. In analogous fashion, the work of ethnomethodologists concerned with members' practical actions in preferring anything could be seen to rest at least in part on the work of the conversational analysts, or at least analysis of the two topics would be mutually informative. While the latter are pursuing their problematic--the structure of conversational practice--those interested in higher level phenomena can embed their work in the analysis of talk, and vice versa, without having to take the related problem up in detail, since it is not the topic of study per se. The analysis of accounts for example rests implicitly on features of talk that the conversational analysts have taken as topic, but have analyzable properties of its own. The latter should form the specific research problem, rather than having to undertake basically two studies, i.e., the social organization of talk and the production of accounts, nor apologize for using "talk" as a resource. Especially insofar as we want to disseminate our work to others, standard presentational practices and space limitations prevent the analysis of all the more general processes plus the specific problem under study.

We basically see ethnomethodological work varying in terms of the level of problem. Only to a minor degree, then, is there intrinsic conflict between analysis of conversational practice on the one hand and the social creation of social problems on the other. By virtue of the fact that these are different rather than competing levels, there is every reason to conceptualize the integrative potential of our enterprise. This will be effected by each of us explicitly attending at the level of analysis of our studies, nothing where they fit in the whole enterprise, rather than feeling obligated to include analysis of other levels, especially those higher on the continuum of generic verses substantive (or microscopic versus macroscopic) process. In short, with attention to these issues, we will be better able to pursue our individual problems of interest, at the same time seeing and articulating the integrated and cumulative character of our program as a whole.

REFERENCES

Attawell, Paul. "Ethnomethodology Since Garfinkel". *Theory and Society,* I, (Summer) 1970; p. 179-210

Carpenter, G. Russell, "One the Epistemology of Ethnomethodology: Notes on the Structure of Ethnomethodology". Unpublished manuscripts, Indiana University, 1975

Cicourel, Aaron. "Ethnomethodology" in Thomas Sebeok and A.A. Abramson et al (eds) *Current Trends in Linguistics.*, 1972

____. *Method and Measurement in Sociology*. New York: Free Press, 1964

____. *Theory and Method in a Study of Argentine Fertility*. New York: John Wiley, 1973

Denzin, Norman. "Symbolic Interactionism and Ethnomethodology" in Jack Douglas (ed) *Understanding Everyday Life*. Chicago: Aldine, 1970

Garfinkel, Harold and Harvey Sacks, "On the Formal Structures of Practical Actions" in John McKinney and Edward Tiryakian, *Theoretical Sociology*. New York: Appelton, Century-Crofts, 1970

Garfinkel, Harold. *Studies in Ethnomethodology*. Englewood Cliffs: Prentice Hall, 1967

Glaser, Barney and Anselm Strauss. *The Discovery of Grounded Theory*. Chicago: Aldine Publ. Co., 1967

Hadden, Stuart C. *The Social Creation of a Social Problem*. 1973 Unpublished Ph.D. dissertation, Washington State University, Pullman Washington, 1967

Hadden, Stuart C. and Marilyn Lester. "Talking Identities: People's Practices for Producing Themselves in Interaction". Submitted for publication, 1975

Handel, Judith. Paper presented at Ethnomethodology Conference, University of California, Los Angeles, 1974

Leiter, Kenneth "Getting It Done". Unpublished Masters Paper, University of California, Santa Barbara, 1969

_____. *Telling It Like It Is: A Study of Teacher's Accounts*. Unpublished Ph.D. dissertation, University of California, Santa Barbara, 1971

Lester, Marilyn. *News as a Practical Accomplishment*. Unpublished Ph.D. dissertation, University of California, Santa Barbara, 1974

Mehan, Hugh and Houston Wood. *The Reality of Ethnomethodology*. New York: John Wiley, 1975

Molotch, Harvey and Marilyn Lester, "Accidents, Scandals and Routines: Resources for Insurgent Sociology" *Insurgent Sociologist*, Vol. IV no. 3, 1973, p. 1-12

Molotch, Harvey and Marilyn Lester, "News as Purposive Behavior" *American Sociological Review*, Vol. 39, no.1, 1974 p. 101-112

Sacks, Harvey, Emmanuel Schelloff and Gail Jefferson, "Simplest Systematics For the Analysis of Turn Taking In Conversation" *Language*, Vol. 50, 1974 p. 696-734

Sacks, Harvey, "An Initial Investigation of the Usability of Conversational Data for Doing Sociology" in David Sudnow (ed) *Studies in Social Interaction.* New York: Free Press, 1972

Sacks, Harvey, "On the Analyzability of Stories by Children", in Sudnow, *Ibid*

Sallack, David, "Class Consciousness and the Everyday World in the work of Marx and Schutz", *Insurgent Sociologist*, Vol. IV, no. 3, 1973, p. 27-37

Sanders, William, "The Accomplishment of Information by Police Detectives". Paper presented at annual meetings of Southern Sociological Society, Washington, D.C., 1975

West, Candace and Don H. Zimmerman. "Sex Roles, Interceptions, and Silences in Conversation in Thorne, B. and N. Hanley (eds) *Language and Sex: Difference and Dominance.* Rowley, Mass: Nowoury House, forthcoming

Zimmerman, Don H. and Melvin Pollner, "The Everyday World as a Phenomenon" in Jack Douglas (ed) *Understanding Everyday Life.* Chicago: Aldine Pub. Co., 1970

Zimmermann Don H. and D. Lawrence Wieder. "The Problem of the Competent Recognition of Social Action and the Phenomenon of Accounting" paper presented at American Sociological Association meetings, Denver, Colorado, 1971

ENDNOTES

1 It is to be remembered that while grounded theory provides a research program, some variation can and does take place in the precise way in which each stage is undertaken.

2 It often happens as well, that in the process of writing one memo, an idea for another occurs. Following the grounded theory process, one will usually stop the first memo, start the second to get the idea on paper, then finish the first, etc. One can thus have several memos going at once which continues until all relevant codes have found their way into memo writing.

Part II

Methodology Revisited

Reprinted from *The Discovery of Grounded Theory*, Aldine Publishing Co., New York, 1968.

THE CONSTANT COMPARATIVE METHOD OF QUALITATIVE ANALYSIS*

Barney G. Glaser, Ph.D.

Currently, the general approaches to the analysis of qualitative data are these:

1. If the analyst wishes to convert qualitative data into crudely quantifiable form so that he can provisionally test a hypothesis, he codes the data first and then analyzes it. He makes an effort to code "all relevant data [that] can be brought to bear on a point," and then systematically assembles, assesses and analyzes these data in a fashion that will "constitute proof for a given proposition."[1]

2. If the analyst wishes only to generate theoretical ideas -- new categories and their properties, hypotheses and interrelated hypotheses -- he cannot be confined to the practice of coding first and then analyzing the data since, in generating theory, he is constantly redesigning and reintegrating his theoretical notions as he reviews his material.[2] Analysis after the coding operation would not only unnecessarily delay and interfere with his purpose, but the explicit coding itself often seems an unnecessary, burdensome task. As a result, the analyst merely inspects his data for new properties of his theoretical categories, and writes memos on these properties.

We wish to suggest a third approach to the analysis of qualitative data -- one that combines, by an analytic procedure of constant comparison, the explicit coding procedure of the first approach and the style of theory development of the second. The purpose of the constant comparative method of joint coding and analysis is to generate theory more systematically than allowed by the second approach, *by using explicit coding and analytic procedures*. While more systematic than the second approach, this method does not adhere completely to the first, which hinders the development of theory because it is designed for provisional testing, not discovering, of hypotheses.[3] This method of comparative analysis is to be used jointly with theoretical sampling, whether for collective new data or on previously collected or compiled qualitative data.

Systematizing the second approach (inspecting data and redesigning a developing theory) by this method does not supplant the skills and sensitivities required in generating theory. Rather, the constant comparative method is designed to aid the analyst who possesses these abilities in generating a theory that is integrated, consistent, plausible, close to the data -- and at the same time is in a form clear enough to be readily, if only partially, operationalized for testing in quantitative research. Still dependent on the skills and sensitivities of the analyst, the constant comparative method is not designed (as methods of quantitative analysis are) to guarantee that two analysts working independently with the same data will achieve the same results; it is designed to allow, with discipline, for some of the vagueness and flexibility that aid the creative generation of theory.

If a researcher using the first approach (coding all data first) wishes to discover some or all of the hypotheses to be tested, typically he makes his discoveries by using the second approach of inspection and memo-writing along with explicit coding. By contrast, the constant comparative method cannot be used for both provisional testing and discovering theory: in theoretical sampling, the data collected are not extensive enough and, because of theoretical saturation, are not coded extensively enough to yield provisional tests, as they are in the first approach. They are coded only enough to generate, hence to suggest, theory. Partial testing of theory, when necessary, is left to more rigorous approaches (sometimes qualitative but usually quantitative). These come later in the scientific enterprise (see Chapter X).

The first approach also differs in another way from the constant comparative method. It is usually concerned with a few hypotheses couched at the same level of generality, while our method is concerned with many hypotheses synthesized at different levels of generality. The reason for this difference between methods is that the first approach must keep the theory tractable so that it can be provisionally tested in the same presentation. Of course, the analyst using this approach might, after proving or disproving this hypotheses, attempt to explain his findings with more general ideas suggested by his data, thus achieving some synthesis at different levels of generality.

A fourth general approach to qualitative analysis is "analytic induction," which combines the first and second approaches in a manner different from the constant comparative method.[4] Analytic induction has been concerned with generating and proving an integrated, limited, precise, universally applicable theory of causes accounting for a specific behavior (e.g., drug addiction, embezzlement). In line with the first approach, it tests a limited number of hypotheses with *all* available data, consisting of numbers of clearly defined and carefully selected cases of the phenomena. Following the second approach, the theory is generated by the reformulation of hypotheses and redefinition of the phenomena forced by constantly confronting the theory with negative cases, cases which do not confirm the current formulation.

In contrast to analytic induction, the constant comparative method is concerned with generating and plausibly suggesting (but not provisionally testing) many categories, properties, and hypotheses about general problems (*e.g.*, the distribution of services according to the social value of clients). Some of these properties may be causes, as in analytic induction, but unlike analytic induction others are conditions, consequences, dimensions, types, processes, etc. In both approaches, these properties should result in an integrated theory. Further, no attempt is made by the constant comparative method to ascertain either the universality or the proof of suggested causes or other properties. Since no proof is involved, the constant comparative method in contrast to analytic induction requires only saturation of data -- not consideration of *all* available data, nor are the data restricted to one kind of clearly defined case. The constant comparative method, unlike analytic induction, is more likely to be applied in the same study to any kind of qualitative information, including observations, interviews, documents, articles, books, and so forth. As a consequence, the constant comparisons required by both methods differ in breadth of purpose, extent of comparing, and what data and ideas are compared.

Clearly the purposes of both these methods for generating theory supplement each other, as well as the first and second approaches. All four methods provide different alternatives to qualitative analysis. Table I locates the use of these approaches to qualitative analysis and provides a scheme for locating additional approaches according to their purposes. The general idea of the constant comparative method can also be used for generating theory in quantitative research. Then one compares findings within subgroups and with external groups (see Chapter VIII).

TABLE I. USE OF APPROACHES TO QUALITATIVE ANALYSIS

Generating Theory	*Provisional Testing of Theory*	
	Yes	No
Yes	Combining inspection for hypotheses (2) along with coding for test, then analyzing data	Inspection for hypotheses (2)
		(1)
	Analytic induction (4)	Constant comparative method (3)
No	Coding for test, then analyzing data (1)	Ethnographic description

THE CONSTANT COMPARATIVE METHOD

We shall describe in four stages the constant comparative method: (1) comparing incidents applicable to each category, (2) integrating categories and their properties, (3) delimiting the theory, and (4) writing the theory. Although this method of generating theory is a continuously growing process -- each stage after a time is transformed into the next -- earlier stages do remain in operation simultaneously throughout the analysis and each provides continuous development to its successive stage until the analysis is terminated.

1. *Comparing incidents applicable to each category.* The analyst starts by coding each incident in his data into as many categories of analysis as possible, as categories emerge or as data emerge that fit an existing category. For example, the category of "social loss" of dying patients emerged quickly from comparisons of nurses' responses to the potential deaths of their patients. Each relevant response involved the nurse's appraisal of the degree of loss that her patient would be to his family, his occupation, or society: "He was so young," "He was to be a doctor," "She had a full life," or "What will the children and her husband do without her?"[5]

Coding need consist only of noting categories on margins, but can be done more elaborately (*e.g.*, on cards). It should keep track of the comparison group in which the incident occurs. To this procedure we add the basic, defining rule for the constant comparative method: *while coding an incident for a category, compare it with the previous incidents in the same and different groups coded in the same category.* For example, as the analyst codes an incident in which a nurse responds to the potential "social loss" of a dying patient, he also compares this incident, before further coding, with others previously coded in the same category. Since coding qualitative data requires study of each incident, this comparison can often be based on memory. Usually there is no need to refer to the actual note on every previous incident for each comparison.

This constant comparison of the incidents very soon starts to generate theoretical properties of the category. The analyst starts thinking in terms of the full range of types or continua of the category, its dimensions, the conditions under which it is pronounced or minimized, its major consequences, its relation to other categories, and its other properties. For example, while constantly comparing incidents on how nurses respond to the social loss of dying patients, we realized that some patients are perceived as a high social loss and others as a low social loss, and that patient care tends to vary positively with degree of social loss. It was also apparent that some social attributes that nurses combine to establish a degree of social loss are seen immediately (age, ethnic group, social class), while some are learned after time is spent with the patient (occupational worth, marital, status, education). This observation led us to the realization that perceived social loss can change as new attributes of the patients are learned. It also became apparent, from studying the comparison groups, under what conditions (types of wards and hospitals) we would find clusters of patients with different degrees of social loss.

As categories and their properties emerge, the analyst will discover two kinds: those that he had constructed himself (such as "social loss" or "calculation" of social loss); and those that have been abstracted from the language of the research situation. (For example, "composure" was derived from nurses' statements like "I was afraid of losing my composure when the family started crying over their child.") As his theory develops, the analyst will notice that the concepts abstracted from the substantive situation will tend to be current labels in use for the actual processes and behaviors that are to be explained, while the concepts constructed by the analyst will tend to be the explanations.[6] For example, a nurse's perception of the social loss of a dying patient will affect (an explanation) how she maintains her composure (a behavior) in his presence.

After coding for a category perhaps three or four times, the analyst will find conflicts in the emphases of his thinking. He will be musing over theoretical notions and, at the same time, trying to concentrate on his study of the next incident, to determine the alternate ways by which it should be coded and compared. At this point, the second rule of the constant comparative method is: *stop coding and record a memo on your ideas.* This rule is designed to tap the initial freshness of the analyst's theoretical notions and to relieve the conflict in his thoughts. In doing so, the analyst should take as much time as necessary to reflect and carry his thinking to its most logical (grounded in the data, not speculative) conclusions. It is important to emphasize that for joint coding and analysis there can be no scheduled routine covering the amount to be coded per day, as there is in predesigned research. The analyst may spend hours on one page or he may code twenty pages in a half hour, depending on the relevance of the material, saturation of categories, emergence of new categories, stage of formulation of theory, and of course the mood of the analyst, since this method takes his personal sensitivity into consideration. These factors are in a continual process of change.

If one is working on a research team, it is also a good idea to discuss theoretical notions with one or more teammates. Teammates can help bring out points missed, add points they have run across in their own coding and data collection, and crosscheck his points. They, too, begin to compare the analyst's notions with their own ideas and knowledge of the data; this comparison generates additional theoretical ideas. With clearer ideas on the emerging theory systematically recorded, the analyst then returns to the data for more coding and constant comparison.

From the point of view of generating theory it is often useful to write memos on, as well as code, the copy of one's field notes. Memo writing on the field note provides an immediate illustration for an idea. Also, since an incident can be coded for several categories, this tactic forces the analyst to use an incident as an illustration only once, for the most important among the many properties of diverse categories that it indicates. He must look elsewhere in his notes for illustrations for his other properties and categories. This corrects the tendency to use the same illustration over and over for different properties.

The generation of theory requires that the analyst take apart the story within his data. Therefore when he rearranges his memos and field notes for writing up his theory, he sufficiently "fractures" his story at the same time that he saves apt illustrations for each idea (see Step 4). At just this point in his writing, breaking down and out of the story is necessary for clear integration of the theory.

2. *Integrating categories and their properties.* This process starts out in a small way; memos and possible conferences are short. But as the coding continues, the constant comparative units change from comparison of incident with incident to comparison of incident with properties of the category that resulted from initial comparisons of incidents. For example, in comparing incident with incident we discovered the property that nurses constantly recalculate a patient's social loss as they learn more about him. From then on, each incident bearing on "calculation" was compared with "accumulated knowledge on calculating" -- not with all other incidents involving calculation. Thus, once we found that age was the most important characteristic in calculating social loss, we could discern how a patient's age affected the nurses' recalculation of social loss as they found out more about his education. We found that education was most influential in calculations of the social loss of a middle-aged adult, since for a person of this age, education was considered to be of most social worth. This example also shows that constant comparison causes the accumulated knowledge pertaining to a property of the category to readily start to become integrated; that is, related in many different ways, resulting in a unified whole.

In addition, the diverse properties themselves start to become integrated. Thus, we soon found that the calculating and recalculating of social loss by nurses was related to their development of a social loss "story" about the patient. When asked about a dying patient, nurses would tell what amounted to a story about him. The ingredients of this story consisted of a continual balancing out of social loss factors as the nurses learned more about the patient. Both the calculus of social loss and the social loss story were related to the nurse's strategies for coping with the upsetting impact on her professional composure of, say, a dying patient with a high social loss (*e.g.,* a mother with two children). This example further shows that the category becomes integrated with other categories of analysis: the social loss of the dying patient is related to how nurses maintain professional composure while attending his dying.[7] Thus the theory develops, as different categories and their properties tend to become integrated through constant comparisons that force the analyst to make some related theoretical sense of each comparison.

If the data are collected by theoretical sampling at the same time that they are analyzed (as we suggest should be done), then integration of the theory is more likely to emerge by itself. By joint collection and analysis, the sociologist is tapping to the fullest extent the in vivo patterns of integration in the data itself; questions guide the collection of data to fill in gaps and to extend the theory -- and this also is an integrative strategy. Emergence of integration schemes also occurs in analyses that are separate from data collection, but more contrivance may be necessary when the data run thin and no more can be collected. (Other aspects of integration have been discussed in Chapter II.)

3. *Delimiting the theory.* As the theory develops, various delimiting features of the constant comparative method begin to curb what could otherwise become an overwhelming task. Delimiting occurs at two levels: the theory and the categories. First, the theory solidifies, in the sense that major modifications become fewer and fewer as the analyst compares the next incidents of a category to its properties. Later modifications are mainly on the order of clarifying the logic, taking out nonrelevant properties, integrating elaborating details of properties into the major outline of interrelated categories and -- most important -- reduction.

By reduction we mean that the analyst may discover underlying uniformities in the original set of categories or their properties, and can then formulate the theory with a smaller set of higher level concepts. This delimits its terminology and text. Here is an illustration which shows the integration of more details into the theory and some consequent reduction: We decided to elaborate our theory by adding detailed strategies used by the nurses to maintain professional composure while taking care of patients with varying degrees of social loss. We discovered that the rationales which nurses used, when talking among themselves, could all be considered "loss rationales." The underlying uniformity was that all these rationales indicated why the patient, given his degree of social loss, would, if he lived, now be socially worthless; in spite of the social loss, he would be better off dead. For example, he would have brain damage, or be in constant, unendurable pain, or have no chance for a normal life.

Through further reduction of terminology we were also discovering that our theory could be generalized so that it pertained to the care of all patients (not just dying ones) by all staff (not just nurses). On the level of formal theory, it could even be generalized as a theory of how the social values of professionals affect the distribution of their services to clients; for example, how they decide who among many waiting clients should next receive a service, and what calibre of service he should be given.

Thus, with reduction of terminology and consequent generalizing, forced by constant comparisons (some comparisons can at this point be based on the literature of other professional areas), the analyst starts to achieve two major requirements of theory: (1) *parsimony* of variables and formulation, and (2) *scope* in the applicability of the theory to a wide range of situations,[8] while keeping a close correspondence of theory and data.

The second level for delimiting the theory is a reduction in the original list of categories for coding. As the theory grows, becomes reduced, and increasingly works better for ordering a mass of qualitative data, the analyst becomes committed to it. His commitment now allows him to cut down the original list of categories for collecting and coding data, according to the present boundaries of his theory. In turn, his consideration, coding, and analyzing of incidents can become more select and focused. He can devote more time to the constant comparison of incidents clearly applicable to this smaller set of categories.

Another factor, which still further delimits the list of categories, is that they become *theoretically saturated.* After an analyst has coded incidents for the same category a number of times, he learns to see quickly whether or not the next applicable incident points to a new aspect. If yes, then the incident is coded and compared. If no, the incident is not coded, since it only adds bulk to the coded data and nothing to the theory.[9] For example, after we had established age as the base line for calculating social loss, no longer did we need to code incidents referring to age for calculating social loss. However, if we came across a case where age did not appear to be the base line (a negative case), the case was coded and then compared. In the case of an 85-year-old dying woman who was considered a great social loss, we discovered that her "wonderful personality" outweighed her age as the most important factor for calculating her social loss. In addition, the amount of data the analyst needs to code is considerably reduced when the data are obtained by theoretical sampling; thus he saves time in studying his data for coding.

Theoretical saturation of categories also can be employed as a strategy in coping with another problem: new categories will emerge after hundreds of pages of coding, and the question is whether or not to go back and re-code all previously coded pages. The answer for large studies is "no." The analyst should start to code for the new category where it emerges, and continue for a few hundred pages of coding, or until the remaining (or additionally collected) data have been coded, to see whether the new category has become theoretically saturated. If it has, then it is unnecessary to go back, either to the field or the notes, because theoretical saturation suggests that what has been missed will probably have little modifying effect on the theory. If the category does not saturate, then the analyst needs to go back and try to saturate it, provided it is central to the theory.

Theoretical saturation can help solve still another problem concerning categories. If the analyst has collected his own data, then from time to time he will remember other incidents that he observed or heard but did not record. What does he do now? If the unrecorded incident applies to an established category, after comparison it can either be ignored because the category is saturated; or, if it indicates a new property of the category, it can be added to the next memo and thus integrated into the theory. If the remembered incident generates a new category, both incident and category can be included in a memo directed toward their place in the theory. This incident alone may be enough data if the category is minor. However, if it becomes central to the theory, the memo becomes a directive for further coding of the field notes, and for returning to the field or library to collect more data.

The universe of data that the constant comparative method uses is based on the reduction of the theory and the delimitation and saturation of categories. Thus, the collected universe of data is first delimitated and then, if necessary, carefully extended by a return to data collection according to the requirements of theoretical sampling. Research resources are economized by this theoretical delimiting of the possible universe of data, since working within limits forces the analyst to spend his time and effort only on data relevant to his categories. In large field studies, with long lists of possibly useful categories and thousands of pages of notes embodying thousands of incidents, each of which could be coded a multitude of ways, theoretical criteria are very necessary for paring down an otherwise monstrous task to fit the available resources of personnel, time, and money.

Without theoretical criteria, delimiting a universe of collected data, if done at all, can become very arbitrary and less likely to yield an integrated product; the analyst is also more likely to waste time on what may later prove to be irrelevant incidents and categories.

4. *Writing theory*. At this stage in the process of qualitative analysis, the analyst possesses coded data, a series of memos, and a theory. The discussions in his memos provide the content behind the categories, which become the major themes of the theory later presented in papers or books. For example, the major themes (section titles) for our paper on social loss were "calculating social loss," "the patient's social loss story," and "the impact of social loss on the nurse's professional composure."

When the researcher is convinced that his analytic framework forms a systematic substantive theory, that it is a reasonably accurate statement of the matters studied, and that it is couched in a form that others going into the same field could use -- then he can publish his results with confidence. To start writing one's theory, it is first necessary to collate the memos on each category, which is easily accomplished since the memos have been written about categories. Thus, we brought together all memos on calculating social loss for summarizing and, perhaps, further analyzing before writing about it. One can return to the coded data when necessary to validate a suggested point, pinpoint data behind a hypothesis or gaps in the theory, and provide illustrations.[10]

PROPERTIES OF THE THEORY

Using the constant comparative method makes probable the achievement of a complex theory that corresponds closely to the data, since the constant comparisons force the analyst to consider much diversity in the data. By *diversity* we mean that each incident is compared with other incidents, or with properties of a category, in terms of as many similarities and differences as possible. This mode of comparing is in contrast to coding for crude proofs; such coding only establishes whether an incident indicates the few properties of the category that are being counted.

The constant comparison of incidents in this manner tends to result in the creation of a "developmental" theory.[11] Although this method can also be used to generate static theories, it especially facilitates the generation of theories of process, sequence, and change pertaining to organizations, positions, and social interaction. But whether the theory itself is static or developmental, its generation, by this method and by theoretical sampling, is continually in process. In comparing incidents, the analyst learns to see his categories in terms of both their internal development and their changing relations to other categories. For example, as the nurse learns more about the patient, her calculations of social loss change; and these recalculations change her social loss stories, her loss rationales and her care of the patient.

This is an inductive method of theory development. To make theoretical sense of so much diversity in his data, the analyst is forced to develop ideas on a level of generality higher in conceptual abstraction than the qualitative material being analyzed. He is forced to bring out underlying uniformities and diversities, and to use more abstract concepts to account for differences in the data. To master his data, he is forced to engage in reduction of terminology. If the analyst starts with raw data, he will end up initially with a substantive theory: a theory for the substantive area on which he has done research (for example, patient care or gang behavior). If he starts with the findings drawn from many studies pertaining to an abstract sociological category, he will end up with a formal theory pertaining to a conceptual area (such as stigma, deviance, lower class, status congruency, organizational careers, or reference groups).[12] To be sure, as we described in Chapter IV, the level of generality of a substantive theory can be raised to a formal theory. (Our theory of dying patients' social loss could be raised to the level of how professional people give service to clients according to their respective social value.) This move to formal theory requires additional analysis of one's substantive theory, and the analyst should, as stated in the previous chapter, include material from other studies with the same formal theoretical import, however diverse their substantive content.[13] The point is that the analyst should be aware of the level of generality from which he starts in relation to the level at which he wishes to end.

The constant comparative method can yield either discussional or propositional theory. The analyst may wish to cover many properties of a category in his discussion or to write formal propositions about a category. The former type of presentation is often sufficiently useful at the exploratory stage of theory development, and can easily be translated into propositions by the reader if he requires a formal hypothesis. For example, two related categories of dying are the patient's social loss and the amount of attention he receives from nurses. This can easily be restated as a proposition: patients considered a high social loss, as compared with those considered a low social loss, will tend to receive more attention from nurses.

REFERENCES

* We wish to thank the editors of *Social Problems* for permission to publish this paper as Chapter V. See Barney G. Glaser, *Social Problems*, 12 (1965), pp. 436-45.

1. Howard S. Becker and Blanche Geer, "The Analysis of Qualitative Field Data" in Richard N. Adams and Jack J. Preiss (Eds.), *Human Organization Research* (Homewood, Ill.: Dorsey Press, Inc., 1960), pp. 279-89. See also Howard S. Becker, "Problems of Inference and Proof in Participant Observation," *American Sociological Review*, (December, 1958), pp. 652-60; and Bernard Berelson, *Content Analysis* (Glencoe, Ill.: Free Press, 1952), Chapter III, and p. 16.

2. Constantly redesigning the analysis is a well-known normal tendency in qualitative research (no matter what the approach to analysis), which occurs throughout the whole research experience from initial data collection through coding to final analysis and writing. The tendency has been noted in Becker and Geer, *op. cit.*, p. 270, Berelson, *op. cit.*, p. 125; and for an excellent example of how it goes on, see Robert K. Merton, *Social Theory and Social Structure* (New York: Free Press of Glencoe, 1957), pp. 390-92. However, this tendency may have to be suppressed in favor of the purpose of the first approach; but in the second approach and the approach presented here, the tendency is used purposefully as an analytic strategy.

3. Our other purpose in presenting the constant comparative method may be indicated by a direct quotation from Robert K. Merton -- a statement he made in connection with his own qualitative analysis of locals and cosmopolitans as community influentials: "This part of our report, then, is a bid to the sociological fraternity for the practice of incorporating in publications a detailed account of the ways in which qualitative analyses *actually* developed. Only when a considerable body of such reports are available will it be possible to *codify* methods of qualitative analysis with something of the clarity with which quantitative methods have been articulated." *Op. cit.*, p. 390. This is, of course, also the basic position of Paul F. Lazarsfeld. See Allen H. Barton and Paul F.

Lazarsfeld, "Some Functions of Qualitative Analysis in Social Research," in Seymour M. Lipset and Neil J. Smelser (Eds.), *Sociology: the Progress of a Decade* (Englewood Cliffs, N.J.: Prentice-Hall, 1961). It is the position that has stimulated the work of Becker and Geer, and of Berelson, cited in Footnote 1.

4. See Alfred R. Lindesmith, *Opiate Addiction* (Bloomington: Principia, 1947), pp. 12-14; Donald R. Cressey, *Other People's Money* (New York: Free Press of Glencoe, 1953), p. 16 and *passim*; and Florian Znaniecki, *The Method of Sociology* (New York: Farrar and Rinehart, 1934), pp. 249-331.

5. Illustrations will refer to Barney G. Glaser and Anselm L. Strauss, "The Social Loss of Dying Patients," *American Journal of Nursing*, 64 (June, 1964), pp. 119-121.

6. Thus we have studies of delinquency, justice, "becoming," stigma, consultation, consolation, contraception, etc.; these usually become the variables or processes to be described and explained.

7. See Glaser and Strauss, "Awareness and the Nurse's Composure," in Chapter 13 in *Awareness of Dying* (Chicago: Aldine Publishing Co., 1965).

8. Merton, *op. cit.*, p. 260.

9. If the analyst's purpose, besides developing theory, is also to count incidents for a category to establish provisional proofs, then he must code the incident. Furthermore, Merton has made the additional point, in correspondence, that to count for establishing provisional proofs may also feed back to developing the theory, since frequency and cross-tabulation of frequencies can also generate new theoretical ideas. See Berelson on the conditions under which one can justify time-consuming, careful counting; *op. cit.*, pp. 128-34. See Becker and Geer for a new method of counting the frequency of incidents; *op. cit.*, pp. 283-87.

10. On "pinpointing" see Anselm Strauss, Leonard Schatzman, Rue Bucher, Danuta Ehrlich and Melvin Shabshin, *Psychiatric Ideologies and Institutions* (New York: Free Press of Glencoe, 1964), Chapter 2, "Logic, Techniques and Strategies of Team Fieldwork."

11. Recent calls for more developmental, as opposed to static, theories have been made by Wilbert Moore, "Predicting Discontinuities in Social Change," *American Sociological Review* 29 (1964), p. 322; Howard S. Becker, *Outsiders* (New York: Free Press of Glencoe, 1962), pp. 22-25;

and Barney G. Glaser and Anselm Strauss, "Awareness Contexts and Social Interaction," *op. cit.*

12. For an example, see Barney G. Glaser, *Organizational Careers* (Chicago: Aldine Publishing Co., 1967).

13. "...the development of any one of these coherent analytic perspectives is not likely to come from those who restrict their interest exclusively to one substantive area." From Erving Goffman, *Stigma: Notes on the Management of Spoiled Identity* (Englewood Cliffs, N.J.: Prentice-Hall, 1963), p. 147. See also Reinhard Bendix, "Concepts and Generalizations in Comparative Sociological Studies," *American Sociological Review*, 28 (1963), pp. 532-39.

Reprinted from *Discovery of Grounded Theory*, Aldine Publishing Co., New York, 1967.

THEORETICAL ELABORATION OF QUANTITATIVE DATA

Barney G. Glaser PhD

Quantitative data is so closely associated with the current emphasis on verification that its possibilities for generating theory have been left vastly underdeveloped. However, in some of our best monographs discovery cannot be stopped; it breaks through both verifications and preconceived conceptual schemes to provide us with very interesting and important theory.[1] Yet, since the authors are still so focused on testing provisionally what they have discovered, their work is mostly written in the hedging rhetoric of verification. The result is that their statements present tests as merely "plausible suggestions". The plausibly suggested test should not be construed with our goal of the purposeful generating and suggesting of theory. The generating capacities of these sociologists and the richness of their research are therefore not given the fullest impetus.

Typically, discovery made through quantitative data is treated only as a byproduct of the "main work" - making accurate descriptions and verifications. When discovery forces itself on an analyst, he then writes his induced hypotheses as if they had been thought up before the data were collected, so that they will seem to satisfy the logical requirements of verification.[2] Purposeful generation of grounded theory is found usually, if at all, in short papers where a single carefully worked-out explanation of a hypothesis is offered, after an analytic wrestle between the rhetoric of tentative qualification and alternative explanations and the carefully researched, accurate data - a slight beginning for an adequate theory.

When the sociologist consciously starts out to suggest a theory plausibly, rather than test it provisionally, then he can relax many rules for obtaining evidence and verifications that would otherwise limit, stultify or squelch the generation of theory. He must give himself this freedom in the flexible use of quantitative data or he will not be able to generate theory that is adequate (as we have discussed it) in terms of sampling, saturation, integration, density of property development, and so forth. In taking this freedom he must be clear about the rules he is releasing (which could not be relaxed for purposes of accuracy and verifications) and he should explain his position to readers. *The freedom and flexibility that we claim for generating theory from quantitative data will lead to new strategies and styles of quantitative analysis, with their own rules yet to be discovered.* And these new styles of analysis will bring out the richness of quantitative data that is seen only implicitly while the focus remains on verification. For example, in verification studies cross-tabulations of quantitative variables continually and inadvertently lead to discoveries of new social patterns and new hypotheses, but are often ignored as *not* being the purpose of the research.

In this chapter we shall present one new strategy of quantitative analysis that facilitates the generation of theory from quantitative data. It is a variation of Lazarsfeld's elaboration analysis of survey data.[3] In our presentation we shall indicate how, at strategic points, the rigorous rules for accuracy of evidence and verification can be relaxed in order to further the generation of theory. To be sure, there are many styles of quantitative analysis with their own rules. Our focus here is an illustration of how these numerous other styles can also be flexibly adapted to generating theory. However, we do touch on some existing general rules of quantitative analysis (e.g., indexing and tests of significance); the way they are relaxed for purposes of generating theory could apply to many styles of analysis. And we shall also develop some general rules governing how to relax the usual rigor of quantitative analysis so as to facilitate the generation of theory.

The organization of this chapter is based on the successive stages of building up to theory from quantitative data. We discuss in turn the most frequent source of data used for generating theory, how one indicates his categories and properties with the data, how one discovers hypotheses with his conceptual indices, and how the hypotheses are then theoretically elaborated. In an appendix to this chapter we provide examples of theoretical elaboration. For some longer examples of certain specific points, we have referred the reader to other literature.

SECONDARY ANALYSIS OF QUANTITATIVE DATA

The sociologist whose purpose is to generate theory may, of course, collect his own survey data, but, for several reasons, he is more likely to analyze previously collected data - called secondary analysis. Surveys are usually financed for providing large-scale descriptions of current populations; and the sociologist whose interest is in theory may not wish to be involved in this part of a study, for it takes considerable time and concentration that might otherwise be used for theoretical analysis. It is easier to analyze previously collected data, for then his only responsibility is to generate theory. Sometimes, of course, after the large-scale descriptions have been accomplished, the director of the study returns to his data to engage in secondary analysis for generating a theory on an idea initially stimulated by the earlier descriptive phase.

Generating theory is a more limited, narrowly focused effort (even though the theoretical concept may be very general) than presenting the broad description of a population given by the total survey. The description may involve thousands of questionnaire items, while the theoretical analysis only requires consideration of a few hundred.[4] Therefore, the tasks of description and of analysis can conflict unless the sociologist has adequate money and time (a likelihood only for the study director and a few assistants). Theoretical analysis of quantitative data is, of course, an opportunity to be taken by many sociologists other than study directors or their assistants,[5] and so most generation of theory from quantitative data will be based on secondary analysis.

Comparative analysis requires secondary analysis when populations from several different studies are compared, such as different nations or factories. Comparative analysis of groups internal to one study does not require secondary analysis, but again it often is.

Trivial data, such as found in market surveys on consumption of products, can also have very important theoretical relevance. For example, from a study of meat consumption one can gain knowledge about the life styles of social classes. Secondary analysis is a necessity in such cases because sociologists with a theoretical bent do not usually collect such data.

When using secondary analysis of quantitative data for generating theory, one point must be kept clear. Because of the heavy emphasis on accurate evidence and verification of hypotheses, the analyst usually wishes to start out with the facts as facts. One limitation of secondary analysis is the difficulty of pinning down the accuracy of findings in what is necessarily a secondhand view - often without much knowledge of collection procedures and meaning of data. Also, since populations are in constant change, we have no way of knowing whether a survey accomplished some years ago for other purposes still applies meaningfully to the specific population.

This problem of accuracy is not as important for generating theory about a type of social unit as it is for describing a particular social unit or verifying a hypothesis. What are relevant for theory are the general categories and properties and the general relations between them that emerge from the data. These can be applied to many current situations and locations as very relevant concepts and as hypotheses of interest to sociologists and laymen, regardless of whether the specific descriptions yielded by the data are currently accurate for the research population. Secondary analysis, then, is uniquely well suited for the generation of theory but is often severely limited for description and verification - for which it is still mostly used, with a typical preamble about "limitations."

Another limitation of secondary analysis that makes its use in description and verification questionable, but does not affect the generation of theory, is the representativeness of the population studied. Accuracy is, of course, crucial in description and verification, and the sample must therefore be carefully chosen by some form of random sampling. Secondary analysis of a random sample chosen for other reasons may introduce systematic and random biases into the secondary study, making claims to accuracy questionable. Indeed, it is often difficult to ascertain from previously collected data what kind of sample was taken for what purpose, since record may have been destroyed, lost, misplaced or made unavailable. Many important questions concerning the sampling become unanswerable, such as how many people did not respond, how many cards were lost, and how many questionnaires were not usable. But when theory is the purpose (as stated in Chapter II), there are two reasons why the representativeness of the sample is not an issue. First, the direction of a relationship used to suggest a hypothesis is assumed to exist until disproved, in both biased and unbiased populations; and, second, theoretical (not statistical) sampling guides the choosing and handling of the data.

What is more important for generating theory is the scope of the population, which can be increased when the analyst is less concerned about representativeness. Representativeness usually requires some purification of the original sample to obtain a clear-cut population for a smaller study; the sociologist takes for his analysis carefully stratified samples from a larger survey sample. This tactic cuts down on scope by weeding out the possible (but never proven) "contaminating" influences of some respondents. For example, one may wish to take all scientists out of a national survey for study, but then, if he purifies the group by weeding out all but the PhD's, he loses the population scope that could have been afforded by keeping the scientists with the MD's, MS's, and BS's.

CONCEPTS AND INDICES

In the last decade, the flexible use of concepts and their empirical indices in quantitative analysis has been advanced greatly by Lazarsfeld. A number of publications[6] have carried his work on the "process by which concepts are translated into empirical indices." We wish to mention here only a few general points and urge the reader to study the footnoted references for the general argument and the examples.

When the discovery and generation of theory is the goal of a survey analysis, "crude" or "general duty" indices (as described in detail by Lazarsfeld) suffice to indicate the concepts of the theory and to establish general relationships between them, which in turn become the basis for suggesting hypotheses for the emerging theory. Similar crude indices, usually a single questionnaire item or a simple summation index of two to six items, are often interchangeable when based on similar, but different indicators. "Interchangeability of indices," as Lazarsfeld demonstrates, means that we obtain the same findings in cross-tabulations with other variables when two indices of the same category are based on reasonably similar but different sets of indicators. Therefore, the analyst does not have to be certain that he has the most accurate index, judged on the basis of either precision or the best set of indicators.

Crude indices, when correlated with other variables, also yield the same relationships in direction as the more precise indices yielded by factor analysis, latent structure analysis, a Guttman scale, or elaborate scales involving dozens of items. Since for generating theory we are only looking for general relationships of direction - appositive or negative relation between concepts, and not either precise measurement of each person in the study or exact magnitudes of relationship - it is easier, faster, and considerably more economical to use the crude index. Even when crude indices result in obvious misclassification of some cases, they still yield the information necessary for generating a grounded theory.[7]

Crude indices of categories or properties can also be based on either a single questionnaire item or a series of items summed into an index. However, for indices of the core categories, it is perhaps preferable to use two to six item summation indices, since the category will usually be based on at least two dimensions and each should be indicated by at least one item. Further, crude indices need only be dichotomized to obtain comparative groups, not cut into several groups. Whether an index is cut in two, three, or four groups, the same general relation will appear when it is cross-tabulated with another variable, provided that the cutting point is statistically established with criterion variables as a meaningful break in the data.[8] Dichotomizing an index is financially economical and saves cases for cross-tabulation when the number of cases is small and when the analyst engages in the multivariate analysis of three or more variables. Indeed, even if a trichotomous index is used, the analyst, except in cases of exceptional patterns, still ends up talking about the general positive or negative relation between two variables.

When generating theory, validation of a core index - demonstrating that the index measures the concept to a sufficient probable degree - need not be a special operation in which a theoretically relevant relation between two variables is sacrificed from the substance of the analysis itself to prove the validity of the argument, as is typically necessary in verifications.[9] If the index "works" - that is, if it is consistently related to a whole series of variables that, when put together, yield an integrated theory - this is validation enough of a core index. Integration of the theory is, in fact, a more trustworthy validation of an index than the standard method of merely showing that an obvious relationship exists between the index and another questionnaire item, and that therefore the index must measure what it is supposed to measure.[10]

For example, the core index of "professional recognition" in *Organizational Scientists* (by Barney G. Glaser) could easily have been validated by showing that professional recognition is positively related to receiving promotions, but instead the whole book shows the validity of the index by the way the substantive theory on scientists' organizational careers is integrated.[11] In fact, the theory becomes integrated around the core index of recognition because of the multiple relationships with that index, indicating that the theory works - it provides relevant explanations and consequences of organizational careers. Lazarsfeld's methods for specifying concepts and for selecting sub-sets of items to construct indices of the concepts are excellent for ensuring that categories will fit the data and will work or be relevant. This fulfillment of the two major requirements of grounded theory explains why the index becomes validated by the whole theory.

We make these statements in the service of generating theory. If the analyst wishes to describe or verify, these issues must be argued on different grounds, because his problems of precision, dichotomization, and validation of indices are different. The analyst must therefore be clear about his purpose. However, most survey analysts are *not* clear, because Lazarsfeld never has made the distinction between the purpose of generation and those of verification and/or description with accurate findings. He writes not of theory but of "empirical propositions" and "statistical relations". We see clearly how his work on concepts and indices is valuable for generating theory through conceptual indices and general relations between them. But others who wish to discover "facts" and verify hypotheses, especially by secondary analysis, must argue for Lazarsfeld' methods on their own. Indeed, there are many sociologists who use his methods and stay on the empirical level of description or harp on their findings in the verification rhetoric, even when attempting to suggest theoretical hypotheses.

The survey analyst chooses his categories in the same manner as the researcher doing qualitative analysis. An initial scheme of concepts and hypotheses, usually applied to quantitative data in attempting verifications, is not needed. Concepts whose fit will be emergent are found in previous descriptive or qualitative data on the same subject. Also, categories and properties emerge during the collecting and analyzing of quantitative data as readily as they do with qualitative. It must be remembered that qualitative data suggesting a category may also be used as another slice of data for the quantitative analysis.

The theoretical relevance of the concept is soon demonstrated by whether or not its index actually works in a multitude of cross-tabulations. If the index does not work, then the analyst should question the theoretical relevance of his concept before he questions the method of index formation. In quantitative analysis it is typical to observe a non-emergent category derived from a logic-deductive theory (say, on self-image, role conflict, or status congruency), forcibly indexed - and then found to be related to nothing of theoretical relevance. The analyst then finds fault with the precision of the method of index formation, rather than with the relevance of a category derived from an ungrounded theory, since he seldom questions his faith in the logic-deductive theorist when the latter is a charismatic figure in the profession Much survey analysis fails for this reason, but we hear of failures only through our friends; tact prevents citing examples.

It is possible to index any category, but while, with emergent categories,the analyst is almost sure to discover many relations between indices, "ought" categories from ungrounded theories are a risk. To stay on the empirical level, using no theoretical categories, is one alternative to taking the chance of directing theoretical research through logically deduced categories such as "anomie" or "authority relations." Yet people who do not trust logic-deductive theory, but who wish to do theoretical work, could very safely attempt discovery of grounded theory as another alternative.

DISCOVERING HYPOTHESES

In generating theory, preconceived hypotheses are not necessary for correlating or cross-tabulating two variables (called runs) with indices of core categories and properties. Indeed, the rule for generation of theory is *not* to have any pre-set or valued hypotheses, but to maintain a sensitivity to all possible theoretical relevances among the hundreds of possible runs afforded by large surveys. In contrast, necessarily preconceived hypotheses direct exactly what two variable correlations to use as tests in verificational studies. Indeed, verificational rules state that data should be collected for tests *after* the hypothesis has been formulated - though they seldom are. For generating theory the data can be collected at *any time*. As we have said, it is usually collected beforehand because most discovery and generation is a secondary analysis of data collected for other purposes, and because the hypotheses come after the analysis - they are suggested from findings, not tested with them.

In order to saturate all possible findings for suggesting hypotheses, the analyst may take his core concepts and run them with literally *every* other questionnaire item in the survey that seems remotely relevant to his area of interest.[12] At this point the theory of the core indices starts to emerge.

TABLE 1

COSMOPOLITAN ORIENTATION

Motivation to Advance Knowledge

	High	Low	Difference
Personal contacts outside organization are very important			

as sources of scientific informat	56%	35%	+21%
	High	Low	Difference
If had to, would prefer to move to a university	72%	43%	+21%
Belonging to an organization with prestige in the scientific world is of the utmost importance	40%	21%	+19%
Very strong involvement with close professional work associates	40%	26%	+14%
Very strong sense of belonging to section (principal research work group)	44%	27%	+17%
Basis research, as a result of clinical program, is likely to			
- benefit	42%	56%	-14%
- suffer	40%	29%	+11%
Those who would worry about a substantial emphasis on applied as well as basic research	38%	19%	+19%
Base for each per cent	(186)	(146)	

LOCAL ORIENTATION

	Motivation to Advance Knowledge		
	High	Low	Difference
Having an important job in the organization is of the utmost importance	30%	12%	+18%
Association with high-level			

persons having important responsibilities is of the utmost or considerable importance	55%	42%	+13%
Having a very strong sense of belonging to the organization	31%	19%	+12%
Interested in a higher level job in the organization which entails stimulating or advising subordinate professionals about their work	77%	67%	+10%
Interested in a higher level job entailing administrative planning or coordination	68%	56%	+12%
Base for each per cent	(186)	(146)	

Clusters of items are discovered as associated with the index. Indeed, this strategy (an unbelievable "sin" in verificational studies) virtually discovers theory for the analyst by providing associations to be conceptualized and analyzed. He induces a theory simply from the general relationships he has found. He need not concern himself with theoretical explanations of what he has found in comparison with what he was supposed to find, as is done in verificational studies.

One comparative strategy for generating theory from findings is to compare clusters of relationships within the context of the emerging theory. For example, in Table I we see that "motivation to advance knowledge" (a crude index) is consistently related to two clusters of items, those indicating a cosmopolitan orientation - toward the profession - and those indicating a local orientation - toward their research organization. Thus we discover and suggest theoretically that highly motivated scientists within research organizations devoted to basic research (a structural condition) possess the property of being local-cosmopolitans.[13] Table II bears out the suggested hypothesis,

TABLE II

Consecutive addition of hours perweek spent on various work activities

	Motivation to Advance Knowledge		
	High	Low	Difference
21 or more hours: own research	76%	61%	+15%
36 or more hours: plus other professional productive work	63%	49%	+14%
41 or more hours: plus nonproductive professional work	69%	48%	+21%
51 or more hours: plus other organization activities for total work week	55%	48%	+17%
Base for each per cent	(186)	(146)	

by showing that in their work activities highly motivated scientists are both local and cosmopolitan oriented: as more working hours and activities are added to the work week, the highly motivated scientists spend more time on both professional and organizational activities.

CONSISTENCY INDICES

These two variable runs showing clusters of associations are analyzed comparatively in two ways: *within* and *between* consistency indices. A consistency index is a list of single questionnaire items which all indicate the same category, such as cosmopolitan, and all relate separately to the core index in the

TABLE III.

Percentage of Researchers with High Motivation as Related to Their Prievious Experience

Background Experience	Previous Experience %	No Previous Experience %	Difference %
Emphasis on advance of knowledge:			
University employment	65	45	+20
	(180)°	(152)	
Research and teaching	61	42	+19
	(247)	(85)	
Ph.D. Education	62	40	+22
	(164)	(58)''	
		55	
		(110)#	
Emphasis on application of knowledge:			
Medical or clinical practice	58	55	+3
	(244)	(88)	
Hospitals	57	55	+2
	(111)	(121)	
Industry	58	56	+2
	(78)	(254)	
Private practice or business	58	56	+2
	(36)	(296)	

Government agencies	48	61	-13
	(117)	(215)	
U.S. Public Health	47	58	-11
Service	(68)	(264)	

° Figures in parenthesis indicate number of cases.

'' Education less than doctorate.

M.D.

same consistent direction. The indicators are not added together first and then related to the core index, as in summation indices Summation indices are best for the categories to which a core index is to be related. This strategy allows the analyst to see how the core concept relates to each individual indicator of another category. If inconsistencies in associations between the consistency index and the core index occur for what appeared to be substantively consistent indicators, they are quickly caught and compared for the underlying meaning of the differences within the set of indicators and the emerging theory.

For example, in Table III we see that *within* the consistency index of applied experience, high motivation to advance knowledge (not to apply it) is not related to previous experiences in private or group practice, hospitals or industry.[14] These particular applied experiences, then, we theoretically suggest, neither engender nor inhibit motivation to advance knowledge. But the problem remains: why is motivation negatively related to applied experience in government agencies and the U.S. Public Health Service, or (theoretically) why do these experiences inhibit or reduce motivation to advance knowledge? We suggest that it is because these two experiences, in contrast to the first four, imply routine service in the application of knowledge.

If all the items on "experience in application of knowledge experiences" had been combined first in a summation index, and then related to motivation, these inconsistent comparisons of groups within the consistency index (from which we discovered strategic structural conditions varying the core category) would have been missed; hence, so would an important hypothesis of the theory: the effect of "routine" applications on the scientist' motivation to advance knowledge. The property of "routine application" would have been missed had the analyst simply constructed a summation index, since all the items on applied experience would have seemed internally consistent when tested - all items positively related to each other. Therefore there would have been no suspicion that correlating applied experience index with another index was actually summing inconsistencies.

Comparisons *between* different consistency indices are also used as a strategy of comparative analysis. We saw in Table I that, since high motivation is positively associated with both a local and cosmopolitan orientation, the analyst can suggest, on the basis of this comparison between consistency indices that scientists highly motivated in research are local-cosmopolitans in a basic research organization.

These two comparative strategies - comparing within and between consistency indices associated with a summation index - occur in three or more variable associations also; but then the analyst is using additional analytic strategies, which we discuss in the next section. Also, once a detailed analysis of an association with a consistency index is accomplished, then the consistency index can be summed and dichotomized for further analyses with three or more variables. These analyses are more

TABLE IV. RELATION OF RECOGNITION TO SCIENCE EXPERIENCE FOR RESEARCH WORKERS WITH HIGH MOTIVATION

Science Experience	High Recognition	Low Recognition	Difference
	%	%	%
Full	76	69	+7
	(46)°	(52)	
Some	68	42	+26
	(75)	(99)	
None	44	35	+9
	(23)	(37)	

° Figures in parenthesis indicate the number of cases.

complicated, requiring reduction of details and the saving of cases for cross-tabulation. For example, the first part of Table III shows motivation to advance knowledge related to a consistency index on one kind of previous experience in science - experience emphasizing advancement of knowledge. Table IV shows the summation index of previous experience in science related to two other summation indices - motivation to advance knowledge and professional recognition - for the theoretical purpose of suggesting hypotheses bearing on the interaction between the three indices.

TEST OF SIGNIFICANCE

Statistical tests of significance of an association between variables are not necessary when the discovered associations between indices are used for suggesting hypotheses. Selvin[15] has argued that this rule should be relaxed for *all* survey analysis, but he can take this stand only because he has not made the distinction between the generating and the verifying or describing purposes of research. He questions whether these tests are appropriate with survey data, since the statistical assumptions necessary to use them cannot be met with such data and also are ineptly applied according to general sociological theory. His critics, however, seem to be more concerned with keeping the tests of significance to ascertain accuracy of evidence used for verification and description.[16] We wish to stay clear of this controversy because we are making an argument concerned only with these tests in relation to the generation of theory.

Testing the statistical significance of an association between indices presents a strong barrier to the generation of theory while doing nothing to help it, since the resulting accuracy (if on can actually trust the test) is not crucial. These tests direct attention away from theoretically interesting relationships that are not of sufficient magnitude to be statistically significant. The analyst usually does not think of the associations as a grounded foundation for an hypothesis, although weak associations may be highly theoretically relevant. Also, the test, not the relationship, may be weak.

Believing that he has no findings relevant for generating theory, the analyst also usually neglects to ask what the partial relationships look like under several conditions. It is easy to forget that partials may be statistically significant even if the general relationship is not, because the partials can cancel themselves out. "Canceling out" means that the relationship may be positive under one condition and negative under another; so that when combined the partial relationships cancel themselves out to result in a weak general association. However, it is theoretically very relevant and interesting to be able to say how conditions minimize, maximize, or cancel out a relationship. Also, even if partials are weak, the theoretical relevance of a weak relationship between two indices may be the weakness itself.

Believing in tests of significance can also dissuade one from trusting consistent but weak relationships within and between consistency indices. Yet consistency validates the merit of relationships when it comes to the plausible reasoning required in a credible theoretical analysis.[17] And, as just noted, whether the level of the relationship is zero, weak, or strong, it may, if relevant, be grist for the theory.

A belief in tests of significance can also, in the process, direct one's attention away from theoretical relevance of content toward confusing statistical significance with theoretical significance, and a statistical method labeled "analysis" with theoretical analysis. Merely being statistically significant does not mean that a relationship is or should be of theoretical relevance. Such relevance depends on the meaning of the association as it relates to the theory. Also, the statistical analysis methods (for example, "factor analysis," or "analysis of variance") are not theoretical analyses. They are merely techniques for arriving at a type of fact. It is still up to the analyst to discover and analyze the theoretical relevances of these facts. In sum, the basic criterion for generating theory is theoretical relevance, and the analyst should sample his quantitative findings on this basis.

In place of making tests of significance, the sociologist can establish working rules to fit his particular situation. For example, two rules for establishing an acceptable percentage-difference level are not to consider any relationship of, say, less than 10 per cent difference; or any relationship in which three people are changing their minds or being misclassified would change the percentage to below an established level. These levels change with the number of cases used, smaller numbers of cases requiring a higher percentage-difference level. Selvin has also developed an internal replication procedure for establishing the possibility that a relationship exists.[18]

Standing by the rules that he may have initially established for his research is pertinent only to the beginning phases of generating theory. When the analyst has achieved theoretical relevance with his data, consistency arises in percentage-difference levels as well as in content, and he will readily learn to understand when and why a lower difference is relevant as well as a higher one. The absence of a relationship becomes just as important as an increase above the consistent percentage level, for any degree of association (or lack of it) may be part of the theory. For example, in Table III the relationship of motivation to previous experience varies at consistent percentage-difference levels-positive (20 per cent) to zero (2 per cent) to negative)-12 per cent) - thus theoretically indicating that these levels are engendered by experiences emphasizing basic research, unaffected by those experiences emphasizing applied research, and inhibited by experiences involving routine service in applied research. In Table V, a consistent percentage-difference

TABLE V. EFFECT OF RECOGNITION ON SCIENTISTS' SATISFACTION WITH DIVERSE ORGANIZATIONAL PERSONNEL°

	Organizational Position of Scientists		
	Junior	Senior	Supervisor
Assisting personnel			
Very and fairly satisfied	+10%	+5%	+11%
Scientific personnel			
Very satisfied	+16%	+5%	+22%
Leadership			
Very satisfied	+28%	+26%	+12%
Fairly satisfied	-11	+11	+16
Institute director			
Very competent	+10%	+7%	+28%
Fairly competent	+7	+2	...

°This is a table of differences accounted for by high compared to low recognition.

level of 10 to 16 per cent shows in comparative relief the theoretical relevance of the stronger and weaker relationships as conditions varying the effect of recognition on satisfaction with organizational personnel.[19]

LIBERTIES IN PRESENTATION OF DATA

When quantitative data are reported in verificational and descriptive studies, typically each association is given in table form with a technically exact discussion of it; and then the finding is qualified by tentative statements and alternative explanations or interpretations. This style of presentation need not be used in generating theory, nor, in fact, could it be used. The multitude of relationships on which grounded theory is based is so large that this style applied to each relationship would make the report of the theory unreadable - too long, cumbersome, and slow-moving - to colleagues and quite inaccessible to laymen. It is particularly important that both colleagues and laymen readily understand the theory,[20] since quantitative data are usually not as interesting to read as qualitative, and do not carry the reader along as easily. Therefore, the analyst must take some liberties both in presenting tables and in making statements about them. Needless to say, the liberties in presentation should not in any way change the data upon which the theory is based; it is just that for generating theory not all data must be presented and stated in exact detail. Since the possibilities are great, each analyst must decide on various liberties according to his particular directions of effort.

Let us consider here a few general liberties of presentation. Unlike Tables I through IV, Table V is a table of percentage difference. The proportions that were compared to arrive at the differences are left out, since they were not necessary for the theoretical analysis. If it is necessary to know about a particular set of proportions, they should be mentioned in text. However, the focus of the analysis in this table was on comparing percentage differences for indicating direction and magnitude of many relationships: that is, differences in satisfaction with organizational personnel accounted for by the high and low recognition achieved by scientists at different stages of their organizational careers. Both the direction and magnitude of these relationships were important for the analysis; if only direction of relationship had been important, the table could have been further simplified by leaving out numbers and using only plus and minus signs. These flexible renditions of quantitative evidence are in the service of generating theory. No information is lost, distorted, or purposely concealed. It is just that only enough information is presented to show, in the simplest possible manner, the grounded basis of the emerging theory. Verification requires a more detailed rendition of the data - showing all N's, sub-N's and compared high and low percentages - so that the reader can verify the verification for himself.

Because of the overabundance of separate associations necessary in generating theory (literally hundreds, in contrast to the few necessary in verificational studies), another general liberty may be taken in presenting tables, particularly two variable tables. Unless a whole configuration of consistency indices are shown together in a table for visual comparisons, it is enough to state in the written text two variable associations in their direction and (if necessary) magnitude; presenting a table would be repetitious. When theoretically necessary, proportions and N's can be provided in a footnote.

While verificational studies require exactitude, statements about associations can be more flexibly written when theory is the goal. For example, "more successful investigators have satisfactory research facilities provided to them as a reward by the organization" is a statement that assumes the reader understands that three liberties have been taken with this reporting of a two-variable table. First, the "successful" investigators have been *compared* with less successful investigators - the statement is comparative. Second, "more" means *proportionately* more - the comparison is relative, not absolute. And third, that the organization provides these research facilities as rewards to the successful investigators is a theoretical *inference* from the finding that they simply have more satisfactory research facilities than the less successful investigators. Such a hypothesis is more readable than the precise, literal statement: "A higher proportion of those scientists with high professional recognition than those scientists with low professional recognition have satisfactory research facilities. We tentatively suggest that these facilities are provided as rewards to the more successful scientists by the organization."

These three liberties in writing can also sometimes be taken when rendering three-variable tables, and the table need not be put in text. But more often, as noted in the next section, three-variable tables have complex purposes - for example, an interaction table showing the joint effects of two variables on a third (example 4 below). A table and some explicit reporting of it are required for the theoretical inference to be easily understood as being based on evidence.

THEORETICAL ELABORATION

The previous section presented the first step in our style of theoretical analysis of quantitative data: saturating core indices with all possible two-variable runs; discovering relationships among the runs with theoretically relevant consistency indices, summation indices and single questionnaire terms; then analyzing the findings with theoretical inferences. The next step, which cannot be neglected, is *elaboration analysis* - to make three or more variable analysis in order to saturate categories further by developing their properties and thereby achieving a denser theory. Thus, the discovery of relationships among indices provides the analyst with beginning suggestions for a theory, plus a theoretical direction and focus for its elaboration.

By "elaboration" we mean that the two-variable associations, which are the basis of theoretical hypotheses, must have their structural conditions specified; their causes and consequences sought, with possible spurious factors checked for; and their intervening variables (delineating processes between the variables) discovered. Although this, of course, is Lazarsfeld's elaboration analysis, [21] we shall contribute something new to his method for our own purpose of generating theory. The next several paragraphs assume an understanding of elaboration analysis (which can easily be gained by a study of Hyman's rendition of it[22]). The notions on consistency analysis discussed in the previous section are subsumed in elaboration analysis.

Lazarsfeld has provided three ways of ordering the variables in an elaboration analysis: (1) temporal, (2) structural level of complexity, and (3) conceptual generality. Temporal ordering is simply the time sequence of the variables involved. Structural complexity is an ordering in terms of the encompassing structural levels that characterize the unit of analysis under study. For example, a nurse can be characterized by the ward she works on, the hospital she works in, the city in which the hospital is located, and the nation where the city is. Conceptual generality is an ordering by degree of abstractness of the variables. For example, a nurse says that all patients should be bathed every day, which is specific opinion derived from a broader attitude of obeying all hospital rules, which attitude in turn derives from a basic value in medicine that nurses should obey hospital rules.

Lazarsfeld's elaboration analysis is seldom used in research, except for the simple task of specifying the conditions of a finding; for this task, one need not understand or expressly use his formula. The reason for this lack of use is simple: the only type of ordering of variables that Lazarsfeld has actually worked out is temporal ordering - the other two types have only been suggested. [23] Since survey data is typically cross-sectional in time, analysts are hard put to establish clear-cut, *factual* time orders in which colleagues will have confidence, because of the emphasis on accurate facts in verification and description.[24] Usually there is too much temporal interrelation among cross-sectional survey variables - over time, either one could, and probably does, result in the other. Thus, elaboration analysis is often stopped in its tracks before it has a chance to prove its usefulness. And the analyst who does not give it a chance stifles, rather than stimulates, his theoretical imagination. He has been taught not to let his imagination range on data that he cannot himself believe completely accurate, much less argue for their credibility with his colleagues. He has been taught to be skeptical of such strategies for survey data to the point of keeping an empty head about data field unreliable.

Elaboration analysis is stimulating because the finding its produces *fit* the thought patterns of sociological theory. With it, the analyst can show interpretations, processes, conditions, causes, spurious factors, and consequences with actual data - not an interpretation of the data. The analyst can literally speak through elaboration tables. He need only infer from his indices the conceptual level of his talk since the tables proved the theoretical arrangement of the variables. But if temporal ordering is believed impossible in most cases, how can we allow theory to emerge from elaboration tables?

THEORETICAL ORDERING

The theory ran emerge from these tables if, first, the analyst decides that his purpose is to generate theory, for then the accuracy of temporal ordering that would be required for verification and description is no longer crucial. He must then proceed to order his variables *theoretically*: a new principle of ordering. Lazarsfeld comes close to suggesting this principle with his "substantive" orderings by structural complexity and conceptual generality, for these are two specific examples of the general principle of theoretical ordering. But Lazarsfeld misses developing a general theoretical ordering principle because he does not consider their underlying similarity, nor how and why they can be used for the generation of theory. He misses this consideration because he is involved exclusively in establishing facts for description and verification. He never comes close to understanding that temporal sequence can be handles theoretically as well as factually.

Theoretical ordering of variables occurs by two strategies: (1) running all possible three-variable associations with each theoretically relevant two-variable association; and (2) running particular tables to fill in gaps or to answer questions, which emerge as the theory develops, by arranging elaboration tables according to the dictates of the theory. From the findings in both strategies there emerge theoretical orderings of variables already integrated with core categories and hypotheses. The analyst then infers or suggests them as his theory.

Theoretical ordering of variables by all possible three-variable associations on core two-variable relationships is done by comparing the partial association percentage differences to the percentage difference of the original relationship. When the partials vary above and below the original relationship, then the analyst discovers conditions that minimize and maximize his core relationship. From these findings he generates theory stating "under what conditions" a phenomenon exists. Some of these conditions are antecedent to the original association and may be suggested as partial causes; others, which occur at the same time, may be called contingencies. When the partials are equal to the original relationship, then a particular condition does not vary the relationship. The analyst either regards it as theoretically relevant or ignores the finding.

When both partials are less than the original relationship (they never completely disappear), then the analyst must theoretically suggest whether the third variable is (1) an intervening variable, thus suggesting a theoretical process between two core variables, or (2) an antecedent variable. An antecedent variable that reduces partials may have several theoretical meanings. The original relationship may be spurious; that is, both original variables are the consequences of the third variable. This finding may be theoretically very relevant. For instance, "the more fire engines that come to a fire, the greater the damage" is a spurious relationship, with both factors accounted for by size of the fire. The antecedent variable may also suggest a process in which the third variable leads to one of the original variables, which in turn leads to the other. This inference can be tested with the second strategy of theoretical ordering, which is to answer the question "Is this a process?" by rearranging the table to fit, thus testing for the theoretically assumed ordering of an intervening variable. If the inference proves correct, the analyst has found a value-added process - without the first variable the other two variables do not occur in process.[25] Thus the analyst can actively check on his theory as it emerges, by testing assumed theoretical orders. (This will be illustrated shortly.) Third, the antecedent variable may be a cause of a cluster of two variables. These two variables always occur together and therefore are truly, not spuriously, associated, but they do not occur without the discovered cause, which the analyst might wish to call a necessary condition. Thus fire engines and fires are truly associated, but are not found together unless someone has put in the alarm.

The first strategy of theoretical ordering is based on emergence: the data provides possible orders for the analyst. He need only induce theory about what he has found. This can be difficult when he has to overcome current training in quantitative analysis. He must remember that he is only looking for plausible orders among variables to suggest a theory. He is not looking for the "facts" of a description or verification. *He must think developmentally by remembering that only the data is static or cross-sectional - not his mind!* Although the data may admit of no temporal sequence, his creative imagination can consider any ordering principle for the related variables, and this principle becomes his ingenious suggestion. With imagination and ingenuity he can theoretically order his variables by time, structural complexity, conceptual generality, or in any other theoretical manner. His job is to suggest a theory based both on the *theoretically relevant order* of elaborated relationships and on the *content* of the variables he employs. He cannot think methodologically or statistically with symbols such as t factors or x leads to y; he must think *theoretically* about the content of his indicated categories and infer why the order of their possible relationships may be as he found them. In short, he must free himself from the exact rules of elaboration ordering as applied to descriptive and verificational studies, so he can be flexible in an imaginative, post hoc theoretical analysis of what he has discovered from the four elaboration possibilities; antecedent or current conditions (PA and PI), antecedent or intervening variables (MA and MI).

In generating theory as it emerges, the analyst first discovers two-variable relationships; second, he discovers their elaboration. Then he moves into a third stage, in which he starts generating possible further elaborations of two-variable relationships within the previous elaboration, using the second strategy of arranging variables to test theoretical orderings. He looks through his data to find indicators for the concepts he thinks are related in theoretical ways to his emerging theory. Then he arranges his elaboration tables to test if they bear out his hypotheses (for suggestions, not verification), or to discover what actually happens. At this stage of the analysis, he is theoretically sampling his data as directed by his emerging theory and he is actively directing his further runs accordingly; much as the field researcher directs his final work toward theoretically sampling data on hypotheses for filling gaps and answering the remaining questions in order to saturate categories. And much as the field worker at this stage moves quickly between situations, achieving greater relevance with smaller amount of data, the quantitative analyst may literally cam in the IBM machine room, having successive tables run to continually check his hypotheses as he thinks them through and theoretically samples his data for them.[26] At this stage an active dialogue of discovery and generation develops between himself and his data. He knows what his data should look like in various runs, and the runs set him straight. By this time the analyst has looked at hundreds of tables, trying to discover what he anticipates finding because of directions provided by the first two stages of his research. Consistency and elaboration analysis join together to provide him a grounded basis for his theory. (The appendix to this chapter gives examples.)

CONCLUSIONS

The point of this chapter has been to illustrate the careful relaxation of rules surrounding quantitative analysis, a relaxation for generating theory. The styles of quantitative analysis are multitudinous, so our discussions here include but few illustrations pertaining to the rich veins in quantitative data that can be mined when analysts relax their rigor.

One topic that we have not yet dealt with in this chapter bears mention: comparative analysis within and between surveys. To be sure, the discovery of relationships and their elaboration are all based on comparative analysis of subgroups that are readily found in the same body of data. However, sociologists have yet to explore the many possibilities for generating theory by the active creation of diverse comparison subgroups within a survey (beside core index and typoligies), and by the active search for comparison subgroups in other surveys. The various survey-data libraries scattered around the nation now facilitate comparisons between surveys.

We can suggest a few general rules for beginning this kind of exploration. The analyst can use *similar* groups for comparisons between surveys; they do not have to be identical. For example, "working class" may be indicated by residential area in one study, income in another, and low degree of organizational affiliation in another (remembering that crude indications are sufficient and interchangeable).[27] Further, the analyst should search for ways of comparing quickly and easily the multiple comparison groups within many different, particularly large, surveys, since one or two surveys can easily run this on data, and what is needed for a dense, adequate theory is a great amount of data. Also, multiple comparisons should be sought and flexibly done with qualitative data on other relevant groups.

In making these multiple comparisons, the analyst should constantly focus on generating and generalizing a theory, not on the comparison of differences to verify or account for a fact. Generating from differences is not easy to manage with quantitative data, since sociologists are trained to verify, and verification from differences comes very easily with quantitative data. Verifying and accounting for facts by differences are subsumed in the process of generating theory; they are not the product of quantitative research for this purpose.

APPENDIX TO CHAPTER VIII: EXAMPLES OF THEORETICAL ELABORATION

Following are several examples of theoretical ordering of elaboration tables, which tell the analyst if it is possible to suggest a theoretical statement. We focus particularly on the second strategy of theoretically arranging tables to discover possible orderings for hypotheses.

1. *The discovery and generation of a performance-reward process.* In a study of organizational scientists, the analyst discovered that scientists' motivation to advance knowledge was positively associated with professional recognition for doing so. This finding suggested the theoretical inference that recognition from others maintains motivation.[28] The analyst then elaborated this relationship by suggesting the following theoretical ordering: if recognition (which indicates previous performance) maintains motivation, then motivation should result in high quality performance in research and this, in turn, should result in more professional recognition. This ordering could then be suggested as a circular, snowballing, reward process for performance within science. The problem then became to order the elaboration tables to test if theoretically (not factually) this process was grounded.

In Table VI, the magnitude of association between recognition and performance is *diminished* when the intervening effect of motivation is removed. Therefore, high motivation tends to be a link between receiving recognition and accomplishing further high quality research performance, tentatively demonstrating the performance-reward process as a grounded basis for a theory of this process. As a social patter, this circular process will continue if the performance measured here results in new recognition.[29]

TABLE VI

Recognition

	Average	Less	Difference
High performance	56%	44%	+12%
	(144)	(188)	
Proportion with high performance and:			
High motivation	60%	53%	+7%
	(96)	(90)	
Low motivation	46%	37%	+9%
	(48)	(98)	

At this point the analyst suggested that, besides research performance, it was also possible to predict behavior associated with research on the basis of intensity of motivation. This assertion was borne out by one indicator of research behavior: the amount of time in a typical work week that the scientist puts into his own research activities. Fifteen per cent more of the highly motivated investigators worked 21 hours a week or longer on personal research. Furthermore, 11 per cent more of those who worked 21 or more hours a week on their own research had a high quality performance score. (Note the discovery of two additional associations.)

TABLE VII

Motivation

	High	Low	Difference
High performance	57%	38%	+19%

	(186)	(146)	
Proportion with high performance who put:			
21 or more hours per week into own research	60% (142)	43% (89)	+17%
Less than 21 hours per week into own research	48% (44)	35% (57)	+13%

Next, in theoretically ordering motivation, personal research time, and performance (Table VII), it can be suggested that the highly motivated investigators will tend to put more time into their own research work, and that this time in turn will tend to result in higher quality performance. The magnitude of association between motivation and performance is *diminished* when the intervening effect of personal research time is removed. This finding then adds a subsidiary link to the circular performance-reward process (diagramed below).

PERFORMANCE-REWARD PROCESS IN SCIENCE

->Recognition ->Motivation ->Time in Own Research ->Performance->

This theory is based on one possible one-time sequence. The reverse time is also possible: some investigators may have developed a high degree of motivation because they put in more than 21 hours per week. Hard work could generate interest. Therefore, we may have another time sequence in the performance process - longer hours in research leading to high motivation, resulting in high performance. However, this cannot be suggested because the data leave it ungrounded. In comparing proportions downward in Table VII, among those with high motivation 12 per cent more of those who worked 21 or more hours a week on their own research had a high performance score. Among those with low motivation, 8 per cent more who worked 21 hours or more a week on personal research had a high performance score. The original relation between time in own research and performance is 11 per cent. So high motivation, instead of being an intervening variable between time and performance, is a condition that creates a slightly stronger relation between the two. This is, of course, the time sequence originally assumed, which shows it to be the only theoretically grounded sequence.

This example indicates the discovery of two-variable relationships and their theoretical elaboration in order to generate a processual theory. The theory is suggested, not tested, because obviously the temporal ordering is theoretical, not factual; the data were collected on one day, except for the performance index, for which data were collected three months after the survey. However, *even theoretical ordering provides checks on itself*; even when the two elaboration tables were rearranged, the order of the process did not change.

2. *Structural complexity process.* In the same study of organizational scientists, the following consequences of two different promotion systems in the organization were discovered.[30] The "recommend" system (in which initial consideration for a scientist's promotion was based on a supervisor's recommendation) resulted in more discrepancies between rank and actual responsibilities and in more unsatisfactory evaluates of the system than did the "routine" system (in which initial consideration for promotion was based on periodic reviews). Theoretically, it seemed that a process was involved, whereby the relative frequency of perceived discrepancies resulting from each promotion system was a reason for the relative number of unsatisfactory evaluates of each system. The analyst then arranged an elaboration table to test for this theoretical order (Table VIII), and the findings supported it - the partial associations (22 and 25 per cent) were less than the original association (29 per cent), showing that discrepancies were an intervening variable between systems and evaluations. This theoretical process was supported by another consistency finding that among scientists in the "recommend" system there was considerably less satisfaction (29 per cent) with chances for a promotion.

TABLE VIII

Promotion System

	Recommend	Routine	Difference
Evaluate promotion process as unsatisfactory:	58% (184)	29% (145)	+29%
Proportion who evaluate promotion process as unsatisfactory and who observed discrepancies:			

Frequently	83%	61%	+22%
	(59)	(28)	
Occasionally	45%	21%	+24%
	(125)	(117)	

Here the theoretical ordering of variables is based on structural contexts at different levels, and assumes that the more encompassing level has a greater effect on the lesser level rather than vice versa. Thus "promotion systems" is a contextual unit that caused discrepancies in rank and responsibilities among personnel; while "discrepancies" is a property of the system that provides a structural condition affecting the way scientists evaluate their systems' promotion procedures. Thus, mixed into this structural level process are contextual properties of individuals or structural conditions under which they have a career (promotion procedures and characteristic discrepancies in rank and responsibility); consequences for individuals (discrepancies) and for a system (evaluations); properties of a system (procedures, discrepancies, and dissatisfied individuals); properties of individuals (evaluations), and so forth - depending on how the analyst wishes to render and focus his theory. In short, even within this simple structural process, as found in one elaboration table, the analyst can find much grist for sociological theory.

3. *Theoretically rearranging a table to test for alternative career processes.* The question arose about how those scientists who planned to move to relieve the pressure of a currently unsuccessful career have made his decision.[31] They may (1) decide to leave the organization, and then choose the goal they plan to work for - perhaps still basic research (by going to a university) or perhaps a change to practice or applied research (by going to either a private, industrial or governmental research or "practice," and this change would necessitate leaving their organization as soon as possible.

Table IX is arranged to test for the sequence of factors in the first process: "plans to move" is tested as an intervening variable, coming between degree of recognition and preference for a preferred affiliation in a university, if the move is made. Since the original relation is nil, we discover that this theoretical elaboration test for an intervening variable is a test if the nonexistent original relationship was actually a canceling-out of a strong positive relationship (between recognition and preference under the condition of planning to move soon) and a strong negative relationship (between recognition and preference when planning to stay on in the organization). Thus this table corrects our theoretical ordering by yielding a finding that suggests that unsuccessful scientists who plan to move (11 per cent in Table X) have not as yet planned to go on with either basic research or applied research or practice. They are still just planning to move because of a poor career, and they have not decided where or for what purpose.

TABLE IX

	Recognition		
	High	Low	Difference
Prefer move to university	62%	63%	-1%
	(144)	(188)	

Proportion who prefer move to university and who plan to:

Move soon	66%	69%	-3%
	(12)	(36)	
Stay for time being or	58%	57%	+1%
permanently	(130)	(152)	

Table X is arranged to test the second-mentioned process in making plans to move. Preference for the university or for other organizations is tested as intervening in the decision to move as soon as possible made by those who lack recognition. Again, planning to move because of low recognition is not a result of planning to change work goals - both partials are not less than the original relationship of 11 per cent. What this table tells us is that the scientists' plans to move as soon as possible materialize (15 per cent) under this condition of a certain preference for moving to a university where their research goals would be the same. On the other hand, plans to move soon hardly materialize (7 per cent), if at all, when the scientists prefer an organization offering them another work goal.

TABLE X

Recognition

	High	Low	Difference
Plan to move as soon as possible	8%	19%	-11%
	(144)	(188)	
Proportion who plan to move as soon as possible and who prefer to move to:			
University	10%	25%	-15%
	(84)	(111)	
Other organizations	7%	14%	-7%
	(60)	(77)	

Thus, theoretical arrangements of elaboration tables, while not necessarily bearing out our theoretical guesses, discover for us what is going on (in, say, the decision to leave an organization because of a failing career). They fill gaps in the total theory of organizational careers and answer our specific questions.

4. *Specifying joint effects of conditions.* Seldom are both partial associations less than the original association; the most frequent finding specifies antecedent or contingent conditions that minimize and maximize relationships. These finding yield perhaps the most frequent of theoretical statements: the varying conditions under which a phenomenon exists. As we have said, the specification of conditions may apply to a single index, but as an elaboration procedure it applies to two or more variable relationships. Antecedent conditions (such as previous research experience, Table III) may, if the theory warrants, be suggested as partial causes. Conditions occurring at toughly the same time are called contingencies, denoting whether a relationship is contingent on a condition that makes it more or less pronounced. Further, for his theory the sociologist may choose to reverse the temporal order of his specifications of conditions to obtain statements on the varying consequences of diverse aspects of a condition (types, dimensions, or degrees of the condition). Thus, this type of elaboration table yields

findings that suggest several ways to generate a theory.

TABLE XI. PERCENTAGE WHO ARE VERY SATISFIED WITH JOB SECURITY

	Felt Recognition		
Organizational Position	High	Low	Difference
Junior Investigator	67%	43%	+24%
	(57)	(84)	
Senior Investigator	70%	58%	+12%
	(40)	(60)	
Supervisor	73%	73%	---
	(47)	(44)	

Joint effects is another theoretically interesting way of talking about the specification of conditions. In Table XI we see the joint effects of scientists' organizational position and degree of professional recognition on their satisfaction with the security of their job in the organization. A standard means for rendering this table is to say that when we hold organizational position constant, professional recognition only makes for job security in the investigator position. But "holding constant" is a notion used in verification of theory, when the analyst is trying to reduce the contaminating effects of any strategic variable not in focus with his variable of interest.

To view the table in terms of joint effects of two conditions on a third lend itself better to generating theory, since no variable is assumed a constant; all are actively analyzed as part of what is going on. For example, in Table XI we see that as a scientist's organizational position advances (or for the theory, as his career advances), professional recognition becomes less important for job security (the percentage differences decrease). Another joint effect for theoretical inference is that, as the scientist's career advances, he becomes more secure in the organization through seniority, and less dependent upon his degree of professional recognition for this security (under "low recognition" security percentages increase with position). Or the analyst might say that a scientist with professional recognition to his credit tends to have a secure job no matter what his organizational position. (See percentages under "high recognition.") Thus, statements of joint effects tell us how conditions interact together to affect a third variable - and this is theoretically rich and relevant information.

TABLE XII. PROPORTION OF JUNIOR INVESTIGATORS WHO ARE VERY SATISFIED WITH SECURITY OF JOB

Promotion

System	*Recognition*		
	High	Low	Difference
Recommend	63%	37%	+26%
	(30)	(51)	
Routine	69%	50%	+19%
	(26)	(32)	

Two other ways of making inferences about this table are in terms of "differential impact" and "differential sensitivity."[32] For Table XI the analyst can say that position has a differential impact on the relationship between recognition and security. In Table XII, we see the *differential impact* of promotion systems on junior scientists' satisfaction with job security under different conditions of professional recognition. These, again, are forms of contextual and conditional comparative analyses. Referring again to Table XI, the analyst can say that the security of the scientists with low recognition is very sensitive to organizational position, while the security of scientists with high recognition is insensitive to organizational position - thus indicating the *differential sensitivity* of the successful and unsuccessful in their job security.

Finally, the analyst can generate minimal and maximal *configurating* conditions (a useful theoretical model) for his theory from a joint-effects table like Table XI. To be at the beginning stages of a career without recognition is to feel comparatively little satisfaction with job security. Maximum security comes at the peak of one's career in the organization, because of tenure. Though it took professional recognition to achieve this position recognition is no longer a condition for job security.

We could suggest more ways to generate theoretical statements form joint-effects tables, as well as from the first three illustrations of elaboration tables. However, we wish only to conclude from these brief illustrations that *if quantitative data is handled systematically by theoretical ordering of variables in elaboration tables, the analyst will indeed find rich terrain for discovering and generating theory.* We hope by our slight but purposeful loosening of the rules, via our principle of theoretical ordering, that elaboration analysis will be used more than heretofore. Its richness for research has not yet been tapped because of difficulties in using it on cross-sectional survey data to produce accurate facts for description and verification.

REFERENCES

1. For examples see James Coleman, "Research Chronicle: The Adolescent Society," and Seymour Martin Lipset, "The Biography of a Research Project: Union Democracy," in Philip Hammond (Ed.), *Sociologists at Work* (New York: Basic Books, 1964).

2. This way of presenting one's work in a publication on research is not chicanery, but an established form in many circles of science. See Bernard Barber and Renee C. Fox, "The Case of the Floppy-eared Rabbits: An Instance of Serendipity Gained and Serendipity Lost," *American Journal of Sociology,* 64 (1958), pp. 128-29.

3. Paul F. Lazarsfeld, "Interpretation of Statistical Relations as a Research Operation," in Lazarsfeld and Rosenberg (Eds.), *The Language of Social Research* (Glencoe, III.: Free Press, 1955).

4. For example, compare the theoretical analysis in Barney G. Glaser *Organizational Scientists: Their Professional Careers* (Indianapolis: Bobbs-Merrill, 1964) to the description from the same study using over 100 different IBM card decks and comprising four volumes. *Human Relations in a Research Organization,* Volumes I and II (1953) and *Interpersonal Factors in Research,* Parts I and II (1957) (Ann Arbor, Mich.: Institute for Social Research). For another example see Hanan C. Selvin, *The Effects of Leadership* (New York: Free Press of Glencoe, 1960).

5. See Barney G. Glaser, "The Use of Secondary Analysis by the Independent Researcher," *The American Behavioral Scientist* (1964), pp. 11-14.

6. Paul F. Lazarsfeld, "Problems in Methodology," in R. Merton, L. Broom and L. Cottrell (Eds.), *Sociology Today* (New York: Basic Books,

1959), pp. 47-67; "Evidence and Inference in Social Research," *Daedalus*, LXXXXVII (1958), pp. 100-109; and, with Wagner Thielens, *The Academic Mind* (Glencoe, Ill.: Free Press, 1958), pp. 402-407.

7. It is at this point, Lazarsfeld suggests, that technicians, who perhaps have no generative powers, take flight into precision by blaming their crude methods and trying to refine their indices instead of thinking about what they have found.

8. In constructing a sumation index, the analyst first obtains one more group than the number of indicators he is using: four indicators lead to five groups. Before combining these groups he should cross-tabulate the five groups with a criterion variable - he knows the relationship exists - to find out between which groups the direction of the relationship changes. He then combines all those groups positively related to the criterion variable and all those negatively. He cannot just dichotomize the index where he pleases, because he may reduce its discriminating power by combining positive and negative degrees.

9. For an example see Lazarsfeld and Theilens, *op. cit.*, pp. 89-90.

10. This is a specific case of Zetterberg's rule that the total integration of a theory tends to make any one of its parts "highly plausible." See Hans L. Zetterberg, *On Theory and Verification in Sociology* (Totowa, N.J.: Bedminster Press, 1963), Chapter 6.

11. Glaser, *op. cit.*

12. If the analyst has enough time and money, he can run the index open (use all groups) and then dichotomize them at the breaking point for each item. This will yield more diverse information on each relationship and make the index more sensitive. This strategy is an alternative to dichotomizing on a criterion variable, but is cumbersome; and once the analyst is sure his break in the index is the most sensitive one, it may seem a wast of time for the yield of information.

13. For the theoretical discussion of Tables I and II, see Glaser, *Organizational Scientists: Their Professional Careers, op. cit.,* Chapter 2.

14. For the theoretical discussion of Tables III and IV, see Barney G. Glaser, "Differential Association and the Institutional Motivation of Scientists," *Administrative Science Quarterly,* 10 (1965), pp. 81-97.

15. Hanan Selvin, "A Critique of Tests of Significance in Survey

Press, 1955), Chapter VII.

23. See Lazarsfeld's introducton to Hyman, *ibid.*

24. The elvaluator of an article for one journal remsrked on an elaboration table, "More generally the whole arghument about establishment vs. persistence (or stability) of the relationships suffers because the author really has no time trend data - and that is necessarily implied in statements about persistence or stability." The paper was rejected because temporal order was not an incontrovertible fact.

25. See, for a discussion of this type of process, Neil Smelser, *Theory of Collective Behavior* (New York: Free Press of Glencoe, 1963), Chapter I.

26. This is a frequent activity among some survey analysts; see coleman's discussion of continually having tables run as he thiks them through, *op. cit.,* pp. 203-04.

27. See Herbert H. Hyman, *Political Socialization* (Glencoe, Ill.: Free Press, 1959), for examples of combining similar categories for comparative analysis.

28. Glaser, *Organizational Scientists: Their Professional Careers, op. cit.*, Chapter III.

29. See *ibid.*, p. 32.

30. *Ibid.*, Chapter III.

31. *Ibid.,* Chapter VIII.

32. *Ibid.,* Chapter IV.

Chapter 11

Reprinted from *Anguish*, Sociology Press, Mill Valley, CA, 1970.

CASE HISTORIES AND CASE STUDIES

Barney G. Glaser and Anselm L. Strauss

This is a *case history*. It consists of a *story* about a lingering dying trajectory, along with an accompanying *theoretical commentary* about this story. To distinguish a case history from a case study as types of sociological enterprise is essential. In this chapter therefore, we shall discuss several distinguishing properties of case histories and studies from two vantage points: (1) the focus and purpose of each, and (2) the use and source of theory of each. We shall emphasize the case history approach to make clear what we have intended by this book. Also, we wish very much to stimulate the publication of case histories. They have passed out of fashion in sociology, although they still retain illustrative and pedagogic uses at least in psychology and anthropology.

THE FOCUS OF CASE HISTORIES

The focus of a case history is a full story of some temporal span or interlude in social life - a biography, and occupational career, a project, an illness, an evolution, a disaster, a ceremony, and evolvement, and so forth. The story is about *one social unit* - such as a person, a status, and organization, a process, a type of behavior, a relationship, a group, or a nation.

Many published cases have taken the form of "life histories,"[1] but they can be about other social phenomena. The theme of a case history, for instance, can be an occupational career, as in Sutherland's book on the professional thief,[2] although the career may be secondary to a particular phase or phases in the career,as in Warner's case study of the rise and fall of a local political hero.[3] A case history may have s its major theme the evolution of family relations;[4] the total span of a lengthy, complicated public ceremony;[5] the events that follow a precipitation of an imaginary disaster;[6] or the evolving pattern of events after an actual disaster.[7] There is no reason why long case histories could not have other temporal themes: the evolution of relationship between business firms or among other organizations, the evolution of an organizational crisis or the breakdown of a battalion's morale.[8]

The research goal in a case history, then, is to get the fullest possible story *for its own sake*. In contrast, the case study is focused or verification and/or generation of theory.[9] There is no attempt at obtaining the fullest possible story for its own sake. Fullness of description refers only to what data is needed for the constructions designated by the abstract purposes of the researcher. Of course, verification and generation of theory require even less data on the full story that a description requires. In sum, the case history gives prominence to the story - and to the "story line" - whereas in the case study the story is subordinated to abstract purpose.

In the case study, single or multiple cases are used, since the process of analytic abstracting-out eliminates and confusion over the various stories behind the different case. Indeed, multiple cases are the requisite basis of broader generalities which are derived from comparisons. In contrast, most case histories have been and probably will be about single cases. Nevertheless, it is possible to do multiple case histories. These can be done under two conditions. First, each case is short enough so the book-length case history is not excessive. Typically, case histories, because of the focus on the full story, are quite long. Second, the analyst has a theory that integrates the multiple case histories together in his commentary. Otherwise he had only a series of single case histories.

To achieve this theoretical integration, he can sample theoretically for his case histories.[10] This means that if he has a case history, ak a theory to explain and interpret it then he can decide - on theoretical grounds - about other possible case histories that wold provide good contrasts and comparisons. For example, our case history of Mrs. Abel, a hospital in a tuberculosis hospital: thus we would be comparing two kinds of hospital careers. The resulting comparative analysis is different from that used in case studies for description, verification, or generation. In the case studies, one analyzes similarities and differences to establish empirical generalizations and variations and to verify and generate theory.[11]

Case histories, particularly long ones, seem to have declined in favor among sociologists, largely because of the advances in research methods which have supported the analytic and abstract thrust of the discipline. In spite of this neglect, sociologists continue to incorporate case histories as data within their case studies, and sometimes a case study itself is actually a case history. These stories embedded in data of a study may be short or long, consist of pure and unedited interviews or field notes or may be slightly constructed from the data because of the researcher's abstract orientation. The stories are not likely to be as full as the stories yielded by purposeful case history collection of data, but may be sufficiently full to be rendered as a case history. The fullest are more likely to be found within single book-length case studies. For example, in *Doomsday Cult* we have the story of the rise and failure of a "far-out" religious group.[12] Mrs. Abel's story was a lucky "find" on our part which occurred while we were collecting data for and publishing a study of dying in hospitals.

Our point is that these case histories are collected by chance and sensitivity, but many are unpublished, or lie buried within case studies, and are destined never *per se* to see the light of day because sociologists today are not doing case histories. We say, "Look there may be a good story in your study, why not write it also." We wish researchers to review their materials for such stories and publish them - the more varied, the better.

In view of the focus on analytic abstraction in current sociological work, it is perhaps preferable to do the research analysis first. Once this responsibility is off the researcher's chest, he can then enjoy the fun of writing a case history of his data. Also at this juncture he has the advantage of knowing or having discovered a theory history. An obvious alternative - and more efficient - is purposively to collect case histories from the start with the intent of writing them up, whether this collection is done along with a case study or as the sole purpose.

In and of itself, the case history is an enterprise of great merit in sociology. One need not always do an abstract study. Through a story, which is *explained and interpreted with theory*, the sociologist can show a type, an average, an extreme or an exemplar case. The case history then provides a very dense, readable imagery for sociological theory. (Currently, novelists much more than sociologists take on this task, but for their own purposes and with much less explicit theory. Their theory is also less integrated and frequently less complex than we wish for sociological purposes.) A sociologist can show how well a theory may work by usefully and relevantly taking apart a single case history from a sociological view. This is the beginning of developing adequate *applied* social theory, an important task facing sociology today. A case history becomes a way of showing laymen how our theory might be used on single cases - possibly on their own case. From the history, people can gain much understanding of general phenomena through its theoretical interpretation and explanation.

This task of doing a case history is at one end of the continuum of abstraction in sociological work. At the other end is the generation of theory by multiple case studies and comparative analysis. (Between are the studies which involve descriptions and verifications, the former being closer to case histories.) *The fullest understandings of social phenomenon come, we believe, from dense case histories on one end of the continuum and from densely generated grounded theories on the other end of the continuum.* In between we have shredded, abstract descriptions; puzzle solving of portions of the theory; and verifications of portions of the fuller understandings found at either end of the continuum.

THEORY AND CASE HISTORIES

We turn now to a discussion of the relation of theory to case histories. For the most part, theory is *applied* to case histories in separate commentaries which explain and interprets parts of the story, as we have done in this book. These commentaries usually appear after each section of the story. Though undoubtedly it will happen, generating new theoretical notions from the story is only a by-product, not the main purpose of a case history. As for the reader, his typical tempo of reading is probably first to read the story, then the commentary, then reread the story for a greater understanding of it. The theoretical purposes of case studies, in contrast, are to generate and verify theory, with parts of the story being selectively interwoven with the theory as evidence and illustration.

Some case histories are published with virtually no theoretical commentary. This occurs when the author assumes that his readers are so familiar with a current theory that they can explain and interpret his case history without guidance. For example, in life histories published by anthropologists, often the reader is assumed to be familiar with anthropological theory and so can intelligently interpret the story without guidance. Similarly, Howard Becker has remarked - in introducing a new edition of Clifford Shaw's *The Jackroller*[13] - that when this classic life history was first published sociologists read it as a piece of a large "mosaic" made up of the many sociological publications then issuing from the University of Chicago. Hence little explicit theoretical commentary was necessary for the readers of this case study. When only a little theoretical commentary accompanies a case history, generally it will appear at least in the beginning and end of the case, and refers the reader to a current theory that applies.

We shall discuss next those case histories requiring or accompanied by considerable theoretical commentary and analysis. What theory should be used for these case histories? The answer is: a theory which fits and is relevant to the data of the history. We suggest therefore that it be a theory grounded in the data of a substantive or a formal area to which the case history belongs. Logically-deducted theory based on speculations and assumptions seldom does justice to a case history and is very likely to distort the story. In our book, Mrs. Abel's story was analyzed with theory grounded in our study of dying in hospitals. Thus we shall apply our substantive and formal theories on dying to her case. They work very well. This reflects back on the usefulness of grounded theory: generating theory from the data of systematic research. However, sometimes the theory to be applied is formulated only on a formal level, as when psychiatrists utilize psychiatric theory to interpret a life history, (say, of a suicide)[14] or as when Sutherland discusses the life and occupation of a professional thief using the general sociological theory of occupations and culture current in his day. Another example is that the story of a person's rise in the military can be commented upon in terms of a grounded formal theory of organizational careers.[15] Thus case histories will vary in accordance with the level of generality of the theory or theories applied. The author must, of course, use the level of generality best suited to bringing out what he deems are essentials of his case history.

To be sure, the author need not use only one theory for his commentary. He can use several theories at different levels, provided he is clear about their individual use. For example, with Mrs. Abel we used our substantive theories on managing pain and dying trajectories[16] and our formal theory of awareness contexts.[17] This led to multiple interpretations and explanations at certain points, but mainly the theories were used successively. In contrast, case studies are usually devoted to one theory, with the exception of some description that use multiple, theoretical ways of describing an area. Since the theory (or theories) is applied to the case history, presumably it already exists. If none applicable exists, whether formal or substantive, then one can be generated for the task by the researcher.

An adequate method is to generate a substantive theory from the class of substantive data to which the story belongs. One cannot generate, however, an adequate theory *solely* from the case history necessary for the comparative analysis that will yield a sufficiently dense and integrated substantive theory.[18] The several cases need, however, only be studied sufficiently for generating theory. As we have shown in the *Discovery of Grounded Theory,* the amount of material needed for generating theory on each case may be very limited compared to a full history. The resulting substantive theory may be written "on its own" in an article, but also can be developed in the theoretical commentary made on a case history. A small amount of substantive theory can go a long way in explaining a case history. The research and generation may go fairly fast. To arrive at this theory, however, the analyst should be prepared to take as much time as needed.

The purpose of a theoretical commentary in explaining and interpreting the case history is to give a broadened picture of the particular case. *The theory puts the case within a more general context of understanding what could have happened under varying conditions, and therefore why it happened this way within this particular case.* The particulars of the case, then, are interpreted generally as "what actually happened" within a range of several probabilities and alternatives. No longer can the case history be considered simply as a typical exemplar or an idiosyncratic occurrence, as is the tendency when the reader does not know the general perspective afforded by the theory. In contrast, the authors of case studies strive for generalization and testing theory and the story is a means to those ends. In case histories, theory is in the service of generalization and specifying the story context by placing it within a theoretical context and is best done, as noted earlier, when the theory is comparative.

To achieve this general understanding of a case history, some stylistic aspects of the theoretical commentary are clear to us now. Primarily, the analyst must use his theory selectively; that is, he uses only those parts of his theory that are most relevant to bring out a general understanding of the case. This requires mastery of the whole theory, and sensitivity in choosing its diverse possible applications to the case. Also, in developing the commentary the story is kept paramount and the theory subdued, although the theory prescribes what aspects of the total story will appear in the commentary. In short, the theoretical analysis is kept implicit throughout a running commentary on the story. In contrast, in case studies the emphasis is on making the theory explicit and structured.

THEORETICAL COMMENTARY IN EXISTING CASE HISTORIES AND STUDIES

In the sociological literature today only a thin line distinguishes most case histories from case studies, if they are distinguishable at all. There are few clear examples of case histories, like Sutherland's *The Professional Thief*. Most monographs and articles, particularly descriptive studies, have bits of case histories woven into them which function in the service of the researcher's more abstract purposes. Thus, what we have today mainly is a matter of degree in differentiating case studies from histories. Let us analyze some of these case studies to see what they can tell us also about the type and potentials of theoretical commentary in case history analysis.

Whether a case study is long or short, it is important to ask how the author writes his theoretical commentary into the publication. Among the relevant dimensions are: the *amount* of theory, its *level* of generality, its *source*, its degree of *systematization, and the density* with which it is formulated. We have already commented upon amount, source, and level of theory used in case histories. A few brief comments on systematization and density in case studies will suffice for understanding our ensuing analysis. In some case studies, the theoretical commentary is well wrought, nicely integrated - it "hangs together" systematically.[19] On the other hand, some theoretical commentaries are decidedly "loose," consisting merely of a collection of theoretical statements because little systematization is attempted. Theoretical commentary also may exhibit degrees of density. The theory may be "thin" (although systematically stated); whereas some theoretical commentary is densely detailed at several levels of generality and gives readers a sense of "depth" or rich context, whether or not the theory is relatively systematized.

With these five dimensions of theory in mind, one can usefully characterize the theoretical commentary of any case study *or* history *with some preciseness.* We emphasize the preceding phrase because ordinarily their functions are thought of in very general terms -what they illustrate, yield understanding or, or give evidence for sometimes is even left understated. The question however is: illustration, understanding or evidence for *what?* If we combine the five dimensions of theory, we have 32 cells by which to characterize the commentary. Thus a case might fall into a cell representing a theoretical commentary that is considerable in amount, highly generalized, systematic, dense, and drawn from outside the body of data which yielded the case. Psychoanalytic commentary about psychiatric "cases" is of this type. Our case history of Mrs. Abel falls into a cell representing theoretical commentary that is considerable in amount, substantive, systematic, dense, and is theory formulated by the authors from research in the same substantive areas to which the case pertains. We commented less, however, than would have been necessary if two volumes on dying had not previously been published by us. A case study like Festinger's[20] utilized theory that is general and systematic, with the virtual exclusion of substantive theory about sectarian behavior because the senior researchers were intent on verifying a systematic general theory.

Sometimes a case study may fall into more than one cell. For instance, a case study of Bostonian Italians by Herbert Gans uses both general theory drawn from outside his research and substantive theory which emerged from his research.[21] The same technique for locating long cases can be used with short cases - the latter can be used to illustrate, for example, a general or substantive theory or an item of either type of theory. The commentary can be systematic or not, dense or not, drawn from outside the research or from its research data.

Stylistic features of cases (study or history) presentations sometimes appear to be related to cell position. When, for instance, the theory is general, systematic, dense, drawn from outside a case, and considerable in amount, then the commentary is likely to be extensively discussed before and/or after the case itself, with systematic discussion of "important" events in the case. General theory left more implicit than explicit leads the author merely to present or sum up the overall case, relating it to a body of general theory, rather than discussing it intensively. In monographs, when sizeable cases are introduced, their contribution to the monograph's style is also related to cell position. For instance, a substantive theoretical commentary drawn from outside the research must be introduced to the reader and related to the case: in detail if the theory is systematic and dense, but in far less detail if only bits of a theory are used or are applied without much density. On the other hand, substantive theory which is discovered by the author of a case does not require introduction as such, but is more likely to be woven into the case itself or even into its very construction. Even the stylistic use of very short cases, in monographs or articles, seems partly to reflect the theory's cell position - as when, following stratification theory, an author presents and interview (or interview fragment) from three interviewees arranged by their social class position;[22] or when numbers of cases are presented serially and each analyzed in turn, as Shibutani did with cases about "rumors" in order to develop an excellent substantive theory about rumor.[23]

There is another reason for emphasizing the relationship of style and type of theoretical commentary. The use of cases or case histories within long case studies probably is more inventive, and certainly more various, than researchers realize. Many researchers incorporate cases - both short and long into their publications without a clear focus on how they do so, since their attention almost invariably is much more on analysis and evidence than on the cases themselves. In a previous publication by one of us (and his co-authors),[24] several different kinds of cases were introduced, in a variety of ways and for a variety of reasons.[25] None of the authors were fully aware - and probably their readers are even less aware - of the range of types, nodes, and functions of their cases. Since case histories are so widely used by social scientists, a much closer scrutiny of them is warranted, both by those who publish cases, in any form, and by their readers. Both share the responsibility of course for fuller recognition of how cases are used and for what purposes. Closer scrutiny should lead to increasingly innovative uses and construction of case histories. We hope this further attention might also lead to increasing publication of long case histories - and also to more effective case study monographs.

Another important question - related especially to a case study's style and its type or theoretical commentary - is what kind of *comparative analysis* is offered by the author? When his publication includes two or more cases, then some kind of contrast will be drawn between or among them, either explicitly by the researcher or implicitly by the reader, and usually by both. Even when a case study publication consists of only a single case, (say a riot) its author is very likely to make comments which indicate how this case differs and is similar to other cases; if not, his readers unquestionably, unless they are very uncritical, will draw such contrasts for themselves. Such comparative analyses are not always of the same type or made for the same purposes. For instance, Gouldner's early study of bureaucratic function in a factory was a one case research, designed to elaborate and correct a theory of bureaucracy derived mainly from Max Weber.[28]

The range of purposes and styles of comparative analyses reflected in the above case *studies* can be better appreciated by contrasting several single case *histories*. Thus Sutherland's case history of the professional thief uses comparative analyses in two principal ways. First, he explicitly comments, mainly in amplifying footnotes, to show how other "con men's" lives and activities are usually similar, but at times dissimilar. Second, Sutherland also makes clear comparisons among different types of professional thieves to distinguish them from con men. Third, he implicitly contrasts their careers and activities with other types of criminals. The analysis is carried out partly in rather descriptive terms and partly in terms of general sociological theory.

On the other hand, the classic life history by Thomas and Znaniecki begins with a three-fold typology of men, and then offers the personal history of a Pole who exemplifies one type. Commenting in footnotes and before and after the case, they make comparisons with other Polish emigrants in accordance with the general and substantive theories thoroughly discussed in the preceding four volumes of their five volume work.

In our own commentary on the case history of Mrs. Abel, the other contrasts, with the type of pain and dying trajectories exemplified by her story, are explicitly and repeatedly made, both in general and with regard to specific details of the patient's story. Internal comparisons also are made of various phases of Mrs. Abel's pain and dying trajectories, as well as with corresponding phases in other types of pain and dying careers.

The types of comparative analyses used in the above case studies and histories can be highlighted further by contrasting them with the article by Shellow and Roemer about "The Riot That Didn't Happen" because Shellow and Roemer helped to prevent its occurrence.[29] This non-riot is described as a "case," and the theoretical analysis explicitly contrasts it only with riots that have occurred. The analysis turns around the conditions for riots which were absent because of certain tactics used by the police who were consulting with the researchers.

We are emphasizing the differential styles and the comparative analyses utilized in various case studies and histories for two reasons. First, we wish to advocate a more self-conscious use of these analyses in studies and in commentaries for case histories. Since researchers seem very little aware of their comparative use of cases, elsewhere we have detailed how comparative analyses differ immensely from publication to publication; the same can be said of the case materials on which comparative analyses are made.[30]

Second, and much the more important reason, we wish to advocate that researchers publish from their data *many more* case histories, *selecting* cases in accordance with clearly thought-out comparative analyses. Probably most lone case histories have tended to be selected on the basis of luck in obtaining them or are pulled out of larger bodies of data because they were "fuller" than other cases; while short case histories within monographs and articles are more likely to be presented, or constructed, because they illustrate or give evidence for points that the researcher is attempting to establish. Yet this selection is likely to be deficient if the researcher is not quite clear as to the functioning of his comparative analysis - and in terms which we have used earlier, his conception cannot be quite clear if he does not know how his analysis related to the level, source, systematization of density of his theory. Moreover, his theory should provide the basis for selecting the case histories which when presented will give the best merging of theoretical commentary and case history material.

In conclusion, we hope that sociologists by using this book both as an example and as a starting point will clearly demarcate case histories from case studies and will start doing the former with the same clarity of purpose that now characterized the latter - the publication of case histories surely has considerable merit as part of the total sociological enterprise.

ENDNOTES

1. W.I. Thomas and F. Znaniecki, *The Polish Peasant in Poland and America* (New York: Alfred A. Knopf, 1918.

2. Edwin H. Sutherland, *The Professional Thief* (Chicago, Illinois: The University of Chicago Press, 1937).

3. W.L. Warner, *The Living and the Dead* (New Haven: Yale University Press, 1959), pp. 9-100.

4. Oscar Lewis, *The Children of Sanchez* (New York: Vintage Books, 1961).

5. W.L.Warner, *op. cit.*

6. Leon Festinger, Henry W. Reichen, and Stanley Schachter, *When Prophecy Fails* (Minneapolis, Minnesota: University of Minnesota Press, 1956).

7. L. Schatzman, *Community Reaction to Disaster,* Ph.D. Thesis, Indiana University, 1960.

8. Tamotsu Shibutani, *Improvised News: A Sociological Study of Rumor* (Indianapolis: Bobbs-Merrill Company, Inc., 1966), see Chapter 5, pp. 129-63.

9. See, for example, in the same Bobbs-Merrill series *ibid.,* on

advanced studies in the social sciences, Alvin W. Gouldner and Richard A. Peterson, *Technology and the Moral Order* (1963), Julius Rosh, *Timetables* (1963, and Fred Davis, *Passage Through Crisis* (1964).

10. Barney G. Glaser and Anselm L. Strauss, *The Discovery of Grounded Theory* (Chicago: Aldine Publishing Company, 1967), Chapter 3, pp. 45-79.

11. *Ibid.,* Chapter 2, pp. 21-45.

12. John Lofland (Englewood Cliffs: Prentice-Hall, Inc., 1966).

13. (Chicago: The University of Chicago Press, 1967).

14. Cf. the comments by Jack Douglas in his, *Social Meanings of Suicide* (Princeton: Princeton University Press, 1968), pp. 258-64.

15. See Barney G. Glaser (ed.), *Organizational Careers: A Sourcebook for Theory* (Chicago: Aldine Publishing Company, 1968).

16. Barney G. Glaser and Anselm L. Strauss, *Time for Dying* (Chicago: Aldine Publishing Company, 1968).

17. Barney G. Glaser and Anselm L. Strauss, *Awareness of Dying* (Chicago: Aldine Publishing Company, 1965).

18. See *Discovery of Grounded Theory, op. cit.,* chapter 6, pp. 117-61 for a discussion of integration and density of theory with respect to several studies.

19. Cf., Howard Becker, Blanche Geer, Everett C. Hughes, Anselm Strauss, *Boys in White* (Chicago: University of Chicago Press, 1962).

20. *Op. cit.*

21. *The Urban Villagers* (New York: The Free Press of Glencoe, 1962).

22. Lee Rainwater, *Family Design* (Chicago: Aldine Publishing Co., 1965), pp. 73-79.

23. *Op. cit.* One critical reader has remarked, however, that Shibutani's cases sometimes seem directly related to the evidential points he draws from them, but sometimes he merely applies to them a distant - and perhaps "not too pertinent" - theory drawn mainly from Park and Mead.

24. Anselm L. Strauss, Leonard Schatzman, Rue Bucher, Danuta Ehrlich, and Melvin Sabshim, *Psychiatric Idealogies and Instructions* (New York:

The Free Press of Glencoe, 1964).

25. Cf. also Anselm L. Strauss, *Images of the American City* (New York: The Free Press of Glencoe, 1961).

26. Alvin W. Gouldner, *Patterns of Industrial Bureaucracy* (New York: The Free Press of Glencoe, 1954) and C.W. Mills and H. Gerth (eds.), *From Max Weber* (New York: Oxford University Press, 1946).

27. Peter Blau, *The Dynamics of Bureaucracy* (Chicago: The University of Chicago Press, 1955).

28. Michel Crozier, *The Bureaucratic Phenomenon* (Chicago: The University of Chicago Press, 1964).

29. *Social Problems*, Vol 14 (Fall, 1966).

30. *The Discovery of Grounded Theory, op. cit.,* Chapter 2, pp. 21-45.

Reprinted from *The American Behavioral Scientist*, June 1963.

RETREADING RESEARCH MATERIALS:

The Use of Secondary Analysis By the Independent Researcher

Barney G. Glaser, Ph.D.

Analysis of existing data originally collected for other purposes is a remedy for many of the afflictions that beset the inquiring sociologist. It fills the research needs of persons with macro-interest and micro-resources, resolves the student's "all but finished dissertation" problem, palliates the research-team member's occasional ennui and alienation, and far from least can lend new strength to the body of fundamental social knowledge. The prescriptions of Dr. Glaser, of the University of California Medical Center at San Francisco, appear widely applicable.

The use of secondary analysis for the investigation of theoretical and substantive problems is still only a "growing tendency."[1] We can strengthen this tendency by attempting to locate its most likely potential users in the social structure of sociology. To be sure, any sociologist may avail himself of this strategy. However, there are some sociologists with personal needs and career problems for whom the benefits of secondary analysis are particularly appropriate.

The research strategy of secondary analysis-*the study of specific problems through analysis of existing data which were originally collected for other purposes* - dates back to before the second world war. Its impetus came from the rapid accumulation of attitude surveys in which "many applied topics suggested secondary analysis for scientific purposes."[2] The first notable effort at secondary analysis from a theoretical and methodological standpoint was Stouffer's *American Soldier*.[3]

The history of secondary analysis may have curbed as well as stimulated its use, since all writers to date have focused on the importance of secondary analysis of survey data. To apply secondary analysis only to unintensively analyzed piles of survey data is limiting in two ways. First, these analyses "follow up the primary analyses for which the data were originally collected."[4] Some see these "follow-ups" as guided "mopping-ups" of loose ends, obtained by a study director from students for a bare wage or a good grade. Whether or not the charge is valid, this image may conflict with the values of independent, original research and is liable to reduce the use of secondary analysis.

Second, the emphasis on survey data neglects other kinds of data, particularly field data, and hence limits the potential use of secondary analysis. This research strategy can be applied to almost any qualitative data however small its amount and whatever the degree of prior analysis.[5] Survey data may always remain the primary source of material for secondary analysis. However, with the current increase in all types of data collection, it is by no means the only possible source. Secondary analysis is something that the sociologist can do with data of his own choosing.

I begin this paper by discussing the *independent researcher*, the person for whom the use of secondary analysis is highly appropriate, and his position in the division of labor which contributes to knowledge. Then I consider how secondary analysis may help solve the personal needs and career problems, generated by their particular locations in the social structure of sociology, of four types of independent researcher: teacher, student, research team member, and "the otherwise employed."

THE INDEPENDENT RESEARCHER

By independent researcher I refer to only one facet of a sociologist's work life, since in few cases does independence completely characterize his work life. As defined by Lee, an independent researcher is one who engages in research as a personal venture, often on free time, (1) to satisfy his own curiosity, (2) to fulfill a desire to contribute to sociological knowledge, and (3) to do both in conformity with his own conception of a scientist's standard.[6] His research is free of influences and pressures from others' vested interests (he spends his own money or is modestly subsidized by a neutral agency), and he is free to pursue his own problem as far as he likes. He is the only person responsible for and to the research. In this sense he is what Merton has termed a "lone scholar,"[7] but he may, of course, use an assistant, clerical help, or processing machines and may also have the interest and occasional help of his associates.

The importance of the independent researcher is indicated by the 80 per cent increase in sociologists during the last decade, the widening variation in their occupational activities, and the increasing diversity of their organization affiliations.[8] More sociologists than ever are grappling with the typical problem of the independent researcher: *how to mobilize resources to accomplish some basic research.*

SECONDARY ANALYSIS: A LINK BETWEEN INDIVIDUAL AND TEAM RESEARCH

Lee, in his comparison of independent and team research, develops points at which these two forms of mobilization of research resources are in opposition, from the point of view of contributing to sociological knowledge.[9] Secondary analysis as a link between independent and team research can in some measure resolve these conflicts. Both independent and team research have distinct places in the division of labor which contributes to sociological knowledge. The basic cutting point in this division of labor is between *data collection* and *data analysis*.

Large-scale inquiry, typical of social research, requires a team of experts skilled in specialized techniques and methods of data collection as well as large sums to finance the operation.[10] This team effort yields data that is in good measure precise, reliable, and based on carefully chosen representative samples - data that give a sound basis for contributions to sociological knowledge. Collection of high-quality data is very often beyond the financial, specialized skill, physical, and temporal resources of the independent researcher. However, analysis of portions of the data collected is within the resources of the independent researcher, and it is here that he may step into the division of research labor. In providing this link between team research and independent research, secondary analysis has several benefits for the team, for the independent researcher, and for sociology.

The Original Idea: Insofar as "the conception of an original idea is essentially an individual effort," the research "task force" is at a disadvantage in contributing to sociological knowledge. Individual efforts at originality made by team members can easily be influenced by "committee thinking" about research design, by a member of the team whose prestige is based on professional reputation, and/or on his ability to negotiate funds, by vested interests in personnel, methods, theories, and by operational imperatives "such as obligations, pressures, forces or controls rising out of the relation to sponsor, client, or supporter." Hyman suggests that one solution to these problems is secondary analysis.[11] I add to this suggestion the requirement that it be done by an independent researcher, *not a member of the team,* who has negotiated for the data in a manner that insures his complete freedom.

Secondary, analysis by an independent, not of the team, is a significant way of severing collected data from research groups' commitments and pressures. Further, since the independent has not been indoctrinated with the original research design, his ability to engage in a fresh, intensive analysis of the data along different lines is greater than that of a team member. In short, the independent is free of both internal and external pressures. Secondary analysis by a team member is not often so free, in many cases I have observed. Though on his own resources, the team member still may be very much controlled by vested interests, committee thinking, and prestigeful associate members and sponsors.

The Independent's Resources: The independent researcher is seen by many group researchers as "lone and primitively equipped." If the independent works with data collected by a research team, he works with data collected by well-equipped people. During the analysis the use of modern data-processing equipment at many university institutes and centers is usually obtainable for a modest fee by the sociologist, especially if he runs the machines himself during evenings and weekends. Thus, if the independent takes a reasonable portion of team-collected data for studying his theoretical or substantive problem, he needs but modest funds and time for using effective equipment. *It is the costs of data collection that are beyond the scope of the independent researcher, not the costs of data analysis.*

Merton has noted in a discussion of the high cost of research based on original data "how wasteful it is to neglect such available material."[12] It is wasteful of time, money, and data when the independent neglects possible secondary analysis of pertinent available material for the study of a sociological problem and instead spends his precious time and money on data collection. It is also wasteful of talent when a sociologist, who cannot muster the resources for data collection, does nothing when he could be applying his analytical talents to available data. The independent researcher also provides an important link between applied and basic research.[13] Lazarsfeld has noted that "A number of very important theoretical ideas grew out of research done for the purpose of solving a specific (applied) problem...."[14] Secondary analysis of the applied research data by an independent provides the financial and temporal resources for a study of these ideas which otherwise might be doomed to oblivion because of lack of budget for theoretical analysis.

The Independent's Personality: Two principal criticisms leveled against independent researchers are: (1) They are "likely to be more intuitive, impressionistic and subject to the use of 'Verstehen' operation than group researchers." (2) They are "likely to be thought impudent, repugnant, confusing or confused by the more socialized or bureaucratic group researcher: the individualists "do not fit in." "While these attributes may be thought of by some group researchers to be a disadvantage in reliable data collection, they are the very stuff from which comes an original contribution. This is substantiated by Anne Roe's compilation of findings on the personality patterns of productive scientists. Her list is too long to reproduce here; however, a few patterns are of direct relevance to our discussion. "Truly creative scientists seek experience and action and are independent and self-sufficient with regard to perception, cognition, and behavior. They have a preference for apparent but resolvable disorder and for an aesthetic ordering of forms of experience. They have strong egos....which permits them to regress to preconscious states with the certainty that they will return from these states. Their interpersonal relations are generally of low intensity (ungregarious, not talkative, asocial)."[15]

Secondary analysis locates the independent researcher with these attributes in an ideal position in the scientific division of labor - a position benefiting group research, sociological knowledge, and himself. In the analysis of group research data he is free to apply his intuitiveness at will, and since he is not a member of the team, whether or not he can "fit in" is irrelevant. It is a solution for some independents to a growing problem of research organizations - "toleration of the 'oddball'" in teamwork. In a very few (usually richer) organizations the "oddball" is encouraged; in most he is readily sacrificed for the "greater good" of the team.[16]

TYPES OF INDEPENDENT RESEARCHERS

Four types of independent researchers are these: teacher, student, team research member, and the otherwise employed sociologist. Many points about one can be applied to others.

The Teacher: The typical career problem of many teachers, particularly those in universities and major colleges, is that they "are hired to teach...with no specifications of research duties. When they are evaluated, however, either as candidates for a vacant position, or as candidates for promotion, the evaluation is made principally in terms of their research contributions to their disciplines."[17] One solution to this "publish or perish" problem is team research. The teacher who works on a team captained by a strong idea man is usually assured of a worthwhile joint publication. Another solution is secondary analysis, which is particularly suited to the independent-oriented teacher who finds the team solution undesirable.

The economies of secondary analysis go far beyond those of time and money saved in data collection. First, there is an *economy of interest*. The typical teacher is probably more adept in analysis of his substantive field than in techniques of data collection - which have become very specialized. To spend time on learning and relearning these techniques can require a partial displacement of interest. A teacher of high reputation can possibly secure enough funds to employ experts, organizations, or students for his data collection, thereby being free, presumably, to work on whatever interests him in the analysis. However,he will be involved then as and administrator of an operation, possibly having to sacrifice precious time allotted for his major interest.

A teacher may have the time and funds sufficient only to collect data on a social unit that is either different or much smaller than the social unit of his interest. Thus, his research interests must be changed and/or curbed. Since creativity generally rises with ability to work on problems of deep interest,[18] secondary analysis may provide a strategy for keeping at the analysis of one's cherished problem area. Secondary analysis of high quality data also provides an alternative to studying a pet problem on lower quality data which, while within the independent's means to collect, can result in a low research yield for himself, his career, and sociological knowledge.

Second, the economies of time, money, interest, and data combine to *increase research output* and *conserve both research and teaching talent*. Secondary analysis may allow the talented teacher to work on more than one project at a time and more projects over time. This strategy may also help him offset some consequences on teaching of the pressure to publish such as "neglect of teaching, the devaluation of instructional tasks and, perhaps most serious, the gradual erosions of the teaching responsibilities of the senior faculty."[19]

Secondary analysis also implies some responsibilities for the teacher. The theorist who writes theory with no data on the pretext of not having time and/or money for data collection can no longer plead this excuse. He must either live explicitly in a world of speculation or make the effort to find some available material on which to base his theory. And the teacher who escapes from data analysis into pseudo-data collection by making unrealizable research plans and pleading no resources is similarly confronted with the fact that he could be attempting a contribution with available data.

The Student: As an independent scholar, the graduate student is perhaps the most stymied of all by the difficulties of data collection. He typically has little money saved or a job that allows only a small margin of money for research. Even with well-sponsored support, his reputation at best commands little more than a fellowship to live on while he does some inexpensive kind of research. To get his Ph.D. he is supposed to make a substantial contribution to his field. This task is harder because of the poorer the data that he must work with; and poor data is often associated with lack of resources for data collection. Poor data may also preclude excellent training in both collection and analysis. Time spent on research is of utmost importance because only with the degree in hand is his professional career in hand. The time factor may also force him to postpone either family life or a sound life for his family, unless he postpones the degree.[20]

Typical solutions to the problem of collecting data are to take a job on a research team or to do a project for a funded professor or a client through a professor's sponsorship. The proviso involved in these solutions is that the student can have a portion of the data for a dissertation. But these approaches still take *time,* even though the money problem may be solved, and they all leave the student somewhat less than independent given his financial, valuational, and perhaps, emotional vulnerabilities, coupled with his connection with power figures of the initial study.

An alternative solution to the data collection problem is the secondary analysis of data from elsewhere - data which is released completely to the student for his own purposes. He can speed up the time for getting a degree. If he must take full or part time employment, he can work on the data during off hours. He may even be able to start his dissertation while still engaged in course work or studying for qualifying examinations, weaving his analysis into his studies, thereby adding to the meaning of both study and research.

Lastly, secondary analysis is an inexpensive strategy for solving the "serious" ABD degree (All But Dissertation") problem in sociology, "which is primarily one of dollars." An ABD degree is given to "those doctoral candidates who have completed everything for the degree except the dissertation and who are away from the campus on a full-time job."[21] In suggesting secondary analysis as a way of doing a dissertation I have assumed that the original contribution of most students comes from problem development, analysis, and presentation, not from data collection. How and where the student obtains the data should not affect the calibre of his training in research analysis by the professor whose data he has elected *not* to use.

Of course, the student can continue his training in team research while engaging in an independent secondary analysis for his dissertation. Concomitant training in data collection and analysis may provide one solution to an important student problem noted by Lee: "But the primary problem is this: Group research has now so absorbed the interests, aspirations and resources of graduate departments of sociology that the training of individual well-rounded journeymen in sociological research is being eclipsed. The situation has thus arisen that it is becoming fairly difficult to locate young staff members for a college or university who are trained to be liberal arts college and graduate school professors and to carry on the independent research that needs to go therewith."[22] This concomitant training may raise the chances of balancing off the absorbing effect of group research on the student, thereby producing a "well-rounded journeyman" steeped in research technology out of the person who might otherwise become simply a "technique peddler."[23]

This strategy is also an excellent way for the student to do term papers and M.A. theses and to attempt aside (not required) contributions on problems that interest him. The meaningfulness of doing papers, whether required or not, is immeasurably enhanced by analysis of high quality data that are respected by other sociologist. In this sense, the facilitating nature of secondary analysis encourages the student to try more research than is requisite for his program.

The Team Member: In response to the familiar charges that research organizations "stultify the independent thought of, deny autonomy to," and cause displacement of the scientific values and motives of its member, Merton has recently noted that "close inspection of how these institutes actually work will find that many of them consist of individual scholars with associates and assistants, each group engaged in pursuing its own research bents."[24] If group researchers are free to pursue their own research problems, they are mostly, if not only, the senior research associate or director of the team. For it has also been noted that the imagination of the junior members of the team is liable to be stifled to the extent that they "no longer consider it their responsibility and duty to think out problems for themselves but expect problems to be handed out to them by their superior."[25] Insofar as junior researchers are liable to this danger, an independent secondary analysis can help fend off any tendency to lose independence of thought and action and to become buried in and by group research.

The director of a group research is, of course also liable to stultification of thought and autonomy. As one who is responsible for the group he must see that its research commitment is fulfilled and that the sources of income do not dry up before the project is finished, so that his own and team members' jobs are not in jeopardy. As Bennis has noted, in his study of a social research organization, this takes much time and effort away from the director's own research - in essence he is forced to become a "research entrepreneur."[26] This responsibility also means that if the research loses interest for the director, he cannot simply terminate the project or give up his position. Loss of both research time and substantive interest may result in stultification with and alienation from the project, with an attendant loss of sensitivity to relevant problems and increased difficulties in finishing the final report. The probability of stultification and alienation for some directors is increased by the fact that some "social scientists have been more or less permanently diverted from their original research interests, simply because they did not resist the temptation of funds which were available for other projects."[27]

Two ways of handling the problems of stultification and alienation are the use of secondary analysis for "bridging" and "mopping-up" operations. The director initiates a series of small studies on the group's data by students to fulfill course requirements or for low wages. One function of these studies is "bridging;" that is, a widespread hunting for relevant problems and discrete analyses that may rejuvenate the director's interest and sense of relevance, thus providing for him a bridge back to the data. Another function is "mopping-ups"; that is, getting the study done faster with little stress on the budget, picking up loose and tangential ends for a feeling of closure, and mollifying any guilt the director may feel over his lack of involvement in what he is supposed to be involved.

These specific investigations are offered by the director as good training for students, whereas in some quarters they are seen as abuses of secondary analysis. The "bridging" and "mopping-up" implications of these investigations indicate on the director's part a lack of honesty to group members, client or sponsor, and students about his relation to the data and appear as exploitation of free or inexpensive labor to solve his problem.

One way that the director may forestall a sense of stultification with a alienation from the group project is to engage himself in a secondary analysis of his other current sociological interests with data from elsewhere. This may keep him vitalized as a researcher. In addition, trying to contribute to sociological knowledge may also forestall others from leveling at him the annoying but typical criticism of group researchers: he is merely a "technique peddler."[28]

The Otherwise Employed: As an economical and independent way of keeping a hand in research, secondary analysis provides a solution to two problems of the otherwise employed sociologist. This is the person who is in neither teaching nor research but in a staff or administrative position. Such people may be employed in university or research organizations, of course, but it is important to note their considerable increase in many kinds of government, professional, and welfare institutions.[29]

First, accomplishing some basic research may have consequences for this person - who is somewhat removed from the direct activity of his discipline - that are similar to those associated with belonging to a professional association and receiving its journal. Engaging in a secondary analysis would maintain his professional self-image as a scientist participating in the prestigeful world of social research, his feeling of unity with his profession, and his communication with, to forestall isolation from, the sources of sociological knowledge: fellow researchers and their research.[30]

Second, this feasible way of accomplishing contributions to knowledge can potentially provide a path back into teaching or research from other types of employment. That the otherwise employed sociologist has a problem in doing some research is forcefully brought out by two of Caplow and McGee's respondents: "yes, he's getting involved with administration there, and that's the kiss of death for any research." "She hasn't been in positions where productivity was demanded or even permitted,....in her current job there's no time for research."[31] Keeping a secondary analysis going on the side can help reduce some of the loss of those potentially talented contributors to sociology, who take full time jobs that do not require, emphasize, or even permit research.

CONCLUSION

In this paper I have explored an alternative strategy for accomplishing basic sociological research.[32] I suggest secondary analysis as only one possible aspect (not a complete style of a sociologist's research career. I doing this I have tried to locate its very appropriate use in the social structure of sociology, in the sense that it can be used to solve some typical problems faced by different types of independent researchers - again, usually only one aspect of a sociologist's career. Insofar as secondary analysis allows some people to mobilize their meager resources to tempt a sociological contribution, it can help save time, money, careers, degrees, research interest, vitality, and talent, self-images and myriads of data from untimely, unnecessary, and unfortunate loss.

REFERENCES

I am indebted to Alvin W. Gouldner and Howard S. Becker for aid and encouragement in the preparation of this paper.

[1] S.M. Lipset and R. Bendiz, *Social Mobility in Industrial Society* (Berkeley: University of California Press, 1959) p.ix.

[2] P.F. Lazarsfeld and S.S. Spivak, "Observations on the Organization of Empirical Social Research in the United States," *Information Bulletin of the International Social Council,* Dec. 1962, p.4.

[3] P.L. Kendall and P.F. Lazarsfeld, "Problems of Survey Analysis," in R.K. Merton and P.F. Lazarsfeld, eds., *Continuities in Social Research* (New York: Free Press, 1950), pp. 133-136; Lazarsfeld and Spivak, *op.cit.,* p.5; P.F. Lazarsfeld, "The American Soldier - An Expository Review," *Public Opinion Quarterly,* Fall 1949, pp. 377-404.

[4] Lipset and Bendiz, *op.cit.,* p.x.

[5] Obtaining data may be difficult when the amount of available material is small and/or the desired data is seemingly well analyzed. However, given the nature of sociological analysis on the same data one can make very different inferences, conceptualizations, indexes and cross-tabulations, study very different problems, use very different pivotal classifications, methods, and models or analysis. In short, analyzed data potentially can be re-analyzed for different problems with little or no relevant

overlap.

6 A. McC. Lee, "Individual and Organizational Research in Sociology," reprinted in S.M. Lipset and N.J. Smelser, eds., *Sociology: The Progress of a Decade* (Englewood Cliffs: Prentice-Hall, Inc., 1961), p. 159.

7 R.K. Merton, *Social Theory and Social Structure* (New York: Free Press, 1957), p.453, and R.K. Merton, "Sociological Conflict over Styles of Sociological Work," *Transactions of the Fourth World Congress of Sociology,* 1959, Vol. II, pp. 38-39.

8 M.W. Riley, "Membership of the American Sociological Association, 1950-1959," *American Sociological Review,* Dec. 1960, p. 926.

9 Lee, *op.cit.* Direct references to Lee and all *incited* quotations in this section of the paper will refer to his article.

10 On the organizational form of large-scale research and its consequences see Herbert Yuman, *Survey Design and Analysis* (New York: Free Press, 1955), pp. 29-39.

11 Hyman, *op.cit.*, pp. 41, 47. Bendix notes that these pressures can "undermine the independent judgement of the individual social scientist with regard to what *he* regards as significant." R. Bendix, "The Image of Man in the Social Sciences: The Basic Assumptions of Present Day Research," in Lipset and Smelser, *op.cit.*, p. 35.

12 R.K. Merton, "The Research Budget," in M. Jahoda, M. Deutsch and S. Cook, eds., *Research Methods in Social Relations* (New York: Dryden Press, 1954), p.344.

13 Secondary analysis by an independent researcher provides one of the "actual," not "supposed or ideal," relations between basic and applied research sought by Merton and Lerner; see R.K. Merton and D. Lerner, "Social Scientists and Research Policy," reprinted in W.G. Bennis, K.B. Benne, and R. Chin, eds., *The Planning of Change* (New York: Holt, Rinehart and Winston, 1961), p. 56.

14 Lazarsfeld and Spivak, *op.cit.*, p. 27.

15 A. Roe, "The Psychology of the Scientist," *Science,* August 1961, p. 458.

16 N. Kaplan, "Some Organizational Factors Affecting Creativity," IRE *Transactions*, March 1960, p. 1960. See also on this problem B.T. Eiduson,

Scientists: Their Psychological World (New York; Basic Books, 1962), pp. 165-169.

[17] T. Caplow and R. McGee, *The Academic Marketplace* (New York: Basic Books, Inc., 1958), p. 84.

[18] Roe, *op.cit.*

[19] Caplow and McGee, *op.cit.*, p. 231.

[20] On the relation of family life to postponing the degree see L.S. Kubie, "Some Unsolved Problems of the Scientific Career," reprinted in M.R. Stein, A.J. Vidich, and D.M. White, eds., *Identity and Anxiety* (New York: Free Press, 1960), pp. 259-268; and J.A. Davis, *Stipends and Spouses* (Chicago: University of Chicago Press, 1962). Davis' findings indicate that once married, more students postpone the degree than sound family life.

[21] B.Berelson, *Graduate Education in the United States* (New York: McGraw Hill, 1960), pp. 171-172.

[22] Lee, *op.cit.*, p. 163.

[23] With respect to the training of "spiritless technicians" with a lack of "moral sense," see A.W. Gouldner, "Anti-Minotaur: The Myth of a Value Free Sociology," *Social Problems,* Winter 1962, p. 212. On the necessity of having "available (to university departments) a well trained group of young research experts which can be moved from one project to another," see Lazarsfeld and Spivak, *op.cit.*, p. 25 and passim. See also P.F. Lazarsfeld, "The Sociology of Empirical Social Research," *American Sociological Review,* Dex. 1962, pp. 763-766.

[24] Merton, "Social Conflict over Styles of Sociological Work," *op.cit.*, p. 39. Lee has also noted and offered a critique of this contention by group researchers, *op.cit.*, p. 160 and passim.

[25] Hyman, *op.cit.*, p. 39.

[26] W.G. Bennis, "The Social Scientist as Research Entrepreneur," *Social Problems,* July 1955, p. 47.

[27] Bendix, *op.cit.*, p. 35.

[28] Lee, *op.cit.*, p. 164. On the many issues involved in "technique peddling" see also Gouldner, *opcit.,* and Merton and Lerner, *op.cit.*, pp. 68-69, Bendix, *op.cit.*, pp. 35-36, and Lazarsfeld, *op.cit.*

[29] Riley, *op.cit.*, p. 921, Table 8.

[30] On the functions of belonging to a professional organization for professional scientists otherwise employed see A. Strauss and L. Rainwater, *The Professional Scientist* (Chicago: Aldine Press, 1962), Chapter 10.

[31] Caplow and McGee, *op.cit.*, pp. 83-84.

[32] In a forthcoming paper, "The Logic and Legitimacy of Secondary Analysis," I take up the problems of searching for data, dealing with the primary analyst, using old data in contemporary settings (the escape from time and place) and developing new research models afforded by secondary analysis. See also B.G. Glaser, "Secondary Analysis: A Strategy for the Use of Knowledge from Research Elsewhere," *Social Problems,* Summer 1962, for a discussion of the applied research potential of secondary analysis.

Reprinted from *Social Problems*, Vol. 10, No. 1, Summer 1962.

SECONDARY ANALYSIS: A Strategy for the Use of Knowledge from Research Elsewhere

Barney G. Glaser, Ph.D.

In recent years there has been a "rapidly expanding demand for sociologists' services" by organizations and groups for aid in solving their operation problems.[1] When a prospective client approaches the social scientist with a problem and asks what research can do to help solve it, he will generally focus this question in one or two ways: 1) what research knowledge already exists that may help and/or 2) what research can be done directly in the present situation?[2] This paper will discuss one strategy for applying existing research in the hope that it may help social scientist cope more effectively with the expanding demand for applied social research.

In the application of scientific knowledge *'discovered elsewhere'* to the solution of an operating problem, the social scientist must face certain important questions of comparability between the past research and the present or operating situation. They are comparability of 1. populations, 2. situational dynamics, 3. problems under study, 4. variables or concepts, and 5. past findings with present hypotheses. If these questions are ignored, the social scientist may err in two ways. He may either prematurely reject important prior research because of glaring manifest differences or he may accept uncritically all findings and insights as relevant to the present situation.

In discussing ways of handling these questions of comparability, Likert and Lippitt focus only on strategies for obtaining data on the *present situation.* These are "budding off" conferences, research application conferences, research review conferences, focusing a specific operating problem, direct consultation on a solution of an operating problem, in-service seminars, and a technique for quick analysis of the present situation.

Obtaining data from the *past research* for the necessary comparisons may equally be a problem. The social scientist may find, in returning to the original publication, that concepts are not clear; populations are not specified; situational dynamics have not been dealt with; the right variables have not been taken up or, if they were, relevant interrelations have not been done; and analysis of problems has taken too dissimilar a tack. He may ask: what would have happened if the author had done this or that with his data?

If the social scientist is able to apply the strategy of secondary analysis, inability to make comparisons or apparent noncomparability with the present situation may not be sufficient cause for discarding potentially applicable past research. On the contrary, past research is just beginning to be tapped for its relevance to solving present problems. With this strategy one does not have to depend solely on the previous analyst's approach and bent of mind. Lipset and Bendix have defined secondary analysis as "the study of specific problems through analysis of existing data which were originally collected for other purposes."[3]

We suggest that through the use of secondary analysis the social scientist may be better enabled to serve his client. First, it widens the potential applicability of a past research by changing its limits from data presented to data collected. Second, with this strategy the social scientist can turn from printed sources to the vast reservoirs of existing data (published and unpublished from) that sit in the basements and files of institutes, bureaus and centers throughout the country. Thus he increases the amount of past research that can be brought to bear on the operating problem.

COMPARABILITY

The first phase in secondary analysis is to face the questions of comparability. If the *populations* of the past research and present situation are somewhat similar but the social scientist is not sure how similar, he can find out the characteristics of the past population and make specific comparisons. If the past population is inappropriate as is, he can carve out of it a comparable sub-group. The latter is a powerful operation afforded by secondary analysis. By using it one can take a past study of a seemingly incomparable population and end up with sub-population that is comparable.[4] For example, if the social scientist is asked by a group of science-oriented pathologist how best to defend their place in both science and medicine which is being challenged by Ph.D.' and clinical pathologists respectively,[5] he can turn to national samples of college graduates or to surveys of research organizations and take out of the total group the sub-group of pathologists for study. In this sense the base of selection of past research is broadened considerably. The social scientist need not be content with or constrained by the population units designed by the primary analyst, hence left with a limited number of useful past researches. This strategy will alert him to the use of data that normally would not be considered or thought of as applicable to present problems.

When he turns to *situational dynamics* the social scientist can again do the necessary secondary analysis for making comparisons. If the science oriented pathologists who have come for his help are under siege in an affiliated hospital, he might want to sort out of his past populations those pathologists who are safe at basic research in a government subsidized, non-profit, medical research organization. Of course, these comparisons overlap with population comparisons to some extent, and both are limited by the amount of data collected in the past research. But in using secondary analysis social scientists are not limited by the amount of data presented in the past research publication.

As to *concepts or variables,* again the social scientist is not limited by the level of thinking of the primary analyst. Likert and Lippitt suggest that the primary analyst try "to move to a level of theorizing... which makes it possible for a wide range of practitioners to see how generalizations apply to analysis of their problems." To be sure the social scientist can raise the level of abstraction or reconceptualize the past research without resorting to secondary analysis. But suppose the variables in the past research do not come close enough to his conceptualization of the present situation. By secondary analysis he can take up variables that were not presented in publication, he can clarify unclear variables that were presented, and most important of all he can construct variables (indexes) which indicate the present concepts. For example, if his hypothesis is that science-oriented pathologists who are losing their identity will tend not to defend their place in medicine and science, and if he has no measure of identity, it may be a simple matter to combine a few items to obtain this measure.

When it comes to comparisons of *past problems and findings to present problems and hypotheses,* the social scientist is even freer of the primary analyst's purposes. It does not matter if the problem analyzed in the past research resembles the present problem. If the data are comparable with respect to population, situation, and variables, then the social scientist merely analyzes it according to the specific operating problem. This is the very essence of secondary analysis. He may, of course, use existing findings, but he is quite free to take the data to its limits for his own purposes. Thus he may look at all possible relations between variables to search for findings that are needed for application to the present problem. Here most of all secondary analysis changes the limits of application of past research from data published to data collected.

It has been suggested to me that in some instances one need not even be content with the limits of the data collected. If the data come from an organization, the social scientist may be able to return to it. By interviewing people who were there in the past or studying pertinent documents he may be able to return to it. By interviewing people who were there in the past or studying pertinent documents he may be able to fill in for the present analysis gaps in the past data.[6] This may even be accomplished, though perhaps less effectively, by letters of inquiry and by requests for document copies.

OTHER BENEFITS FROM SECONDARY ANALYSIS

Economies: This strategy has many other useful consequences for the application of research done elsewhere. If the people with the operating problem do not have enough money for an adequate study of their situation, secondary analysis is a much less expensive process and can, through use of a number of past researches, potentially provide a sufficient amount of data. If the present situation requires action in a short time, secondary analysis can usually be done more quickly than collecting and analyzing new data. If the operating problem is of such a nature that a study of the situation would be inadvisable, secondary analysis provides a way to study the problem elsewhere.

Readiness: Likert and Lippitt state that clients will utilize social science only if they are ready for its help. This readiness depends on (1) a problem sensitivity, (2) an image of potentiality and (3) a general experimental attitude toward innovation. In order to create this readiness for utilization of research the social scientist should try to develop these elements in his clients. New research is not feasible if the clients are not ready for it; and past research as published may be too barren from the point of view of comparability to be used for creating readiness. However, a secondary analysis which shows clients that what was done elsewhere can be done for them may be a very useful device in developing a problem sensitivity, and image of potentiality and a feel for research, hence readiness. At the same time, it also may provide an empirically based design for guiding future research in the present situation, both by suggesting gaps to be filled in and providing findings to validate and to further analyze.

Application Testing: Application of social research provides some unique problems that secondary analysis may help solve. If past research meets the criteria of comparability and a particular finding seems applicable to the present situation the client may be eager to apply it. This may put the social scientist in the awkward position of having to challenge the application in some measure. He must suggest limits of generalization, he must warn against over-simplification; he must explain how a finding needs considerable testing before application. He must stress, as Hyman suggest, that findings to be applied should first be analyzed as much as possible in terms of the realities of the present situation in order to judge their potential consequences.[7] At this point it is likely that the past research will let the social scientist down. The previous finding may not have been tested or tested enough in a manner appropriate to the present situation. The social scientist is faced with the conflict of wanting to apply a fact to ready clients which his expertise says he cannot do. Secondary analysis is a potential way out of this dilemma. With this strategy the social scientist can do the necessary sub-group comparisons and characterizations. He can bring out the associated norms, beliefs, values and sentiments. He can look at the variations that strategic contextual variables make in the finding. He can analyze the potential side-effects of implementing policy based on the finding.

Application Variables: Another problem is that variables which have theoretical importance do not necessarily have practical importance. Using secondary analysis, the social scientist can take comparable past research, particularly that which is theoretically oriented, and search for strategic application variables. He can develop their importance by looking at their distribution in various sub-groups, showing their relation to other acknowledged strategic variables, and looking for crucial cutting points. He can also look for the controllable variables in the study which are more important for application than the noncontrollable ones, even though the latter may be stronger determinants of the phenomena under study and therefore more emphasized in a theoretical approach. Gouldner has indicated other properties of variables useful in applied social science:[8] they are easily translated into lay concepts; they will not impede intended change when collected, studied or implemented; they are accessible, reliable and efficient; they provide preferential entry to the situation and they are latent to the client with the operating problem. Returning to original data will allow scanning for variables with these properties, hence their potential use in solving the operating problem.

CONCLUSION

This paper has been written to suggest a strategy for practice that is also being used for theory development.[9] The social scientist will be guided in its implementation by the requirements of the operative situation and the controls surrounding the past research data. In some cases he may obtain the data easily; in others he may find it more appropriate to ask the primary analyst or custodian of the existing data to have a few tabes run. Sometimes the data may not be relinquished, but if code books or schedules can be obtained he can send in orders for the necessary machine work. To be sure, secondary analysis is not limited to quantitative data. Observation notes, unstructured interviews, and documents can also be usefully reanalyzed. In fact, some field workers may be delighted to have their notes, long buried in their files, reanalyzed from another point of view. Lastly, secondary analysis of past research for application purposes need never hinder the researcher from writing up the theoretical side. Man is a data gathering animal. This paper suggests a strategy for using the data he gathers.

REFERENCES

[1] Talcott Parsons, "Some Problems Confronting Sociology as a Profession," *American Sociological Review,* 24 (1959), pp. 555-557.

[2] Rensis Likert and Roland Lippitt, "The Utilization of Social Science," in *Research Methods in the Behavioral Sciences,* Leon Festinger and Daniel Katz (eds.), New York: Dryden Press, 1953, p. 583. All references to Likert and Lippitt are taken from their introduction to this article and their first section, "Using Knowledge and Theory Derived from Research Elsewhere," pp. 581-602.

[3] Seymour M. Lipset and Reinhard Bendix. *Social Mobility in Industrial Society,* Berkeley: University of California Press, 1959, Preface, p.x.

[4] If this sub-group is taken from a large survey or a field project that has gone on for years and is, itself, too large to handle conveniently for the purpose of application to a situation elsewhere, it is a simple matter to take some kind of systematic sample (e.g., random, stratified, etc.) of the sub-group of IBM cards or field notes. Thus, it can be reduced to a more manageable size for faster results and smaller cost of processing.

[5] For a discussion of this problem see Mary Rue Bucher, "Conflicts and Transformations of Identity, A Study of Medical Specialists," unpublished Ph.D. dissertation, University of Chicago, 1961.

[6] Suggestion made to author by Robert K. Merton.

[7] Herbert H. Hyman, *Survey Design and Analysis,* New York: The Free Press of Glencoe, 1955, p. 336.

[8] Alvin W. Gouldner, "Theoretical Requirements of the Applied Social Sciences," *American Sociological Review,* 22 (1957), pp. 92-102.

[9] On the traditional use of secondary analysis for theory development see Paul F. Lazarsfeld and Sydney S. Spivak, "Observations on the Organization of Empirical Social Research in the United States," *Information Bulletin of the International Social Science Council,* XXIX (December, 1961), pp. 5, 6, 27 and 30.

Part III

Generating Grounded Formal Theory

Reprinted from *Theoretical Sensitivity*, Sociology Press, Mill Valley, CA, 1978, Chapter 9.

GENERATING FORMAL THEORY

Barney G. Glaser, Ph.D.

The methodology detailed in the preceding chapters was developed from generating substantive theory. This process generates theory that fits the real world, works in predictions and explanations, is relevant to the people concerned and is readily modifiable. Countless studies make us quite sure of this effort.

We are far more humble when it comes to generating formal theory. We remain convinced that it should be grounded, but are not sure yet, as with grounded substantive theory, of the resolutions to many specific problems of generation. For example: In choosing a core variable for a formal theory, what are the grounds for its relevancy, how does one integrate the theory, where next to theoretically sample,how dense should formal theory be? Indeed why generate formal theory at all? Once the analyst is cut loose from the grounding of a specific substantive areas, answers to these questions are not readily apparent. At times it seems that formal theory can "go" just about any way that an analyst desires.

In this chapter we shall touch on these problems, by giving answers to strategies developed through many years of experience in doing research and in writing at varying levels of conceptualization, including two formal theory monographs.[1] We shall also give our thoughts on these problems, which have supplemented our experience and somewhat outdistanced it.[2]

In the first section we consider the diverse sources of generating formal theory, with special attention to the link that substantive theory provides between data and formal theory. In the next section we discuss the differences in comparative analysis operations between substantive and formal theory, with special attention to theoretical sampling. Then we present a section on theoretical sampling for generating formal theory. Then we present a section on theoretical formulation with focus on density and integration. Lastly, we give our view of why generating formal theory is of value. Again, we reiterate that these ideas barely open up the methodology of generating grounded formal theory.

SOURCES OF FORMAL THEORY[3]

The several sources of formal theory can usefully be classified in three ways: Grounded in systematic research, ungrounded, or a combination of both grounded and ungrounded. Speculative or ungrounded formal theory derives from any combination of several sources; whims and wisdom of usually deceased great men, conjecture and assumptions about the "oughts" of life, and other extant speculative theory. The usual method of developing such theory is to deduce logically from these sources. The weaving in of some grounded theory usually helps, but does not save nor even compete well with the theorist's emphasis on speculative sources.

As we have argued in *Discovery*, this speculative, derived formal theory does not meet our criteria of fit, "works," relevance, and easy modification. Indeed, because it is ungrounded, when applied to data such theory forces the data in many ways. The theory dictates, before empirical examination, presumed relevancies in problems, concepts, and hypotheses, and the kinds of the indicators that "should" apply - to the neglect of emergent relevancies of processes, concepts, and their properties and indicators. Its fit and its predictions also are suspect; while modification of the theory when it does not work is regarded as requiring systematic conclusive proof, certainly not warranted by a few exceptional (often crucial) incidents. This forcing of the data by speculative formal theory has two untoward consequences: (1) Some theorists, especially when young, are dissuaded from advancing and extending theories which appear useless, (2) while others settle for description made at low conceptual levels.

The principal sources of grounded formal theory consist both of the data of diverse systematic research and the substantive theories generated from such data. In combination and separately these sources give rise to several bases of grounding: (A) One substantive area formal theory which uses "rewriting-up" techniques, (B) direct formulation from data from diverse substantive areas when no substantive theory exists, (C) expanding a single, existing substantive theory with comparative data of other areas, and comparative analysis of several existing substantive theories which is perhaps the most powerful of these approaches. The latter is powerful because its coverage of more diverse properties of the formal theoretical area makes it apply to more diverse substantive areas with minimal qualifications. The "rewrite" approach is, however, both the weakest and the more prevalent in sociology. (D) Lastly, we consider the BSP approach to generating formal theory and, (E) cumulative knowledge.

From Substantive to Formal Theory: Before considering these bases of grounding let us briefly consider the essential difference and a few relationships between substantive and formal theory.

By *substantive theory* we mean theory devolved for a substantive or empirical area of sociological inquiry - such as patient care, race relations, professional education, geriatric life styles, delinquency, or financial organizations. By *formal theory* we mean theory developed for a formal or conceptual area of sociological inquiry - such as status passage, stigma, deviant behavior, socialization, status congruency, authority and power, reward systems, organizations or organizational careers. Both types of theory may be considered "middle-range."[4] They fall between the "minor working hypotheses" of everyday life and the "all-inclusive" grand theories.

Substantive and formal theories exist on conceptually ordered distinguishable levels of generality, which differ only in terms of degree. In any one study each type of theory can shade at points into the other. The analyst, however, should focus clearly on one level or the other, or on a specific combination, because the strategies vary from arriving at each one. For example, in an analysis of the organizational careers of scientists, the focus was substantive (scientists' careers), not formal (organizational careers.)[5] With the focus on a substantive area, the generation of theory can be achieved by doing a comparative analysis between or among groups within the same substantive area. In this instance, comparisons were made among the career stages of junior investigator, senior investigator, and supervisor within two different promotional systems of the organization. Generation of the substantive theory also can be furthered by comparisons of the organizational careers of scientists with other substantive cases within the formal area of organizational/careers, such as the careers of lawyers or military officers. Those comparisons would be used to illuminate the substantive theory about scientist's careers.

However, if the focus of level of generality is on generating a formal theory, the comparative analysis is made among different kinds of substantive cases and their theories, which fall within the formal area, without relating the resulting theory back to any one particular substantive area. The focus of comparisons, to continue with our example, is now on generating a formal theory of organizational careers, not on generating a theory about a single substantive case of an organizational career. In *Organizational Careers,* the comparisons were between theories.

A. *"Rewrite" Techniques:* One version of rewriting techniques is simply to omit substantive words, phrases, or adjectives; instead of writing "temporal aspects of dying as a nonscheduled status passage," one would write "temporal aspects of nonscheduled status passage." Substantive theory can also be rewritten up a notch: Instead of writing about how doctors and nurses give medical attention to a dying patient according to his social loss, one would talk of how professional services are distributed according to the social value of clients.

In each version of the rewriting technique, the social scientist writes a one-area formal theory on the basis of his substantive theory; he does not generate the former directly from the data. These techniques produce only an adequate *start* toward theory, *not* an adequate formal theory itself. *The researcher has raised the conceptual level of his work mechanically; he has not raised it through comparative understanding.* He has done nothing to broaden the scope of his theory on the formal level by comparative investigation of different substantive areas. He has not escaped the time and place of his substantive research. Moreover, the formal theory cannot fit or work very well when written from only one substantive area (and often only one case of the area), because it cannot be developed sufficiently to take into account many of the contingencies and qualifications that will be met in the diverse substantive areas to which it will be applied. All that happens is that it will be modified by other theories and data through the comparative method, because by itself it is too sparsely developed to use in making trustworthy predictions and explanations beyond the substantive area. Thus, in our view, the one-area formal theory still remains, in actuality, treated as a substantive theory possibly later to be generalized by comparative analysis. To be sure such theory is a strategic link in advancing from substantive to formal theory, as it can be used in the comparative analysis of several substantive theories.

B. *Data:* The linkage provided by substantive theory is not omitted when generating a formal theory directly from diverse sets of data. It is natural to the process of generating that parts of a substantive theory will emerge from the initial set of substantive data, before the theory's level of conceptualization is raised by comparing it to data from other substantive areas. This process leads to great changes in the variable structure of the theory. For example, there is a drop-out of what are only contextually significant variables - time, place, conditions, of each substantive area.

C. *Substantive Theory:* The linkage between research data and formal theory, provided by substantive theory, is twofold. It occurs when a particular substantive theory is extended and raised to formal theory by the comparative analysis of it with other research data. The linkage occurs also when the substantive theory is comparatively analyzed with *other* substantive theories. The theory arrived at when comparing substantive theories is more general and more qualified.

Substantive theories typically have important general relevance and become, almost automatically, springboards or stepping stones to the development of a grounded formal theory. As stated in Chapter 6, the core variable has general implications and can be followed through on to generate a formal theory of the core. For example, a substantive theory on the comparative failure of scientists leads directly to the need for a theory of comparative failure in work (or even more generally in all facets of social life)[6]. Or substantive theory on deviance disavowal of people with visible handicaps leads to a formal one concerned with deviance disavowal by a much wider range of persons.[7]

Other relevant aspects provided by substantive theory for formal theory are the providing of *initial* direction in developing relevant conceptual categories, conceptual properties of categories, hypotheses relating these concepts, and in choosing possible modes of integration for the formal theory. We emphasize "initial" because as the formal theory is generated from comparing many substantive theoretical ideas from many different cases - the relevant categories, properties, and hypotheses will change in the process of generating theory. Also, in integrating formal theory, formal models of process, structure, and analysis may be useful guides to integration, along with models provided by the comparatively analyzed substantive theories.

D. *BPS:*[8] A forth approach, closely related to the above, to generating formal theory is to start with a BSP (or other core variable) and compare its phenomenon in different substantive classes. This is done both by searching the literature for where the BSP is processing on some dimension and through memory of relevant literature, experiences and incidents. This approach requires a mature, experienced grounded theorist for several reasons. He must know a great deal of literature to draw on, he must have had experience in research for worthy anecdotes, he must have the capacity and skill to search much literature quickly and he must be experienced *in knowing when his BSP is merely a logical elaboration.* One can find specks of a BSP everywhere, but unless it was firmly grounded in at least one substantive theory, only the mature, theoretically sensitive sociologist will begin to know empirically if it is indeed relevant anywhere, *even though it sounds relevant.*

For example, it seems that BSP's such as memoing or risk taking are relevant, but we are not that sure, never having seen them be the core variable in a substantive study. We have seen these variables in studies many times, but they never seem to emerge as core or near core. Thus, experience counsels that they would not be worthy candidates for generating a formal theory. In contrast, core BSP's such as cultivating, waiting, or faulting are very relevant BSP cores and are probably worthy of the time and effort to generate a formal theory on them. Our theory of Status Passage was generated on this basis - we had read, researched and experienced many forms of status passage for some years.

In searching the literature, the analyst must be experienced, skilled at and sensitive to looking for the BSP in both its more general and more specific, but also different, conceptual forms. For example, to generate a formal theory of cultivating he can look at the more general processes of servicing and the more specific ones of courting, soliciting, prospecting, selling and persuading, as he varies his substantive classes of data. And the analyst can look for comparisons in BSP's that seem closely related; such as delivering, collecting or rewarding. As this theoretical sampling proceeds, much that is preconceived and/or logically elaborated tends to be corrected by comparisons.

In writing a theory from this source of focusing on a BSP or core variable, the analyst should be careful not to mislabel the theory by referring to a unit - which both specifies it out of generality and shifts emphasis from process to unit. Thus, a general theory of "becoming" should be left as such and not be titled with a unit such as "becoming a nurse", or "becoming a professional", although it might have begun from such a source.

E. *Cumulative Knowledge:* Within these relations between social research, substantive theory and formal theory is an overall design for the cumulative nature of knowledge and theory, hence a moving force for generating higher level formal theory. The design involves a progressive building up from facts through substantive to formal grounded theory. To generate grounded substantive theory, we need many facts for the necessary comparative analysis; ethnographic studies and direct data collection are required. Ethnographic studies, substantive theories, and direct data collection are all, in turn, necessary for building up by comparative analysis to formal theory. This design, then, locates the place of each level of work within the cumulation of knowledge and theory, and thereby suggests a division of labor in sociological work.

For example, after having developed a theory of status passage there is not reason not to link other grounded theory with this theory, providing that extant theory fits well and makes sense of our data. For example, "awareness theory" was linked with our emergent theory of status passage.[9] Useful linkages with other grounded theories possibly will occur to other readers. In turn, our theory of status passage is subject to extension - best done through theoretical sampling and the associated comparative analysis. This extension represents a further specifying of the limits of that theory, thus an inevitable qualification of it.

The cumulative design also suggests that, besides many ethnographic studies, both multiple substantive and formal theories are needed to build up, through discovering their relationships, to more inclusive formal theories. Such a call for *multiple* theories is in contrast to the directly monopolistic implications of logico-deductive theories, whose formulators talk as if there is only one theory for a formal area or perhaps only one formal sociological theory for all areas. The need for multiple substantive theories to generate a formal theory may seem obvious, but it is not so obvious that multiple formal theories are also necessary. One formal theory never handles all the relevancies of an area, and by comparing many formal theories we can begin to arrive at more inclusive, parsimonious levels of formal theory. Parsimonious grounded formal theories are hard won by this design.

If we do not practice such modes of extending grounded theories, we relegate them, particularly if substantive, mainly to the status of respected little islands of knowledge, separated from others - each visited from time to time by inveterate footnotes, by assemblers of readings and of periodic bibliographical reviews, and by graduate students assigned to read the better literature. While the owners of these islands understandably are pleased to be visited, in due course of time they can look forward to falling out of fashion and to being bypassed. This is not how to build a cumulative body of theory.

The formal theory that we are referring to is induced by comparative analysis, and needs to be contrasted with "grand" theory that is generated by logical-deduction from assumptions and speculations about the "oughts" of life. The logico-deductive theorist, proceeding under the license and mandate of analytic abstraction and deduction from assumptions and conjecture, engages in premature parsimony of concepts and integrative model. He is not concerned with the theoretical comparative analysis of data and substantive theories required to achieve a theory that fits and works in explaining and interpreting a formal area of inquiry. If sociologists continue to develop both speculative theory and general theoretical frame works without recognizing the great difference between those formulations and the theory that is genuinely grounded in data, however useful the former types may be as rhetoric or for orientation, when they are taken as theory,they simply help to forestall another generation's discovery and formulation of grounded, truly testable theory. Speculative theory and theoretical frameworks also have had the consequence of turning away many persons from theorizing (because those are the only theories they recognize) in favor of syntheses[10] or publishing minimal conceptual description.[11]

GENERATING FORMAL THEORY BY COMPARATIVE ANALYSIS

The term comparative analysis - often used in sociology and anthropology has grown to encompass several different meanings and thereby to carry several different burdens. Many sociologists and anthropologists, recognizing the great power of comparative analysis, have employed it for achieving their various purposes. To avoid confusion we must, therefore, be clear as to our own use for comparative analysis (generating of theory) in contrast to its other uses (achieving accurate evidence, empirical generalizations, specification of a concept, and verifications of a hypothesis). Generation of theory both subsumes and assumes these other uses but only to the extent that they are in the service of generation. Otherwise they are sure to stifle it.

Comparative analysis is considered a general method, in our use of it, just as are the experimental and statistical methods - and all involve the logic of comparisons. Comparative analysis can, like those other methods, *be used for social units of any size*. Some sociologists and anthropologists customarily use the term "comparative analysis" to refer only to comparisons among large scale social units, particularly organizations, nations, institutions, and large regions of the world. But such a reference restricts a general method to use with only the specific class of social units to which it has frequently been applied. As a general method for generating theory, comparative analysis takes on its fullest generality when one realizes its power applied to social structural units of any size, large or small, ranging from men or their roles, through groups, organizations, to the nations or world regions. (See Chapter 3 on the theoretical coding of structural units.)

Comparative analysis can also be used to compare conceptual units of a theory or theories, as well as data, in terms of categories and their properties and hypotheses. Such conceptual comparisons result, as we have seen, in generating, densifying, and integrating the substantive theories into a formal theory by discovering a more parsimonious set of concepts with greater scope. The basic criterion governing the theoretical sampling of comparison groups in order to compare conceptual units for generating formal as well as substantive theory is their theoretical relevance for furthering the development of emerging categories, properties, hypotheses, and integration of the theory. *Any* groups may be selected that will help generate these elements of the theory. In making his selections, the researcher must always remember that he is an active sampler of theoretically relevant data, and as an active sampler of data, he must continually analyze the data to see where the next theoretical question will take him.

The criterion for selecting theoretically relevant materials is *ideational* to provide as broad and diverse a range of theoretical ideas on the formal area as possible. *This range of ideas may be contrasted to and does not necessarily mean, a broad range of data or of authors.* Ideas that fit theoretical areas or problems are the criterion of placement - not how much of an author or of a kind of data is used. The ultimate range of authors need not be great. It depends on the state of knowledge of the field.

Thus, materials are chosen to provide as many categories, properties, hypotheses, and problems on the formal theory as space permits - which, in turn, provides the range of elements for developing the formal theory. Many materials will come from exploratory qualitative research, not all of which are published yet are found in footnotes.[12] In qualitative research we usually find an abundance of general categories, hypotheses, and problems, in contrast to their sparseness in quantitative research. Also, qualitative research discussions are easier and richer to read, especially for interested readers outside of sociology. The ideas of many of the materials may be applicable to several parts of the theory. But each is put where it will contribute the most ideationally to the generation of formal theory.

As said in discovering substantive theory, because groups are chosen for a single comparison only, the analyst has no definite, prescribed, preplanned number and types of groups to compare for all or even most categories but he can cite the substantive class of groups. In research carried out for discovering formal theory, the researcher also *cannot* cite the diverse classes of substantive groups from which he collected data until the research is completed. In an extreme case, he may then find that the development of each major category may have been based on comparisons of different classes of groups. In the usual case there is considerable overlap of classes of comparison groups.

In theoretical sampling for formal theory, no one kind of data on a category nor any single technique for data collection is necessarily appropriate. Different kinds of data give the analyst different views or vantage points from which to understand a category and to develop its properties; these different views we have called "slices of data" in *Discovery*. Theoretical sampling allows a multi-faceted comparative investigation: There are no limits to the techniques of data collection, the way they are used, or the types of data required. The result is a variety of slices of data that would be bewildering if one wishes to evaluate them as accurate evidence for verifications. However, for generating formal theory this variety is highly beneficial, because it yields more diverse comparative information on categories than any one mode of knowing (technique of collection).

Among the slices of data that can be used in formal theory as opposed to substantive theory is the "anecdotal comparison." Through his own experiences, general knowledge or reading, and the stories of others, the social scientist can gain data on other groups that offer useful comparisons. Anecdotal comparisons are especially useful in developing core categories. The researcher can ask himself where else has he learned about the category, and make quick comparisons to start to develop it and sensitize himself to its relevancies.

Rules of comparability of groups used in descriptive and verification studies do not apply in generating formal theory because group comparisons are conceptual. Two typical, complementary rules of comparability mentioned in Chapter 3 as irrelevant are especially so when generating formal theory is the goal. One rule states that to be included within a set of comparison groups a group must have enough features in common with them. Another rule is that to be excluded it must show a "fundamental difference" from the others. These two rules for verificational and descriptive studies attempt to hold constant the strategic facts or to disqualify groups where the facts either cannot actually be held constant or would introduce more unwanted differences. In sum, one hopes that in this set of purified comparison groups spurious factors will not influence the findings and relationships and render them inaccurate.

These rules hinder the generation of formal theory. Weeding out spurious factors is not important in generating since they are just one more theoretical idea to be included in the theory. Indeed, concern with these rules - to avoid spuriousness and inaccuracy - diverts attention away from the important sets of fundamental differences and similarities among groups which, upon analysis, become important qualifying conditions under which categories and properties vary. These conditions should be made a vital part of the theory. Further, these two rules hinder the use of a wider range of classes or groups for developing categories and properties. Such a range, necessary for the fullest possible development of formal categories, is achieved by comparing incidents or ideas from *any* group, irrespective of differences or similarities, as long as the data indicates one similar category or property.

When theoretically sampling for comparison groups, several matters must be kept in mind. The analyst must be clear on the basic types of groups he wishes to compare in order to control their effect on the generality of both *scope* of population and *conceptual level of* his theory. As the analyst gradually shifts the degree of conceptual generality from substantive to formal theory, he must keep in mind the class of groups he selects. While the logic and process of comparative analysis remains the same, the process becomes more difficult because of the more abstract conceptual level and wider range of groups. When the aim is to discover formal theory, the analyst will definitely select dissimilar substantive groups from the larger class, in order to increase his theory's scope while transcending substantive areas.

He will also find himself comparing groups that seem to be

noncomparable on the substantive level but which on the formal level are conceptually comparable. Noncomparable on the substantive level here implies a stronger degree of apparent difference than does the term dissimilar. For example, while fire departments and emergency wards are substantially dissimilar, the conceptual comparability is still readily apparent; both deal with emergency systems which render immediate assistance. Since the basis of comparison between substantively noncomparable groups is not readily apparent, it must be explained on a higher conceptual level. For example, one could start developing a formal theory of social isolation by comparing four apparently unconnected monographs: *Blue Collar Marriage, The Taxi-Dance Hall, The Ghetto,* and *The Hobo*[13] All deal with facets of "social isolation." For another example, Goffman has compared apparently non-comparable groups when generating his formal theory of stigma.[14]

The analyst who wishes to discover formal theory, then, should be aware of the usefulness of comparisons made on high level conceptual categories among the seemingly noncomparable. He should actively seek this kind of comparison, do it with flexibility, and be able to interchange the apparently noncomparable comparison with the apparently comparable ones. The noncomparable type of groups comparison can greatly aid him in transcending substantive descriptions of time and place as he tries to generate a formal theory.

Density: Making a distinction between category and property indicates a conceptually systematic relationship between these two elements of theory. A category stands by itself as a conceptual element of theory; for example, a reversal. A property, in turn, is a conceptual aspect or element of a category; for example, the degree of clarity of a reversal. Categories and properties vary in degree of conceptual abstraction. Synthesis and integration of the theory may occur at many levels of conceptual and hypothetical generalization, whether varying from substantive to formal theory or within the formal level of abstraction. Levels of conceptualization, then, is one aspect of the density of generated grounded theory. Another aspect of density is how densely a category is developed in terms of its theoretical properties. Yet, another consideration of density is how well the theory is integrated within its full range of conceptualization. We believe, of course, that a grounded substantive theory warrants much densification so that it will fit a multitude of situations in its area. A dense theory lends itself to ready modification and formulation in order to handle yet new qualifications *required* by changing conditions in what is "going on." A dense theory helps relate very abstract levels to data.

A formal theory should also be dense, but in generating a formal theory *de-densification* occurs.[15] As substantive theories are compared there is a "fall-out" of substantively specific variables, as cross contextualizations generates the most general codes on underlying uniformities. Thus, parsimony and scope increase with comparison of different substantive classes.

The richness of substantive theory comes from the multiplication and proliferation of codes from the most abstract down in pyramiding fashion to smaller, lower abstraction codes. In contrast, the richness of formal theory comes from de-densifying by a parsimony of underlying general ideas which "lump" or condense some generally relevant substantive codes together as specific others "fall-out". Formal theory is extensive compared to the intensiveness of substantive theory.

Obviously, as the analyst extends the scope of his theory by including new substantive classes, his theoretical sampling is guided by the less dense, higher abstracting, recording process. As the abstracting process continues, formal theory densifies to the degree the scope of generality is increased by including more substantively relevant codes from different classes. In so doing, the analyst must guard against easily slipping into logical elaboration, by being sure all his comparisons are of grounded ideas.

Integration: The integration of a dense formal theory is accomplished quite differently from that of a substantive theory. The latter, as we have seen, is integrated by the emergence of a natural integration which occurs in the data of the area under consideration. Not so for formal theory; integration of small segments of a formal theory do emerge from substantive theory as it is generated. But, substantive integration is likely to disappear along with fall-out, condensing, and depyramiding of substantive codes.

In large measure the total integration of the formal theory can become arbitrary, since core relevance is hard to be sure of. Hence, formal theory can be usefully integrated by one or more theoretical models. In *Status Passage* we chose a cumulative build-up of several core categories of status passage, each of which has clear relationships to the other. Thus, to recapitulate direction and timing combine to make shape of status passage; and desirability provides the motivation to control shape and to go through a single status passage and through multiple status passages whether alone, in aggregate or in concert.

This mode of integrating the theory readily can be seen as arbitrary, in light of possible alternative modes. We originally worked on fifteen core categories of status-passage, which could have been reduced differently than finally chosen; and of course we did not work on all possible core categories. Again, logical elaboration is too easily slipped into if the analyst is not careful, and goes the way of "neatness" and "completeness."

A modeled integration does not make a formal theory ungrounded, it merely makes it somewhat less grounded than if integration were achieved by the emergence of a natural integration, which includes the higher level abstraction codes. This raises the question: Can a formal theory be integrated on a grounded basis, if substantive integration does not hold? The answer, yet to be completely shown by more studies, is *perhaps*. One way is for the analyst to use the most general codes of the stage of a grounded BSP as his integration scheme.[16] The analyst then begins to theoretically sample in a variety of substantive areas for each stage of the process. For example, in diet health optimizing there are three stages; pollution, purification and compromising purification with small amounts of pollution.[17] If the analyst were to develop an optimizing formal theory, he could theoretical sample for each stage in various substantive areas.

Limits for theoretical sampling do not revolve around saturation, as with substantive theory, since we think it is probably impossible to saturate categories for the formal theory. There are always new substantive areas to sample. Saturation in fact revolves only around the temporal limits, monetary resources, personal interest and knowledge of the analyst. But no matter, since new data and ideas merely modify an ever-developing formal theory by adding density, parsimony and scope while de-densifying substantive specific codes. Another analyst, not personally saturated, can always pick up where the analyst left off.

The grounded area which yielded the BSP makes the analyst sensitive to how to begin theoretical sampling and coding by using the original substantive areas to vary the scope of his theory and generate the fall-out of substantive specific variables and condense those that uncover the cross-contextual uniformities of the formal theory. As the formal theory codes emerge they are integrated by the general stages of the BSP, however modified. The chances that the stages will vary from the substantive integration are great if the variation that they account for in the formal theory problem is different from that of the substantive theory. But, however, the stages may change, they will be a grounded integration that emerged for the formal theory by cross-substantive comparative analysis of an emergent substantive integration. The above discussion also applies to the dimensions of a basic structural condition, such as shifts, or of other core variables.

The BSP integration of a formal theory has some advantages in degree over an arbitrary modeled formal theory. It tends to be more relevant since it started from substantive relevance and the comparisons verify and modify the relevance. Its applicability is also more apparent for the same reason. It is more understandable to readers because of its emergent "natural" integration. Arbitrary integration tends to lead to a highly dense unrelieved formal theory since all seems relevant - logically - as more comparisons generate more codes. This was the problem of *Status Passage*. The theory will also seem closer to reality, if it appears grounded in the original substantive concern; thus it will have more grab, imagery and fewer gaps. Also the formal problems seem more relevant when they are grounded in data, not in "sociological" interest. Parsimony and scope probably do not vary significantly between the two types of integrations.

Further, a formal theory based on a BSP integration can be used tentatively to open up a substantive area. This is only provided that the BSP has an emergent fit, and the analyst has not enough resources to emerge a substantive theory from systematic research, which would clearly be more favorable. In this sense a formal theory can be a useful consultation tool. Let us examine this area.

APPLIED FORMAL THEORY

Our colleagues often ask: "Of what use is formal theory?" We assume that they accept the standard uses of formal theory: Guiding substantive research; opening up substantive areas for thought, research, and scholarship; verificational studies of formal theory; modifying and extending it and integrating it with other theory to increase its scope with parsimony. These are quite worthy of *grounded* formal theory as opposed to the blind alleys of logical formal theory.

An applied use for grounded formal theory exists, especially one based on a BSP. This is based on the fact that it is not generalized to other populations but *generalized to basic social processes that underlie the issues and problems of diverse substantive areas* - for which there is *yet no grounded theory* (see Chapter 6). This general relevance, this transcending of substantive areas, makes grounded *formal* theory, a viable, applicable tool in, for example, consultations and during negotiations. It is also useful for critiquing other sociology.

When using grounded formal theory, the social scientists need not know all there is to be known about the substantive area. A little substantive knowledge related to the emergent fit of principle indicators, allows the formal theory to be applied. For example, theory about emergency systems that is based on the standard systems of a city, can be applied to developing a new system, such as a type of "crisis intervention." The consultant finds that the mind-absorbing and mind-opening aspects of such formal theory make sense to the client, and soon he becomes able to supply his own indicators and substantive information. Moreover, a theorist qua consultant can contribute to the research enterprises of colleagues, by stimulating thought about the implications of their data (already or soon to be collected) concerning matters suggested by grounded formal theory. We have found the theory of status passages useful both for research consultation and pragmatically addressed consultation.[18]

Often in the latter kind of consultation there is neither time nor money for the research needed to develop a relevant substantive theory or there is yet nothing to research, or no way to research the data. Cogent suggestions are needed, and grounded formal theory is most applicable in these instances. Our theory of status passage, for instance, is fairly obviously applicable to help, guide, and articulate many institutionalized status passages now in their formation, expansion, or "having problems"; such as new kind of training programs, illness careers, and novel styles of socialization.

We have underlined the applied capability of grounded formal theory as an emerging area for sociological endeavor and theory. Applied social theory - in contrast to applied social research - only becomes realitist with the development of grounded theory that fits, works, is relevant and is readily modifiable, and it seems that formal theory is more readily applicable than substantive theory to different classes of substantive areas.

One clear consequence of both its high density and tight integration of ideas in favor of a plethora of examples is the relatively unrelieved nature of our book *Status Passage*. It goes slow for the attentive reader. We can only advise readers to read it quickly at first for the main ideas and for their integration into the theory; then to read at a slower pace in order to study their densification. The reader may, however, read sections of chapters with another perspective more suitable to whatever he is currently studying. For example, he may study the chapters on reversibility and temporality to help his study of "promotion".

Giving more examples would simply have resulted in fewer ideas and narrower scope; this would undermine the basic power of the theory. Indeed, we had only presented about one third of what we had generated for reasons of space and sanity. This is a typical fate of formal theorists.

REFERENCES

1. Barney G. Glaser and Anselm Strauss, *Status Passage, A Formal Theory* (Chicago: Aldine-Atherton, Inc., 1971) and Barney G. Glaser, *Organizational Careers: A Sourcebook for Theory* (Chicago: Aldine Publishing Co., 1968). See also Strauss and Glaser, *Chronic Illness and The Quality of Life* (St. Louis: Mosby, 1975).

2. The future of grounded formal theory requires that we do another book devoted to its methodology, *after* much more experience is gained.

3. Much of this section may also be found in slightly altered form in chapter 9 of *Status Passage,* op. cit., and the introduction of *Organizational Careers,* op. cit.

4. Robert K. Merton, *Social Theory and Social Structure*, (New York: The Free Press, 1957).

5. Barney G. Glaser, *Organizational Scientists, Their Professional Careers* (Indianapolis: Bobbs-Merrill, 1964).

6. Barney G. Glaser, "Comparative Failure of Scientists," *Science,* Vol. 143, March 6, 1964, pp. 1012-14.

7. Fred Davis, "Deviance Disavowal," *Social Problems*, Vol. IX (1961) pp. 120-132.

8. This subsection rests heavily on memos received from Odis E. Bigus, Department of Sociology, The University of Tulsa, Oklahoma.

9. Glaser and Strauss, *Time for Dying* (Chicago: Aldine Publishing Co., 1968).

10. John Lofland, *Deviance and Identity* (New Jersey: Prentice-Hall, 1969).

11. David Sudnow, *Passing On, the Social Organization of Dying* (New Jersey: Prentice-Hall, 1967).

12. Erving Goffman, *The Presentation of Self in Everyday Life* (New York: Doubleday Anchor, 1959) and Everett C. Hughes, *Men and Their Work* (Illinois Free Press, 1958), for examples of masters referring to unpublished student work.

13. Respectively, Mirra Lomarovsky (New York: Random House, 1962), Paul Cressey, Louis Wirth, and Nels Anderson (all with University of Chicago Press).

14. Erving Goffman, *Stigma* (New Jersey: Prentice-Hall, 1963).

15. Bigus, *op. cit.*

16. Bigus, *op. cit.*

17. Richard R. Hansen, *In Quest of Optimal Health: The Natural Health Movement in the United States* (Dissertation, Department of Sociology, University of California, Davis, 1976).

18. Hans L. Zetterberg, *Social Theory and Social Practice* (New Jersey: Bedminister Press, 1962).

Reprinted from *Organizational Careers*, Aldine Publishing Co., Chicago, IL, 1968.

*ORGANIZATIONAL CAREERS: A FORMAL THEORY

Barney G. Glaser, Ph.D.

INTRODUCTION

In general, organizations obtain work from people by offering them some kind of career within their structures. The operation of organizations, therefore, depends on people's assuming a career orientation toward them. To generate this orientation, organizations distribute rewards, working conditions, and prestige to their members according to career level; thus these benefits are properties of the organizational career. To advance in this career is to receive more or better of all or some of these benefits. Generally speaking, therefore, people work to advance their organizational careers. But also, generally speaking, people do not like to talk about their careers or to be asked about them in everyday conversations with many or unknown people. In this sense, a person's own organizational career is a sensitive or "taboo topic." Discussions with others about one's career occur only under the most private, discreet conditions. As a result, while people may talk abstractly and generally about careers, these discussions are typically based on a combination of the little they know of their own career and much speculation. They often have very little particular or general knowledge based on actual careers. These observations apply also to a large sector of the sociological community, as indicated by a brief perusal of the table of contents of sociological monographs and readers on organizations. The topic of careers is seldom discussed and almost never concertedly focused upon.

Several sociologists, however, have written on careers in general in their focus on problems of work and professions. Many of their discussions, of course, clearly refer to organizational careers, though these sociologists are writing on the general topic of occupational careers. There is a difference between these two topics. An occupational career is a very general category referring to a patterned path of mobility wherever it may take people geographically, organizationally, and socially while following a certain type of work. An organizational career, in contrast, is a specific entity offered by an organization to people working in it, using its services, or buying its goods.

286

Purposes of This Reader

Since so much of what we all do is linked with organizations, it is very important to consider an organizational career as a special entity and develop our understanding of it. We hope to achieve this purpose partially by bringing together many articles on careers that fit the category of organizational work careers. This act of itself will initiate much general understanding.

We also wish to start the generation of a formal, grounded theory of organizational careers by initial comparative analysis of these articles.[1] In its beginning operation, a comparative analysis for generating theory starts with the general understandings gained by reading about the same problem from the perspective of several different organizational careers. Pursuit of the comparative analysis brings out several other purposes of this reader.

For the interested reader, whether sociologist or non-sociologist, this book brings together a very rich body of comparative knowledge, experience, and thought on organizational careers. The general understandings, concepts, and strategies gained by merely reading it will aid the reader in "making it" in his own career. This is important to so many of us whose work life is tied up with an organizational career. With little information on which to base our decisions, we are continually trying to decide and manage how to move through the organization to some advantage. The comparative analysis afforded by this book just naturally leads one to an applied sociological perspective.

For the sociologist, this reader may have several benefits. Teachers may use it simply as a body of information on work careers. But they may also use it for teaching students the techniques of comparative analysis and of generating theory from data.[2] Sociologists (students and teachers alike) will find the comparative materials a stimulant and guide to scholarship and research on organizational careers. The comparisons will lead the sociologist to develop relevant categories, hypotheses, and problems and to discover important gaps in our knowledge of particular organizational careers and in our budding theories. The end result, we trust, will be the stimulation to develop more formal theory for various aspects of organizational careers.

Lastly, this reader will indicate how, in many instances, the analysis of organizations can be usefully accomplished through a theory of the careers of its members. The properties of their organizational careers are prime determinants of the behavior of the people who man the organization. This is, however, a neglected topic in most sociological analyses and descriptions of organizations. The focus of explanations of behavior is typically upon goals and work expectations, authority and power structures, rational decision-making, efficiency demands, and working conditions. Organizational careers appear to be too sensitive or taboo a topic to acknowledge as a determinant of a man's behavior, with its subsequent effect on the organization. Perhaps the self-interest it implies as the motivation behind behavior, which is presumably in the service of the organization, is not supposed to be acknowledged.

Furthermore, the articles published in this volume only describe, by and large, various aspects of a career. The concept of "organizational career" is itself seldom used in them as a way of describing the organization as a social structure or explaining organizational behaviors, problems, or facts. If employed in this way, a theory of organizational careers would itself be a very relevant tool by which to analyze organizations.[3]

Part I

TOWARD A THEORY OF ORGANIZATIONAL CAREERS

A general theory of organizational careers can be aided by initial formulations from the "classic" articles in this section on careers in general. These articles come from successive generations of sociologists who, because of their training and/or teaching at the University of Chicago, have been stimulated to take up the topic of careers in their research, scholarship, and thought. In these articles we find many basic dimensions and problems of careers which provide a general perspective helpful to guiding the comparative analyses necessary to generating and integrating the various aspects of a theory of organizational careers. Further, they provide a general focus on careers of all kinds which show the context for our more delimited focus on "organizational careers."

An organizational career is one type of status-passage (Hughes). It is a passage from one status to another through the type of social structure frequently called by sociologists either an "organization," a "formal organization," a "complex organization," or a "bureaucracy." This career is linked with the organization either by a job in which the person does the work of the organization in which the person receives the work of the organization - patient, customer, consumer, and so on. In this reader, we consider only articles on job-related organizational careers, with one exception (Glaser) in Part VIII.

A formal theory of organizational careers should consider several interrelated central units of analysis: the person having the career, other people associated with the person, the career itself, the organization, and the society (or its sector) in which the organization exists. Consideration of these units in analyzing a particular career is always, of course, subject to their particular relevance. However, the formal theory must consider them in order to guide analyses that make any particular unit relevant.

From the point of view of the person, several basic aspects of organizational careers emerge in the articles of this section. Some organizational careers advance persons to different - usually more skilled - work; some merely advance the career while the work stays the same; and some make the work easier or less skilled while advancing the career. There is no necessarily direct relation between the career and the kind of work involved at each stage. It depends on the type of career offered by the type of organization. Organizational careers guide the person into kinds of interpretations, perspectives, or meanings of his work and his performance of it, his responsibility, his powers, rights, and privileges, and his identity, and they guide others' appraisals of the person on these dimensions (Hughes). Further, the organizational career structures, at each stage, the various people within and outside the organization that a person will work and associate with, At each stage of his career the person faces new organizational (and family) concerns which tend to vary his motivation for continuing the career and his loyalty and commitment to the organization. At each stage of the career the person faces a turning point in his work life and identity, some being relatively incidental and some being traumatic, requiring transitional periods and occasioning choices about leaving the organization or taking an alternative career direction within the organization.

The organizational career literally moves the person through the organizational structure or freezes him in one place. Thus several facets of organizational mobility must be considered for a theory of organizational careers (Becker and Strauss). To what degree is the career clearly ordered, and stages and rates of advancement and promotions routinized? Sometimes the career must literally be created by the person having it as he goes along. Careers will vary in the clarity of definition of each stage or rank and how people are led to expect the next direction in their career - they may be moved up, down, sideways, or kept in place. These attributes of career vary in terms of the size of the organization, its general stability, whether and how it is changing, and whether it moves people along individually or by cohorts (all together) at one's particular stage or for one's group. We must discover theory for how people start their careers moving when blocked, stimulate promotions, prevent or refuse changes in their position, avoid undesirable positions or demotions whey they cannot "keep up," gauge their career timetables (Roth) and compare them to other people's, handle the uncertainties of movement through the organizational career, become sponsored, give up the career, develop possessiveness or proprietary rights over positions which they must sometimes be talked or forced into vacating, switch careers on the wave of their movements, move between organizations, and so forth.

From the point of view of the organization, the following articles highlight several basic concerns linked with organizational careers. In order to keep itself manned, the organization must continually fill positions through recruitment and replacement. Recruitment usually refers to filling positions at the beginning of the career, but it can also refer to bringing in people from the outside to all levels. "Recruitment programs" refer to the beginning and highlight the continual need of organizations for new, young people, ranging from those who are highly trained to severely unskilled. Replacement usually refers to the filling of vacated positions, which occurs for several reasons that relate to movements of people in their careers. The organizational problem is how to manage existing turnover, how to plan, generate, and procedurally order succession between positions, and, once people are moved between positions, how to train and help them take over their new responsibilities. The organization must also establish procedures (however codified or surreptitious) for filling highly skilled positions, positions of power, undesirable positions, lower rank positions, and for serving people from the organizational career - retiring or firing them. In resolving these problems in some fashion, the organization provides a broad shape and style of career for its people, several patterns of interdependence between careers, a context (often shifting) for these careers, and a ground for routinizing careers, for starting new careers, and for differentiating old careers into several new ones.

The organizational career has several relationships with society (Wilensky). Many people in various sectors of society are untouched by organizational careers in their own work. Some people just find non-organizational work as their condition. Others vehemently look for these sectors of society and work in them exclusively. But since ours is a society whose principal institutions are run by complex organizations, these people must in their current, daily rounds deal of necessity with others in the midst of their own organizational career - a contingency strongly influencing many dealings.

The organizational career provides for people a stability in life plan, style, and cycle, engendering their motivation to work. This stability is one of the sources of a stable organization and thus leads to stability in the organizational sectors of society. This stability is clearly seen in the continuity of employment, style, and plan of life in the governmental sectors of civil service and the military. It is also felt in the instability effects on society of transient and temporary work and of undesirable workers for which careers are non-existent. The educational institutions of our society are devoted to providing stable numbers of people to fill career positions of importance to organizations that firmly integrate society. Organizational careers also, however, force upon vast numbers of people a residential mobility that generates problems of stability for many facets of society, such as transportation, record-keeping, ownership, financial responsibility, community involvement, and so forth. Clearly the facets of organizational careers that relate to society are in need of much research and theory development. This reader does not provide much on this subject.

To move toward a formal theory of organizational careers we must generate many theories on the many aspects of organizational careers in relation to people, the organization, and society. As these are developed they become integrated, however tightly or loosely, and represent a general formal theory. The articles in this section merely open up pathways to research and theory development.

The remainder of the book presents articles on several of the current foci of studies of organizational careers: recruitment, motivation, loyalty, promotion, demotion, succession, moving between organizations, and career patterns. These articles provide the beginning grist for a comparative analysis designed to generate formal theory for these problems. However central these problems are, there are doubtless many more of high relevance upon which we have little or no research and theory. The articles in this book provide many leads to these other relevant areas of organizational careers by their text and, importantly, by their lack of generality of scope which indicate the neglected gaps in our knowledge of subjects relevant to the study and theory of organizational careers. The task remains for sociologists to start discovering grounded theories on aspects of organizational careers for integration into a formal theory.

Part II

RECRUITMENT TO ORGANIZATIONAL CAREERS

There are two points of view to consider in generating theory on the recruitment of people to an organizational career. One is the view of the person recruited - how he appraises the organization, its career and his prospects within it. The other is that of the organization - how it proceeds to screen and decide upon what people to hire or otherwise bring into the organization and under what conditions it might try them out.

Recruitment begins with the process by which the organization or the recruit reaches the other (Marcson, Caplow and McGee, Smigel). The organization might actively go out looking for recruits, usually with an image of the "right type" of man (social background, values, style, education, and so forth) for the job and the organization. They might tap the resources of third parties (people or other organizations) that specialize in (as well as, perhaps, engage in for personal reasons - for example, a sponsor) mating recruits and organizations. The organization may go to employment agencies, placement bureaus, referral systems, alumni organizations, or noted sponsors; ask influential clients; seek recruits through personal contacts; and so forth. These third parties put them in touch with the "right" potential recruits, thus providing initial screenings and narrowing their field of choice (Sills). The needs of the organization for quantity and/or quality in recruits direct them to the various kinds of third parties. For example, sponsors put them in touch with the quality person, employment agencies with large numbers of lesser skilled people.

Organizations also develop their own programs for reaching recruits directly. They might advertise in journals and newspapers or other media. They may employ public relations firms to guide their advertising. They form hiring departments which start recruitment programs such as visiting college campuses or high schools, interviewing students, and inviting possible recruits with the appropriate social background to come to the organization for a talk (Smigel). They develop procedures for "bating" recruits, at the right moment in their lives, with favorable images of the organizational career. They highlight its most socially favored, if not its most general goal, and its "great" working conditions. They use current myths to reinforce the prestige of belonging to the organization. They offer the recruit potential association with favored models - a general, a scientist, an outstanding executive, a famous lawyer - to encourage him with this form of subtle training for advancement. They may also offer him post-hiring education. They figure out limited ways of hiring the recruit, such as with one-year contracts, initial rotating assignments, options, clear temporary or try-out periods, or no commitments, in order to keep him in the recruiting process for a few years to see if he is really worth taking into the organization for a particular type of career. Thus the recruit may not just be hired, but brought into the organization gradually.

Recruitment is then a process going on for a period of time both inside and outside the boundaries of the organization. It is a process of screening, wooing, and eliminating before the career actually starts. It might vary from being a fairly simple process of solicitation and short test period to, as in the cases of academic organizations and law firms, a highly elaborated process, sometimes requiring time and effort seemingly far beyond what the particular requirements of the position and person would seem to demand.

Elaborate procedures of recruitment, focused on "choosing the right man" or making sure that no one who gets as far as an interview on organizational premises is later refused a job, have other vital consequences. These procedures involve large numbers of others in the organization, whose careers will be interdependent with that of the recruit (Caplow and McGee). These others will know that they have been consulted, have had some say and commitment to a decision, and can protest if comparative discrepancies in the organizational career offered to the recruit might cause personal or general morale problems. Other organizations, such as the army, simply ignore the wishes and problems of other members who will have interdependent careers with the recruit. Fitness for these positions is arrived at on the basis of objective, technical criteria, not on subtle, personal, and organizationally sensitive ones embodied in elaborate procedures.

Another condition affecting recruitment procedures is how easy will it be to get rid of people who do not work out. This condition influences how important it is to screen and try out recruits. Some organizations can never fire or "lay off" a person once the career has started. Other organizations can simply ask the man to leave. Yet others must go through an extended "edging out" process.

Organizations must also contend with their position among other organizations in the competitive market for recruits. Sometimes their procedures must work very fast to win out in intense competition. Other times they have months to decide, even if the competition is stiff.

The organization must also screen people for its future as well as its current requirements and provide images of careers that entice recruits into a long-range or short-range view of possible commitment. Thus some recruits will plan on becoming executives in later years, and others will plan on a short stint for experience and their record before moving on to a more permanent career.

The recruit might actively go out and seek entrance to organizational careers by applying at personnel offices and going to placement agencies. He may also ask friends, make visits to strategic people, and drop the word that he is available into the "right" grapevine or referral systems. Of course, finding the latter two might be difficult, impossible, or a simple matter, depending on the type of career of the recruit and his current location in the organizational world. It is often hard to negotiate a rise from lower prestige organizations to higher ones.

Recruits from educational institutions might be routinely listed in a placement bureau. This source of third party might be the approved method for becoming recruited. It also might be a residual source of poorer careers, and hinder receiving the best chances if they come only through private, informal sponsorship channels. Depending on his previous educational institution, the recruit may or may not have to be active in seeking a start in an organization. Graduates from the best universities might have to be active and gracious in putting off too many offers from recruiters that come to campus; graduates from other educational institutions might simply go through placement bureau channels with no stigma attached; or they might be just cast free to find a job (for example, trade school graduates).

After contact with an organization the recruit may have to jockey for and then negotiate his offer, if the organization allows such space. This "offer space" is usually found in organizations with higher skilled careers that compete with other organizations. Workers' careers usually start with a flat "take it or leave it" offer that the union has negotiated.

The recruit may have to make a decision about his occupational career at the same time that he selects an organization, or his career status may automatically be fixed as a consequence of being hired for a job.

The decision to accept the organizational career will also include considering *anticipated consequences* for family life, ability to moonlight, kinds of colleagues and need for colleagues (stimulating, none, or chance for contact with them, etc. [Riesman]) and probable type of career (how routinized, how rapid advancement in position and salary can be). The recruit may anticipate consequences from the described working conditions, responsibilities, and kind of identity he will receive and feel; from juxtaposing organizational with personal goals; from the size, kind, and prestige of the organization; and so forth.

Many of these anticipations may be inaccurate because of lack of experience and knowledge both generally and specifically with the organization and because of belief in the "bating" recruitment rhetoric of the organization. But, however accurate or inaccurate the anticipations, the recruit will usually find - some months after joining the organization - that because of the experience and knowledge he gains, the reasons for which he started the career are not the reasons he stays with the career.

Theory on recruitment processes of organizational careers may usefully begin being generated along the lines of these general categories and properties obtained from the comparative analysis of the following articles. Surely we must also discover the relationship of these processes to societies that depend upon the organizational careers of large numbers of people for its stability, growth, and change.

Part III

CAREER MOTIVATIONS WITHIN THE ORGANIZATION

Career motivations never quite stand still. The shifting in direction and objects of motivations is accounted for by the changing conditions of organizational life and begins upon entering the organization. The career motivations that lead to recruitment may change once the person becomes involved in the organizational career. The major condition that changes the objects of career motivations is the person's stage of career with its associated problems and contingencies. He may be at the stage where many prospects for advancement stimulate him into working hard and striving for a better position. He may have arrived at "a" top or be leveled off before reaching this limit. This condition generates motivations to hold down a position until retirement, slow down work (if safe), or look elsewhere for a different career. When his performance is judged poor by others, he may lack advancement or be demoted, which is likely to undercut his motivation to work hard and continue pursuing the organizational career.

As the person advances, his motivations to achieve certain goals of the organization are continually being modified by current and changing associations with people in and outside the organization and by his increasing knowledge about the organization's activities and reward systems (Marcson). He revises the "best" goals to pursue for a person at his stage. For example, while young his goals may focus on the basic work of the organization. Later they may (and typically do) become administrative goals and perhaps empire building. New goals of work and career may be literally forced on him, thus forcing a shift in motivations. Truly the person's motivations toward work, goals, and career levels and movements must keep up with his career as it changes. If they do not, he will be out of line with where he is and what is expected of him. This condition makes him liable to the dissatisfactions that come with discrepancies between what he expects and what he is supposed to expect and will, in fact, obtain among the alternative career directions and top levels available to him at this stage.

The diversity of kinds of specific careers and their associated work and goals varies with the size and kind of organization. The person's abilities, training, and sponsors condition how many of these career options he may be able to take. These factors, by providing opportunity, engender the motivation necessary to take them. The army, for example, has many diverse kinds of specific working careers for its members to pursue. There are, however, several kinds of general types of organizational careers with fairly distinctive, associated motivations, as admirably summarized by Kornhauser, which occur no matter what is entailed in the person's particular work and organization.

The person may be seeking an organizational career of *service* to people, organization, and/or country, whether he is a highly trained professional, an expert, or merely a willing worker. The *service* career may range from a missionary to fee-for-service career with consequent variation in motivations. The person may be a careerist (see Wilensky and Janowitz), seeking only to reach the top of the hierarchy, as constituted, as fast as possible in order to have power and control and to better his general social condition and rank. He may be motivated principally toward a *professional* career among colleagues, wherever they may be found in the world, using the organization as only a base of operations. He may seek a *simple organizational career* of constant work with financial and job security, whether white or blue collar. This career is trimmed with modest aspirations, if any, to lower or middle level supervisory positions, which motivations themselves can become easily cooled off by lack of promotion and opportunity (Chinoy). In these careers, seniority and its security benefits provide the movement and the motivated goals, unless seniority ends in loss of current position and salary in a particular organization (Seidman). The person may have no career motivations and simply flounder around between jobs within and between organizations, oblivious to or ignorant of the career each job might offer him.

Motivation toward these various types of careers may be initially generated from boyhood ambitions, current social values, religion, geographical regions linked with rural and urban values, more recognized kinds of success, and goals of various professional, educational, and trade schools, before being modified by colleagues and arrangements within the organization. Therefore, the modification that occurs after joining the organization is a result of past motivations and present shiftings occurring within the organizational career.

Since career motivations are ever-shifting, it is apparent to organizations that motivations can be molded to suit their requirements of a proportionate distribution of people into various types of careers. Their tool is to develop incentive or reward systems to keep the motivations for particular careers at constant levels of intensity. By this maneuver they maintain the division of labor relatively intact even as it is changing. Organizations may also carefully recruit people from a sector of society or particular educational institutions with the right motivation for careers (the sons of officers get commissions readily in the army). They also may develop indoctrination programs of a great variety to instill a necessary kind of motivation in the person beginning a career. Some organizations regularly send their men back to schools (colleges or in-service schools) for re-indoctrination on the prime goals of the organization and their associated career potentials.

Sometimes, as a way of controlling its members' motivations to work hard and thereby move ahead in the career, organizations will develop elaborate hierarchies for advancement (Dreyfuss). These hierarchies can even be artificial in the sense of not corresponding to the division of work and its relative evaluations on skill and prestige. This excessive gradation keeps employees scrambling in the competition for advances and benefits of the organizational career instead of relaxing and grouping for confrontations with higher management on working conditions. If employees realize what is happening, it dampens their motivation to pursue a career that gets them nowhere.

Another way of controlling its members' motivations (at the other end of the gradation range) is to offer to most employees a career at one organizational level with slight salary increases for seniority. Thus, from the start, their aspirations are cooled down and they learn to pursue the one goal of their job and hope they last long enough for the salary increments.

In any event, whether careers are spoken of in general or specific types, motivations toward career and work are intimately linked. Sometimes they are discernibly different and alternatively boost each other, with incentive systems for work that hold out career movements as rewards and career rewards that set the person up for new work. Sometimes they are virtually the same - to work for one's career is to do what the organization wants (for example, basic research). A formal theory of careers must lead to describing, understanding, and accounting for these relations in career and work motivations.

Part IV

LOYALTY AND COMMITMENT TO THE ORGANIZA- TIONAL CAREER

As we have seen in the in the last section, there is one type of organizational career motivation that has received considerable attention in research and theory development - the person's loyalty or commitment to the organization. This loyalty is profoundly affected by how he perceives the organization as a base for his career. The following articles present some of the research and theory development on this subject.

Several conditions affect the person's loyalty to his organization. One major condition is whether the person is an expert or professional who is motivated to have a career as such among colleagues, such as a career "in science" or "in law." The problem then becomes to what degree, if at all, he is devoted to his current organizational base and its career. Some experts or professionals may feel no loyalty or commitment to the organization, so devoted are they to a professional career which transcends the boundaries of all organizations. They are called "cosmopolitans," in distinction to "locals," who are devoted mostly to the organizational career (Gouldner). The organization may need such experts and simply put up with their lack of commitment and turnover, knowing that, as they get older, more of them will be likely to become involved in their particular organizational career.

Many structural conditions, however, engender a "local-cosmopolitanism" among organizational experts - those devoted to both organizational and professional careers. One is how many alternatives they have for moving to other organizations. Only by having opportunities to move to other organizations of equal or higher caliber can an expert be oblivious in commitment to his current organizational career. Without these opportunities he cannot realistically transcend his organization's boundaries in pursuing a career. Lack of alternatives elsewhere becomes a condition for developing loyalty to an organization and commitment to a career within it. This condition obtains even though groups of colleagues elsewhere are still used as reference groups on matters of profession. Two conditions restricting opportunities for other organizations are: (1) the fact that there are no better or more prestigious organizations to move to at the expert's level of career; and (2) the fact that the expert's performance would not allow a move to an equal or better organization with an advance in rank.

The former condition particularly applies to people in the top levels of their career in the "best" of the organizations available. Moving elsewhere becomes a moot question. Their local-cosmopolitanism is usually focused on empire building and running their current organization to suit their needs for compatible working conditions (Glaser). These people have been rewarded for successful work at several stages of their career by their current organization; and they have overcome several organizational obstacles to reaching the top of their career (Grusky). For these career rewards they have provided the organization with hard work and prestige by their expertise. The result is a "deepening involvement" process, by which a cosmopolitan becomes a committed local as he grows within the organizational career.

The latter condition - where performance does not warrant an advantageous move - arises for experts that are in the beginning or middle stages of their careers. For them to move may easily involve a loss in organizational prestige and perhaps a loss in career level. They must work hard to stay where they are and hold their own in competition for advancement. Thus their cosmopolitanism becomes readily infused with local commitment because this is how they have to "make it," unless they change their type of work or go to a less prestigeful organization.

Another condition making cosmopolitans into local-cosmopolitans is the normal acculturation process of learning to work in the organization (Avery, Marcson, in Part III). As the beginning expert tries to learn what is expected of him in practicing his expertise, he starts focusing on organizational goals and problems: he learns to do what will be locally rewarded; he learns how an expert in his field makes it in the organization; and he starts enjoying organizational career rewards. As a result of this continuing process of partially working on organizational goals, and consulting with others more devoted to the organization than he, he is brought around to organizational thinking without realizing it and becomes a local in this measure. If the organization's goals are divergent with the expert's professional goals, the expert is clearly developing a commitment to both professional and an organizational career, with some ensuing built-in conflict. If the organization's goals are the same as the professional goals involved, then the expert's organizational career is "the" way of having a professional career. And though we may view him as a local-cosmopolitan, he may simply feel that he is only professionally oriented - a cosmopolitan - and that loyalty to the organization which provides a synonymous professional and organizational career is part of this professional orientation.

In the study of loyalty and commitment to organizations the sociologist should always be sensitive to what level(s) of the organization the person is committed or loyal (Glaser, Bennis). To focus only on the total organization as the unit of loyalty is to neglect those who are loyal only to particular work groups, departments, wards, branches, institutes, or other units within the organization, while feeling no loyalty (or even antagonism) to the organization itself. From the point of view of the total organization, it might not matter to which and how many levels of its structure a person is loyal. Loyalty to one level may be enough to ensure hard work and striving for the appropriate organizational career. Further, these structural levels of focus for loyalty are bound to change as the person rises in his career.

The non-expert in an organization may appear after more research to be a somewhat simpler case of loyalty to the career. Not having any strong occupational reference groups outside the organization, he will probably be a devoted local working his way up in the organizational career. If not, he will be either oblivious to his possible career within the organization or looking for a change to another organization for personal preferences.

Also an employee's career, if at the lower levels of the organization, may require little in the way of loyalty except responsible attendance and continued employment to prevent the organizational headache: "turnover." Then the less loyalty, the better for the organization with it must, according to changing conditions, lay off, demote, or discard workers. Loyalty to lower and middle levels by non-expert employees seems to take a temporal form. The organization requires them to speak and work in the interests of the company against all possible intrusions merely while on the job - for example, the sales lady, clerk, or secretary.

Obviously the following articles indicate a narrow view of research to date on loyalty and its relation to organizational careers - narrow in the sense of problems posed and an over-focus on experts. We need a more general approach in research to generate a grounded theory of loyalty to the organizational career.

*Formal Theory extracted from Reader based on constant comparative analysis of 63 articles.

1 Barney G. Glaser and Anselm L. Strauss, *The Discovery of Grounded Theory* (Chicago: Aldine Publishing Company, 1967), Part I.

2 For the latter two purposes, we suggest that it be used in conjunction with Glaser and Strauss, *ibid.*

3 For an example of this type of organizational analysis, see Anselm Strauss, Leonard Schatzman, Rue Bucher, Danuta Ehrlich, and Melvin Sabshin, *Psychiatric Ideologies and Institutions* (New York: Free Press of Glencoe, 1964).

Part V

SOURCES AND STRATEGIES OF PROMOTION

The idea of the successful individual as an independent entrepreneur has changed. Today it refers to the person who has reached the top levels of an organizational career. "Getting ahead" refers now to a process of advancement in an organizational context of associates, superiors, and rules of promotion in a hierarchy (Mills). Further, this success achieved by the "bureaucratic crawl," can by itself never end up in the person being among "the very rich" (Mills). Thus, in deciding upon an organizational career, a person must consider how rich he wants to be. Perhaps the top salary of an organizational career is enough. If more is desired then the person must choose an organizational career that raises the probability of providing the person, on the side, as he moves up, with an accumulation of advantages that he can parlay into a fortune. The long crawl, then, pays off only if it is transformable at some point into the "big jump" to riskless fortune-making.

For most people, however, this extreme form of success is not the goal. For them it is reaching the top, which boils down to how to be continuously promoted as long as possible. This question leads to another: What accounts for promotions at each stage of an organizational career? Organizational rhetorics usually state that promotions are made on the basis of some combination of ability, competence, merit, and/or seniority. Everyone suspects, however, that also other informal processes and factors are involved. To put it in Mills' terms: "now the stress is on agility rather than ability." He was emphasizing "personality" factors, which is partially a correct emphasis, as the several articles in this section indicate. Let us consider some of the social structural sources and strategies of promotion brought out in these articles that are of major relevance for a formal theory of promotion in organizational careers.

One organizational condition affecting advancement is how many different career lines are offered a person at his stage (Martin and Strauss). Any one stage of a career may be considered a "testing point" for the person to see which of the next career lines he might be ready for (Roth). The test may be considered to last for years, requiring this experience in a position; it might be scheduled as a formal examination or some combination of knowledge, experience, and performance, and so forth. The testing becomes one source of whether the person is ready for a promotion and for which career line. This readiness is one aspect of the timing of promotions. Another temporal aspect is whether the organization requires that the person be moved up after a certain time in his present position irrespective of readiness. The "up or out" rule of academic life, airlines, and law firms, for example, forces either advancement or departure from the organizational career in many instances (Caplow and McGee). The larger the organization, usually the more complex the timing and alternative career lines for advancement.

302

Another prominent source of promotion in organizations is the process, both ordered and unordered, of selecting persons for promotion. Large organizations may have elaborately ordered processes for considering each man routinely when he is ready - has been in a position a prescribed length of time (Janowitz). This routine appraisal is usually based on performance, merit, and seniority. However, with these ordered procedures may be juxtaposed, unordered, informal processes which become more elaborate and decisive of promotion as one nears the top of the career. For example, in the army, as one advances the "tapping system" becomes more important for the next step. An officer is tapped for advancement by superiors because of his outstanding accomplishments, his unconventionality, and his ability to fit personally into the next highest group of colleagues.

The formally ordered procedures are fairly well known to people in the organizational career. They may even be printed in handbooks. Besides being routinely considered, the person may have to receive evaluations or recommendations from certain superiors, some of whom may be informal sponsors and others whose favor must be won by strategies varying from "buttering them up" to shows of high-quality work. Standardized procedures allow people some expectation as to the inevitability of their next promotion. These procedures specify how much control people might achieve over their promotions through gaining information and through indicating points in the structure of the process to exert pressure on those involved in the procedures. Indeed, using controls allowed by the ordered procedures is a test in itself on ability to advance. For example, sometimes attending a transitional school is necessary for the next promotion (a war college, graduate work, flight school, and so forth (Roth)). The test, then, is on the person's ability to achieve an assignment or entry to this school, as well as doing qualifying work once in it. The resort to strategic sponsors and their power is an important strategy here. Learning how and when during his career to apply for the school assignment is vital also. Achieving a skip in stages of career may also be necessary sometimes to be in an advantageous position for a crucial promotion. Being at the right place at the right time, knowing of this place and how to get there again may be necessary for a promotion.

Ordered promotion procedures are liable to change by several contextual conditions. Changing race relations in the community may have changed the requisite composition of various races of ethnic groups at some levels of the organizational career. Perhaps more Negroes must be in the upper levels of the union (Kornhauser) or army. Perhaps law firms have started to hire more Jewish lawyers and then to take them into partnership. The police force may be required to hire any nationality. Also the changing size of the organization shifts conditions for advancement. Expansion creates positions, making advancement easier. Cutting back the size freezes many who might otherwise advance. How many different sites the organization has may affect advancement. It may be hard to promote a man to a level where others feel he is not their equal, even though he is ready to be advanced. If, as in the case of the army, large industries, government, or banks, the promotion can be combined with a move to a new site, formal advancement is less liable to being blocked.

At the other end of the continuum from ordered procedures are ad hoc, unordered promotion processes. Patterns, ordered only by the changing conditions of people and organizational life, of course, may be seen within these processes. The law firm, for example, would appear to use a very flexible process of elimination (Smigel). There are several facets to this process. The person does not really know what will happen to his career until it is about to happen. Promotion does not occur as a discrete jump up in rank but as a growing process of excellence in work and involvement in the firm so that it becomes the natural step to move the man into an associate position or partnership. This natural move up may take years, but usually not more than ten for partnership. It also becomes a natural occurrence that others are eliminated or leveled off, so that when partners are finally chosen, only a few of an initial group of recruits remain to choose from.

Another unordered process is clique system advancement (Abegglen). The clique may be composed of family, friends, or close classmates from a school. The informal reciprocal obligations existing between members of the clique require that they all (eventually) advance together in relative position. If one advances, he pulls the others along with him. Sometimes sectors of the clique advance and the rest are soon brought up. Other times the clique moves up in toto. Outsiders to the clique have little chance in rising on the organizational career line taken over by the clique. This clique system may overlap processes of elimination or of sponsorship, but it tends to be broken down by a formally ordered system of advancement, unless it controls this order. For example, cliques in law firms may be obvious because of the homogeneity of the ruling partners on several dimensions, such as religion, social class, and law school.

Family and social class cliques used to run the army, but this is a thing of the past, due to both the increased size of the army and the formal promotion procedures causing great heterogeneity among officers. Cliques typically survive best in small organizations, with their reduced requirements of providing careers for large numbers with diverse expertises.

Sponsorship is also another unordered process of achieving promotions. It tends to exist alongside any other type of ordered or unordered process of promotion. It is usually very effective, since people with power can find ways of bringing up others they are sponsoring, whether using formal procedures, informal strategies, or combinations of both. Sponsorship, however, can break down in organizations where merit or seniority is of such high importance that to merely suggest advancement for a private or particularistic reason is to be liable to favoritism, which might hurt a candidate's chances of winning in the competition for a promotion. Another condition hindering sponsorship is when the sponsor himself looses power or position. Those persons he is sponsoring may be carried away with him, loosing out to people sponsored by those in power. Other properties of sponsorship varying a person's chances for promotion are how many sponsors one has and whether they are within the organization or important people outside of it (a dean, a client, or a politician, for example). Sometimes sponsorship dominates all promotion procedures (Hall). This domination creates some codification of its criteria and boundaries of effectiveness among sponsors. However, since sponsorship tends to occur in a closed awareness context,[1] candidates usually never know what will happen or how to achieve advancement except by orders from their sponsor. Several articles in this section discuss other properties of sponsorship, such as how people control the organization by it (Kornhauser), or the reciprocal obligations and mutual needs of sponsors and their candidates (Hall).

No matter what promotion process or combination thereof is operating, sociological researchers have discovered a strong emphasis on promoting the "right" man for the job: a vital condition for many a person's advancement. The image of the right man may be based on idealized reasoning about who is best for this job or stage of career, or it might be based on clear-cut personal attributes and achievements of the candidates. Usually, but not always, these properties of the person become deciding factors for picking a person from a group of candidates that have an adequate level of ability for the job. These attributes may be age, sex, religion, ethnicity, family background, wife, political preference, or club affiliation. Patterned clusters of these attributes develop for levels of the organizational career (Collins, Dalton). To violate them by promoting the wrong type of person can cause troubles for the organization, as strikes, walk-outs, factional fights, or low morale. The organization usually adheres to these clusters unless itself and its context change sufficiently that contrary promotions are not damaging to the organization. Individuals try to break through these patterns by working excessively hard so they will be advanced irrespectively (for example, Jewish lawyers in Gentile firms, or an Admiral Rickover type). They then become the token breakdown of the pattern, the exception that proves the rule for the stage of the organizational career in question. Another tactic is for a person to get behind a man soon to retire so he is the only effective successor and will have to be advanced although not the right type.

Clearly this is a well-studied area of organizational careers, because of its central importance to the notion of careers as an advancement process. But, clearly also, we need more generation of formal theory on promotions which can be accomplished by comparative analysis of our current substantive theories and knowledge, combined with studying the many other kinds of organizational careers yet unresearched. (See also Part VII on succession for other categories and properties of promotion.)

1 Only the sponsor and a few strategic others know what is going on. See Barney G. Glaser and Anselm L. Strauss, *Awareness of Dying*, (Chicago: Aldine Publishing Company, 1965).

Part VI

MANAGING DEMOTION

Promotion is the successful aspect of being moved through an organizational career. However, as we have said, not all movement is up; some is down and is likely to be awkward or painful to the demotee and the organization. Thus, one central problem arising for a theory of demotion in organizational careers is how a demotion is managed by both the organization and the person and his associates. This problem breaks down into two aspects. How can people ascertain that a demotion has in fact occurred; and once sure of it, what are the strategies for coping with its consequences?

We are fortunate to have More's article, which sets down eleven different empirical forms of demotion, as a starter on how to define demotion in organizational careers. To be sure, these are not the only forms, as indicated in the articles by Martin and Strauss, Goldner, and Dalton. They are only the more clearly definable ones. Many organizations will purposely try to obscure demotions to prevent the strains it is likely to produce in the person and his associates. Whatever the degree of clarity or obscurity, demotions occur in three general forms, singly or in combination. A person may be demoted through a change in his job, in his relative position within the organizational career, and in his current organization.

Job refers to the performance required, working conditions, salary, and other benefits and deficits associated with the job. Demotions of this nature can be very obscure and subtle, as well as quite clear.

Relative positions within the organizational career refer to the number of its stages and the number of people at each stage. Demotions of this sort, if the hierarchy itself is clear, are usually clear. They can be obscured with several organizational tactics, however, such as by adding new positions over a person, so that while he is being promoted it is actually a demotion, by obscuring advancement criteria, by horizontal mobility (Martin and Strauss) with subtle changes in job content and/or honorary rewards, by sinecure positions (Dalton) which can be established for either high or low competence people, by "zig-zag" mobility (Goldner) which combines demotions and subsequent promotions to the point that the person is not sure where he is relative to others nor where he started, and by filling similar positions with both successes and failures. A clear strategy used by organizations is to elaborate harmless positions and even promote people into them (Abegglen). This is used by organizations which cannot fire people because it has given life commitments or tenure.

Changing a person's current organization can be a clear demotion based on the differential organizational prestige or benefits resulting from the change. Some changes are initiated within and by the organization to different sub-organizations, such as the army and large banks. Others are initiated by the person, such as going from a top university to the "bush" leagues, or going to work in a low-prestige restaurant (Whyte). In some cases of changing organizations, the demotion is relatively lower but still respectable; in other cases a lowly evaluated organization may itself indicate outright failure for the person.

Besides degree of clarity, another aspect in defining a demotion is the relative failure which is indicates. A clear demotion might have occurred, but the person might not have lost much relative to his previous position or others' positions (for example, the promotion sideways or upwards to a harmless position). This demotion, then, is only a slight comparative failure, which can be easily overlooked, and more easily so if it has been obscured. Another kind is being passed up by others moving up or by not achieving levels which favored models have arrived at. The clearer these forms of comparative failure, the more painful they are likely to be. However, they may indicate nothing more than the lack of outstanding success, while still indicating moderate success (Glaser). Also slight comparative failures are likely to be differentially perceived by many demotees, ranging from some feeling distraught and some feeling that they have actually been promoted. The range of perceptions varies with the degree of clarity of the demotion and the possible interpretations of relative failure (Smigel). In contrast to slight changes the relativity of demotion in some cases is a clear failure to perform adequately or a loss of a prestigeful position and job. People in these circumstances approach absolute failure in their own minds and those of others.

The relativity and clarity of demotions is born from the balance of pressures the organization is under to obtain levels of excellence or adequacy of performance and people's desire to achieve or rest at such levels. Linked with this balance is that of the relative degrees of security or insecurity in a position which the organization provides for stimulating the appropriate level of performance. Then, when a change in the person's position, job, or organization occurs, he and others may judge by the established balances whether a demotion has occurred. These balances on performance and security stimulate people to compete in certain ways for promotions and for avoiding demotions by, for example, taking risks with innovations, putting out careful, routine work, and so forth.

Once a demotion is defined and its relative failure calculated, how is it handled by the demotee and organization? Some people, of course, desire it, especially older people who no longer want to work so hard to compete and would rather relax in an easier job with adequate salary. Others rationalize with a "peaking out" theory: they have peaked out in ability to compete for positions in the organizational career and now they only can stay put or move down. This theory can be normalized by the organization for all its members, so all expect to "peak out" and demotion therefore is accepted as an inevitable part of the career (Goldner). Others say demotion is the "price one pays" for going too high in the career. Obscured demotions may simply be never mentioned by people, since they are the easiest for a person to deny, especially if the organization is providing fringe rewards (for example, trips, salary increase, and so forth) at the same time. They may devote themselves to a family or leisure pursuit to the neglect of further "making it" in a career.

Demotion can be a stigma for a person when it is clear enough to ascertain and the relative failure indicates the person's organizational career is blocked forever or downwardly mobile. Under this condition the stigma spoils the organizational identity and career of the person.[1] In some careers, such as nursing, people can go down or up as often as they desire with no stigma; it is merely accepted as taking another job. In other careers, such as academic, the stigma of loss of position is strong - indeed it may seldom happen for this reason, as suicides may result. Organizations will endeavor at times to cover the stigma by various strategies, such as by normalizing the final stages of career with a demotion, as we have said. The organization may retrain them for a "new" job, principally to build up confidence, self-esteem, engage them in educational programs and seminars to show them the vital "relevance" to the organization of their new work, and so forth. These organizational responses to the stigma of demotion (see More, Martin and Strauss, and Goldner for other responses) may be summed up in trying to "cool-down" (Glaser) the unfortunate person to a level of self-appraisal and career expectation commensurate with his career movements. Cooling-down the person is necessitated by the strong responses of depression, apathy, hostility, irritability (see Whyte), withdrawal, and so forth, with which many persons meet a stigmatizing demotion. When not cooled down, the person is likely to be a disruptive force in the organization, making trouble, avoiding cooperation, and exercising undue influence or authority over others.

Some of our best theory on organizational careers has been written for the problem of demotion. But it is only a beginning in the study of this, often subtle, type of relative organizational failure; it is only a beginning for the comparative analysis necessary to generate a formal theory of demotion in organizational careers.

1 Erving Goffman, *Stigma* (Englewood Cliffs, N.J.: Prentice-Hall, 1963).

Part VII

ORGANIZATIONAL SUCCESSION

What is a career movement, from the point of view of a person, is, from the point of view of the organization, the succession of people into and between positions. Thus, in managing promotions, demotions, simotions (horizontal mobility), and recruitment of individual careers, the organization is managing its succession requirements and problems, and in so doing it is creating much interdependence of organizational careers. Organizational succession refers to the flow of people into, through, and out of the organization at all levels. Succession to top leadership has always been a well-publicized and studied (but special) problem for people inside and outside of organizations, particularly large ones. The organization, however, must manage problems of succession at all levels, which are perhaps not as crucial as succession to leadership, but are nevertheless quite important. In some cases the public can also become quite concerned with succession problems at lower levels of careers, such as with the turnover rate of nurses in hospitals, layoffs resulting in unemployment problems for a city, or shortage of blue and white-collar workers. The following articles indicate the substantial amount of work on this aspect of organizational careers. But this work is a mere beginning for generating a dense, inclusive formal theory of succession by comparative analysis. It is also over-focused on professionals and executive upper ranges of organizations. It seems sufficient, however, to provide us, upon analysis, with the beginning formulation of a general process of succession which, in turn, can theoretically guide further research for generating of grounded theory on this dimension of organizational careers.[1]

The general process of succession would appear to have three stages. First, a vacancy occurs. Second, the organization fills the vacancy by a replacement. Third, there is a take-over of the position by the replacement. At each stage there are sub-processes. A small organization may undergo this process infrequently. A larger organization may be continually and multiply undergoing this process with many people at many levels. The process may be planned and routine or serendipitous and unplanned for all levels or only particular levels of the organizational career and for either or all stages of the processes. The planning may be designed for individual successions or continual, multiple successions of large numbers of people. Individual succession occurs mainly in line-succession: people in relative order can only move up on one hierarchical line of, say, one administration or one department. Continual, multiple successions are typically planned for echelon-succession: people are moved to the next career stage on schedule, irrespective of their current hierarchical lines. Examples of echelon-succession are found in the civil service, army, banks, and academic organizations. Hierarchical lines, thrown out of order by such promotions, simotions, or demotions, may be brought back to order by moving people between different hierarchies after or during the move. Now let us consider some of the major properties and sub-processes of each stage of this process of succession as grounded in the following articles.

Vacancies of career positions occur in two essential ways: voluntary or involuntary departures by a person (see, particularly, Caplow and McGee, Smigel and Dalton). Voluntary vacancies mostly occur from promotions and resignations for health, current interpersonal incompatibilities, early retirement, travel, occupational drift, and better or "unbeatable" offers for organizational careers elsewhere. Involuntary vacancies occur from routine retirement, demotions, simotions, death, routine rotations, "weeding out," or elimination processes, dismissals, and layoffs for poor performance or lack of business, operations, or funds. No matter how well-planned succession may be, there are still several serendipitous sources of both individual and multiple vacancies on voluntary or involuntary bases. Thus, replacement, no matter how well-planned and anticipated, can pose crucial problems for the organization when vacancies in strategic positions come as a surprise. The timing of vacancies can either generate or eliminate problems of replacement. Vacancies can also occur when new positions are created during organizational expansion or change.

Replacement for a vacancy can be a most crucial decision for the organization. In multiple vacancies and replacements at lower levels of careers this step may be highly planned and not organizationally significant, even if adversely affecting the local work force (for example, the building trades.) But even in these routinized replacements, hidden troubles for the organization may be brewing, such as when the "wrong" man is made a foreman, head clerk, or supervisor, causing disruption and morale problems among workers (See Part V). Sometimes replacement is avoided by doing away with a position vacated by an individual. This may create consternation among one or two other people who perhaps had wished to move up to this position.

Replacement is crucial because three vital organizational conditions are at stake: organizational stability and change (Gouldner, Gusfield), interdependence of organizational careers (Levenson, Gusfield), and the social-psychological processes of position-holding at stages of a career (Strauss, Dalton). Questions of organizational change and stability or continuity are a direct concern in choosing a successor or planning for multiple routine successors. The desire to avoid change, provide continuity, or institute change in a preferred direction at whatever level of the organization is a significant factor in making appointments. The person is judged on how he will handle the take-over and manage a change or the stability of his sector of the organization. This judgment is based on his experience, his clique affiliations, his education, personality, influencibility, political preferences, and so forth. Indeed, the wish to institute organizational change is often implemented not by changing social structure or systems but by replacing people in strategic organizational positions.

The interdependence of organizational careers involved in choosing a replacement or a series of them is a touchy problem for the organization with hierarchical lines. One promotion to a vacancy can set off a chain reaction of necessary successions all the way down the line, generating intense competition between contenders for the vacancies that occur. Planned succession for hierarchical lines is an effort to reduce the disruptive consequences of such chain reactions. Sometimes a replacement bypasses several others on the line who, say, are not sufficiently competent or too old for the vacancy. These others may feel thereby a deep sense of demotion and cause trouble. Also the whole sentimental order supporting the career for the hierarchy in question may be challenged, causing trouble and disenchantment with the career, resignations, and organizational ineffectiveness (Trow).

Impending vacancies and choices of a replacement engenders what Levenson has called "anticipatory succession" among people lower in the hierarchy. This occurs less in organizations with echelon-succession since they can move up irrespective of mobility in their current hierarchy. In anticipation of who will get the appointment, potential successors compete with each other, debate, wager, guess who will be appointed, form cliques of support for candidates, and temporarily take over the vacancy to show ability. The interdependence of careers is clearly indicated in all the maneuvering. Once a successor is chosen, interdependence takes on other dimensions. Some people behind the promoted person move up themselves or realize that they are behind moving channels of mobility. They are promotable in time. Others stuck behind a person who did not get the position realize that they may be blocked from moving up, unless they are good enough to bypass a superior. They become for the time being non-promotables and perhaps disillusioned with their career. Others, after a series of successions, will not know how promotable they are in the future; their careers have now become interdependent with new people. People start maneuvering to get from blocked to open hierarchical lines. Each line also has its range of possible promotions, some making the upper management a possibility and others only middle or lower. In small, family-owned organizations no one may ever reach the top except a family member. The interdependence of careers signified in sponsorship processes also figures into who is chosen as successor and who might be left behind.

The motivational aspects of being a successor generate social-psychological problems and processes when changing positions. Some people eager to move up have virtually given up their present position before leaving it by their zealous anticipatory succession for the next position. The organization may have a problem in keeping them patient and doing a good job until the succession occurs. Another organizational process is to "groom" people beforehand for succession by providing them broad or focused experience, schools, and indoctrination. Also they may require being trained in different demeanor and loyalties for the new position. Some people will not be severed from their old position; they are too satisfied with their career and work. The organization must either coach or coerce them to give up cherished activities and move up. They may be persuaded to succeed with realizations that they cannot remain in one place because they are not getting any younger, that the organization needs their expertise in higher level capacities, that it "does not look right," that they or their work may be outmoded soon anyway or that they could be fired, that they may never have another chance to rise, and so forth. Once advanced they are given tolerance periods to readjust their identity and learn the new job. Also their new subordinates or equals who were formerly equals or superiors respectively must have time to adjust to new relationships.

Since the foremost consequence for an organization when a successor (or series of them) takes over a position is organizational change, stability, or continuity, the succession process must be watched closely by organizational members in top administration. Through succession an organization controls potential change or stability. The closeness of watching varies with the increase in size, complexity, and decentralization of an organization and with its rates of successions (Grusky). Control is initially achieved through bureaucratic routines for succession and ultimately through delicate decisions on how specific replacements will act when they take over. How will these people's loyalties, motivations, ability to supervise and work, and social life change or affect the new position and ultimately the organization?

People are asked or made to take over positions for essentially two reasons of control: (1) changes must be made on some organizational dimension (Gouldner) or changes must not be made; and (2) continuity must be maintained or social order must be perpetuated (Gusfield). These changes or continuities refer to such dimensions as goals, morale, staff problems, effectiveness, values, work loads, and so forth, of the sector of the organization involved.

A condition that generates a need for change and a successor who can handle it is a desire for improvements, such as more efficiency, effectiveness, or profits; better service; different management-worker relations; aggressiveness; and so forth. Doing away with waste, unofficial reward patterns, graft, and other kinds of "takes" stimulate the need for improvements in the operation of the organization. In Gouldner's case the successor used the strategy of "strategic replacements" to gain control for changes. He started a chain reaction of succession. While some improvements resulted, his changes, especially in the unofficial reward system, were so drastic as to generate a strike. A successor must be chosen according to his ability to make changes paced temporarily in a reasonable way to allow others in the organization to change accordingly.

A condition that generates a need for continuity and stability is the need on leadership's part to perpetuate its regime and underlying values (Gusfield). This leadership may take on an age-graded generational stand against a new one moving up in the organizational career with different life experiences, education and values. Large unions, corporations, and voluntary organizations often experience this conflict between generations. Two frequent strategies to perpetuate the regime are rigged, controlled, or fixed elections and "pipe-line succession." The latter refers to successors being picked years in advance and then put in positions that legitimately guarantee their takeover of leadership positions when the time comes, however serendipitous. This strategy can occur as far down the levels of the organizational career as top leadership deems necessary. It can take many years to break through this resistance to change, as we often see in political organizations.

In summary, the following articles, as discrete efforts to study and theorize about organizational succession, upon comparison integrate into a beginning formal theory on the process of succession in organizations. This theory is very useful for continued theoretical sampling in research for generating more theory on this area of organizational careers.

1 See Barney G. Glaser and Anselm L. Strauss, *The Discovery of Grounded Theory* (Chicago: Aldine Publishing Company, 1967), Chapter 3, "Theoretical Sampling."

Part VIII

MOVING BETWEEN ORGANIZATIONS

At first thought it might seem that moving between organizations is a fateful career step, perhaps requiring changes of great moment to the person. This may easily be the case, but it is not necessarily so. The move may also come as a matter of course in a routine career pattern. A useful way to begin analysis of the significance to a person's career of a move between organizations is to classify it as one of four general kinds of moves. Does the move entail a change in type of organizational career and does it entail a change in organizations or in sub-organizations of a parent organization?

Classification of Moves Between Organizations

		Type of Career	
		Same	Different
Parent	Same	1. Least Change	3.
Organ-			
ization	Different	2.	4. Most Change

In the above chart of this classification, we have shown the probable relative amount of change involved for the person. This relative amount of change does not necessarily indicate the degree of impact nor the dimensions of change for the person. This question, as yet, lacks grounding in research for generating formal propositions. Let us consider examples we have for each cell.

Changing only sub-organizations (Cell 1) is a characteristic of organizational careers in large complex organizations, such as the armed or civil services, school systems (Becker), banks, large industrial organizations, and so forth. A person can put in for a transfer in order to change his working conditions (such as Becker's school teacher) or geographical location, and this change can mean very much to the person. These volitional transfers are likely to be either horizontal, as with teachers, or vertical, as in the army or banks. Organizations may decide on these transfers as part of their work requirements, or for advancing or demoting a person. Routine transfers can occur every few years as an organizational policy (for example, in the army). Thus, the main factors in perhaps making this a change of great importance to the person are different working conditions and/or geographical location or a demotion.

The same career but in different organizations (Cell 2) we would judge as having relatively more impact of change on the person than Cell 1. Still pursuing his career, his move, if volitional, is likely to be linked to an equal or advanced career level. The prestige of the new organization may be a factor in this calculation. However, now he must adjust not only to new working conditions, but also to new organizational policies influencing his work and career, and, perhaps, to a new geographical location. If the move is the result of a well-calculated career plan, the adjustment to the new organization is probably a welcome challenge and not too bothersome a change, such as with the academic career pattern of "outbreeding," or with scheduled student careers (Glaser). This welcome change is particularly the case with executives of technical firms such as IBM, who take jobs in business or industry running a technical department for more money, higher rank, and better working conditions. This type of fruitful move of experts is a typical pattern. Nurses, as we see in Pape's article, engage in "touristry" as a career plan in the early stages of their careers. Touristry is moving between organizations for the purpose of travel to different parts of the nation or world while pursuing a career in organizations whose conditions facilitate this mobility.

While the changes may be welcome if the person moves between organizations as part of his own plan, it can be a most unwelcome change if the organization gets a person a job elsewhere in order to get rid of him. The move might entail a demotion as well as subtle discharge.

However, it might entail a promotion, but in a lower prestige organization (for example, to a "bush-league" college), so while his career is ostensibly advancing, he is on balance going down. Calculation of the career changes in these moves is up to the people involved, and differential calculations of the same move are prevalent.

Changing sub-organizations and type of career (Cell 3) may entail a complete career change within the organization by the person starting afresh in a different sub-organization. This may occur, for example, in switching from staff to line or from enlisted to officer corps. The person obtains a new start from the organization among people who do not know him nor can easily associate him with his previous career motivations, identity, and competence. The person may request this fresh start or the organization might consider it the most advisable way to save or help him in starting out again. Besides coming as a planned new start, a complete change in career may necessitate a change in sub-organization, come with this change, or be forced on the person by the organizational change. It also might come at a normal stage in a person's present career where he has the option to change or go on as he is; for example, researcher-scientists reach a point where they decide to stay in research for the remainder of their careers or switch to administration. In any case, it seems that the impact of this change is greater than Cell 2, because a new career, sub-organization, and working conditions must be adjusted to, even if the general organizational policy is the same.

Changing one's career within the organization may be an advantage offered by a large organization that becomes part of a person's career plans. But also it is a function of the alternatives the person has for moving to new organizations (Wilensky). If the person has no alternatives elsewhere for his new career, he is "locked in" the current organization and must continue "as is" or try for a new career in a new sub-organization. And unless he has some type of tenure, he is likely to be quite dependent on his current organization's desires as regard whether he can switch, and if switching whether he will be better off. His ability to negotiate his changes depends in part on his ability to move to another organization, and to have this ability known. This latter ability will vary strategically with his age, training, and competence, and the prestige of his current organizations. His satisfaction with his current type of career is also relevant. Some people who realize that they should change organizations or sub-organizations, which might require a new career, cannot make the change because of "love" for their work.

Changing both career and organization entails, on the face of it, the most changes in store for the person. These changes may be "drastic" for the person and take a long time to adjust to if they were not desired or planned for. Sometimes people never adjust to them. If desired and part of a career plan, they are likely to be met with a welcome challenge to make good in a new alternative to work life. Indeed, when these changes are made as careful career planning, we must look at the underlying sociological changes involved, for they may not be as great as the apparent changes. For example, Etzioni shows that in their changing careers and organizations, army officers going into private organizations as executives choose the same type of "compliance structures" they were used to in the army. Thus, on this important organizational dimension, there tended to be no change.

A central category from the person's point of view in these four types of moving between organizations are his career plans. Glaser presents one useful scheme for their analysis. In this scheme it is important to include with "3 - influences upon the actor," the organizational conditions under which moves are facilitated or hindered. Some organizations, such as educational institutions, make moves automatic between organizations or sub-organizations. Others facilitate moves, as by the standard employment practices of hospitals and the licensing of nurses. Others hinder moves as much as possible through union requirements, blackball lists, promises to never rehire a person, and so forth. In "2.a - motivations of the actor," it is important to specify his intentions with regard to staying with the organization and its career. Does the person intend to stay for a long time or for a short, necessary experience? Is he using the organization as a stepping stone to another in his career? If so, is this an open or closed maneuver? Is the organization a formal stepping stone, such as a hospital for interns? Is the person passing through the organization on the way down, up, or just drifting?

A central category from the point of view of the organization pertaining to moving between organizations is that this provides a type of interdependence between them. This interdependence is probably most relevant with people staying in the same career but applies to all four types. Once in the new organization the person can give away secrets of the old organization, or he can be used as a future contact or liaison man with his former organization. If he can keep some foothold in the former organization, as with friends or holding a nominal position, the person can also interlock the organizations, such as on the directorates. This moving may also indicate a "raiding" relationship between organizations. The raiding of scientists between government, industry, and university organizations carries with it the potential impact of a linkage of some sort for the benefit or deficit of either or both organizations.

Part IX

EXECUTIVE AND WORKER CAREER PATTERNS

Career pattern is a broad general category which describes a person's career or a type of career. In our case, a career pattern occurs within an organizational structure which sets limits to its requirements and is a partial determinant of it. Organizational career patterns may be contrasted to the general notion of occupational career patterns, which may or may not be organizationally bound for periods of time. Much of what we have discussed in the previous eight introductions provides the elements of organizational career patterns. These elements may be brought together under two dimensions of career patterns - shape and time. Further, we have presented in this section articles on executive and worker career patterns which are usually considered in writings as "extremes" of a range or as "very" different. In comparing them on the various elements of shape and time, the reader will see that these patterns can be quite similar in many respects, even if different on the level of social prestige with which each is generally held. Indeed, some variations within types of executive or worker career patterns may be far greater than between them.

The shape of an organizational career pattern can be described by two properties - length and direction. Length refers to where it begins and where it ends on the organizational hierarchy, and how many positions there are in between terminals. Length, then, specifies the type of career hierarchy involved and the sector of the organizational hierarchy the length covers. Thus, for example, some organizational careers of manual workers (Harper and Emmert, Blauner, Chinoy in Part III) have only one or perhaps two positions and are at the bottom of the organizational hierarchy, such as auto, postal, and textile worker careers. However, some manual careers, such as chemical workers, may have an elaborate set of positions to advance through, as many executive patterns have. However, it is usual to find that the higher upon the organizational hierarchy, the more the number of positions in a career pattern.

Where the career begins in the organization depends on the tributaries to recruitment (Mills), such as education, friendships, experience, apprenticeship, and so forth, as well as processes of recruitment. Where it ends depends on its ceiling within the organizational hierarchy and retirement requirements. From the point of view of the person terminating his career passage, ending a career pattern depends on his capabilities and age, and the various factors we have discussed which account for promotion and demotion. Ending an organizational career is a dimension upon which we have no body of focused research or theory; otherwise it would have been an important topic to include as a section in this reader. Like recruitment, and movement within the career, it is necessary to study the organizational processes and conditions of terminating or retiring from a career. Our discussion of demotion and dismissal touches only a few properties of ending a career.

The second property needed to describe the shape of an organizational career pattern is the direction of its movement. Demotion, simotion, and promotion combine to generate a career pattern. These movements may account for several shapes in direction of movement, besides the classic image of a direct line up to the ceiling of the pattern. There may be reversals in direction when the career "peaks out" and moves down. There may be repeatable movements as a career goes up and down with promotions and demotions. There may be plateaus accounted for by horizontal mobility. The shape may have a tree image, when at critical points alternative career lines may be equally well chosen. The direction of movement may be not to the top but away from the organization to private practice (Strauss and Cohen).

The shape of a career pattern may be prescribed and standardized by the organization, thus providing members a clear, concrete image of the path to success (Janowitz). However, the same organization, along with these conventional careers, may also allow unconventionally shaped careers which are developed out of the adaptive capacities of persons molding a new form of career for themselves. These adaptive career patterns, it would appear from the Janowitz and Mills articles, are developed by people who are determined to reach top leadership and who, in their self-made quest and by the sponsorship of other top leaders, jump over many of the conventional positions. The two main sources of prescribed career patterns are the organization's type of work or production and the requisite division of labor. Adaptive career patterns tend to ignore the requirements of these sources.

To graph an organizational career pattern one needs to know, besides the length and direction of its shape, the temporal aspects of its movement. These aspects include length of time in a position, rate of advancement between positions, duration of the whole career to various retirement points and transitional periods such as schooling, temporary positions, or coasting through preparatory jobs. Transitional periods are provided for by transitional statuses which structurally block out a portion of time for the person. For example, training periods provide a "student's" status, or temporary positions provide an "acting" status.[1]

Temporal aspects of career patterns may be handled in many ways by the organization. They may vary on the degree they are routine and scheduled as we have seen in promotion. They may vary on the degree they are well ordered so that the movement of one person through a career pattern is temporally articulated with the movement of another person at a different stage of the same career. The interdependence of personal careers within the same pattern, when temporally articulated, will not be likely to disrupt the organization, as we saw in the discussion on succession. Temporal movements, such as advancement, demotion, or retirements may be formally, privately, or secretly announced, or never mentioned. For example, a life insurance organization uses secret phone calls to a person to announce the timing of impending career moves. Secret or private announcements may easily change the behavior of a candidate at his current work, resulting in clashes with former associates that are inexplicable to them because they are unaware of their causes. Temporal aspects of career patterns are also deduced by people from various kinds of signs or cues left by the organization about impending movements.

The organization may provide either or both a lifetime career pattern or a passing-through career pattern. The latter has a built-in expectation or intention that the person will move to another organization after a specified time (for example, internship or residency in a hospital). Passing-through career patterns may and may not be articulated with the career patterns of other organizations. They are for hospital organizations, being scheduled on a yearly basis. This articulation results in a system of career patterns between hospitals from studentship, through internship and residency, to practice.

Organizational career patterns change in shape and temporal aspects throughout historical time (Mills and Warner and Abegglen), because of changing social conditions of education, employment, and technology, and because of changing organizational structures. For example, executives now tend to start with higher education at middle levels of the organization compared to thirty years ago when they tended to leave high school or grammar school and start out as laborers and become "self-made" men. Thus a specific career pattern for an organization is liable to continual modification by the pace of history. For example, the recruitment of army officers has continually changed from drawing upon upper-class sons to candidates from any social class or race who can cope with the changes in technology, required expertises, and organizational complexity. Also, recruitment is affected by changing social and race relations and by new patterns of upward mobility through education. The current multiplication of "professionals" and their changing patterns of work within and outside organizations has generated new organizational career patterns. Automation has, with its development and spreading use, generated new organizational career patterns. It remains to accomplish the necessary study and research for generating theory on the trends of changing organizational career patterns.

1 On transitional statuses see Barney G. Glaser and Anselm L. Strauss, "Temporal Aspects of Dying as an Non-Scheduled Status Passage," *American Journal of Sociology,* 71 (July, 1965): 48-59.

ORGANIZATIONAL TURNOVER:

An Illustration of the Grounded-Theory Approach to Theory Construction

James L. Price

ABSTRACT

This paper suggests one type of grounded-theory strategy to explain turnover better. The strategy consists of three steps. The first step is to specify demographic variables likely to be related to turnover in a nonspurious manner. The second step is to investigate empirically the relationship between these demographic variables and turnover. Existing theories of turnover, it is argued, should not be used in these investigations. Finally, the third step uses the demographic variables to located theoretical variables not presently incorporated into current theories.

Glaser and Strauss' (1967) work on the grounded-theory approach to theory construction, written in reaction to the dominant Parsonian approach of the forties and fifties, had a major impact on theory construction in sociology during the seventies. The grounded-theory terminology became part of the sociological lexicon and many scholars busied themselves in constructing theory by this approach. Grounded-theory thus took its place alongside the highly valued middle-range theory approach in the sociological pantheon. Lately, however, the grounded-theory approach seems, at least impressionistically, to be increasingly ignored. One seems to see few scholars explicitly using this approach. This paper illustrates one type of grounded-theory approach to the construction of theory; the aim of the paper is to reaffirm the basic strategy embodied in Glaser and Strauss' work.

The study of turnover in the field of organizations is chosen to illustrate this type of grounded-theory approach to theory construction. Any area of study in sociology would serve equally well to illustrate the approach; the topic turnover is selected because of the author's research in this area. As in most research on turnover, the focus will be on the voluntary separations of employees from work organizations, commonly referred to as "quits." New entrants into work organizations, plus employees forced to separate, will be ignored.

The core of the strategy advanced is the location of a set of empirical generalizations regarding turnover. Once these generalizations have been located, an effort can be made to specify theoretical variables implied in the generalizations. The strategy has three steps. Before describing the steps, however, key terms used to present the strategy--demographic variable, empirical generalization, and theory--must be discussed.

Methodological issues, such as data collection and measurement, will be ignored. Although important in a comprehensive strategy to explain turnover better, these issues are not within the concern of this paper.

PRELIMINARY DEFINITIONS

A demographic variable is specific as to time and place. "Length of Service" is an example of a demographic variable widely used in the study of turnover. Seniority is another name for length of service. Demographic variables are sometimes referred to as "proxies," "correlates," and "surrogate variables."

Most demographic variables use the individual as the unit of analysis. The previously cited length of service is an illustration. Some demographic variables, however, use the social system as the unit of analysis. The "existence of a trade union" in an organization is an example of variable with a social system (the organization) as the unit of analysis. One or more specific trade unions do or do not represent the employees of an organization. This paper will use demographic variables with both the individual and the organization as the unit of analysis.

Researchers who study turnover often use demographic variables as measures of theoretical variables. For example, an important theoretical variable used in theories to explain turnover is general training, that is, the degree to which the skills and knowledge of an individual can increase the productivity of different organizations (Becker 1964, pp. 7-36). Amount of education, a demographic variable, is often used as an measure of general training (Barnes and Jones 1974), especially by economists who refer to variables of this type as "proxies." Most researchers, however, do not distinguish between demographic variables and theoretical variables, using them both interchangeably in theories.

Demographic variables are inferior measures of theoretical variables. Education, to refer to the previous illustration, measures many ideas in addition to general training, since the amount of time spent in school is correlated with "just about everything," as the saying goes. (Material documenting the importance of education will be cited later.) Better, if one wishes to measure general training, to construct a set of measures designed only to assess the transferability of skills and knowledge between organizations. Price and Mueller (1986a, p. 264) attempted to construct such an index of general training in their study of hospital absenteeism and turnover. Despite their inferior psychometric properties, demographic variables, because of their easy availability, will, unfortunately, probably continue to be widely used to measure theoretical variables.

Empirical generalizations are observed uniformities between variables (Merton 1957, p. 95). With length of service and turnover as variables, an example of such a uniformity is the statement that *employees with low lengths of service will usually have higher rates of turnover than employees with high lengths of service* (Price 1977, pp. 26-88). With the existence of a trade union and turnover as variables, a second example of such a uniformity is the statement that *organizations whose employees are not represented by a trade union will usually have higher rates of turnover than organizations whose employees who are represented by a trade union* (Freeman and Medoff 1984, pp. 94-110). There is nothing *causal* about empirical generalizations; length of service and the existence of a trade union are merely *related* to turnover. Empirical generalizations are, in short, not propositions.

Theories are basically sets of interrelated propositions (Zetterberg 1965, pp. 9-29). An illustration is Price and Mueller's theory (1986a, pp. 9-33) which consists of nineteen causal statements (propositions) linked together to explain turnover. Theories, of course, vary by their level of confirmation: some have been well confirmed, whereas others have only begun the process of confirmation. The previously mentioned Price and Mueller theory is moderately well confirmed. Theories also consist of more than sets of interrelated propositions. In addition to the propositions, the full statement of a theory must also include definition of theoretical variables, specification of empirical assumptions, indication of the linkages between the theoretical variables of the propositions, and description of scope conditions. The propositions are, however, the core of a theory. This view of a theory, in its essentials, appears to be widely shared by theorists (Cohen 1980; Homans 1967; Merton 1957; and Wallace 1971).

Demographic variables should not be used in theories. The propositions of a theory should include only theoretical variables,that is, concepts which are not specific as to time and place. It is acceptable, to return to the previous illustration, to use general training but not education in theories of turnover because general training is analytical, whereas education, as commonly used, is specific as to time and place. What is being argued is that the nature of theories requires the exclusion of demographic variables. Important theories in economics (Fuchs, 1983) and psychology (Homans 1961) do not include demographic variables and major sociological theorists, such as Merton (1957) and Cohen (1980), exclude these variables in their view of theories. A recently published frame of reference for the study of organizations (Price and Mueller 1986b) also contain no demographic variables.

The basic terms used to describe the suggested strategy have been defined. What must be done next is to set forth the three steps of the strategy.

THE FIRST STEP OF THE STRATEGY

The first step of the strategy is to located demographic variables likely to be the nonspuriously related to turnover. Once located,these variables will then become part of empirical generalizations, like length of service and existence of trade unions in the preceding illustrations. The first step thus consists of the tentative statement of empirical generalizations.

"Nonspurious" in the present context means the exclusion of theoretical variables from the analysis. A demographic variable is nonspuriously related to turnover when it is statistically significant after turnover is regressed (assuming this type of analysis) on a set of demographic variables. If turnover is regressed on both demographic variables and theoretical variables, most of the demographic variables will not be statistically significant, especially if the theoretical variables include most of the determinants of turnover (Price and Mueller 1986a, pp. 25-29). *The reason is that the theoretical variables captures what it is about the demographic variables which have an impact on turnover*. A later section of the paper will present an argument for the exclusion of theoretical variables from the suggested strategy. To exclude theoretical variables is, of course, to exclude theories since the former are embodied in the latter.

There are two major sources of these demographic variables. First, a sizeable number of these variables have already been used in the study of turnover. The problem is to select those variables likely to be nonspuriously related to turnover. There are a great many of these variables in the literature and few of them have been studied with statistical controls. Gender is a noteworthy example. Early research on turnover seemed to indicated that females had higher rates of turnover than males. However, when controls were used, it appears as if the early relationships between gender and turnover was spurious (Price 1977, pp. 39-40). The second source of these indicator variables is the literature of the behavioral sciences. Sociologists have, for instance, made extensive use of these variables in their research. Whether or not these variables will be nonspuriously related to turnover, however, is another question. Variables from these two sources will now be described.

Examination of the turnover literature yields 11 promising individual demographic variables and three which use the organization as the unit of analysis. Fourteen empirical generalizations regarding turnover thus appear promising. "Promising" in this instance means likely to be nonspuriously related to turnover. The 11 individual variables are as follows: age, length of service, education, occupation, shift, recent turnover experience, marital status, existence of children, race, source of referral to the organization, and previous employment. Each of these variables requires comment; following these comments, the three organizational variables will be discussed.

Reviews consistently indicate that age and length of service are negatively related to turnover (Cotton and Tuttle 1986). Although the data are not totally consistent (Mobley 1982, p.98), education appears to be positively related to turnover (Cotton and Tuttle 1986). Blue-collar workers and *unskilled* blue-collar workers have higher rates of turnover than, respectively, white-collar workers and *skilled* blue-collar workers (Price 1977, pp. 31-34). Most reviews indicate that rates of turnover are higher among night-shift employees than among day-shift employees (Pettman 1973). A new variable, which is strongly supported by research, is recent turnover experience: employees who have recently quit are more likely to quit again than employees who have not recently quit (Price and Mueller, 1986, pp. 107-129).

Unmarried employees and employees without children are more likely to terminate their employment than married employees and employees with children. Price and Mueller (1986a, pp. 261-262) use marital status and the existence of children as two measures of kinship responsibility. It appears that whites have higher turnover than blacks (Steinberg 1975).

Applicants for employment referred to the organization by formal sources, such as employment agencies and advertising, seem to have higher rates of turnover than applicants referred by informal sources, such as employees and relatives (Mobley 1982, p. 99). Finally, employees who were unemployed when they applied for a job are more likely to quit than employees who left a previous job to take their present job (Weiss 1984).

Questions can be raised about each of the 11 demographic variables. Age and length of service are, for example, highly related and it is possible that only length of service is nonspuriously related to turnover (Young 1965). The empirical generalizations are, in short, not well established. These questions can only be resolved by empirical research, the next topic of the paper. All that is being asserted at this point is that these 11 variables appear likely, on the basis of current data, to be nonspuriously related to turnover. The empirical generalizations appear plausible.

Three demographic variables which use the organization as the unit of analysis also appear promising. First, there is the existence or nonexistence of a trade union in the organization, a variable already discussed. Second, organizations which do not have pension plans appear to have higher rates of turnover than organizations which have such plans (Folk 1963). Third, organizations located in more urbanized areas have more terminations than organizations located in less urbanized areas (Saul 1977/78). Other social demographic variables could be cited--country, industry, and level of employment are illustrations (Price 1977, pp. 29-31, pp. 34-35, and pp. 38-39)--but they do not appear as valuable in the construction of theories as the three organizational variables described. The United States, for example, has more turnover than other capitalistic democracies. This generalization, however, is not too helpful, since there are a multitude of differences between the United States and these other societies.

Examination of the behavioral science literature--the second major source of demographic variables--yields six additional variables whose widespread use make them worth of investigation: dual career in the family, ethnicity, religion, political preference, current class position. and home ownership. Comments are required about each of these seven variables.

Dual careers, it should be emphasized, must be distinguished from situations where the husband/father and wife/mother simply work. When both adults in the family have dual careers, they have long-term commitments to occupations and/or organizations; these commitments are absent when both adults simply work. Ethnicity is often confused with race (Steinberg 1981). Ethnicity is viewed, in this paper, as nationality. An individual born in America is, ethnically, an American. Religion should be approached in terms of self identification regarding the major denominations in the United States. Political preference can also be examined in terms of self identification regarding the major political parties. Home ownership includes the purchasing of a residence as well as its full ownership; the most comment alternatives are various forms of rental.

It is not clear whether or not these six additional variables will be nonspuriously related to turnover. Nor is it clear how these variables are related to turnover, whether there is, for example, a positive or negative relationship. However, given the widespread use of these six variables in behavioral science research, it would seem prudent to investigate them.

THE SECOND STEP OF THE STRATEGY

The second step of the strategy is to investigate empirically the relationship between the 20 demographic variables and turnover. The empirical generalizations must, in brief, be firmly established. Since the goal is to specify variables nonspuriously related to turnover, some form of multivariate analysis must be used. Statistical controls are, in short, a necessity.

Age will be used to illustrate the goal of this research. If age continues to be statistically significant after turnover is regressed on the other demographic variables, the conclusion will be that there is something about age *per se* that is having an impact on turnover. There is something about age, in other words, that is producing the negative relationship between age and turnover. This "something" is captured by one or more theoretical variables for which age is a proxy. The goal of this research is to have a set of variables which are nonspuriously related to turnover. In short, the goal is to have well-established empirical generalizations regarding these variables and turnover. It will probably require a series of investigations to find a set of demographic variables nonspuriously related to turnover. These investigations should encompass different industries, occupations, and countries. The greater the number of differences encompassed by these investigations, the greater the confidence that can be placed in the results of the investigations. It is, of course, not known how many variables will continue to be statistically significant after these investigations. The hope is for as many variables as possible, since the location of theoretical variables appears to be facilitated by a substantial number of variables. Each variable is a clue and one prefers as many clues as possible.

As previously indicated, theories should not be used in these empirical investigations. This suggestion will be elaborated later in the paper.

THE THIRD STEP OF THE STRATEGY

The third step of the strategy is to concentrate on the location of theoretical variables. Assume, for instance, that education continues to be statistically significant after the multivariate analysis. In short, it can now be stated that there seems to be something about more education *per se* which produces more turnover. The problem is to locate the theoretical variables which produce this result--to find, in other words, the theoretical variables for which the amount of education is a surrogate variable.

There is a sizeable literature dealing with the impact of education on the individual (Hyman, Wright, and Reed 1975; Hyman and Wright 1979). This literature should be reviewed to locate theoretical variables not presently incorporated in current theories. It is impossible to indicated these variables until this literature has been reviewed. There are also other ways to locate theoretical variables than by literature reviews. Such reviews are, however, one way to locate these variables.

A sizeable number of theoretical variables should result from this review. The problem will be to select which variables to investigate further, since many--perhaps most-of these variables will have no impact on turnover. The selection problem will be complicated by the fact that the literature review for each demographic variable will yield a set of theoretical variables. Existing knowledge about turnover, plus plausibility, can be used to select the theoretical variables to investigate further. If, for instance, the review indicates that education, to return to the previous illustration, is positively correlated with motivation to work hard, there are some data which support the idea that motivation (discussed as "work ethic") reduces the amount of turnover (Mowday Porter, and Steers 1982, pp. 107-133). Motivation may thus be worthy of further investigation. If, on the other hand, the review indicates that education is positively correlated with mental maturity, it is plausible that mental maturity might have an impact on turnover, since such a property might make it easier for employees to retain their jobs. Mental maturity may also be worthy of further investigation. Even with some data and thinking in plausible terms, it will be difficult to select the theoretical variables to investigate further.

The critical importance of the second step of the suggested strategy now becomes clear. It will require a substantial investment of time and energy to review the literature about the impact of education on the individual, to continue with this example. This investment can be justified only if one is confident that education is nonspuriously related to turnover; the research performed to implement the second step should provide the basis for this confidence. Since several demographic variables are likely to survive the multivariate analysis, literature reviews must be conducted for each of these variables, thus increasing further the resources invested in locating additional theoretical variables. Before concentrating on the location of theoretical variables, one must be confident that the demographic variables examined are nonspuriously related to turnover. The empirical generalizations must, in brief, be well established before one can search for theoretical variables.

The description of the strategy leaves the location of theoretical variables to the third stage of the strategy. It is possible, of course, that the location of additional theoretical variables will occur at any time. Empirical research on the demographic variables (the second stage) may, for example, suggest additional theoretical variables. One cannot obviously program the exact stage at which these variables will be located. It is likely, however, that most of the variables will be located when the literature is reviewed about the demographic variables that survive the multivariate analysis; the third stage will thus probably concentrate on the location of these variables.

THE USE OF THEORIES

It is recommended, as previously indicated, that theories--this, in effect, means the theoretical variables of these theories--not be used in the empirical investigation of the demographic variables. Turnover, in short, is to be regressed (again, assuming this type of analysis) only on the demographic variables. This may appear to be a strange recommendation, since there currently exists a number of theories of turnover (Mobley 1982, pp. 115-132; Mowday, Porter, and Steers 1982, pp. 107-133; Price and Mueller 1981, pp. 9-25; and Price and Mueller 1986a, pp. 9-33) which could be used in these investigations. The recommended exclusion of theories must now be justified.

There are two reasons for excluding theories from the investigations.

First, there is nothing in the recommended strategy which requires the use of theories. The proximate goal of the research is to locate demographic variables which are nonspuriously related to turnover. One wants to be able to state, for example, that "there is something about increased education *per se* which increases turnover." At this time, this is all one wishes to state. Once these demographic variables are located and empirically estimated, they can be used, through intensive reviews of the literature, to find theoretical variables which appear to be related to turnover and which can then be empirically estimated along with existing theories. *The limited goals of the research do not necessitate the use of theories. One does not have to use both theories and demographic variables as controls if one only wishes to make statements about indicator variables.*

Second, the use of a theory would greatly complicate the recommended research. Excluding turnover, the 1986 version of the Price and Mueller model contains 16 (p. 11) theoretical variables. All of these variables require complex indices for valid and reliable measurement. Despite a preference for parsimony, additional research, at least for a while, is likely to add more variables to investigate. The previous reviews cited 20 demographic variables which appeared promising. More of these variables will certainly be forthcoming. The demographic variables do not, of course, need complex measures. Use of the Price and Mueller theory thus requires an investigation of 16 theoretical variables and 20 indicator variables, *at the minimum*. It is much simpler to exclude the theories from the investigation.

SUMMARY AND CONCLUSION

This paper has suggested one type of grounded-theory strategy to explain turnover better. The strategy consists of three steps. The first step was to locate demographic variables likely to be related to turnover in a nonspurious manner. Twenty variables were located. Additional variables will certainly emerge, so these 20 are a minimum list of the variables. The second step of the strategy was to investigate empirically the relationship between these 20 variables and turnover. Since the purpose of the investigation was to located nonspurious variables, some form of multivariate analysis, such as regression techniques, must be used. Theories, because they are not required and because of their added complexity, should not be used in these investigations of the demographic variables. The third step of the strategy was to concentrate on the location of theoretical variables that will explain the empirical generalizations produced by the second step of the strategy. What must be done in the third step is to review the literature about the demographic variables nonspuriously related to turnover. The purpose of the review is to locate theoretical variables not presently incorporated in existing theories of turnover. Once these variables are located, they can be estimated with one of the existing models. The hope is that use of these new variables will increase the explanatory power of current theories.

The grounded-theory approach, as expounded by Glaser and Strauss, is rich in insights about the construction of theories. What is being asserted in this paper is that the suggested strategy is an illustration of the grounded-theory approach to theory construction. This grounded approach to theory construction is too valuable to pass into disuse.

REFERENCES

Barnes, W.F., and E.B. Jones. 1974. "Differences in male and female quitting." *Journal of Human Resources* 9:439-451.

Becker, G.S. 1964. *Human Capital*. New York: Columbia University Press.

Cohen, J.L. and J.F. Tuttle. 1968. "Employee turnover: A meta-analysis and review with implications for research." *The Academy of Management Review* 11:55-70.

Folk, H. 1963. "Effects of private pension plans on labor mobility." *Monthly Labor Review* 86:285-288.

Freeman, R.B., and J.L. Medoff. 1984 *What Do Unions Do?* New York: Basic Books.

Fuchs, V.R. 1983. *How We Live*. Cambridge: Harvard University Press.

Glaser, B.G., and A.L. Strauss. 1967. *The Discovery of Grounded Theory*. Chicago: Aldine.

Homans, G.S. 1961. *Social Behavior: Its Elementry Forms*. New York: Harcourt, Brace, and World.

Homans, G.S. 1967. *The Nature of Social Science*. New York: Harcourt, Brace, and World.

Hyman, H.H., C.R. Wright, and J.S. Reed. 1975. *The Enduring Effects of Education*. Chicago: University of Chicago Press.

Hyman, H.H. and C.R. Wright, 1979. *Education's Lasting Influence on Values*. Chicago: University of Chicago Press.

Merton, R.K. 1957. *Social Theory and Social Structure*. Glencoe: The Free Press.

Mobley, W.H. 1982. *Employee Turnover: Causes, Consequences, and Control*. Reading: Addison-Wesley.

Mowday, R.T., L.W. Porter, and R.M. Steers. 1982. *Employee-Organization Linkages*. New York: Academic Press.

Pettman, B.O. 1973. "Some factors influencing labor turnover." *Industrial Relations* 4:43-61.

Price, J.L. 1977. *The Study of Turnover*. Ames: Iowa State University Press.

Price, J.L. and C.W. Mueller. 1981. *Professional Turnover: The Case of Nurses*. Bridgeport: Luce.

Price, J.L., and C.W. Mueller. 1986a. *Absenteeism and Turnover among Hospital Employees*. Greenwich: JAI Press.

Price, J.L. and C.W. Mueller, 1986b. *Handbook of Organizational Measurement*. Scranton: Harper Collins.

Saul, P.N. 1977/78. "Job satisfaction, performance and tenure: A predictive study based on a model of an organization and an underutilized statistical technique." *Organization and Administrative Sciences* 8:189-206.

Steinberg, E. 1975. "Upward mobility in the internal labor market." *Industrial Relations* 14:259-265.

Steinberg, S. 1981. *The Ethnic Myth*. New York: Atheneum.

Stolzenberg, R.M., and J.D. Winkler. 1983. *Voluntary Terminations From Military Service*. Santa Monica: Rand.

Young, A. 1965. "Models for planning, recruitment and promotion of staff." *British Journal of Industrial Relations* 3:301-310.

Wallace, W.L. 1971. *The Logic of Science in Sociology*. Chicago: Aldine Atherton.

Weiss, A. 1984. "Determinants of quit behavior." *Journal of Labor*

THE DEVELOPMENT OF GENERIC CONCEPTS IN QUALITATIVE RESEARCH THROUGH CUMULATIVE APPLICATION

Jacqueline P. Wiseman

ABSTRACT: Because of their close contact with the actual flow of human group life, qualitative research projects frequently have as a bonus the development of insightful concepts of generic quality that catch some essence of social interaction and/or structural conditions. Yet little attention has been paid to the way these concepts are modified and strengthened *over a series of projects*. The lack of regard for this methodological issue may lead to the false impression that qualitative research is not cumulative. In this paper, I urge qualitative sociologists to be aware of cumulative concept development as a major methodological tool, and to demonstrate how concepts derived from one research project are extended and modified in subsequent projects. Additionally, I show how this approach aids in both illuminating aspects of a given research context, while at the same time drawing attention to hitherto unnoted relationships among concepts. In this way, more systematic strategies for developing generic concepts and cumulative understanding of human group life through qualitative research is possible.

INTRODUCTION

In 1967, Glaser and Strauss alerted sociologists to the technique of developing theory through constant referral to, and comparison with, related substantive material as it is gathered during a research enterprise. As the theoretical framework developed from an initial analysis of a phenomenon accumulates and accommodates data from parallel sources, it is modified and elaborated by being constantly "grounded" through reference to this data, for which it, in turn, is used as an enhanced analytic tool. At the same time, the gathering of data is increasingly focused as this analytic framework becomes more and more specific.

Glaser and Strauss' concerns were the building of useful theory, and as a result, enhancing the analysis of the data being gathered on which the developing theory was also based. This "grounding" of theory could be accomplished by two types of comparative operations: 1. location of numerous similar situations and/or groups *within* a given research project that could be used to modify the theory as a result of their variation (e.g., theory concerning nurses' attitudes toward different types of dying patients [Glaser & Strauss, 1967:49-60]); and 2. application of the theory from one project to other various *similar* interactions occurring in different research topics (e.g. theory expanded by comparing status passage of dying persons to status passage of, for instance, change from the single to the married state.) They also suggest that this latter type of comparison should broaden the theory further, although they do not discuss possibilities more specifically (Glaser & Strauss, 1967:83-90).

This paper extends their notion of refinement of theory through constant comparison with the substantive data, to *conscious awareness of concept development* over a series of research projects with no apparent similarities.

The fact that a concept emerges from, or is usefully applied to, numerous social worlds that may vary considerably in size, content, and characteristics of personnel, offers one of the real intellectual joys of sociology. The transcendental quality of some concepts as labels for various types of behavior or structural attributes makes them transferable. The concern here is to show how each application of these concepts to a parallel situation, can further refine it, if sociologists remain aware of what configuration of circumstances bring about what kinds of modifications or elaborations in the concept. This should improve the generic quality of concepts by exposing subtle shading of applicability.

When concepts are developed through cumulative application to various research contexts, their usefulness is expanded because added dimensions of the concept are articulated. Such an intellectual exercise calls attention both to what is universal in the concept as well as to its many possible forms[1] as they develop out of various contexts. Additionally, this unfolding differentiation alerts the researcher to nuances and unnoticed ingredients in each situation or research context to which the concept is applied (and by this application is modified). Thus, by examining the increasing dimensions of the concept, a repertoire of the attributes found in types of research contexts that bring out certain modifications in the concept can be developed and knowledge of the research subject is increased simultaneously. Additionally, relationships *among* concepts become clearer through this procedure.

Most important, the ultimate result of such development of the generic quality of concepts through attention to the details of their refinement plays a significant role in making qualitative research *cumulative*. This is because although much of qualitative research is admittedly based in settings/ social situations that are difficult or impossible to replicate in the traditional sense of the word, the concepts that emerge from, or are inspired by, the data can have a replicable life of their own through repeated application. Thus, it is the generic development of useful analytic concepts, as well as exposure of connections among them, that can be the generalizable building blocks of qualitative sociology. Further, this process often provides insights into the nature of human group life for situations seemingly unrelated to their origin. To accomplish this, however, we must pay attention to nuances revealed in concepts through repeated application.

In this paper, I will use my own research to illustrate how concepts can be developed, enriched, and sometimes interrelated, as they are applied to more than one research context. Two types of concepts will be discussed - those focused on types of *interactive behavior* and those concerned with *structural qualities* of personal existence.

Interactive Behaviors	Structural Qualities
Defining encounters	Social anchors
Acting natural	Social margin
Depending on implied contracts	Role vestiges
Codifying emotions	Baked resources
Behavior scripts	Quasi-primary relationships

While presentation of research contexts are in chronological order (because that is the way the concept modifications emerged), the order is actually irrelevant. In fact, by mentally applying new concepts *post hoc* to old research projects, possible modifications become evident as, do hitherto undiscovered nuances in the setting and/or situation.

More importantly than the order in which the concepts are generated, applied, and reapplied to gain their maximum development, are the dynamics of the research context. It will be seen that over and above the general sociological field of endeavor on which the research is focused, are significant attributes or characteristics of the setting, the situation, or the relationships of people that affect a concept, even while being analyzed by it. As the aspects of topics of investigation vary, so do the attributes of concepts when applied across various research contexts.

Thus, the characteristics of the contexts are significant for the modification of concepts in that they transcend the sociological field of their origin.

PROCEDURE

To discuss systematically the methodology of concept development through analytic application to diverse sociological investigations, the following procedure will be used:

With each study, the general field of endeavor and its significant attributes will be outlined briefly. Following that, some concepts that developed from, or were applied to, this research context will be presented. Each will be defined in a way that indicates its analytic usefulness as well as its derivation[2] where appropriate.

Following this, the next research setting will be presented in terms of its general field of inquiry and its significant attributes. Concepts from the prior study will be applied progressively where useful analytically, and their alteration discussed in terms of its reflection of the dynamics of the new research context. Additionally, new concepts, arising from this research setting/situation[3] will be presented and will join the group of concepts to be applied to subsequent research contexts (or mentally applied, *post hoc* to published material).

Some of these concepts originated with me as a way to describe my findings. Others originated with me but have obvious roots in earlier works. Still others originated with me but have obvious roots in earlier works. Still others are taken from the terms used by respondents to describe their own actions or feelings, while a fourth class of concept originated with other researchers and were used to analyze my own data. The research cases presented involve deviants and their significant others, persons in primary group relationships, and social outsiders.

INITIAL EMERGENT CONCEPTS - A STUDY OF SKID ROW ALCOHOLICS

In the first study, intended as a contribution to the field of deviant behavior, the interaction between Skid Row alcoholics and agents of social control is the research focus (Wiseman, 1979a). Research settings include Skid Row and various treatment or control institutions. The power differential between the down-and-out drinking man and persons who "process" them is substantial.

Of the three concepts that emerged from this study that can be traced through other studies, one seems to be the discovery of a behavior and the other two are of a structural nature. While all three started out imbedded in a deviant context, this becomes insignificant to the usefulness of the concept in subsequent applications.

The three concepts are: (a) defining encounter; (b) social anchors; and (c) social margin.

QUALITATIVE SOCIOLOGY

Defining encounters refers to the way in which brief contacts between Skid Row alcoholics and agents of social control result in each defining the character and possible consignment to a role of the other. Such decisions set behavior of each toward the other in motion. This concept is related to the work of Goffman (1961) and W.I. Thomas (1967). It is also related to labeling theory (Becker, 1963, Lemert, 1951; Kitsuse, 1962).

Social anchors refers to the connections and relationships that most people have with family, employee/colleagues, and friends, that give in a storm during trouble. Skid Row alcoholics lack these anchorages because their social bridges have been burned as a result of their heavy drinking and accompanying misbehavior. The concept has diverse origins and is widely used, such as in Eckert's (1980) study of the elderly who live in single room occupancy hotels.

Social margin is related both to defining encounters and to social anchors. It refers to the "margin for error" people allow each other before negative labeling and possible termination of the relationship. The concept is useful in explaining why a Skid Row alcoholic who has undergone treatment is allowed very few missteps before being called a "hopeless drunkard," "unworthy of employment," or "not to be trusted," while other persons can make the same social errors without having the label applied so quickly. A concept very close to social margin is *deviance credits* (Hollander, 1958), which Hollander defines as the degree of idio-syncratic behavior of an individual tolerated by a group. Hollander points out that people possess deviance credits in varying degrees, as a result of past behavior, and other interactional and structural qualities.

FIRST MODIFICATION OF CONCEPTS - A STUDY OF WOMEN MARRIED TO MIDDLE AND WORKING CLASS ALCOHOLICS

In the second study (Wiseman, forthcoming), my focus remained on deviant behavior, but attention shifted to the non-deviant partner of the drinking man, thus also adding to the literature on the family. Wives of alcoholics in America and Finland were studied in order to compare the impact of problem drinking on these women and their marriages in two cultures with somewhat different drinking norms. The setting was the home rather than institutions of social control and the power relationship was reversed. In these still-intact middle and working class marriages, the drinking husband had more power in the long-term dyadic relationship than did the wife. These shifts in focus, settings, and the dynamics of the relationship resulted in the first modification of the prior concepts. In addition, two other new concepts emerged from the data: (a) acting natural, and (b) role vestiges.

Defining encounters takes on a temporal dimension when applied to wives of alcoholics that is lacking in the brief manner with which Skid Row alcoholics and agents of social control "size each other up." When wives try to decide whether their husbands are alcoholics or just men who periodically drink too much, they go through an extended career of ambivalence. During this period, they weigh the incidents that suggest alcoholism, and those incidents that seem to rule against it. They try to make the decision based on cumulative increments of evidence. Certain types of behavior will be "straws" that tip the scales, so to speak, toward a diagnosis of alcoholism. Then they go back in their minds over evidence they ignored earlier and reassess its significance to make it congruent with their final diagnosis.

Obviously, this prolonged judgmental career means that my earlier concept of defining encounters must be expanded to accommodate structural and relationship differences in the two situations. Between indigent alcoholics and agents of social control, there is no history of a permanent relationship as there is with husbands and wives. The first encounter of the former could result in a final definition, inasmuch as no lengthy and intimate background relationship exists for comparison. Second, agents of social control have no reason to maintain ambivalence over an extended period. In fact, they have a vested interest in avoiding ambivalence so that organizational decisions concerning clients who have almost no power to resist the label can be expeditiously made. Wives, on the other hand, take more time and weigh evidence with much greater care, because the final "diagnosis" of alcoholism in their husbands is devastating to their relationship. Furthermore, husbands have the power to resist a wife's label, a factor that aids in protracting final decisions.

Social margin and social anchorage also apply in this study, but with a difference. Both can be lost by association. Wives of alcoholics find family and friends restrict relational contacts, fearing they will be asked for help that will drain their resources. Wives are cut off from social gatherings and friendships because of the behavior of their inebriated spouses.

Acting natural is a concept that grew directly out of the data and refers to a term wives, themselves, use to describe the outward manner they assume when their tears, threats, cajoling, and reasoning fail to convince their husbands to stop drinking. Feeling that perhaps the pressure they are putting on him may actually be causing the husband to drink to excess, the wives decide to cease taking *any* notice of the drinking and drunken behavior. Instead, when in his presence, they pretend that everything is all right. Both American and Finnish wives refer top this charade as "acting natural."[4] *Post hoc* application to Skid Row alcoholics indicate that the concept would be useful to describe how these men act when they have been drinking, but still want to pass for sober (in order to gain admission to a shelter or to get a free meal). Thus there appears to be a social need at times to act natural to cover true status when one is both psychologically disturbed (i.e. unhappy about something) or physically affected (i.e. as a result of alcohol ingestion).

Role vestiges is my concept used to describe the way in which wives of alcoholics cling to and enact the role of wife, even after their husbands ignore their presence in the home. These women make meals they know will not be attended and conversation they know is not heeded, acting as though the doing of these things will aid in preserving the role. Looking back at the data on Skid Row alcoholics, it can be seen that no role vestiges remain for these men at the "bottom of the barrel." Any other roles they may have had are usually totally - not partially - gone.

SECOND MODIFICATION OF CONCEPTS - A STUDY OF
THE FRIENDSHIP RELATIONSHIP

Opportunities for this modification of concepts that were developed in the past studies emerged, not from a shift in the context of deviant behavior, but because of a new focus on voluntary relationship interaction (Wiseman, 1986). The dynamics of friendship relationships were explored - how people make friends, keep them, and sometimes lose them; what they see in their friends, and what they think their friends see in them. The emergence of new concepts or the application of concepts from other investigations include: (a) implied contracts; (b) banked resources; (c) codifying emotions; and (d) scripts for behavior.

Defining encounters. Friendship is a voluntary relationship based on the attraction between two persons for no apparent gain other than the pleasure of each other's company.[5] Inasmuch as the data on the friendship-making process indicates there is both "friendship at first sight" (a sort of mutual realization of empathy), and friendship evolving out of a long career of association (such as when co-workers become friends), the defining encounter, when associated with the process of friendship-making, has dichotomous forms in terms of timetables and emotional charge. Being voluntary, friends are independent of both institutional purpose (in contrast with alcoholics and agent of social control), and a long prior intimate relationship with its attendant expectations (such as was the case with wives of alcoholics). These differences may account for the breadth of time-span involved in defining encounters of friends.

Social anchorage was originally used to refer to the ties with family, friends, and employers that indigent male alcoholics (and families of middle-class male alcoholics) lose as a result of their heavy drinking. In that case, these significant persons are lumped together as possible sources of social connections and help during times of trouble and gradually fade away in response to deviant behavior (problem drinking).

The friendship data indicate that social anchorages provided by friends are not perceived in quite the same way as that provided by family. With the family, it is expects; with friends, it is seen as a gift having family-like qualities. Thus, this study differentiated types of social anchors by those that are expected (because of blood ties), and those that were a pleasant surprise. This differentiation may also explain why wives of alcoholics are more likely to be upset when they are deserted by their parents and their husbands' family than when such action is taken by close friends.

Social margin. Friends are expected to allow each other special margin for error because of their closeness. Thus, this concept can refer to more than a characteristic of persons that varies with their social power. It can be a special expectation of close friends, which, if not fulfilled, will cause rancor between the grantor, who apparently did not extend enough margin, and the grantee, who expected more.

Dependence on *implied contracts* was adapted from Rubington's (1964) study of the alcoholic, Grady, who "broke out" when he felt a "contract"''''' between himself and the administrators of the alcoholic treatment center where he was an employee (and a former client) had been broken. This "contract" was never discussed; it was a relational expectation arrived at unilaterally by Grady.

Data from the friendship study indicates that friends similarly rely on implied contracts with each other. They almost never discuss these special expectations, however. This absence of openness is not because the relationship lacks the intimacy necessary to allow them to come to some agreement about what one expects of the other, but rather because the relationship *is* so very close that the discussion of such matters would seem so unnecessary as to denigrate it.

Thus, the friendship data indicate that implied contracts can occur in other than the institutional settings where people are in a secondary relationship to each other. Among friends, where the relationship is primary, special expectations of implied contracts can grow out of the unique characterizations each individual has of the relationship. Some persons (especially friends), who experience disappointment in the breach of an implied contract, may reflect Shibutani's (1961) concept of interpersonal role relationships when they say, "Of all the persons I know, I would have expected John to help" Of course, implied relationship contracts can also reflect general cultural expectations as, "I would think that any real friend would..."

Looking back at earlier research, Skid Row alcoholics testify that the first time they hear such statements from a judge, doctor, or counselor as, "I am sending you to jail (the mental hospital, a mission) where they will help you, "they believe this and see it as a promise of helpful treatment. They, therefore, feel cheated when treatment of alcoholism turns out to be "sitting around in a circle talking," and/or work therapy. They shortly learn not to depend on these implied contracts.

Cynicism begins here for these Skid Row men and although they behave outwardly as required by agents of social control, they have no faith in them nor respect for them. They also have definite ideas as to how a "good" social worker, psychologist, or even policeman and jailer should act toward them. Failure to measure up to these standards makes such professionals humbugs and exploiters in their eyes. This cynicism and absence of reliance on implied contracts works both ways. Agents of social control also lose patience with the lack of sincerity on the part of the alcoholics whom they feel they are trying to help.

For the wife of an alcoholic, the implied contract she initially operates with is that the marital relationship is strong enough for him to accept her diagnosis of his problems as well as her suggestions for overcoming it. To find that she is wrong is heartbreaking and drastically changes the meaning of the relationship for her. Thus the breach of implied contract can vitiate a close relationship between two equal individuals, change the meaning of a marital relationship, and create cynicism between low status people and the institutions on which they are dependent.

Banked resources is a concept closely allied to implied contracts. Although friends claim they do not keep a mental balance sheet on who did what for whom, they definitely believe that good deeds ought to be remembered by the beneficiary. Further, good deeds should create resources possibly to be called upon in like or comparable fashion when needed (in terms of loans, temporary housing, et cetera). Thus, a person must have resources (and share them) in order to have some banked with the recipient for possible future needs.

Parenthetically, *social margin for error* is considered by many to be a banked resource with friends, as, for example: "Well, I forgave her when she did thus and so; why shouldn't she forgive me for doing this and that?"

Skid Row alcoholics, of course, can expect little in the way of banked resources with anyone, since they take more than they are in a position to give. Wives of alcoholics who share their husbands' stigma also suffer the continual diminution of social resources with him. Eventually, these women see that their husbands are not to be counted on as a resource, and neither are relatives nor "couple-friends." Some women will, at this point, attempt to make new friends (often with women who are also married to men with a drinking problem) on whom they can rely in a crisis - a new source of possible banked resources, inasmuch as each can offer the other special understanding and support.

Codifying emotions is a concept originating with Hochschild (1979; 1983), and refers to the way in which people talk themselves into feeling a socially proper emotion. For example, an individual might think "I should be enjoying this party..." and then will "psych" him/herself into feeling the expected sense of gaiety. This concept is useful in contrasting the need for such internal self-coaching with the sense of "being one's natural self" with a friend, where the joy of being together develops unselfconsciously, rather than by "emotional labor."

Wives of alcoholics codify their emotions in the opposite direction - toward calmness. They try to talk themselves out of believing their husbands are alcoholics. Later, they try to distance themselves from their husbands during social events after his drunken behavior has reached the crisis state (e.g. "I handled it [his drunken antics in public] by pretending that he was somebody else's husband"). As the husband's drinking career proceeds, however, a substantial proportion of wives say that they "gear themselves up" to a point where they can take steps to live their own lives without considering their drinking husbands. (One even refers to "recipes for action" which she writes for herself." Thus, emotion work can move toward either detachment or involvement.[6]

Inasmuch as codifying emotions is an attempt to "stir up" genuine emotions, Skid Row alcoholics, most of whom have developed an overriding cynicism, do not testify that they do much of this.

Acting natural does occur with friends, but in an interesting reverse mode of its use by wives of alcoholics. Since one of the joys of a good friendship, as reported from the data, is feeling entirely natural in the company of a friend, persons who are angry with a friend sometimes act *stiffly* natural, in this way sending the friend a message of estrangement.

This studied loss of spontaneity is one means by which angered and hurt friends convey to one another the altered state of their relationship. They seem to be saying, "Things are bad between us. Because of our past relationship, I'll continue to be polite, but I won't be spontaneous." Therefore, unlike wives of alcoholics who act natural in an effort to save the relationship with their husbands, friends take this stance to distance or break a relationship that has gone sour (or alert a friend to be concerned and to take ameliorative steps).

Scripts for behavior based on ranking of the relationship. This is a concept suggested by Libby (1976) and Schwartz and Laqws (1977), both of whom studied various categories of sexual intercourse relationships such as romantic, procreative, recreational, friendly, and exploitive. Their data indicate that each type has a behavioral and expectational "script." My friendship data indicate individuals also categorize their friends. Using intimacy as a criterion, they define friends on a continuum from best or closest, to good, colleagues and persons for special activities, to mere acquaintances. Each of these designations calls for scripted behavior concerning such aspects or the relationships as degree of familiarity, amount of togetherness time, and friendship bank expectations.

Looking back at previous studies, it can be seen that scripts also have strategic qualities. Drinking men on Skid Row learn that scripts also have strategic qualities. Drinking men on Skid Row learn a script in order to manipulate their way (during defining encounters) into an institution when they need shelter. Wives of alcoholics also carry a mental script -acting the part of the good wife in a happy marriage so as not to disappoint relatives and friends. By "covering" the true facts, they hope their husbands will eventually reform, leaving no one the wiser about his former problem. It is also easier to *act natural* if you know the script expected. Thus, in these cases, knowing and using script expectations allows people to manipulate others.[7]

Role vestiges do not emerge from the data on friends. Apparently persons in this relationship are less likely to cling to a role as it slips away than are wives of men with a drinking problem. Rather, friends often let the role go without a struggle or even hasten demise of the relationship by leaving the dyad first - perhaps so as to avoid a more painful, lingering end, hurtful to their pride. It may be possible also, that a given friendship role is not seen as essential to identity as that of wife, for instance, and not worth the struggle to maintain in shadow form.

THIRD MODIFICATION - THE CLOSE BUT FLEETING RELATIONSHIP

In this study (Wiseman, 1979b), an explanation of the unusual friendliness between strangers who are customers in second-hand clothing stores is offered by analyzing how various exigencies of the social structure of the store encourage, or make necessary, much more intimate behavior than is found in ordinary retail clothing establishments. Thus, it is primarily an urban ethnography. From this study I have selected one concept that has proved useful in the analysis of other social action in similar, but not equivalent, situations: quasi-primary relationships.

Quasi-primary relationship is a concept that originated with me. It refers to interactions between people who have not had the time nor opportunity to develop a close personal relationship, but who, pressured by an immediate need for assistance and by the structural exigencies of second-hand clothing stores, (few dressing rooms, absence of size labels, inadequate mirrors), must turn to each other for aid. These people help each other with intimate problems of selection, fit, zipping, and suggestions on alterations or mending, which would not normally be shared with a stranger, Yet, once through the checkout stand, the ambience changes, the closeness ends, and each customer goes a separate way with no expectations of further social intercourse (particularly if there is a status differential).

This setting, and the relationships it encourages, provides the possibility of a mental exercise in the application of the concept of quasi-primary relationship to other social situations. Such an attempt can help a researcher surface some nuances of the concept, as well as see how a situation and/or setting can contribute to the development of close but limited relationships.

For instance, among Skid Row men there are bottle gangs that are also transient, quasi-primary relationships. Usually this is the greatest degree of closeness that one finds in this area because of evanescent living arrangements. It is obviously the symbiotic, yet nondemanding, aspect of the relationship that helps hold these groups together. However, there is also evidence that this represents an enjoyable, friendly relationship (Rooney, 1961). On the other hand, wives of alcoholics, who have had a close relationship with their husbands, find it deteriorating to a quasi-spousal relationship over the course of his drinking. Soon she is merely pretending to care about him for the sake of the children, while planning to leave as soon as she can. These two situations indicate that quasi-primary relationships may be an initial step to closeness (and enjoyable in their own right) or a movement toward disengagement.

On the other hand, understanding the conditions in which quasi-primary relationships emerge, clarifies why some of the concepts presented earlier are not applicable to second-hand store patron relationships. The absence of *social anchors* is actually a positive factor in a scene where strangers call upon each other for aid. Both are expected to disengage once the major purpose of their interaction has been accomplished.[8] In such cases it is safe to talk to anyone. Likewise, there is no *role vestige* to cling to and no apparent need to *codify emotions*. Deep feelings are not involved in these intimate, but brief and utilitarian *defining encounters*. The compiling of *social margin* is not possible nor necessary because the encounters are so truncated.

FORTH MODIFICATION - A STUDY OF SOCIAL OUT-SIDERS

This study focused neither on close personal relationships of fairly long duration, nor fleeing quasi-close relationships, but on the social position of persons who are marginal to the society in which they live - newly arrived immigrants (Wiseman, 1985). Their interactions with spouses, parents and children, as well as relationships between themselves and others of the same ethnic background and with citizens of the host country are overshadowed by their immigrant status. In terms of sociological focus, the study is concerned primarily with family dynamics under stressful, problem-producing situations. The immigrant experience appears to offer both a way of modifying or elaborating among concepts.

Maines (1978) points our that there are two parts to migration - that of bodies and selves. That is, people may take their bodies to a new land, but psychologically remain firmly anchored in the old country, at least for a time. Sooner or later, they must decide where they will be *socially moored* (Erikson, 1978). Then they must choose the country left behind, the host country, or their ethnic enclave there. As a concept, social mooring appears similar to *social anchoring*. However, applying this concept to the immigrant condition allows us to see how it can be further elaborated. Earlier,the concept "social anchors" was used to refer to interpersonal bonds; social mooring refers here to bonding with a geographic and cultural place. Both are different ways of belonging.

A part of this decision by immigrants concerning where to be *socially moored* will come from *codifying their emotions*. In one direction they could talk themselves out of their sense of uprootedness and give up *vestiges* of old country *roles,* developing acceptance for the norms and values of the host country. Moving in another direction, they can solve their sense of alienation by joining forces with others of like national origin in an ethnic enclave.

Immigrants often try to cover all bases. They will cling to vestiges of old-world roles which do not fit in the host country or their place of employment, but aid their acceptability in an ethnic enclave, where one exists. In many cases, the immigrants develop *quasi-primary relationships* with the natives as protective coloration, and real primary relationships in the ethnic enclave. Later as the assimilation process begins to accelerate, immigrants may take on host-country ways and be forced to cover these changes when in the presence of members of the ethnic enclave by *acting natural.* Thus, role vestiges and quasi-relationships take on a continuum aspect.

Within each setting, there is a special (and often quite different) *script.* Thus, scripts for behavior can reflect a concrete place and cultural situation as well as grow out of categorization of an individual dyadic relationship. Furthermore, in a life situation calling for the mastery of many scripts, such as facing the immigrant, a social actor is *"on"* a great deal more than the ordinary individual and is "acting natural" in more than one way, which can be quite demanding. Broadhead (1980) discusses the strains of this kind of existence when he speaks of people who must articulate multiple identities. Ultimately, immigrants may not follow all details of expected subcultural behavior in each world where they have membership, but strategically choose cultural elements from each (Fine & Kleinmann, 1979). Then by *codifying their emotions,* they develop and follow hybrid scripts in order to handle the amalgam of subcultural norms they have created as a means of survival.

Each day, *defining encounters* must continue both inside and outside the family as immigrants and their children see each other adopt host country norms as well as those of ethnic enclave peers. But now we see defining encounters in another light, because the data here tell us that they are made on an explicitly comparative basis. For example, second-generation immigrant children compare the way their parents act and live with the parents of school friends; wives compare spousal behavior with that accorded by the husbands of native women; and immigrant husbands compare their wives' current behavior with that of old-country norms. Defining encounters thus are broadened not only by time, prior relationship, and participant's stake in it, but by cross-cultural comparison.

Looking back, of course, one realizes that some type of comparison was always implicit in the earlier studies. For instance, what (or who) was the yardstick by which agents of social control measured indigent alcoholics? What kinds of husbands were wives using as a model against which they compared their own, when they were trying to decide whether their spouses were alcoholics or not? Had I studied the family relationships of immigrants first, I might have looked at defining encounters in a more comparative mode.

A relationship between *social margin, banked resources,* and *implied contracts* becomes apparent by applying these concepts to the existential position of immigrants. In the intake country, these newcomers have little social margin, can count on no banked resources, and implied contracts are often ephemeral. (They sometimes do, of course, have some formal contracts and/or promises of employment by the host country.) Their relative powerlessness in the area of what we call social networks of the receiving country citizens is apparent to them. This is one of the attractions of the ethnic enclave (which often provide an informal credit union, assistance networks, and sociability).

Later, if these immigrants develop relationships with host country citizens, they may find they are losing margin within their ethnic enclave. Their children may experience what turns out to be a *quasi-primary relationship* when the friendships they make at school do not carry into other phases of life - especially when they reach puberty and wish to date. In as much as misunderstandings are an ever-present danger of relying on *implied contracts,* or by an unsuitable choice of scripts to fit the relationships, it should come as no surprise that these expectations are frequently abrogated where cultural differences exist. Parents may also find that the implied contracts they thought they had with their children (for example, in terms of their presumed filial responsibility) may be substantially eroded.

Parents learn that their children, born and schooled in the host country, are not the *banked resources* they were in the old country. For example, in the intake country they cannot be counted on to support elderly parents, nor do they plan to carry on the family business if there is one. Upwardly mobile or freedom oriented immigrant wives and second generation children may feel their families are "holding them back." Parents are seen by their children as actually *losing margin* with host country citizens rather than offering a source of useful banked resources. Thus, the worth of the banked resources is an issue that does not appear in the friendship data, but through application to immigrant families becomes a more fully realized generic concept.

SUMMARY OF CUMULATIVE FINDINGS

In the process of applying these concepts, I noted the ways in which different settings/situations presented new factors that resulted in modification of the meaning of the concept. By codifying what seems to be significant or basic in these research contexts, in terms of their effects on concepts developed and/or applied elsewhere, we begin to understand how a constellation of factors could exert pressure to modify concepts. These concepts allow us to learn more about the nuances of the setting/situation as well. Possible relationship between concepts can also emerge. Not all of the factors that can result in concept modification or elaboration are found in the five studies presented, nor are all concept relationships uncovered. If the number of cases were doubled, other pressures for modification and further permutations would result.

Each of the factors that affect the application of concepts will be discussed briefly and consistencies in their effects will be noted. It will become apparent from this codification that several causes can coalesce.

FACTORS THAT SHAPE INTERACTIVE CONCEPTS

The emotional valence between principals in the relationship. As a result of emotional closeness, persons in primary relationships make decisions during *defining encounters* much more carefully than those in secondary relationships. *Acting natural* can be intended calming by spouses who still love their husbands or it can be obviously stilted among friends who are drifting apart. The break of an *implied contract* differs greatly if the expectation involves a spouse, a friend, or a stranger representing an institution. For a spouse or a friend, the reaction is hurt feelings; with a stranger, it is cynicism and/or anger. *Codifying emotions* varies by the type of relationships extant when a decision is made to create (or call up) a positive or negative emotion. *Behavior scripts* and their use as representative of the status of a relationship (or to create such a status) depend on the current relationship as a starting point for acceptable interaction.

The distribution of power among principles. The effects of power differentials among principals is notable in *defining encounters* where power to resist a definition changes the ability of the judge to make a quick diagnosis. *Acting natural* seems to be a strategy of the less powerful in handling the more-powerful. The *breach of implied contracts* can create cynicism in low status individuals who feel betrayed by those of higher status, or anger and disappointment if the high status person feels betrayed by the lower. Among equals, it can vitiate the relationship. (It is obvious from the prior discussion that the emotional valence between persons can affect reactions to the breach as well, and thus some research on the relationship between these two factors would be useful in further clarifying the generic aspects of this concept.)

It is possible that persons with the least amount of power do more *codifying of emotions* than those with the most. *Behavior scripts,* strategically used, could aid power gains. However, this did not specifically surface in the research presented.

The importance of the interaction to the identity of principals. For persons whose own identities are affected by a decision when *defining another during an encounter,* the definition will be very carefully made - in contrast to cases in which no ego is at stake for the judge and the decision is a bureaucratic one. *Acting natural* can be seen as an attempt to save either the egos of a loved one (among wives of alcoholics) or oneself (among friends). This helps to account for the differences in performance. People *codify emotions* only when they stake their identity on the maintenance of proper feelings; thus there is less need for it where encounters are quickly over and not truly primary, or where "natural feelings" are allowed full way. *Behavior scripts* represent the status of a relationship, and thus may also affect the identity of participants either positively or negatively.

The goal of the interaction for each principal. If the goal of the interaction is either to maintain the relationship or to terminate it, the way in which the interactive concept applies will change drastically. *Defining encounters* can be either quickly handled for bureaucratic efficiency, or carefully and thought fully managed when the goal is seen as a decision of major importance. Thus, people can *act natural* to smooth a situation or to telegraph problems; they can *codify their emotions* so as to remain cool or to get up courage to make a relationship break. Emotions can also be codified in order to maintain a relationship. People can be guided by a *behavior script* to meet or set the boundaries of a relationship or in order to manipulate it.

The effect of applicable normative or cultural criteria, or the existence of an accepted exemplar guiding interaction. These are factors more often implicit than stated.[9] When people make a decision concerning the identity or behavior of another, what are they using as a standard? In *defining encounters,* there is an unstated comparison utilized both by institutional representatives and wives as they judge or diagnose heavy drinking males, which is either concerned with amenability to rehabilitation or criteria for differentiating social drinking from problem drinking. *Implied contracts* are often created out of trust in a close, emotional relationship (such as a marriage or a friendship), or are more business-like (such as a reliance on an institutional promise, as do alcoholics with agents of social control and immigrants with the host country). A breach in the former case could be one cause of hurt feelings; in the latter case, cynicism. *Emotions are codified* in keeping with normative expectations and change as these norms do; *behavior scripts* are often selected normatively or with the aid of assumed cultural expectations, and thus vary by them. Even *acting natural* has some reference point to cultural expectations of mundane behavior.

MAJOR FORCES WHICH SHAPE STRUCTURAL CONCEPTS

In keeping with this type of concept, the changes are not as focused on relationships, as on variation or degrees of a structural attribute present, absent, or changing.

Structural variation by means of acquisition: Achieved, ascribed, expected, or unexpected. Social anchors can be ascribed through family where they are an expectation, and achieved through friends where they are perceived as a gift. Social anchorage can be selected, as in the case of a country. *Social margin* can be either ascribed or achieved, and can be lost through misbehavior. If ascribed through association, it can be lost the same way. *Banked resources* are usually achieved, but if ascribed, they often refer to family and are taken for granted until lost.

Quasi-primary relationships are brief and offer social enjoyment with only momentary social commitment. They are less ascribed or achieved than fortuitous and usually represent a brief symbiotic partner ship. There is some indication that quasi-primary relationships may be a stage in a continuum between a close relationship and a relationship break.

Structural variation by mechanisms of maintenance or loss. Social anchors and *social margin* can be maintained by normative behavior and lost by deviant behavior. The loss of social margin may be a first definitive step toward the loss of social anchorage. Social margin can be remade with difficulty by consistently good behavior over a considerable period of time. *Role vestiges* are maintained by continuing to do role duties even if counter-role personnel are no longer interested. If not necessary to identify, role vestiges are not maintained. *Banked resources* are maintained by exchanges of favors and can be lost by overdrawing or devalued by reassessment of the "banker," as in the case of second generation immigrants and their parents.

POSSIBLE RELATIONSHIP AMONG CONCEPTS

Perhaps because of its concern with persons managing identities in several subcultures at once, the study of immigrants surfaced the most possible relationships among concepts, although a few were noted in other studies.

Social margin can be a banked resource, as can be an implied contract. When following a social script, some persons, are, as they see it, also "acting natural." Social anchoring can be a decision that requires codifying of emotions, the learning of new social scripts, while at the same time clinging to role vestiges. The loss of social margin often precedes the loss of social anchors. When a close relationship deteriorates into a quasi-one, some participants may cling to a role vestige.

CONCLUSIONS

The preceding discussion indicates how concepts that transcend specific areas of sociological investigation can be applicable to diverse settings and situations where they have great analytic utility. In the process of these applications, the concepts themselves are elaborated and/or modified. By tracking these developments through many data analyses, and comparing them in the manner parallel to that of Glaser and Strauss' grounding of theory through constant reference to substantive data, we can see how the differential dynamics of social life create major forces which shape generic concepts. Furthermore, the relationship of these concepts to each other becomes more apparent by seeing them applied in parallel, but different research projects. Finally, certain aspects of research settings/situations are highlighted by noting how the application of the concept changes across investigations. Behavioral and structural factors can form any complex configurations that result in illuminating nuances of concepts as they are applied.

Concepts are the building blocks of theory. Thus, their enrichment and/or elaboration is a step toward more specifically forced theory. This cumulative refinement can become the generalizable product of our qualitative research efforts. Such a methodological approach also underscores what attracts qualitative researchers to their craft - the marvelous versatility of human beings as they confront their situations and construct their reactions.[10]

ENDNOTES

1. This tracing of the development of behavior concepts through parallel but different situations can be seen as an attempt to systematize what Simmel discussed in essays on substantive issues, but which where never outlined as thoroughly as his theory of social forms. Simmel's major interest was what he considered to be stabilized forms of interaction found in a multitude of disparate settings. Primarily structural, they included such relationships as in-group out-group, superiority and subordination, dyadic (and triadic) relationships, the division of labor, and conflict and competition, to name but a few (Levine, 1971: Levine, Carter, & Gorman, 1976; Mayntz, 1985). Within these forms of interaction, however, Simmel saw social life as pulsating and oscillating (Wolff, 1950:385), bound to "fit" to a great degree within the form's parameters, yet possibly moving "ahead" of it (resulting in adjustment of the form, or lingering for time "behind" a form that had changed). This paper is concerned with developing more completely the concepts pertaining to the content of interaction through application to parallel settings/situations. This differs from Sylvan ad Glassner (1985) who are interested in developing Simmel's forms through computer modeling, using the interaction within a form as it applies to different situations to help create formal variations.

2. Those concepts originating with sociologists other than myself, which I have applied to my own research, have a longer history of cumulative application than shown here. My own concepts, as utilized by others, may also have more permutations than are shown in this paper.

3. The terms settings/situations will be used to refer to all types of research settings, social relationships among principals and their interactive behaviors, in all types research contexts and their structural

characteristics.

4. Acting natural and being natural are two different types of behavior. There is a strain to acting natural, because a person must try to act as he/she thinks significant to others will accept as "natural." The concepts is also related to Goffman's discussion in "Insanity of Place" (1968) in which spouses of the mentally ill keep them under secret surveillance to prevent them from harming themselves, while the observed (and disturbed) person pretends not to notice. As a result, both are "acting natural" and neither is feeling so.

5. People do seek friends for other purposes, such as enhanced reputation through association, anticipated economic gain and so on, but such motives remove the relationship from the realm of pure friendship.

6. Codifying emotions can be differentiated from "acting natural" in that there is no need when "acting natural" to *convince one's self* that the act is or should be genuine. Yet, each can lead, as McGraw (1961) has said, to believing in what one started out only acting - although by a slightly different route.

7. Persons operating with an exploitative sexual script will often disguise their true intentions by using a romantic or friendly script.

8. Prostitution is another example of a quasi-primary relationship, inasmuch as it is intimate in order to reach a goal, but further commitment by either party is understood to be undesirable.

9. Swidler (1986) has noted that cultural strictures should be viewed as "tools" for strategies of action, proper behavior, or judging the behavior of others.

10. The last portion of this sentence paraphrases Herbert Blumer (1971, 1978).

REFERENCES

Becker, Howard S.

1963 *Outsiders*. New York: The Free Press.

Blumer, Herbert

1971 *Symbolic interactionism*. Englewood Cliffs, New Jersey: Prentice-Hall.

1978 Colloquium presented at Sociology Department, University of California, San Diego.

Broadhead, Robert S.

1980 Multiple identities and the process of their articulation: the case of medical students and their private lives. *Studies in Symbolic Interaction.* 3:171-191.

Eckert, J. Kevin

1980 *The unseen elderly: A study of marginally subsistent hotel dwellers.* San Diego: Campaniel Press.

Erikson, Robert

1978 Social mooring: An aspect of welfare. *International Journal of Contemporary Sociology* 15:145-162.

Fine, Gary Alan & Sherryl Kleinman

1979 Rethinking subculture: An interactionist analysis. *American Journal of Sociology* 84:1-20.

Glaser, Barney G. & Anselm L. Strauss

1967 *The discovery of grounded theory: Strategies for qualitative research.* Chicago: Aldine.

Goffman, Erving

1961 *Asylums,* New York: Anchor Doubleday.

1968 Insanity of place. *Psychiatry* 32:357-388.

Hochschild, Arlie R.

1979 Emotion work, feeling rules and social structure. *American Journal of Sociology* 84:551-575.

1983 *The managed heart.* Berkeley & Los Angeles: The University of California Press.

Hollander, E.P.

1958 Conformity, status and idiosyncrasy credit. *Psychological Review* 65:120.

Kitsuse, John

1962 Societal reaction to deviant behavior: Problems of theory and method. *Social Problems* 9:247-257.

Lemert, Edwin M.

1951 *Social pathology*. New York: McGraw-Hill.

Levine, Donald N.

1971 Introduction in Georg Simmel, *On individuality and social forms.* (pp.ix-lxv). Chicago: University of Chicago Press.

Levine, Donald N., Ellwood B. Carter, & Eleanor Miller Gorman

1976 Simmel's influence on American sociology: I. *American Jounral of Sociology* 81:813-45.

Libby, Roger

1976 Social scripts of sexual relationships. In S.Gordon and R. Libby (eds.) *Sexuality today and tomorrow: Contemporary issues in human sexuality* (pp.172-3). N. Scituate, MA: Duxbury Press.

McGraw, Charles

1961 *Acting is believing*. New York: Holt, Rinehart and Winston.

Maines, David R.

1978 Bodies and selves: Notes on a fundamental dilemma in demography. *Studies in Symbolic Interaction* 1:241-265.

Mayntz, Renate

1985 Georg Simmel. In Adam Kuper and Jessica Kuper (Eds.) *The social science encyclopedia.* (pp. 251-257). London: Routledge & Kegan Paul.

Rooney, J.F.

1961 Group processes among skid row winos: re-evaluation of the undersocialization hypothesis. *Quarterly Journal of Studies on Alcohol* 22:444-460.

Rubington, Earl

1964 Grady "breaks out": A case study of an alcoholic's relapse. *Social Problems* 11:372-80.

Schwartz, Pepper, & Judith Long Laws

1977 *Sexual scripts*. Hinsdale, IL: The Dryden Press.

Schibutani, Tamotsu

1961 *Society and personality.* (pp. 323-266). Englewood Cliffs, NJ: Prentice Hall.

Swidler, Ann

1986 Culture in action. *American Sociological Review* 51:273-286.

Sylvan, David & Barry Glassner

1985 *A rationalist methodology for the social sciences.* Oxford, England: Basil Blackwell.

Thomas, W.I.

1967 *The unadjusted girl.* New York: Harper & Row.

Wiseman, Jacqueline P.

1979a *Stations of the lost: The treatment of skid row alcoholics.* Chicago: University of Chicago Press.

1979b Close encounters of the quasi-primary kind: Sociability in urban second-hand stores. *Urban Life* 8:23-51.

1985 Individual adjustments and kin relationships in the "new immigration": An approach to research. *International Migration* 23:349-368.

1986 The sociology of friendship: Bonds and binds in a voluntary relationship. *Journal of Social and Personal Relationships* 3:191-211.

(Forthcoming) *The other half: Wives of alcoholics.* Philadelphia: Temple Univeristy Press.

Wolff, Kurt H.

1950 *The sociology of Georg Simmel.* Glencoe, IL: The Free Press.

AWARENESS CONTEXTS AND GROUNDED FORMAL THEORY

Anselm Strauss

The reasons for developing formal theories, as well as how *to* and how *not* to write them, are subjects about Barney Glaser and I have written many pages together. But we have never offered a set of concrete images for how one might develop a particular formal theory. I shall try to do that today, perhaps in an overly personalized way, giving a few of the steps I am now following in developing a theory of awareness contexts. My talk is meant to show a theorist at work, rather than to offer a prescriptive set of generalized steps in the formulation process. My hope is that you will neither take my illustration as the only mode of doing this necessary job in social science, nor dismiss my style of working as idiosyncratic or as feasible only for someone who already has considerable experience in discovering theory.

When listening to this sketch of my procedures, you will notice that some are exactly like those recommended for developing substantive theory. The analytic work begins immediately with the collection of data - it does not await the piling up of data. Analytic memos are written continually. The first phases of the analytic work - which may take several months - are focused conspicuously on open coding: the discovery of salient categories, including the core categories of "dimensions." They are also focused on "densification," or on building the relationships among those categories - including noting relevant conditions, tactics, interactions, agents, consequences. Theoretical integration begins through that densification, but is not yet at the forefront of the enterprise. Theoretical sampling, as discussed in The Discovery of Grounded Theory,[1] begins almost at once and largely directs the collection of data. During these early phases, the differences between developing a substantive theory and developing a formal one is that for the latter, theoretical sampling is done across many substantive areas, and the open coding and densification is done at distinctly more abstract levels than in substantive theorizing.

The prevalent mode of formulating formal theory is to move directly from a substantive to a formal theory, without grounding the latter in any additional data. The theorist, for instance, suggests that his substantive findings and perhaps theory, about, say, physician-patient relationships, have implications for a general theory of professional-client relationships - but he does not do the further work of studying the latter relationships comparatively. As we have noted, this kind of rewriting technique produces "only an adequate start toward formal theory, not an adequate formal theory itself. The researcher has raised the conceptual level of his work mechanically; he has not raised it through comparative understanding. He has done nothing to broaden the scope of his theory on the formal level by comparative investigation of different substantive areas. He has not escaped the time and place of his substantive research. Moreover, the formal theory cannot fit or work very well when written from only one substantive area (and often only one case of the area), because in reality it cannot be developed sufficiently to take into account all the contingencies and qualifications that will be met in the diverse substantive areas to which it will be applied.[2] In contrast, the general strategy which we advocate involves the comparative analysis of data drawn from many substantive areas, this analysis directed if possible, along its full course, by theoretical sampling. A good substantive theory can provide an excellent stepping stone for attaining a powerful formal theory; but of course, even a good substantive theory only provides the initial stimulus which moves the theorist toward his or her necessary comparative work.

Three months ago I began the comparative work intended to lead to a grounded formal theory of awareness contexts. Why awareness contexts, other than that they represent an old substantive interest of mine? Awareness-context behavior is universal, occurring everywhere and in very many areas of life. What comes immediately to mind are secrets of all kinds, their protection, penetration and disclosure; also illicit and illegal behavior of various kinds (fraud, corruption, plea bargaining, confidence games). Like negotiation, awareness contexts constitute quite possibly what my friend Fritz Schutze calls, "meso-structures of social order," neither the macro structures nor the microstructures that we are familiar with, but something between, linking both, and very significant for our understanding of social order.

So three months ago, I began my investigation by comparing several kinds of "data in the head" - data drawn from the Awareness of Dying study, and data drawn from what I remembered reading about spies, about the gay world, about "passing," about the handling of stigmatized diseases like leprosy. My aim was to abstract from those data some major categories, or "dimensions," that might possibly pertain to all awareness phenomena. Then, these would suggest theoretical samples to be soon looked at. My initial dimensional analysis resulted in a typed memo, which listed and briefly discussed the following: (1) the kind of informational object at stake (for instance, identity, activity, object), (2) the kinds of information involved, (3) the visibility of the information, (4) the accessibility of the information, (5) the interpretation of the information. Later on I would add to this paradigmatic scheme two additional categories: evaluation of the information, and the convincing of relevant others about the interpretation of the information. I also guessed from these initial data that various structural properties might contribute to variation in the awareness phenomena: number of participants involved in the context, degree of their knowledgeability, the social worlds they came from, the stakes in obtaining knowledge, and so on.

My next memos are not so systematic, they just represent some thoughts about misrepresentation, suspicion, deluding, and also guarding against discovery of secrets. You would think those topics might have led to theoretical sampling of materials on, say, confidence games, or to a fuller scanning of literature on the gay world. But I let that sampling go until later, sensing that virtually anything sampled, this early in the theorizing, would be useful. I turned next to the phenomenon of the misnaming of the identity, recognizing that inaccurate naming left the option, to the mis-named person, of accepting the attributed identity or revealing the "true" identity.

So, my first scrutiny of new data involved looking at a book titled, *The Vindicators,*[3] full of true stories about how various persons had been mistaken for criminals, been punished, but eventually had been vindicated in their protestations of non-criminal identities. Mostly, their vindications came about not through their own efforts - since their resources for discovering why they had been misidentified were slim - but through the efforts of skilled lawyer detectives who had many resources for searching out and interpreting the new and often relatively inaccessible information (evidence) needed to rectify the record. The vindicators needed to convince not only themselves but also the authorities - this was how I realized that "convincing" was also a central category. I called the whole process, "rectification," and wrote notes with such headings as mis-identification, rectifying actions, conditions preventing rectification, and the convincing of relevant audiences. There were other notes bearing on previously recognized categories, especially the major or dimensional ones.

The next memos touched spottily on similar topics, as I thumbed through an old copy of Richard Wright's *Black Boy*.[4] This book also brought home, though I did not need the reminder, how the management of information is a matter of positioning and control, as well as how awareness management cannot be understood except in terms of larger "macro" structural conditions: the larger relationships extant between blacks and whites in the U.S.

Next, I recollected that Orrin Klapp's *Symbolic Leaders*[5] had data bearing on celebrities, whose public and private identities were sometimes discrepant. If so, then a form of public misrepresentation was occurring. Most of Klapp's data on celebrities bear on the manufacture of a false public identity by the celebrity and his or her agents, and its maintenance in the face of a discrepant private life; also the breakdown of hidden private secrets when the public learns of the private life; also the consequences for the celebrity and for others when that happens. But the private and public identities of the celebrity can also be consonant: under what conditions and with what consequences, then, we can ask. Another new concept appears in this memo: "discrediting" - either in the face of unwitting or deliberate disclosure of identity information. I called the latter "public rectification."

Shortly after, I scanned another book in my library, *Disappointed Guests*,[6] essays by Commonwealth students about their disillusioning experiences while in London. I chose this volume next because I suspected another rectification phenomenon might appear. It did: I called it, "rectification by cumulative incident or event" - for the students gradually realized the true British interpretations of their own identities: outsiders and of low value. The attendant conditions, consequences, and some of the interaction and tactic, are noted in this same memo. Cumulative rectification is contrasted with sudden-disclosure rectification, as it appears, say, in the shockingly harsh relevatory incidents in Wright's autobiography - when the child was brutally shown by whites what it meant to be black in the American South. Cumulative rectification was linked, in my notes, especially with the major category of "interpretation of information."

Thus far I have given you only major categories and headings in the memos: these are mostly instances of "open coding" - the developing of categories (and their names) on the basis of analyzing comparative data.

You should imagine also that some of my notes helped to densify the analysis - that is, to put analytic meat on the analytic bones, in the form of relevant conditions, consequences, strategies, tactics, interactions, agents, etc., as specifically noted in the data.

My test theoretical sampling - one I had early thought of but delayed getting to - centered around the following contrast: an awareness context kept closed by an experienced and resourceful team, even by an entire organization, for profitable stakes, against a relatively inexperienced and lacking-in-resource opponent. The actors in this drama were the con and mark: the source of data was Sutherland's Professional Thief.[7] I was especially interested in the division of labor within the confidence team. The category of "betrayal" comes immediately into the foreground, since betrayal is potential whenever more than one person is in on a secret. Later I would begin to explore betrayal in relation to awareness, moving toward a scrutiny of materials on spy organizations. At this point, however, I found myself writing memo-notes about the requirements of certain social worlds for keeping vital secrets hidden, and asking questions about who was most likely to betray these secrets. "It is at the intersections between worlds that we would expect to find the betrayals, the informers, the giveaways, etc." I told myself that it was worth looking closely at such worlds, since they should have special mechanisms for protecting those secrets, and possibly for discovering the secrets of those who would endanger their own. The thief's description of the criminal "fix," and how it operated also reminded me of what I had known so well from research on hospitalized dying: namely, that the management of awareness is part and parcel of people getting their work done - work as they perceive it. Of course, my memos continued to flower with minor notes on such matters as fake and true settings, courtrooms as disclosures sites, an so on.

Picking up now the thread of social world secrets, I analyzed data found in Carol Warren's *Gay World,*[8] especially that bearing on visibility and accessibility of the signs of homosexuality, to outsiders and insiders to the gay world. And I linked the recognition or non-recognition of those signs in space: the sites where they were displayed or muffled. Data on space and movement in space, as they relate to maintaining social world secrets seemed likely also to be salient to a group like the Gypsies, so I looked at a book on them and found a number of their specific and masterful tactics for keeping gypsy activities secret from outsiders. There were good data, too, on conditions under which their tactics occasionally fall, and what consequence then ensue.

You may have been wondering about the sequence of my theoretical sampling. Leaving aside fortuitous circumstances like just happening to own certain books, the sampling really *is* being directed by the continuing analysis. In general, the sampling steps have been directed by one or more of four considerations. First: the further exploration of a major dimension, such as accessibility (relatively easy or difficult), which more or less characterizes the secrecy of the gay world. Second: a structural condition that might saliently affect the awareness context: for instance, the organized character of confidence games; or the organized control of information by the endangered gypsies as they drift through enemy spaces. Third: the deliberate strategy of building maximum structural variation into theory. This is combined sometimes with, fourth, theoretical sampling in terms of other formal theories, such as a theory of status passage or of negotiation, as in the next instance that will be described. (It is very important, of course, to link one's formal theory with others, provided they are grounded, not speculative.)

For it has occurred to me that private secrets and intimate relations - seemingly the polar opposite of social world secrets and relationships - might yield theoretical gold. Murray Davis' *Intimate Relations* provided the test ground for this hunch, giving a wealth of data on a passage (from familiar to confident) manipulated by one or by both persons involved in that passage. My memo touches on that passage itself; on the management of both public and private identities; on the characteristics of crucial and mundane secrets; on the dangers of disclosing; on testing tactics; on levels of dangerous information; on psychological hostageship; on mutual hostages; on failure of disclosure efforts or at convincing; on the interpretation of cues and its timing; on unwitting and deliberate betrayal, on mutual betrayal, on sequential betrayal. In short, I did further open coding, but also I did further densification. I wrote several methodological directives, telling myself to "look into" this and that soon.

The Davis monograph raises an important issue: how can the formal theorist utilize the substantive theory which he finds in such publication? (I can direct you here to pp. 82 91 of *Discovery*, and to my pages on "Discovering New Theory From Previous Theory,"[9] in the Blumer Festschrift (8: pp. 46-53); but here intend to talk only about my procedural steps in building an awareness context theory.) In general, my experiences can be summarized as follows. First: sometimes the substantive theory contains concepts potentially useful for one's formal theory; for example, Davis' "psychological hostages" and "crucial secrets." Second: if the concepts seem useful, then the substantive theorist probably has also offered some analysis of conditions, consequences, and so forth, that are associated with the referents pointed to by the concepts. For instance, Davis has a good analytic discussion of mutual hostages, of conditions and consequences of this, and of phases in moving into those statuses. Likewise, in the Olesen-Whittaker study of nursing student socialization (*Silent Dialogue*)[10] we are given useful analytic information on public-private identities as they related to students' presentations of selves. And in Fred Davis' paper on "Deviance Disavowal"[11] there is a very useful substantive analysis of phases and tactics in preventive rectification by the visibly handicapped. When using such materials, the formal theorist must be careful to bend the original analysis to his formal-theoretical purposes. That is done not only by linking the former, in one's memo writing, with one's own categories - especially with the major dimensional ones - but also by asking further questions that lead to "next steps" in the investigation. For instance, and I quote from a memo here: "identity disavowal, however, can be false, unlike that in the Fred Davis article. And this misrepresentation can be accepted, be found suspicious, or rejected by other persons. What are the conditions for all of that?"

Now, if I am leaving you with the imagery of a fairly deliberate, step-by-step choice of theoretical samples, that imagery would not be accurate. The procedural picture needs to be filled in with at least two additional images of the theoretical craftsman or craftswoman at work. This theorist does not merely work when at the desk or in the library: work goes on subliminally, and while other activities are taking place. So, I have found myself thinking about awareness contexts while walking, driving, even in the duller moments of concert going. Then, quite fortuitously, one also comes across sparking, and even confirming, data in various forms: in newspaper articles, friends' stories, books read for entertainment, in events occurring in one's own life. Everything is grist for the formal theorist's mill, especially perhaps in the earliest phases of the investigation. An anecdote from Malcolm X's autobiography suggests how public identity may be disclosed to the privileged powerless, but not to those perceived as powerful, and therefore dangerous. A reseeing of that great old *Bridge on the River Kwai* gives rise to a memo-note on the failure to distinguish proper priorities of private identity, and the reading or misreading of its signs by other actors in the drama. A chance bit of thinking about the *Taming of the Shrew* leads to a note abut misrepresentation for another's "good." A happenstance reading of a sociological article turns up interesting material on conditions and tactics of awareness management in casual conversations.

It has been my experience that this fortuitous and continuous contribution to the theorist's enterprise is highly useful, both on logical and psychological grounds. Logical, because it helps to build that systematic theoretical structure at which one is aiming. Psychological, because it often gives us that "ah ha!" feeling of delight ("of course!") or surprise (damn, of course I should have thought of that; it's expectable). When the theorist is also a teacher in a graduate program, or a consultant to other people's research, then he finds that these other researchers unwittingly add to his cumulative data, forcing further analysis and memo writing.

One of the more unexpected and exciting dividends, at least for me, is the gradually enlarging substantive scope of the investigation. One begins to think of, and then actually to scrutinize, substantive areas undreamed of earlier in the research. I always knew that I would look intensively at spy organizations, at the making of artistic fakes, and at Goffman's book on stigma. I did not realize that the work of creating a believable drama on the stage would be a target for my inquiry, along with such interesting topics or categories as "believable or credible performances."

Perhaps I should close this performance of my own - hoping it, too, is believable - with an open request for any substantive ares you think could be profitably explored for building this particular formal theory: for, as we said specifically in *Discovery*, of one wishes to develop a *grounded* formal theory, then it should be a "multi-area" theory, based on the comparative analysis of diverse substantive areas, and of numerous incidents drawn from those areas. While I shall not repeat or elaborate further, here, on why we so urgently need grounded formal theories, I certainly hope this talk will encourage you to bend your research efforts in that direction, rather than settling merely for substantive theorizing and even for doing ethnography, however accurate and useful it may be. A good formal theory ought to be at least the equivalent weight of a ton of ethnographies and perhaps a half gross of substantive theories.

REFERENCES

1 Barney Glaser and Anselm Strauss, *The Discovery of Grounded*

Theory. Chicago: Aldine Publishing Company, 1967, pp. 45-76.

2 Barney Glaser and Anselm Strauss, *Status Passage.* Chicago: Aldine Publishing Company, 1971, pp. 179.

3 Eugene Block, *The Vindicators.* New York: Pocket Books, Inc., 1965.

4 Richard Wright, *Black Boy.* New York: Harpers, 1937.

5 Orrin Klapp, *Symbolic Leaders.* Chicago: Aldine Publishing Company, 1964.

6 Henri Jajfel and John Dawson (eds.), *Disappointed Guests.* London: Oxford University Press, 1965.

7 Edwin Sutherland (ed.), *The Professional Thief.* Chicago: University of Chicago Press, 1937.

8 Carol Warren, *Identity and Community in the Gay World.* New York: John Wiley and Sons, 1974.

9 Anselm Strauss, "Discovering New Theory From Previous Theory," in Tamotsu Shibutani (ed.) *Human Nature and Collective Behavior.* Englewood Cliffs, N.J.: Prentice-Hall, 1970, pp. 46-53.

10 Virginia Olesen and Elvi Whittaker, *The Silent Dialogue.* San Francisco: Jossey-Bass, 1968.

11 Fred Davis, "Deviance Disavowal: The Management of Strained Interaction by the Visibly Handicapped," *Social Problems.* Vol. 9, 1961, pp. 120-32. Reprinted in Fred Davis, Illness, Interaction and the Self. Belmont, CA.: Wadsworth Publishing, 1972, pp. 130-49.

DISCOVERING NEW THEORY FROM PRE-VIOUS THEORY: An Exercise in Theoretical Sampling

Anselm Strauss

Recommended by my undergraduate teacher Floyd House, I went eagerly to see Herbert Blumer in his office one hot September afternoon. It was one of the fateful encounters of my life. I found him in his shirt sleeves, feet resting easily on his desk, reading *Life* magazine (for data, no doubt!), and receptive to serious talk about serious issues in sociology. The conversation made of me, already partly won over by reading Dewey, a quick convert to sociological pragmatism. Before many weeks Blumber had won my admiration for his critical mind and tenacious grasp of truly relevant issues in social science. The paper below is addressed to one he raised on that same day - how to close the devastating gap between speculative theory and descriptive empiricism.

Perhaps most readers of this paper will be familiar with *The Discovery of Grounded Theory,* in which Barney Glaser and I discussed strategies designed to further the discovery and formulation of theory.[1] One strategy was the calculated use of theoretical sampling, a process of data collection which is controlled by emerging theory. (In theoretical sampling, the basic question is: What groups or subgroups does one turn to next in data collection? And for what theoretical purpose? Since possibilities of choice are infinite, choice is made according to theoretical criteria.)[2] We emphasized also the need for theory which is dense in conceptual details, noting that much of sociological theory is thin - a collection of loosely integrated categories, none deeply developed. (As we remarked, "stable integration of the theory requires dense property development of at least some categories." and in thin theory it is "difficult to say which of the array are the core categories, that is, those most relevant for prediction and explanation.")[3] Because the *Discovery* book is spiced with an attack upon speculative theory, some readers have assumed we advocate abandoning all previous writing, whether theoretical or empirical, in favor of using only one's intelligence.

In this paper, I shall address two questions relevant to discovering and formulating effective theory when there is already extant grounded theory on which to build. We need not ignore the latter merely to show ourselves master or our own data or to parade our originality? First, how can we use previous theory to discover and formulate more extensive theory? Second, how can we render previous theory more dense, making certain that the final product is also well integrated? The key to both questions is a systematic use of theoretical sampling. This strategy eventually leads, if one goes far enough with the research, to verification and expansion of the theory through actual collection of data. (I shall not focus here on how to verify theory, although how this is done in connection with discovering theory should be clear enough.) I address the above questions because very little grounded theory, even when it is well integrated, is either extensive in scope or very dense in conceptual detail (at all levels of abstraction.)

In his article on "Deviance Disavowal," Fred Davis has offered a useful, grounded theory about (as his subtitle reads) "The Management of Strained Interaction by the Visibly Handicapped."[4] Because this excellent paper is so widely known, there is no need to do more than highlight certain aspects of his carefully presented theory. By way of preface, I should note that this presentation is exceptional because its author tells us exactly what his theory applies to, alerting us to what phenomena it does not apply and to matters over which it glosses. (Thus: "Because of the paper's focus on the visibly handicapped person...his interactional work is highlighted to the relative glossing over of that of the normal" person.) One of the most valuable features of this paper is that it stimulates us to think of variables which Davis does not discuss fully or omits entirely, including those quite outside of Davis' focus when he developed his theory. Indeed, when rereading the article I have often found myself aching to know more about all those untreated matters. The reader bears the responsibility to carry on this unfinished business, of course, if the author does not elect to do so.

Davis's theory is about (1) *strained* (2) *sociable interaction* (3) in *face-to-face* contact between (4) *two persons,* one of whom as a (5) *visible handicap* and the other of whom is (6) *normal* (no visible handicap.) The theory includes propositions about tactics, especially those of the visibly handicapped person. But the central focus is upon *stages of management,* notably (a) fictional acceptance, (b) the facilitation of reciprocal role-taking around a normalized projection of self that is normal in its moral dimension. Emphasis on stages makes this a distinctly processual theory.

The italicized terms in the above sentences begin to suggest what is explicitly or implicitly omitted from Davis' theoretical formulation. The theory is concerned with the visibly (physically) handicapped, not with people whose handicaps are not immediately visible, if at all, to other interactants. The theory is concerned with interaction between two people (not with more than two), or with combinations of normal and handicapped persons (one interacting with two, two with one, two with two). The interaction occurs in situations termed "sociable"; that is, the relations between interactants are neither impersonal nor intimate. Sociable also means interaction prolonged enough to permit more than a fleeting exchange but no so prolonged that close familiarity ensues. Sociable interaction does not encompass ritualized interaction.

But the interaction is not merely sociable, it is face to face - not, for instance, carried out by telephone or through correspondence. This interaction represents the first meeting between the interactants, not a later meeting or one based on an interpersonal tradition. This meeting is only the first of a series of episodes that may lead to a more intimate relationship, and is so recognized by the handicapped person. Throughout this interaction the handicapped person attempts to minimize his handicap, rather than to highlight or to capitalize on it. The normal person also attempts to minimize the handicap, rather than favorably or unfavorably maximizing it. Also, control of the interaction is vested in the handicapped person, who has a willing accomplice in the normal. Moreover, the normal must agree to the game of normalization rather than resisting or being indifferent or even failing to recognize it. In addition, we should note especially that the interaction is strained - that is, the visible handicap tends to intrude into the interaction, posing a threat to sociability, tending to strain the framework of normative rules and assumptions in which sociability develops.

Visible handicaps which pose no particular threat to sociable interaction are not within the province of this theory. Also, because emphasis is on the handicapped person's management of interaction, the theory covers quite thoroughly the tactics and reactions of the handicapped, although it says relatively little about those of the normal. And finally, the theory pertains to a handicapped person who is already quite experienced in managing strained interaction with a normal - who by contrast is relatively inexperienced in interacting with handicapped persons. If we imagine a simple fourfold table, we can quickly supply three contrasting situations involving such experience.

This filling in of what has been left out of the extant theory is a useful first step toward extending its scope. We have supplemented the original theory. (Supplementation does *not* mean remedying defects of a theory.) Supplementation has led to the generation of additional categories, which in turn leads us - unless we cut short our endeavor - to think about those new categories. Thinking about those categories amounts to building hypotheses which involve them, quite as Davis built hypotheses around the categories generated from his data. We can think about those new categories, one at a time: for instance, the nonvisible handicap. We can do this much more efficiently, however, by comparing the new category with others, whether those are newly generated or inherited from Davis.

Imagine what happens in the first episode of face to face, sociable interaction when (1) a person with a relatively invisible (although potentially visible) handicap meets a normal person as against (2) when Davis' visibly handicapped meets a normal. The former situation is not too difficult to imagine, even if we have never been in that situation. Unlike the latter situation, one of its properties may be "secrecy," because the invisibly handicapped, if he is experienced, probably will be much concerned with keeping his handicap thoroughly hidden. If he is more experienced unless his handicap is of recent occurrence; as for instance, a woman recently operated on for mastectomy (cancer of the breast) who now appears in public with a breast prosthesis hidden beneath her dress.

By reaching out for this case as an example, we have begun (in imagination) to sample theoretically; we could, in fact, now either interview or seek existing data not only about such patients but about others who had newly acquired various nonvisible, but potentially visible, handicaps. We can ask, what other kinds of persons (i.e., comparison groups) might those be? Clearly not included are persons who have just suffered strokes or irradicable facial burns or been through not entirely satisfactory facial operations after bad auto accidents. On the other hand, the other groups of non-visibly handicapped persons whom we seek might include those born with stigmata which can be readily covered with clothes, and those with deforming arthritis of the shoulder which is not yet severe enough to show through clothing.

A moment's reflection about those comparison groups of handicapped - visibly or invisibly - tells us that we have generated additional categories. Possibly some may become core categories, among the many being built into our extension of Davis' original theory. Thus, there are invisible handicaps which have been present from birth, others which have been acquired whether recently or some time ago or long ago. There are some, whether visible or invisible, which never grow worse, and others which may grow much worse. Some may be temporary, disappearing over varying amounts of time. Some handicaps are seen by most people as stigmatizing, while other handicaps bring compassion or pity or indifference. They may also cause fear (leprosy) or revulsion (syphilitic noses).

If we pursue this analysis (resisting all temptation to shrug away the new categories, saying "oh that's all quite obvious"), we can eventually develop testable hypotheses about each class of handicapped person as these people interact in sociable or other situations with normal or other handicapped people. The hypotheses are designed not merely to illustrate what happens to this class of handicapped but to add density of conceptual detail to our evolving theory of interaction engaged in by handicapped persons generally.

Think again about women operated on for mastectomy, with their invisible defects. What is likely to be a dominant consideration for them in sociable interaction? Must they guard their secret because the loss of a breast is stigmatizing if it is known? Is the loss more likely to be a dread and guarded secret for unmarried young women than for young mothers? For young mothers than for elderly mothers? (We shall not even bother here with other obvious comparisons such as what happens in encounters with normal men versus normal women.) It should be easy enough to imagine the kinds of hypotheses that might be generated about each of those situations, including those involving tactics to keep secret the loss of a breast. For instance, we can hypothesize that a woman who has been operated on recently will be fantastically concerned with the selection and arrangement of her clothing and with her appearance when she leaves the house, and that she will pay close, if surreptitious, attention to her bosom during the ensuing sociable interactions. If we turn to the experienced women, who have worn their substitute breasts for many years, we can hypothesize that there will be less concern about betraying the secret - so that their social interactions are more like those between two normals. Under what conditions will anxiety, about accidental revelation, make the secret salient again for these more experienced women?

Our selection of secrecy as an important probable feature of the above interactions suggests that it is a core category, standing somewhat or exactly in the same relation to the non-visibly handicapped as does "normalization" to the visibly handicapped. Using the terminology developed in *Awareness of Dying*, we may say that the non-visibly handicapped attempt to keep the context "closed" while the visibly handicapped attempt - with the tacit cooperation of the normal - to maintain a context of "mutual pretense."[5] Secrets and the possibility of disclosure are characteristic properties of closed contexts, not to mention certain tacitly agreed upon matters characteristic of mutual pretense contexts. Note, however, that in our theoretical sampling we have built considerable variation into the probable management of secret handicaps, just as one might for the management of strained interaction by visibly handicapped persons under similar varied conditions.

At this point in his analysis, the theorist has various options. He can pursue further the case of the patient operated on for mastectomy, turning her around as if she were a complexly cut diamond and examining her many facets. The cues for that analysis have been adumbrated. How do these women act in various types of non-sociable interaction? How do they perform in the successive episodes of social interaction, rather than just in the first episode? What happens when women, each of whom has been operated on for mastectomy, meet each other in various kinds of interactional situations? What occurs in intimate interaction when the woman regards her stricken bosom as ugly but her husband does not? Suppose she regards herself as victimized by fate, but he regards her with compassion? As the theorist answers these questions (in imagination or later with data), he builds hypotheses of varying scope and different degrees of abstraction, with his variables crosscutting again and again in his analysis. Thus he continues to build conceptual density into his theory and simultaneously to integrate it.

Instead of continuing to analyze the same comparison group (woman operated on for mastectomy), the analyst has the option of examining other groups, especially those that will maximize the power of his comparative analysis because of the great differences among them. Suppose, for instance, he begins to think about the interactional situation in which Davis' visibly handicapped person is inexperienced while the normal person is exceedingly experienced in handling, say, stigmatized handicaps. Physical therapists are not only experienced - as professionals they are much involved in treating and giving "psychological support" to handicapped clients. We can now hypothesize, either from the professional's or the handicapped person's viewpoint, in sociable, nonprofessional encounters. We might even in imagination (and later, in fact) interview physical therapists about their reactions when they encounter different classes of handicapped. How do they react to those who have handicaps identical with or similar to those of their patients, as against those with dissimilar handicaps (the deaf, the astigmatic, the blind).

If the theorist wishes to build into his theory the phenomenon of handicapped patients interacting with professionals (normals), he can concentrate on comparisons of that type of interaction with the sociable type. His comparisons can include not only the case of the physical therapist managing his varied classes of handicapped clients (stroke, polio, arthritic, auto accident cases), but can include those comparisons with the professionalized interaction of physician and his mastectomy (and other physically handicapped) patients.

The theorist can, of course, decide to delimit his theory - indeed he must draw limits somewhere, restricting it even to as narrow a scope as sociable interaction. Then he will not focus on the non-sociable encounters (except secondarily, to stimulate his thinking about sociable encounters), but will focus steadily on comparisons that will yield him more and more hypotheses about this central phenomenon. Again, he will seek to make comparisons among groups that seem quite dissimilar and among those that seem relatively similar. In each comparison he will look for similarities as well as differences. These comparison groups will, as before, be suggested to him by his emerging theory. There is no end to the groups he will think of as long as his theory proves stimulating.

When does one stop this process so fertile that it seems to have run riot? This issue was addressed in *The Discovery of Grounded Theory,* and I shall not repeat our discussion here. In brief, however, the directed collection of data through theoretical sampling leads eventually to a sense of closure. Core and subsidiary categories emerge. Through data collection there is a "saturation" of those categories. Hypotheses at varying levels of abstraction are developed (they embrace the categories). Those hypotheses are validated or qualified through directed collection of data. Additional categories and hypotheses which arise later in the research will be linked with the theory. If they are only "nice ideas" but link with the theory only distantly or not at all, they must be pruned away lest they distract from the main job of developing and publishing the theory.

Once we have developed this theory (whether or not we have jumped off from someone else's theory), there is no reason not to link other grounded theory with ours, providing this extant theory fits well and makes sense of out data. The one example given above was the linkage of "awareness theory" with our emergent theory. Useful linkages with other grounded theories may occur to other readers. In turn, our own theory is subject to extension, best done through theoretical sampling and the associated comparative analysis. This extension, perhaps it needs to be said, represents a specifying of the limits of our theory and thus a qualification of it.

Turning again to the main strategy illustrated by this paper, I wish to add three further points in conclusion. If we do not practice such modes of extending grounded theories, then we relegate them, as now, mainly to the status of respected little islands of knowledge, separated from others, each visited from time to time by inveterate footnoters, by assemblers of readings and of periodic bibliographical reviews, and by graduate students assigned to read the better literature. While the owners of these islands understandably are pleased to be visited, in time they will fall out of fashion and be bypassed. This is no way to build a cumulative body of theory (We may even discover eventually that one bit of theory never really was theory, a discovery made about Robert Merton's famous anomie paper.) As the Merton example illustrates, another consequence of failing to delimit, extend, and diversify extant grounded theory is that sociologists continue to develop both speculative theory and general theoretical frameworks without recognizing the great difference between those formulations and theory which is genuinely grounded in data. However useful the former may be as rhetoric or for orientation, taken as theory they simply help to stall another generation in its discovery and formulation of testable theory. Speculative theory and theoretical frameworks have also turned away many of our generation from theorizing (because this is the only theory they recognize) in favor of publishing low-level description. Such description is a necessary sociological task, but it is comparable to the collection of specimens and the making of primitive classification by zoologists - a far cry from the creation of effective theory. Until we develop good methods for and the habit of building on extant theory - this paper represents one modest attempt - it will be easy to continue confusing excellent theoretical papers such as Davis's with others that are merely descriptive.

Reprinted from *Time for Dying*, Aldine Publishing Co., New York, 1967.

TIME, STRUCTURAL PROCESS, AND STATUS PASSAGE

Barney G. Glaser and Anselm L. Strauss

In our opening pages, we remarked that the temporal features of work are of the utmost importance for understanding how organizations function. On virtually every page of this book, readers have found materials pertinent to the temporal features of work organizations and trajectories. Now those features will be discussed within the more general context of the sociology of time.

It is useful to begin by thinking of the hospital career provided for a dying trajectory as a succession of "transitional statuses" in the passage between life and death,[1] as it takes place in the hospital. In contrast to Wilbert Moore's concepts[2] of sequence, rate, synchronization, rhythm, routines and recurrence, which simply denote time unrelated to social structure, transitional status is a concept denoting *social structural* time. How does a social system keep a person in passage between two statuses for a period of time? He is put into a transitional status, or a sequence of them, that denotes a period of time during which he will be in a status passage (*e.g.*, he is put on the ICU, thereby denoting a quick passage.) As a concept for ordering social structural time, transitional status has great advantages over Moore's concepts. His concepts help us talk of the social ordering of behavior; but they are not automatically linked with social structure; they are only applied to it, if the analyst is so inclined. In contrast, referring to the transitional statuses of a status-passage, on the other hand, automatically requires locating the discussion within a social structure.

In general, sociological writing about groups, organizations and institutions tends to leave their temporal features unanalyzed.[3] When they are handled explicitly, the focus is on such matters as deadlines, scheduling, rates, pacing, turnover, and concepts or time which may vary by organizational, institutional or group position. The principal weakness of such analysis stems from an unexamined assumption that the temporal properties worth studying involve only the work time of personnel which must be properly articulated - hence deadlines and schedules. Breakdowns in this temporal articulation occur not only through accident and poor planning, but also through differential valuation of time by various echelons, personnel and clientele. But from our analysis the temporal order of the organization appears to require much wider range of temporal dimensions. We have assumed in this book that, for instance, people bring to an organization their own temporal concerns and that their actions there are profoundly affected by those concerns.[4] Thus, woven into our analysis were experiential careers (hospital, illness, and personal, as well as the patient's and the families' concepts of time. In our analysis we have attempted to show how temporal order in the hospital refers to a total, delicate, continuously changing articulation of these various temporal considerations. Such articulation, of course, includes easily recognizable organizational mechanisms but also less visible ones, including "arrangements" negotiated by various relevant persons.

The kind of analysis required when studying temporal order brings our discussion to the two other topics of this chapter - structural process and status passage. Such a conception of how to study temporal order emphasizes the continual interplay of structure and process. Critics who incline toward a processual view of society have frequently criticized - and in our judgment effectively - the over-determinism of structuralists. But that critique need not necessitate an abandonment of the tremendously useful mode of thinking which is called "structural." That analytic mode need only be combined systematically with an allied concern with process. The study of dying trajectories within hospital organizations happens to have led easily to *thinking generally* about "structural process" and "status passage." Let us consider each in turn.

STRUCTURAL PROCESS

One of the central issues in sociological theory is the relationship of structure to process. What implication does this book have for this issue? We have, in previous chapters, discussed explicitly the structural adaptations of hospitals to various phases of dying trajectories. If one considers dying as a process extending over time. then the hospital's structure can be seen as continually changing to handle different phases in that process. Its structure, then, is in process; which phenomenon we call "structural process." We have seen how a person may be brought into one section of the hospital and then moved to another, as his trajectory is redefined or as he reaches certain critical junctures in an anticipated or defined trajectory. Even when a dying patient remains on one ward, he can be moved around within that ward so that different aspects of its "structure" can be brought into play. If he is never moved,the ward's or hospital's varying resources of manpower, skill, drugs or machinery may be brought into play as his trajectory proceeds. What is true for the staff's relationships with a patient is also true for its relationships with his family.

Sociological analysis ordinarily does not join structure and process so tightly as our notion of "structural process" does. Structure tends to be treated as relatively fixed - because it is what it is, then certain processes can occur. Or inversely, because the major goals involve certain processes, as in a factory or in a governmental agency, the structure is made as nearly consonant with the processes as possible. New processes are conceived as leading to new structural arrangements; while innovations in structure similarly lead to associated processual changes. A major implication of our book is that structure and process are related more complexly (and more interestingly) than is commonly conceived.

We have, for instance, remarked how during a given phase of a trajectory a ward may be quite a different place than before. For instance, when the sentimental order has been profoundly disrupted, the structural elements that can be called on are not quite the same as before; some elements no longer exist and may never again exist. If afterward an "equilibrium" is reached, it is a moving equilibrium with the ward calmed down but forever at least a somewhat different place.

So, rather than seeing a relatively inflexible structure, with a limited and determinable list of structural properties, we have to conceive of a ward, hospital, or any other institution as a structure in process. It therefore has a potential range of properties far greater than the outsider (the sociologist) can possible imagine unless he watches the insiders at work. He can be surprised at the ways in which staff, family or patients can call on diverse properties of the hospital or local community, for bringing in resources that he never dreamed existed but which became permanently or temporarily part of the structural processes of the ward.

In a previous work, one of the authors and his colleagues made a similar point, but neither gave it a name nor developed it as we are doing here.[5] It was remarked then that ordinarily state mental hospitals are conceived as places of limited resources, but that their personnel, when observed closely, exhibit great variation not only in how they use the obvious resources of the hospital but also in how they draw upon outside resources. If we interpret that latter set of operations in terms of structural process, we would say that the innovating personnel are making use of the lectures, or asks his own analyst to advise him, however in outside resources (say, a young psychiatrist who asks colleagues directly, on how to handle his subordinates.) These resources are as much part of the hospital "system" - at least for the time being - as anything found in the hospital itself. And they come into play during determinable times: they function neither independently of time nor of circumstance.

Perhaps we need especially to emphasize that the clients of an institution - patients or family members - are also structural features of it. Thus, a Japanese mother who cares for her dying son at a hospital becomes part of the hospital's structure. If the family gathers around during a patient's last days, then the hospital's structure is amplified. If families are banished or voluntarily "pull out" during certain phases of dying, then they do not loom large as structural possibilities for the staff to call on or to handle.[6]

Structural process relates to the various participants' awareness. They will vary, of course, in their awareness of which structural properties are operating, or can be brought to operate, during various phases of the dying process. Misperceptions are involved as well as awareness; a doctor, for instance, may assume that he can call on some structural resource (*e.g.,* an oxygen tank) when it no longer exists. He may discover its "disappearance" too late; or he may never discover his error, if it is not very consequential. Others, such as the nurses, may or may not be aware of the absence or presence of his knowledge. The relationships of these "awareness contexts" to structural processes are neither accidental nor unpredictable, as staff and patients sometimes believe.

Perhaps the point that most requires underlining, however, is that structural process has consequences which themselves enter into the emergence of a *new* structural process. For the sociologist, this fact implies an important directive: part of his job is to trace those consequences that significantly affect the unrolling course of events called "structural process" - not for particular cases, but for *types* of cases. Sociologists, for instance, are not interested in a dying person, but in *types* of dying persons and the patterned events relevant to their dying. When focusing on the consequences of structure and process, it is all too easy to settle for lists of consequences for, say, various personnel or for the repetitive functioning of an organization or institution. But the explicit directive given by the concept of structural process is that the sociologist cannot rest until he has analytically related the interactional consequences to the next phases in interaction - or, in our terms, present structural processes to later structural processes.

THE DYING TRAJECTORY AS A STATUS PASSAGE

It is not necessary to review our substantive theory of dying trajectories, except to remind readers of several points: dying must be defined in order to be reacted to as dying; defining occurs not only at the beginning but throughout the courses of the various trajectories; hospitals are organized for handling various trajectories, including the establishment of specialized locales for handling different types of trajectories; work at those locales is organized in terms of a range of expected trajectories; a principal feature of these trajectories is the attempts by various parties to shape them; this shaping is affected by various cross-cutting variables (such as social loss, experiential careers and awareness); the various parties may differentially perceive the trajectories; the juggling of tasks, people and relationships during the course of anyone's dying opens possibilities for a considerable misalignment of actions that are usually quite well aligned. Our analyses have established that ascertainable structural conditions are related to the above items, and that their important consequences are also explainable - even somewhat predictable, provided one has advance knowledge of the relevant variables.

This substantive theory of dying trajectories has two especially valuable features. First, it is *dense:* it consists of a great number of propositions, so many indeed that the total theory is not easily summarized. One must almost read the book in order to grasp the theory in anything like its complex density. Second, the theory is *integrated:* the numerous propositions are related systematically to each other throughout our total discussion, and in complex fashion - and yet, we trust, with sufficient clarity to indicated the varying levels of abstractness at which they are formulated.

These two features - density and integration - contribute to the theory's *generality.* By this term, we mean that the theory is applicable to the multitude of diverse situations of dying trajectories. We remarked on this in our earlier book, *Awareness of Dying.*[7]

"Through the level of generality of our concepts we have tried to make the theory flexible enough to make a wide variety of changing situations understandable, and also flexible enough to be readily reformulated, virtually on the spot, when necessary, that is, when the theory does not work. The person who applies our theory will, we believe, be able to bend, adjust, or quickly reformulate... theory as he applies it in trying to keep up with and manage the situational realities that he wishes to improve."

This implies that the density, integration, and generality of the substantive theory increase the control that the user can obtain over various contingencies that may arise during the course of dying. To quote again:

To give this kind of control, the theory must provide a sufficient number of general concepts and their plausible interrelations; and these concepts must provide him with understanding, with situational controls, and with access to the situation in order to exert the control.[8]

It scarcely seems necessary to emphasize that such control also stems from the "grounded" origins of the substantive theory: that is, the theory was not conceived prior to the research but evolved during it.

After a substantive theory is formulated, it is useful, when possible, to scrutinize its relationship to an existing formal theory. The aim is twofold: The scrutiny can lead to further formulation of the substantive theory; it can also lead to discovery and development of gaps in the formal theory. A dying trajectory, as we have suggested, can be usefully thought of as a type of *status passage:* the dying person is passing - through "transitional" statuses - between the statuses of being alive and being dead; various other participants are correspondingly involved with and implicated in his passage.[9]

The phenomena of status passages were enduringly called to the attention of sociologists and anthropologists by Van Gennep's *Rites du Passage*.[10] In that book, the French scholar remarked on various types of passages between what, in modern vocabulary, are termed "statuses." Mainly, he analyzed such passages as those which occur between age-linked statuses such as adolescence and adulthood, and between being unmarried and being married. Those kinds of passages have, of course, been very thoroughly studied since Van Gennep's day. Sociologists have also expended considerable effort in studying passages that occur within occupations ("socialization," for instance) and within organizations ("mobility," for instance.) A principal characteristic of most of those passages is that they are governed by rather clear rules, bearing on when the passage should or can be made and by whom (scheduled); the sequences of steps that the person must go through to have completed the passage (prescribed steps); and what actions must be carried out by various participants so that the passage will actually be accomplished (regularized actions). These dimensions are so integral in numerous status passages that anthropologists and sociologists usually have focused on descriptions of the rituals - extremely scheduled, prescribed sequences of regulated actions - that tend to accompany at least certain phases of those passages.

Scheduling, regularization, and prescription are important dimensions of many, but not all, status passages. Each dimension can be absent, or present only to a degree. Furthermore, certain other relevant dimensions may characterize a type of passage. Thus, the passage may be considered (by the person making the passage or by other relevant parties) as in some measure *desirable* or undesirable. The passage may or may not be *inevitable*. It may be *reversible* and, if so, it may even be *repeatable*. The person undergoing the passage may do so *alone,* or *collectively* with any number of other persons of whose passages he may or may not be *aware.* Also, *clarity* of the signs of passage as seen by various people may be very great or very slight. The person making the passage may do so *voluntarily* or have no choice in the matter, have degrees of choice about varying aspects of it. Another dimension is the degree of *control* that various agents, including the central figure, have over various aspects, and during various phases, of the passage. One final dimension is especially noteworthy; the passage may require special *legitimation* by one or more agents.

Our research has shown the importance of distinguishing clearly among such structural dimensions of passage, and among their various possible permutations. When studying particular types of passage, the analyst could focus, according to their relevance, on several characteristic dimensions. Thus, Julius Roth has, without explicitly recognizing that recovery from severe TB can be conceptualized as a status passage, quite correctly emphasized the indeterminant pace of recovery, the ambiguity of signs of recovery as the patient sees them, and the patient's manipulations in getting his condition defined "upward" by the legitimating physician.[11] Similarly, when writing of degradation ceremonies, Harold Garfinkel almost inevitably emphasized legitimacy: the degrading agent must manage to legitimate his activity and his role to make his accusation persuasive.[12] Orrin Klapp's analysis of how people are made into fools also had its appropriate focus: the successful or unsuccessful strategies of the foolmaker, and of the person who either manages or fails to avoid that status and who manages or fails to reverse the passage once cast into it.[13] To note one last example, Lloyd Warner's detailed description of an Australian tribe almost necessarily turned around a discussion of sequential and collective passages, carefully regulated so that entire segments of the tribe were involved at particular times and places.[14]

Analysis of a given status passage may be incomplete, however, if the social scientist focuses only on one, two or three relevant dimensions of the passage. It is also necessary that he trace the structural conditions under which passage is made, say, alone rather than collectively, or voluntarily rather than involuntarily. He must also research the consequences of these structural conditions for the various participants and the groups or institutions to which they belong - as well as their import for social interaction. A systematic analysis will also clarify the "exceptions" - that is, the variable patterns of interaction and consequence that occur when a normally important dimension is absent or modified. We cannot expect hat these tasks can be accomplished unless the analyst is aware that his analysis can usefully be conceived as pertaining to status passages. If not, then he can be expected to make only a very incomplete analysis of his materials, with regard to status passages. Were this kind of analysis conscientiously attempted, it would be detailed, woven densely and quite lengthy. Of course, it is possible to analyze one or two dimensions systematically within a single journal article, but fuller analysis would require much more space, perhaps as many pages as in this book.

The major dimensions of a dying trajectory as a status passage are unquestionably the ones noted earlier, in opposition to Van Gennep's discussions. First, dying is almost always *unscheduled;* second, the sequence of steps is *not institutionally prescribed;* and third, the actions of the various participants are only *partly regulated.* It is also quite relevant that the transitional statuses of dying (though not necessarily death itself when it comes) are usually defined as *undesirable.* Among the other relevant but highly variable dimensions are: the *clarity* of signs that are available to the various participants; the amount of *control* that the participants (including the patient) have over aspects of his passage; whether only the patient is dying; and which, if any, patients in a simultaneous passage are *aware* or particular aspects of that process.

Complex permutations of those interrelated dimensions give rise, as we can now see, to the many variations of dying trajectories described earlier. This book could very well have been explicitly organized around the concept of status passage, with full focus on the systematic permutation of its dimensions. We chose not to write the analysis in that manner, for two principal reasons. First, the substantive theory developed during our research long before we understood its full relationship to a systematically formulated theory of status passages. Second (and more important, since we could have "converted" the substantive theory) we much preferred to present a substantive theory because of the infinitely greater sense of immediacy to dying situations that it would give our readers. After writing the book, we realized that a well-presented substantive theory would pass an especially critical test if it actually measured up to what a formal theory would require of it. When judged by that criterion, the substantive theory of trajectories measures up well. Unquestionably, however, something is lost when an analysis is not explicitly organized in accordance with a formal theory. For instance, some emphases in the "non-scheduling" paper are not at the foreground of analysis in the present book.[15]

It now seems to us that anyone who wishes to develop substantive theory about any phenomenon that might also be usefully seen as a status passage can considerably speed up his systematic guidance of research and his generation of substantive theory by a formal theory of status passage. But he must not do so too rigidly he must avoid operating only within the framework of that formal theory - unless he is principally interested in the formal theory itself. Otherwise he runs the risk of radically closing off the possibilities of developing other aspects of substantive and formal theory. If we had, for instance, focused only (or principally) on status passage, we would not have developed the related substantive theory of awareness contexts. (Readers have seen it used, in crosscutting fashion, in this book.) Thus the total theory would have been more restricted in scope, less complex in its interrelationships, less dense, and certainly less widely applicable to dying situations.

To keep the record accurate, we should add that we began the research with two general ideas. One was that dying "took time," and thus was a process. The other idea, derived from personal experience, was that a collusive game of "evasion of the truth" often occurred around dying people. The second idea evolved organically into a theory of dying trajectories long before we sensed its relevance to a theory of status passages. Therefore, we reiterate that formal theory should be used, but judiciously - and the earlier in the research it is used, the more wary the researcher should be of overcommitting himself to that formal theory.

When the substantive research is brought to a conclusion, what should it contribute to a preexisting formal theory? All too often, research based on (or brought into alignment with) a formal theory adds nothing to the theory; it merely applies it. Relevant substantive research, however, must elaborate, supplement, correct, critically test or in some other way stand in an instrumental relationship to the formal theory. Correspondingly, research that initiates a new substantive theory should lead to suggestions for the formulation and study of a related formal theory.[16]

Since it is our intention to present in another volume a formal theory which combines status passage and awareness context, we shall conclude the present discussion with two general remarks. First: the method used in discovering substantive theory - the systematic use of comparison groups - can be used effectively for generating a formal theory of a status passage.[17] The general procedure is to study simultaneously, or in quick succession, a number of kinds of status passages. The constant comparison of these will quickly draw attention to their many similarities and differences; the analysis generates the formal theory. Probably one need not engage in much firsthand gathering of data, for a number of status passages have been studied or described by social scientists. These materials can be used in "secondary analysis." So can the abundant popular material that an ingenious researcher can bend to his uses - for instance, books like *Diabetes as a Way of Life, Thank God for My Heart Attach, Managing Your Coronary, The Changing Years, What to Do about Your Menopause;* or materials on "getting ahead" in business, or "how to prepare" for motherhood or any other status;; as well as such writings as the book in which John Griffin described how he, a white journalist, "passed" back and forth between the race lines in the Deep South, or the published autobiographies of con men which reveal clearly how they manage the status passages of their "marks."[18] Data represented by such publications can be used flexibly for building formal theory through constant comparisons, since the researcher will be guided by his evolving theory to either new uses of his data or the discovery of valuable new data.

A second point that deserves underscoring is that the same paradigm suggested earlier for substantive research about status passages can be used for developing formal theory about such passages. The theorist cannot be content with isolating and relating a few important dimensions of status passage. His theory must include their structural conditions, their interactional consequences (including relevant strategies), and their consequences for relevant participants and organizations. If this mandate is followed, the formal theory will be dense, integrated, of great scope and of considerable applicability. The theory will also be helpful in guiding new studies of status passages - as well as being useful in critical reviews of older studies.

1. Glaser and Strauss, "Temporal Aspects of Dying as a Non-Scheduled Status Passage," *American Journal of Sociology,* Vol. 71 (1965), pp. 48-59.

2. See *Man, Time and Society* (New York: John Wiley, 1963), Chapter 1.

3. The following pages are adapted or quoted from the introduction to *George Herbert Mead on Social Psychology* ed. by Anselm Strauss, (Chicago: University of Chicago Press, 1964 edition), pp. xiii-xiv.

4. This kind of view is implicit in the writings of G.H. Mead. Herbert Blumer has attempted to make the view more explicit in his writing about Mead and in various papers about symbolic interactionism. *Cf.,* his "Society as Symbolic Interaction," in A. Rose (Ed.), *Human Behavior and Social Processes* (Boston: Houghton Miffling, 1962), pp. 179-92.

5. Anselm Strauss *et al., Psychiatric Idealogies and Institutions* (New York: Free Press of Glencoe, 1965).

6. Herbert Simon makes the point that clients are as much part of an organization as its personnel, but he makes the point statically. See his *Administrative Behavior* (New York: Macmillan, 1948).

7. *Awareness of Dying, op. cit.,* p. 265. For a general discussion of generality, density and integration see our *Discovery of Grounded Theory.*

8. *Op. cit.,* p. 268.

9. Cf. Glaser and Strauss, "Temporal Aspects of Dying as a Non-Scheduled Status Passage," *op. cit.*

10. Translated by M. Vizedom and G. Cafee (Chicago: University of Chicago Press, 1960). The original publication date was 1908.

11. *Timetables* (Indianapolis: Bobbs-Merrill, 1963).

12. "Conditions of Successful Degradation Ceremonies," *American Journal of Sociology*, Vol. 61 (1956), pp. 420-24.

13. "The Fool as a Social Type," *American Journal of Sociology,* Vol. 55, (1949), pp. 159-60.

14. *A Black Civilization* (New York: Harper, 1937).

15. Glaser and Strauss, "Temporal Aspects of Dying as a Non-Scheduled Status Passage." *op.cit.* See also *Discovery of Grounded Theory, op. cit.,* Part I, on relation between substantive and formal theory. On this, see also the introduction to Barney Glaser, *Organizational Careers* (Chicago: Aldine Publishing Company, 1968).

16. For an example of this, see *Awareness of Dying, op. cit.,* pp. 276-80.

17. *Ibid.; The Discovery of Grounded Theory, op. cit.,* Chapters III and IV.

18. John Griffin, *Black Like Me* (Boston: Houghton Mifflin, 1960); crf. Edwin Sutherland, *The Thief* (Chicago: University of Chicago Press, 1937).

NOTES

NOTES

NOTES

NOTES

NOTES

NOTES